J. P. P. (Jean Pierre Paulin) Martin

Anglican-ritualism as seen by a Catholic and foreigner

A series of essays, with an appendix, on the present position of the Church in France

J. P. P. (Jean Pierre Paulin) Martin

Anglican-ritualism as seen by a Catholic and foreigner
A series of essays, with an appendix, on the present position of the Church in France

ISBN/EAN: 9783741182235

Manufactured in Europe, USA, Canada, Australia, Japa

Cover: Foto ©Andreas Hilbeck / pixelio.de

Manufactured and distributed by brebook publishing software (www.brebook.com)

J. P. P. (Jean Pierre Paulin) Martin

Anglican-ritualism as seen by a Catholic and foreigner

ANGLICAN-RITUALISM.

ANGLICAN-RITUALISM

AS SEEN BY A

Catholic and Foreigner.

A SERIES OF ESSAYS:

WITH AN APPENDIX, ON THE PRESENT POSITION OF THE CHURCH IN FRANCE.

BY

ABBÉ P. MARTIN, D.D.,

LICENTIATE OF CANON LAW,
PROFESSOR OF HOLY SCRIPTURE IN THE CATHOLIC INSTITUTE OF PARIS,
AND HONORARY CANON OF CAHORS.

LONDON: BURNS AND OATES.
1881.

NIHIL OBSTAT:

T. E. BRIDGETT, C.SS.R.,
Deputatus ad hoc.

IMPRIMATUR:

HENRICUS E. CARD: ARCHIEP:
WESTMONAST.

Preface.

MOST of the Essays contained in this volume have already appeared in some of the English Reviews. Only three will be absolutely new to our readers, namely, the first, the fourth, and the last; and these may fittingly be associated with the others, since they touch upon subjects intimately connected with those now under discussion by the Anglican and Ritualistic sections of the religious public.

Although we write for all educated persons who interest themselves in great religious questions of the day, yet we address ourselves more especially to two classes of readers—the members of the High Church and of the Ritualistic parties, who, from some points of view, approach more closely to the Catholic Church than any other divisions of the Anglican body.

We have carefully revised those Essays which have been previously published; and, without making any essential alteration, we have modified some expressions, so as to bring our phraseology into more exact accordance with our views. The course of events has thrown light upon many points, and we trust that our experience has been of benefit to us.

On other aspects of the subject, we candidly own that we have seen reason both to modify and to change our opinion; and, whilst ready to do justice to all, we are perhaps less inclined, at the present moment, to approve of Ritualism and Ritualists than was formerly the case. We have also added footnotes, upon some points which seemed to call for especial attention.

Before entering upon our task, we think it right to make answer to a charge that has been brought against us. We are accused of having said "that the Ritualists are *held back by motives more or less ignoble* from acknowledging and following out their inner convictions" (Reply to the Abbé Martin, p. 6).

Our accuser is Dr. Littledale. But, we are aware that others, both Anglicans and Ritualists, have felt somewhat aggrieved by the imputation of what we have termed "interested motives." Dr. Littledale asserts "that this assumption underlies the whole article (What hinders the Ritualists from becoming Roman Catholics?), and no courteousness of mere phrase avails to cloak its real character" (*Ibid.*)

To this charge we reply, that we never dreamed of ascribing such motives to the great mass of Anglican-Ritualists. We have, at the utmost, asserted that some individuals amongst them may have allowed themselves to be swayed by *ignoble motives*, though we should have at all times been reluctant to express the idea in those discourteous terms: and we think that all who have read our papers will acknowledge that, if we have for a moment raised the veil which hides from view the great crises of the spiritual life, we have always endeavoured to do this carefully and lovingly, so as to give the least possible amount of pain.

We have read over with the utmost attention the passage in which we enter upon that critical question, as to the influence which our material interests exercise over our moral and spiritual life ; and we still remain of opinion that, taking into account the large allowances made by us to modify the expression of our views, no doubt can be raised as to the general correctness of our statement. It is undeniable, that the world and the things of this world do act as a terrible drag upon our higher life. This fact no one will dispute. How far then, we may ask, are material interests and human affections likely to prove obstacles in the way of those Anglicans and Ritualists who are to *a certain extent* desirous of union with Rome, and who have a *vague* idea that they are not in the true Church ? This is a question which it does not belong to us to solve, nor should we wish to pronounce upon it. Still, we think that, were it not necessary to make such great sacrifices in order to become a Catholic, there would have been more than even 80,000 or 100,000 conversions in England during the last fifty years.

If, quitting England, we go to France for an instance in point, does any one believe that, unless great pressure had been exercised by the Government, the Seventh Clause of the notorious "Ferry Bill" would have been voted for by one hundred and twenty-nine Senators? We think not. Those Government officials who voted against the Seventh Clause certainly proved thereby that they had the courage of their convictions; whilst, those holding office under Government who voted for it when, in other circumstances, they would have supported the cause of religious freedom, have justly incurred the suspicion of sacrificing their convictions to their interests.

Although we have not, nor have ever had, the slightest intention of giving offence to any one, we willingly withdraw any expressions calculated to hurt the feelings of the Anglican or the Ritualistic clergy, whom we admire for the many noble and generous characteristics which they share with their countrymen at large.

We now leave our readers to decide upon the value of the line of argument pursued by us in the following pages. We trust that they may be read in the same spirit of charity in which they have been written. They were written to guide and instruct, not to grieve nor to wound. We are not fond of controversy, when it is carried on in a bitter or irritating tone; we should always wish to conduct it in such a manner as to make brotherly love the connecting link between all minds in search of truth and of right.

Such has been our sole aim in writing and publishing these Essays; and should we, in how small a degree soever, attain that object, we shall feel ourselves amply repaid.

ABBÉ MARTIN.

ST. ETHELDREDA'S, ELY PLACE, LONDON, E.C.
August 1, 1880.

Contents.

	PAGE
PREFACE	vi

ESSAY
I. ANGLICANISM AND CATHOLICISM 1

II. RITUALISM, PROTESTANTISM, AND CATHOLICISM . . 20

    Originally published in the "Nineteenth Century," February 1878, under the title of "A Roman Catholic View of Ritualism."

III. THE INCONSISTENCIES OF RITUALISM . . . 56

    Originally published in the "Tablet," 1878, pp. 1352 *et seq.*, under the title of "On Certain Inconsistencies of Ritualists."

IV. THE CHURCH, THE STATE, AND THE RITUALISTS . 81

V. WHY DO NOT RITUALISTS BECOME CATHOLICS? . . 122

    Originally published in the "Contemporary Review," August 1878, under the title of "What Hinders the Ritualists from becoming Roman Catholics?"

VI. RITUALISM AND CATHOLICISM COMPARED: A REJOINDER . 160

    Originally published in the "Contemporary Review," December 1878.

VII. RITUALISTIC PREJUDICES AND MISCONCEPTIONS . . 210

APPENDIX.

ON THE PRESENT STATE OF THE CHURCH IN FRANCE . 255

    Originally published in the "Nineteenth Century," December 1879.

ANGLICAN-RITUALISM.

ANGLICANISM AND CATHOLICISM.

IT is scarcely two years since a list of names entitled "Rome's Recruits" appeared, first in the "Whitehall Review," and afterwards as a separate publication.

This pamphlet made, and not without reason, a considerable sensation. There was no great novelty in its contents, the substance of which was more or less familiar to all; but, it brought clearly to light, as a palpable fact, what had hitherto been only vaguely suspected. Gratefully welcomed by some,[1] looked upon by others as ill-judged and inopportune,[2] this pamphlet has already passed through several editions, revised, corrected, and enlarged. According to the latest issue, the total number of noteworthy persons who have been converted from Anglicanism to Catholicism is upwards of three thousand. The editors of "Rome's Recruits" do not profess to give a complete list of all Catholic converts from Anglicanism; indeed, in the preface to their work they expressly state that they have only noted the *élite*—those

"Who held more or less public positions, and whose change of faith was not a matter of merely individual privacy. . . . The list has no pretension whatever to be complete. . . . The list takes no count at all of converts from the lower classes; . . . it is far from being complete even as regards the educated classes."—*Third Edition.*

---

[1] "We are thankful to have the list."—"Church Times," Nov. 22, 1878.
[2] Dr. Littledale's "Reply to the Abbé Martin," p. 13, note.

Nothing can be clearer or more explicit than these words. Notwithstanding which, and with an object which unprejudiced persons will readily fathom, "Rome's Recruits" has been alluded to by some writers as though it gave a full and entire catalogue of Anglican conversions. Moreover, the same writers, whilst assuring us that they do not for a moment pretend to underrate the intellectual status of these converts, yet proceed forthwith to speak of them in very unbecoming and uncharitable terms; and none have gone to greater length in this respect than the "Church Times,"[1] and the distinguished Ritualistic author, Dr. Littledale.[2] The converts are alluded to in a body as a "galaxy of intellect" of which the Anglican Church is well rid; and Dr. Littledale exclaims triumphantly: "Only ten per cent. of the clergy and two per cent. of the laity were persons of any intellectual mark."[3] To this assertion the very reasonable answer has been returned, that, taking the facts as represented by so unprejudiced a person as Dr. Littledale himself, the Catholic Church may well be proud of the result. "That this high compliment may, with truth, be paid, by an avowed antagonist of the Church, to converts to Catholicism from the Establishment is indeed a triumph. On Dr. Littledale's own ground it may even be made an unanswerable argument in favour of Ritualists becoming Catholics, that 10 per cent. of the clergy and 2 per cent. of the laity, or that 58 men and 9 women out of 1816 converts, of real intellectual distinction, or of personal influence, have done what he affirms Ritualists do *not* do—submitted to the See of Peter."[4]

I. If during the last half-century three thousand persons of intellectual or social distinction have become

---

[1] "Church Times," Nov. 22, 1878, "Killed, Wounded, and Missing."
[2] "Reply to the Abbé Martin," pp. 13, 14, and note.
[3] When Dr. Littledale wrote, the list already contained over 1816 names; this is, however, a mere matter of detail.
[4] Mr. Orby Shipley in the Tablet: "Truthfulness and Ritualism," Jan. 17, 1880.

Catholics, it is natural to conclude that the less prominent classes of society have contributed a still larger number of converts. In the absence of official statistics covering this period,—viz., from the year 1830 to the year 1880—we may get a kind of rough average from the printed diocesan lists of conditional baptisms. From 1850 to 1865, these conditional baptisms, in nine out of the thirteen dioceses of Catholic England, amounted to upwards of 37,000.[1] These numbers, implying a similar number of conversions, are divided thus :— from 1850 to 1857, 12,000 ; from 1857 to 1865, 25,000.[2] Here, then, we find these three facts :—1. During the last fifty years there has been a constant and steady flow of conversions from Anglicanism into the Catholic Church. 2. Conversions have increased, and have largely increased, in number as the years went on. And 3. These conversions are to be counted, not by units and tens, but by hundreds and by thousands. Even our opponents acknowledge that those who quit the English Church for the Catholic Church are, intellectually and morally, amongst the choicer specimens of their kind. None can deny that these facts are important in themselves. They become still more important when they are examined one by one, and when all the accompanying circumstances are taken into consideration.

An explanation of this remarkable moral phenomenon has been attempted by Dr. Littledale, who—carried away by an irritability which he doubtless regrets now, and which he will regret more deeply still in proportion as good sense reassumes her sway—has classified under the following heads all converts from Anglicanism to Catholicism :—

"These converts secede—1. From causes of temperament, *i.e.,* because they like it (the Roman system), just as they might like

---

[1] "Tablet," Jan. 17, 1880, p. 76, col. 2.
[2] It seems to us that, without exaggeration, the number of converts may therefore be approximately stated as being from 80,000 to 100,000.

oysters or pastry. 2. From sentimental motives. 3. On practical grounds" (Reply to the Abbé Martin, pp. 38, 39). A little further on Dr. Littledale enumerates these "practical reasons:" "First, is the wish to be free from clerical obligations, and to enjoy the unrestraint of laymanship." This, of course, only applies to clergymen. The following refers to laymen: "Next, residence in some part of the country not yet covered by the rising waters of the Catholic Revival, or where neglect, sordidness, or a narrow and illiterate Puritanism are still dominant." The last is applicable to both clergy and laity. "Finally, in this category come what are in my experience the immense majority of cases, viz., those who, from motives of sheer mental (*Ibid.*, p. 45) laziness and sloth, and of unwillingness to face the spiritual problems of the day for themselves, go out from a communion which bids them prove all things and hold fast that which is good . . . into one whose easier counsel is to use their intellect only so long and so far as it may lead them into the haven of Rome, and thenceforward to abandon all the trouble and sin of thinking, which will be much better done for them by the Church, acting through the agency of a qualified director. I am bold to say that this is, beyond all others, the chief motive and incentive to secession, so far as I have ever been able to examine and test the matter. What its moral value is I leave my readers to decide" (*Ibid.*, p. 46).

If the 80,000 to 100,000 converts to the Church are not satisfied with this explanation, they must be hard to please. And if the Ritualists or the Anglicans raise any objections, either as to the soundness of the reasoning, or as to the language in which it is conveyed, they must be exceedingly "thin-skinned," as the "Guardian" newspaper was pleased to say. In reading these and similar passages, we cannot help pausing to ask, How far is it possible for men to be led astray by party spirit and the heat of controversy? We too, in our turn, "leave our readers to decide what is the moral value" of these explanations of Dr. Littledale. It seems to us that those who, like the majority of Anglican converts, have followed the leadings of their consciences at the cost of great personal sacrifices, should be spoken of with all possible delicacy and respect. To say nothing of the spirit of fairplay, charity demands this.

But if these facts are important—1, in themselves;

2, as regards the accompanying circumstances; and 3, with respect to the converts themselves, we are surprised that neither the "Church Times" nor Dr. Littledale should have thought of bringing out a list of " Church of England Recruits" in opposition to " Rome's Recruits."

We offer this suggestion for their consideration, and we earnestly beg of them to carry it out. "We shall be thankful to have the list." We shall not look upon it as "ill-judged or inopportune." In it will doubtless figure, as "persons of intellectual mark," Père Hyacinthe, Abbé Michaud, Abbé Deramey, Jean Wallon, the Pomponio Letos and Januses of the age. Let such a list as this be drawn up, and then we can compare it with " Rome's Recruits." We fear, however, that we shall have a long while to wait for it!

II. These facts evidently imply the existence amongst Anglicans of the educated and professional classes, and especially amongst the clergy of the English Church, of a state of mental struggle and dissatisfaction, of a moral and intellectual uneasiness, which from time to time reaches the natural conclusion of an exodus, in greater or smaller numbers, from that body. Men do not quit the communion in which they were born, the faith in which they were reared, and around which cluster all their most cherished associations; they do not break asunder all the ties of kindred, of friendship, of schooldays and college life; they do not cut their career as it were in half, and sacrifice all their prospects—they do none of these things, for a passing caprice. Before taking a step which changes the very mould of their lives, they search, they weigh and ponder deeply; and it is only as the result of full conviction that they take the final step, let it cost what it may. We cannot imagine that Dr. Littledale will find many to accept his assurance, that such a step can be taken from motives as trivial as those which create a preference for "oysters and pastry."

Since no effect can be brought about without a cause, it is evident that these 80,000 or 100,000 conversions show that an extensive hidden work of decomposition and reconstruction must be going on in the very midst of the Anglican Church.

Hitherto we have considered these secessions as the effect of a given mental process; but we must now treat them as the cause of a similar mental process in others. Each conversion propagates that mental struggle of which it is itself the fruit; it raises many questions in the minds of those who hear of it. When men, venerable by age or eminent from their antecedents, from the good work they have done in the world, from their social position, or their moral and intellectual worth, take a step of such vast importance, it is impossible for upright, guileless, truthful souls, filled with religious feeling and with faith in the unseen —it is impossible, we say, for such souls as these to refrain from asking, each for himself, these two questions:—1. Why have so many men left the Anglican Communion to join the Catholic Church? and, 2. Does not a moral obligation to take the same step rest upon me also? Can I, with a safe conscience, remain where I am?

These two questions must be asked and answered by all earnest men who desire to justify their own conclusions, both to their consciences and to their fellowmen. But, more especially must they be asked and answered by all members of the High Church and Ritualistic parties. For, of all bodies outside the Church, these approach her most closely in their belief and in their religious practice.

Of all such bodies, they are the most ready to acknowledge, nay, almost to boast of, the shortcomings of their own communion, both in past and present times; and their most earnest desire is to reform it and to bring it gradually so close to the Church as that it shall no longer differ from her in *kind*, but only in *degree*. Since they have found in the Catholic Church numberless good practices which they have adopted in spite of their ecclesiastical superiors, they ought, on pain of being considered illogical and dishonest, to tell us plainly why they accept a portion of the Catholic faith whilst they reject the remainder.

To the first of the questions asked above, Dr. Littledale has furnished an answer which we have already placed before our readers. We do not think that any enlightened and well-bred man—and of such, happily, there are many amongst High Churchmen and Ritualists—would consider this answer conclusive in its reasoning, and still less would he be disposed to endorse the terms in which it is expressed.

Dr. Littledale has also replied to the second question, and his answer takes two lines of argument:—1. We ought to remain in the communion where God has willed that we should be born. Σπάρταν ἔλαχες, ταύτην κοσμεῖ: "Sparta is thy lot, adorn her." 2. The Church of Rome, when closely examined, is no nearer perfection than the Anglican communion. In these few words may be summed up all that Dr. Littledale has written of late on this subject.

Are these two reasons sufficiently full and satisfactory to tranquillise an inquiring mind? Let it be understood that, in asking these questions, we leave it to each individual to answer for himself in the presence of God, face to face with his own conscience, and to remember that the salvation of his soul is at stake.

Not by us can that answer be given. We may offer some slight assistance towards answering it; but still it is each one for himself who must make, after calm and mature reflection, once and for always, the great decision.

It is sometimes said, that Catholics encourage and even urge converts to enter the Church with very little previous reflection or preparation. This is not the case. We, Catholics, cannot indeed remain indifferent to the deliverance of those whom we know to be in error. We pray with all our hearts that it may please God to lead them to His Truth. We do our utmost to make the road plain and the path easy to them. But, beyond this we do not venture, and the Church herself would be the first to blame undue haste in such matters; she would certainly distrust any who came to her not having well counted the cost. We must remember, too, that the Church claims as her own all the baptized who are honestly ignorant of her rights over them.

The Church, therefore, never advises haste in a matter so important both spiritually and temporally; but neither does she encourage that intellectual sloth which puts aside all unpleasant or disquieting questions. On the contrary, she teaches that there are no stronger obligations laid upon man than those of examining strictly the grounds of his belief, and of then following implicitly the guidance of his conscience.

III. To continue: these two questions, which High Churchmen and Ritualists must alike ask themselves, are surrounded by what may be called moral difficulties, in contradistinction to difficulties of an intellectual and social character. We will dwell on these for a few moments.

When we consider the position of members of the High Church and Ritualistic bodies, in relation to Catholics, simply from a philosophical and moral point of view, we must acknowledge it to be one full of danger, more especially for the clergy. If there be one thing in life which we should approach with well-balanced and impartial minds, free from preconceived notions—one thing in which it is necessary that we should guard ourselves most vigilantly against the dangers of self-love and self-esteem, it is in the business of our conversion and salvation; for when the salvation of the soul is at stake, no obstacle should check us, no sacrifice should be beyond our strength. This all must admit.

Now, Ritualists and High Churchmen are exposed to much and serious self-delusion during the combat which takes place in their souls before they can make the truth they seek their own. They deceive themselves and come to a halt midway, whilst others who started with them arrive at the goal—the Church—with apparent ease. And this it is which is the special danger of the Ritualistic clergy.

Let us ask, what is their position at the present moment? The Ritualists are trying to raise the Anglican Church to a doctrinal and practical level, which, if it does not precisely attain the Catholic standard, at all events approaches it in externals, and of which the logical tendency and issue must be the Catholic Church. Thus they occupy a post halfway between Anglicanism and the Church, trying to amalgamate the two systems, and soothing themselves with the chimerical hope of forming some day a link in that re-union of Christian Churches which is the Utopian scheme of some of their number.

Placed thus between two hostile camps, they are attacked at one and the same time by Anglicans and by Catholics. And herein lies the chief moral danger of their position; for, as the Anglicans charge them with being traitors and deserters, they are naturally eager to refute the accusation and to prove incontestably that they are neither the one nor the other.

Is there any foundation for this twofold charge? Are the Ritualists and the more advanced High Churchmen traitors and deserters? If we take the words in the unfavourable sense which usually attaches to them, it is manifestly unjust to apply such epithets to the persons of whom we are speaking. It is only those who forsake the party to which they belong, with the full and deliberate intention of first weakening, and, ultimately, destroying it, who deserve to be called traitors and deserters. Now, the Ritualists do not entertain any such design. They certainly do not wish to destroy the English Church; on the contrary, they wish to reform her, to perfect her, to preserve her. Therefore they are not traitors or deserters in the ordinary sense of those words.

And yet, in point of fact, they are essentially guilty on both counts. They are actually weakening the English Church, and they are steadily paving the way for her disestablishment. Therefore, in spite of their good faith, they lay themselves open to the charges brought against them by their co-religionists; and it becomes necessary for them to prove their innocence by overt acts. Now, there is only one proof of innocence which the anti-Ritualists will accept, though even this they accept with a certain amount of suspicion,[1] and that one proof is, antagonism to Rome. It is their imitation of the Roman Church, and their approximation to her; it is the fact of their not condemning everything Roman, of their praising, admiring, and loving much that is Roman—even whilst abusing Rome—which draws down upon the Ritualists the animadversions alike of High Churchmen, Broad Churchmen, and Dissenters. Therefore, in order to be able to rebut the charges brought against them by all parties in the Established religion, they are forced to take up a hostile attitude towards the Catholic Church,

---

[1] We could give almost hundreds of passages in proof of this. The "Rock," for example, speaks thus of Dr. Littledale's campaign against the Church and her members:—"For ourselves we can speak decisively, that to put forth Dr. Littledale as an opponent of Popery and a champion of the English Church, would be as absurd as to represent Mr. Bradlaugh as an enemy to atheism and an advocate of Christian religion. The cause of the English Church requires no such helpers as he. Men who honestly teach her principles and live up to her teaching are those only who can be accepted as worthy representatives; but to be assailing Popery with one hand and building it up with another is to occupy a position that is simply ridiculous. Dr. Littledale should either totally renounce his Roman teaching or go over honestly to Rome, from whose storehouse of heresy and superstition he has pilfered so many of the treasures which he now sets forth as his own."— "Rock," 1880, p. 184, col. 3.

to speak of her harshly and slanderously, using, indeed, language concerning her such as we have scarcely been accustomed to even from the Evangelical, or from the Nonconformist, or even from the Infidel press.

Such is the pass to which the Ritualists have been brought by stern polemical necessity; and such is the attitude which they have taken up. We have only to read their religious organs, such as the "Church Review," and, more especially, the "Church Times;" we have but to glance at their controversial works— Dr. Littledale's pamphlets, for example—and we shall see that the Ritualists speak and write about the Catholic Church with such levity and disrespect, with such virulence, with such prejudice—we had almost said with such a want of good faith—as we have never yet found in evangelical and dissenting or even in infidel publications, in the "Rock" or the "Record," in the "Christian World" or the "Nonconformist," or in the "National Reformer."

We see Ritualistic writers collect indiscriminately every piece of gossip and scandal, every false report calculated to give an unfavourable impression of the Church; and if any Catholic author or editor meets these attacks and disproves their assertions, no newspaper, as a rule, will publish, and no author will note, the refutation.

We could give many instances in point, taken from Dr. Littledale's writings, from the columns of the "Church Times" and even from the "Church Review," although, generally speaking, the last-named journal is far more moderate in tone, and far more courteous in its phraseology.[1]

It is easy to understand that the attitude which the

---

[1] We have twice contradicted, first in the "Contemporary Review" and afterwards in the "Nineteenth Century," certain slanderous statements respecting the treatment of the Belgian clergy by their bishops. These statements were circulated by the "Church Review," the "Church Times," and by Dr. Littledale. We still await from them an acknowledgment of the absolute incorrectness of their assertions.

Ritualists are in some degree forced to assume, frequently brings about a state of mind very unfavourable either to the perception, or to the acceptance of Catholic truths. Heated minds and prejudiced hearts can neither see nor hear calmly and dispassionately. They are restless and excited, and in this state they can have no clear vision of the Church as she truly is.

This, then, is the chief danger for the advanced Ritualists, and this danger is yet further complicated.

Set upon at one and the same time by their brethren of the Low Church and Broad Church parties, the Ritualists are also exposed to attacks from Catholics, who, actuated by totally different motives, are, equally with Protestants, alive to the inconsistencies of Ritualism—inconsistencies which they are apt to attribute to a lack of earnestness or of reasoning power; whilst they do not fail to remark how unproductive, how wanting it is as a body in real weight, learning, and importance. In speaking thus plainly, Catholics fulfil a great work of charity. We will even go further and say that it is their duty thus to speak; for, as St. Paul says, the truth should be preached "in season and out of season," and in doing this the Church has never been found wanting.

So long as Catholics set about this unwelcome task in a spirit of kindliness and goodwill, they will do a true missionary work, and fulfil a most important duty. It is one which they cannot be censured for undertaking; on the contrary, they will deserve the thanks of all, if only they are actuated by brotherly charity. On the whole there is little fault to be found with the Catholic press on this score. If, occasionally, a harsh word or an unjust expression is employed by a Catholic controversialist, it is from no real want of good feeling on his part. We must lay it to the account of human frailty, and we must remember, further, that the behaviour of the Ritualists themselves has oftentimes been such as to exhaust the patience of their opponents. It is, moreover, quite possible that we may show less consideration towards the Ritualists now than we should have done some time since. How can we read some of the paragraphs of the "Church Times" and the "Church Review," or most of the pages of Dr. Littledale's pamphlets, without feeling hurt by the injustice of their attacks and the unbecomingness and levity of their language? Still, every Catholic writer should remember that he is bound to be impartial and charitable, and to make great allowances for his antagonists, courtesy being all the more due to those who have shown so little of it towards us.

We have now explained why it is that the Ritualists, exposed to a cross fire and charged both in front and in rear, driven out by one party and repulsed by the other, rebuffed by all and welcomed by none, are obliged to constitute themselves as a new religious body, which, though no longer distinctly Anglican, is still very far indeed from being Catholic. This position is undoubtedly, both morally and intellectually, a dangerous one.

But this is not all. We must be permitted to draw attention to another side of the question.

Even if the Ritualists were not denounced as deserters and traitors, their conversion would be a painful process, and one that would cost them very much. Whatever Dr. Littledale may say to the contrary, men do not revel in their wearisome struggle towards the light, as they might in the physical enjoyment of "oysters and pastry." But, these denunciations weigh them down in the struggle ; and the more upright and earnest they are, the more bitterly do they grieve under such accusations, which are especially repugnant to them : and they naturally shrink from taking a step which seems to justify the charges of treason and desertion.

Many souls may have been checked on the very

threshold of the Church by this thought :—" I have been called a deserter and a traitor. If I become a Catholic, not only shall I justify the accusation on my own account, but I shall be the cause of its being brought, with apparent truth, against those whom I am leaving, those who have hitherto been my friends and colleagues."

We know what trivial causes sometimes influence the most important decisions of our lives; and who shall say that such considerations as these may not have kept from us some of the loftiest intellects and the warmest hearts at present outside the Church?

Lastly, there is abundant matter for self-deception even in the good which the Ritualists do, or which they imagine themselves to be doing.

We do not think that we can be accused of injustice towards Ritualists or Ritualism. On the contrary, we have been thought to deal too gently with them, and to look so exclusively at the brighter aspect of men and things belonging to them, as to appear blind to any less favourable view.

We do not deny that good has resulted from Ritualism. But the good which it has accomplished is more interesting as being unlooked-for and out of the usual course, than as being practical or lasting in itself. We have never advanced any such opinion as that which Dr. Littledale, with his usual inaccuracy, has attributed to us, namely, "that the Church of England, whatever its defects may be, is *the* great breakwater against infidelity in this country."[1] We admit that the Anglican Church is *a certain*, though not "*the great* breakwater against infidelity." But, after all, we have no right to complain, for Dr. Littledale has placed us in very good company. We cannot

---

[1] "Reply to the Abbé Martin," p. 47. Cardinal Newman has several times disclaimed the saying attributed to him by Dr. Littledale. See "Difficulties felt by Anglicans in Catholic Teaching." (4th edit., pp. 363, 364.) Formerly it was a *bulwark*, not a *breakwater*, which was spoken of by Protestants.

admit, as he himself says, that Ritualism is "a marvellous revival unparalleled in the history of the world" (Plain Reasons against Joining the Church of Rome, p. 197).

But, whilst making many exceptions to these results attributed to Ritualism, we readily acknowledge that it has done great things; and it is in this very fact that we see a new and a serious source of danger, which is, unfortunately, by no means imaginary.

The Ritualists say that great good has been accomplished; that the Anglican Church is completely metamorphosed from her former self; that God has abundantly blessed all that has been done; and that, if we will only wait patiently, we shall have a Church—once only too evidently human in her origin—transformed into the Church of God's own foundation. They gradually become intoxicated with success, and with the consciousness of their own admirable intentions; and, looking at the past, and at what is now taking place, they affirm that they would be guilty of a breach of duty towards God, towards the Church, and towards their co-religionists, if they were to pass over to Rome; they would deem themselves cowardly, faithless, and ungrateful in so doing. Thus they yield to an overstrained Quixotism of sentiment; and they end by drugging themselves with this maxim above quoted, which is dear to lethargic souls: "Sparta is thy lot, adorn her."[1]

---

[1] Dr. Littledale has displayed great eloquence in presenting the various aspects of this subject, both in pamphlets and newspaper articles. The Abbé Martin, he says, "has spoken truly in saying that the lack of enthusiasm and of the heroic and apostolic spirit has been the most crying defect of the Church of England. He has generously said that Ritualists have got just this very apostolic spirit. There is no doubt at this moment that Roman Catholics in England, and especially Roman Catholic clergymen, are much safer from hostility and molestation than the Ritualist ecclesiastic, who is the one exception made to the equal protection and incidence of the law. For a Ritualistic to become a Roman Catholic, is to pass from the van of battle to the rear, to exchange the cross for the olive-branch. On any theory of Christian conflict, of self-sacrifice and devotion, his nobler and truer post is where the blows are falling thickest, for in that part of the battle is the King."—" Reply," pp. 63, 64.

A very brief reflection must lead to the conclusion that the Ritualistic situation is, both morally and religiously, full of danger; and the Ritualists surely cannot blame those Catholic controversialists who endeavour to point out the inconsistency and the logical inaccuracy of the position, and who in so doing fulfil a great duty and perform an act of the truest charity.

IV. What, then, is the true solution of the two questions which we have asked above? The object of the present volume is to aid those who are anxiously and laboriously seeking an answer, and we will take the simplest and most logical way to attain this end.

Without entering upon an exhaustive discussion of the subject, we will sum up what we have to say in a few words.

The questions referred to may be epitomised as follows:—1. Why is it that the Anglican body and the Ritualistic party, though containing in themselves much that is good, *cannot* be recognised as the Church founded by our Lord Jesus Christ? And 2. Why is it that the Catholic Church, in spite of the inevitable shortcomings of so many of her members, *can* be recognised as that divinely established Church? Or, in other words: What are the reasons which hinder the Anglican body from making part of the one Fold? and what are the reasons which constitute the Roman Church as that one Fold?

The examination of this subject is thus divided into two portions; and it is an examination which all who are on their road from Anglicanism to Catholicism must make carefully, each one for himself. It is under these two heads that the line of argument taken in these essays must be resumed. The first three papers, though far from exhausting the subject, show briefly that the Anglican body, even in the Ritualistic and High Church branches of her communion, where she is seen under her most favourable aspect, can put forward no real claim to be considered as the Church of our Divine Lord.

The Ritualists are specially concerned in this matter; for they all, or nearly all, recognise and lament the many and serious defects of the Anglican system— the absence of defined dogmas clearly enunciated and binding on all her members, the utter confusion of her ceremonial system, the complete abeyance of discipline, the absolute subjection of the Church to the State, which may indeed be more fitly termed the absorption of the Church by the State—the result of which is, that there is no unity in the Anglican Church save in her relations towards, and by the authority of, the temporal power.

The last three papers refer to the second question. Our object has been to show that if the Ritualists do not acknowledge the Divine origin and continuity of the Roman Church, it is because they know her imperfectly, or because they do not know her as she really is.

The second portion of this subject when undertaken by Anglicans, usually occupies more time than the first portion. This is partly because they adopt a defective method: they busy themselves with details, when they should take a general view. They discuss isolated facts, obscured by prejudice, by want of good faith, and by party spirit; consequently they are long before they arrive at any conclusion, and oftentimes they come to no conclusion at all. The only way for them to reach the goal swiftly and surely is, to consider the doctrinal, ceremonial, and disciplinary system of the Church in its entirety.

They have but to cast their eyes on the living Church of Christ, as she stands before them at this moment—they have but to see her as she is, not as she appears in the records of her foes, and they will then say: "The finger of God is *there.*"

Where else will they find such unity of discipline,

ritual, and dogma? Where else will they see more honour given where honour is really due? And how, looking on the Church as one great and consistent whole, can they dare to speak of *maximisers* and *minimisers*?

Undoubtedly, imperfections may be found here and there amongst Catholics; but, these are personal imperfections, they are not inherent in the system. Elsewhere, the imperfections belong more to the system itself than to the individuals who administer it, and who are, for the most part, good and estimable in themselves, whilst the system is miserably defective.

Those High Churchmen and Ritualists who desire to examine the religious difficulty thoroughly and earnestly, should endeavour, in the first place, to adopt a sound method of argument; and, in the next place, should seek to arm themselves against all the inborn ideas and feelings belonging to their position. Their own observation and experience will soon convince them that the Reformation—the counter-Reformation as some love to call it—which they have dreamed of, attempted, and partially carried out, will accomplish, can accomplish, nothing more than it has already done. Beyond the adoption of vestments, the improvement of Church furniture, the holding of missions and retreats, and the establishment of guilds and sisterhoods, it cannot go. Ritualism cannot rebuild the Catholic faith. It cannot reconstruct Church discipline. It cannot even change the Anglican ceremonial. Though it has made some tentative efforts in these directions, the sanction of ecclesiastical authority, which alone gives value to undertakings for religion and renders them lawful, would be wanting to these as to all its other endeavours.

When Ritualists have reached this stage of the argument, they will have more than half solved the second portion of the question. For, in spite of those imperfections inseparable from humanity which are to be found in the Catholic Church, it must be acknowledged that she alone, of all Christian communions, possesses that unity of faith and that strength of discipline, which, without checking development and progress, binds the past and the present together with links uniting the faithful of our own day to the disciples of our Divine Master.

Those who examine these questions calmly and impartially; those who have but one object in life—to find the truth and to make her their own; those who study prayerfully and humbly—will soon see and understand that it is God alone who is the source of all Light and Truth. Those who seek the Truth without His aid, labour in vain, and will never see her as she is. We, too, must ourselves say: "In Thy Light we shall see light" (Ps. xxxv. 10).

RITUALISM, PROTESTANTISM, AND CATHOLICISM.

THERE is much which deserves to attract the notice of contemporary society, and to fix the attention of serious observers, in the singular phenomenon of the religious revival which is termed "Ritualism." It is, in fact, no ordinary phenomenon which has effected this spiritual regeneration in the heart of English Protestantism, by efforts coming from within, and by the action of Protestantism reacting on itself. It offers matter for interesting observations of social psychology; and we doubt whether history affords many instances of such a revival.

Sometimes, indeed, recurring to decadent ages, or to those which are on the eve of dissolution, we encounter nations which are suddenly restored to life, which once more lift up their heads, recover their strength, and renew their youth; but, when we look more closely, instead of pausing on the surface of history, we examine the events themselves, and the causes which produce them, then, it becomes manifest that the revival asserted to be spontaneous was simply the effect of external causes. God, says the Scripture, "created the generations of the world healthful" (2 Wisdom, i. 14). But, in order that a people may be healed, a medicine must be found, and this medicine must be sought outside of that people; since there is no instance of a sick man, who has reached a certain stage of prostration, being able to restore himself to life. Lazarus, indeed, left the grave: but, before he issued from the sepulchre and resumed his place in his home at Bethany, it was necessary for Christ to open the tomb and to release him from his bonds, by uttering the words which restored him to life : " Lazarus, come forth." It is without precedent that the dead should restore themselves to life. When a nation is dead, it cannot live again ; and when a nation is dying, it can only be preserved from the grave by a miracle.

Once, undoubtedly, the Roman Empire was seen to die, and then apparently to revive under a new form, in those European nations which have preserved its laws and usages ; but this was the case only in appearance. It was not really the social system of Rome, whose day was over. That social system gave way to the barbarous era which supplanted it, and which gathered the heritage of its predecessor, seeming to reanimate it, while it was in fact forming an entirely new society. It was a succession, not a resurrection. But, this succession was, under the guidance of Providence, effected so naturally, that it was for some time possible to mistake it for an actual resurrection.

The Catholic Church alone appears to be endowed with the power of endless renewal ; but, this is because in reality she never dies. Peoples go and come ; they enter into her bosom ; they are born, increase, grow old, and die. And this leads to the belief among some men that the Catholic Church dies, although, in fact, she is ever the same, ever advancing, ever young, since God has made, and still preserves, her immortal. We see her beside the cradle of nascent peoples, and find her once more at the deathbed of nations ; and while the world is ever being renewed, she alone does not die. She is always the same, always endowed with a youthfulness which cannot fade, with a vitality which nothing can take from her, and thus it is that she lives on for ever.

The sects, on the other hand, which separate from her, are subject to the conditions of human existence, and share the lot of earthly things. They are therefore no sooner detached from the stem whence they drew their divine life, than they begin to languish and decline, to become extinct, and to die; and as there was a time when they did not exist, so the day comes when they are said to be no more.

Protestantism forms no exception to this law of history. Jesus Christ has pronounced its sentence of death in the parable of the vine; and we can already discern its fulfilment. English Protestantism alone appears to contradict this general law. In what is called Ritualism, the lopped branch seems at this moment to have found a fresh life, and to have recovered an appearance of youth, just when its dissolution was expected.

This phenomenon is certainly strange and unexpected. But, it is still more strange that Ritualism, in coming to life, has everywhere excited, not merely surprise and astonishment, but indignation, anger, threats, and persecution. Ritualism is perhaps more offensive to English Protestants than Roman Catholicism; nor does it, on the other hand, find much sympathy among some Catholics. Protestants persecute the Ritualists, and wish to drive them out of their communion; while Catholics decline, and with too much reason, to receive them, so long as they are not disposed to submit to the Church.

This is a singular fate; and when events which are so intimately connected with the salvation of souls, with the future of a great people, and with the prosperity of the Catholic Church pass before our eyes, ought we not to grant them consideration, in order to ascertain their cause, and to discover their explanation? They contain more than one lesson; and we should be wrong not to gather up the lessons which these contemporary facts afford. So, at least, it appears to us; and for this reason we wish to devote some space to English Ritualism, in order to test its strength, to show its weakness, and to predict its destiny.

I. A religious system that has made the progress which Ritualism has made, in spite of the attacks directed against it, of the obstacles placed in its way, and of the legal prosecutions in which it has been involved, must indeed possess certain strong principles and some elements of vitality. Nor is there any doubt that Ritualism is on the increase, and that its progress has been perceptible, first in England, then in America, and finally in the colonies. It has been assailed on every side, by Protestants and even sometimes, but for very different reasons, by Catholics. The former have sought to extinguish it by the strong hand of the law, "to put it down," while the latter have admitted that the imputations made against it were just; and yet, in spite of dislike on the one hand, and persecution on the other, Ritualism advances. It advances, undaunted either by the blows which were inflicted yesterday, or by those which threaten it on the morrow. Not many years ago a new law directed against Ritualism was passed, the vigour of the ancient laws having been exhausted against its boldest representatives. This new law has been put in force. Some of the Ritualist clergy have been condemned, and the same or a worse fate, viz., deprivation, is preparing for others. Yet, in spite of these facts, and others more hostile, we repeat that Ritualism advances with apparently rapid strides.

Everything which enables us to trace the course of public opinion in England proves this truth beyond a doubt. The Ritualist churches are built more ornate than formerly; the services are less cold, and better attended; church decorations assume a more important place in divine worship; the display of religious sentiment in palpable and visible signs increases; the rising tide is not limited to the members of the Anglican Church : it has even extended to the Dissenting communities, and to the Wesleyans in particular. This fact has of late been particularly manifest, and it has even entered the citadel of ancient Protestantism, or what is called the Low Church, as well as the Broad Church parties.

Nowhere do we now find the negligence and sloth, the physical and moral torpor, the disregard of forms, which forty years ago was general among the religious bodies of England. In London, for example, most of the churches which belong to the Established Church have unconsciously adopted Ritualistic observances, and it is not one of the least curious and hopeful symptoms, to find the most implacable enemies of Ritualism carried away by the movement which they wish to oppose. Progress has been and is made in everything: in doctrine, in worship, in religious practices, in charitable works and institutions; all have been drawn into the Anglo-Catholic current. It is not only the Anglo-Catholics, the Ritualists, the Sacerdotalists, by whom these things are proclaimed and asserted. From them nothing else could be expected, for men are always unwilling to confess themselves vanquished. The power of sentiment is so great, that it easily transforms absolute defeat into victory. It would, therefore, be strange to find any confession of defeat in the writings of the Ritualists; but, in order to proclaim victory, and to appear triumphant, it is necessary to be really powerful and vigorous. It is, in a word, necessary for a man to feel himself master of the situation. And Ritualism makes no secret of this conviction, but proclaims it everywhere. Our enemies, says a Ritualist journal :—

"Our enemies have obtained several legal victories, but these victories have not gone far enough to be of any real service to them. The Catholic (Anglo-Catholic) cause continues to prosper, and loses none of its power of expansion. The transition from the old phase to the new phase, which extends the influence of the High Church party to places which it never reached before, is apparent throughout the country in a thousand ways, consciously or unconsciously." ("Church Review," Dec. 25, 1875.)

The future of the Anglican Church is in the hands of

the High Church party, and of Ritualism, which forms its vanguard.

We could cite many facts which confirm the Ritualist point of view. The Bishop of Winchester's Pastoral Letter, "On the Position of Parties in the Anglican Church" (1875), shows that in the Episcopate itself, generally so hostile to Ritualism, a more moderate tone, a kind of conversion, has insensibly been produced. We might also urge the advances made by the Evangelical party towards the moderate section of High Churchmen, which, from the doctrinal point of view of the Ritualists, does not differ much from the Erastianism of 1840. The Evangelical party seeks to break the bonds which attach this portion of the Anglican Church to Ritualism. They wish to enlist it in a crusade against Anglo-Catholic tendencies, conscious that they are unable to stand alone, and that they represent too insignificant a minority of religious life to make any impression on public opinion.

The admissions which escape from Evangelicals are very conclusive: their organs are continually protesting against Ritualist aggression. Wherever a beautiful church is built, a surpliced choir introduced, a reredos erected, or an old-fashioned hymn-book set aside, the Evangelicals utter cries of horror. "We cannot," says a Ritualistic journal, "call the Holy Communion a mystery, mention sacramental grace, speak of the divine succession of the ministry, or call ourselves Catholics, without provoking a torrent of invective. The flood-gates of wrath are opened on Mr. Mackonochie; but Bishop Jackson (of London) also excites bitterness and irritation, because he has spoken of the forgiveness of sins as accorded in the Holy Communion." ("Church Review," Dec. 1875.)

There is hardly a number of the "Record" or of the "Rock" which does not contain admissions and complaints of the same kind. Ritualism is detected everywhere, and is, in fact, and under different forms, really present everywhere. It is apparent in doctrine, in worship, in the mode of chanting, in religious works and institutions, in publications, in confraternities, schools, guilds, parish missions, and retreats for both clergy and laity. The "Rock" lately published a letter from Count Povoleri, a Continental Protestant, which contains the following remarks. After asserting that three members of the Episcopate, at least, show an inclination towards Ritualism, he cites a letter from the Protestant Primate, condemning certain practices as opposed to Anglicanism, and goes on to say:—

"I am astonished to see, in the majority of the London churches which I have attended, all the ceremonies of the Papal Church. Every gesture, even the most insignificant, every usage, every ornament or decoration which we see on the Continent, may be found in such churches as St. Alban's, St. Michael's, Shoreditch, St. Peter's, London Docks, and, with singular correctness, at St. Paul's, Walworth, where there are three communion tables, at which the Ritualist clergy minister, dressed like the priests who say mass, administer the sacrament, three at each altar, at the same time, just as it is done in the Papal Church." ("Rock," Dec. 24, 1875.)

The progress of Ritualism is therefore an acknowledged fact. The future of the Anglican Church belongs to it: it already encloses the land in its meshes; and wherever in the heart of the English nation there is any remnant of religious sentiment, it is drawn towards Ritualism. Willingly or unwillingly, the attraction exists, even for those who resist it. What does this mean? What is the cause which has thus effected, in the midst of a great people, of a people essentially industrial and commercial, this spiritual revolution which is indeed marvellous and consolatory, and which, if not perverted and distorted to a pernicious end, by sectarian and uncatholic spirit, may conduce to good results in the future?

We trust that we are not mistaken in our belief that

there are, in our day, few subjects more worthy of consideration than the consequences involved in the progress of Ritualism.

II. When we compare Ritualism with other forms of Protestantism, the first thing which strikes a mind well acquainted with the history of sects and doctrines, is the superiority of the former from a simply intellectual and doctrinal point of view. Protestantism is, strictly speaking, composed only of negations. Its articles always begin with, *I do not believe.* Now, it is as impossible to create a system out of negations as it is to form a man out of nothing; and for this reason, Protestantism has, properly speaking, no creed. In order to be a Protestant, it is not necessary to adhere to a precise, definite, immutable dogma. It suffices to oppose the dogmas of Catholicism. This is so true that the most ardent opposers, not merely of Catholicism, but of Christianity itself, are now included in the ranks of Protestantism. A man may be a Protestant, and yet may deny the supernatural, the miraculous, the divinity of Jesus Christ. Strauss has said: "We are no longer Christians, but we still continue to be good Protestants."

The natural tendency of Protestantism is towards Rationalism, in the first instance, as an intellectual principle; and then, towards Materialism, as its practical consequence. If Protestantism did not arrive at this conclusion from its very beginning, it was merely from a want of logic, and owing to its inconsequence. But since, sooner or later, logic asserts its rights, and rigorously deduces the conclusions contained in the principles laid down for it—even among the people, and with those who are least accustomed to reflect or to reason—the day has come when the remnant of Christianity retained by Protestantism at the time of the Reformation has disappeared in order to give place to Rationalism. It is in our own day that this has happened. We stand by to see the intellectual decomposition of Protestantism. In France and in Germany the work is already accomplished. In England it is far advanced.

A system which is composed simply of negations cannot long satisfy the understanding, especially the understanding which has received only an imperfect culture. There is, indeed, a species of intellectual Materialism in which a delicately organised mind sometimes delights, and which consists in dissecting all truths and all systems, without accepting any of them; but, this intellectual Materialism is not found in the mass of the human race. The average man requires something more positive—truths which present themselves with a body as well as with a soul; dogmas which are defined, tangible, and palpable; dogmas which the senses and the mind can grasp and retain, so as to feel that they possess something not wholly unsubstantial. The people cannot be satisfied with negations; they will not accept barren sentiments, even though expressed in language full of beauty.

No observer, of a philosophical mind, can doubt that this is the law of the human intellect; and this is a fact of extreme importance, since it explains why Protestantism and why Natural Religion never have had, and never will have, many enthusiastic followers. Passages worthy of the topic have been written, from a rational point of view, on the worship due to God. M. Jules Simon has written eloquently on the subject; but, this eloquence has not made one worshipper in spirit and in truth. M. Jules Simon, we believe, is himself convinced of the fact. Natural Religion can only make intellectual Epicureans.

Such has been, and is, the fate of Protestantism. In proportion to its inclination to Natural Religion, it has left the masses without faith and without worship; and as for the higher classes of society, it has gradually led them into that intellectual Materialism which we call Rationalism. Jesus Christ and Christianity are not indeed altogether ignored; but they have lost all living force. They have become a mere object of study: they have ceased to be a God and a religion. And if a sense of their beauty still remains, it is powerless to produce the deep influence upon a man's life which is called a conversion.

We repeat, that Rationalism is unable to satisfy either the mind or heart of man. The mind feels the need of a belief, the heart feels the need of love—the need to love and to believe in, not phantoms and chimæras, but living, visible, palpable, almost actual realities. It is necessary for man to have a positive religion, which distinctly tells him: "That is what you must believe, this is what you must do."

No wonder then that we see, from time to time, a reaction take place in the midst of the decomposition of Protestantism, which has been going on for the last three centuries. One such reaction took place in England in the seventeenth century, under Charles I. and Archbishop Laud; another in the eighteenth century, under John Wesley and George Whitfield. But neither of these reactions possessed the energy, the proportions, and the success of the one we are now considering, which is termed Ritualism.

With the energy of men who feel that they are suspended over an abyss into which they are about to fall and perish, those English Protestants who have retained a remnant of faith in the supernatural, in the divinity of Jesus Christ and of His Church, have set to work, and while they reject as elements of ruin and death the two primordial principles of Protestantism, the right of Private Judgment and the all-sufficiency of Holy Scripture, they cling to the remnant of Christian doctrine contained in their formularies, and have thus recovered, one by one, nearly all the beliefs which their ancestors had lost. Where Protestantism says: "I do not believe;" Ritualism says: "I do believe." Protestantism says: "I do not believe in the divinity of the Church; I do not believe in tradition, in the Sacraments, in the Real Presence, in the sacrifice, in the remission of sins, in the priesthood, in the communion and the worship of the Saints." Ritualism says: "I believe in the divinity of the Church; I believe in tradition; I believe in the Sacraments; I believe in the Eucharist, in the remission of sins, in the Sacrament of penitence and of absolution, in the Sacrament of ordination, in the priesthood and the hierarchy; I believe in the communion of Saints, and in the worship which has been generally accorded to them."

Not only does Ritualism say these things, but it causes them to be believed; and we see lettered and unlettered men, the higher classes and the working classes, those who formerly remained strangers to all religious sentiment, apply themselves to practices of devotion. At St. Alban's, Holborn, for instance, nearly as many men as women are worshippers; and it is easy to see that the majority of the men, for the most part between twenty and thirty years of age, belong to the commercial or to the working class. They feel that the void in their intelligence has been filled, and that a body of organised doctrine has supplied the vacuum.

This species of resurrection, effected by Christianity on itself, is certainly a remarkable phenomenon; and perhaps there has been no more striking proof in our day of its power over the mind of man.

III. But, those who sympathise with the Ritualists have asked—How all these innovations could be reconciled with the law; and whether this reconstruction of the Christian creed, effected by means of a reaction against Protestantism, be not founded on the very principle of Protestantism, and of Rationalism, that is, of free examination? It is true that the Ritualists have again adopted ancient dogmas, dogmas which Protestants perhaps did wrong to reject. But, by what authority are they resumed, and what assurance have the Ritualists that it can always be done successfully? What warrant have they that they can always discern the truth in the midst of the negations and the systems accumulated by Protestantism, and that no error will be introduced into their formularies?

This objection is serious, and has been addressed to Ritualists both by friends and by enemies. The partisans of the new movement have not from the first clearly understood on what they must rely in order to justify their position. While advancing, they attempt to show, by study, research, and discussion, that they are introducing nothing absolutely new, or unknown, to their Church. They assert that they are not raising an entirely new building, but that it is merely a reconstruction; that they are restoring dogmas and practices which had a previous existence, and which at any rate were held in honour in all other Christian Churches. In the end, however, one idea has disengaged itself from the facts; one principle has arisen out of the fusion of elements; a flash of light has illumined the sky, and men have begun to speak, not of Tractarians, nor of Puseyites, nor of Ritualists, but of Anglo-Catholics.

The fraction of the Church of England to which we allude has rejected the sectarian spirit in order to adopt the Catholic spirit; and it uses Catholicity as the engine with which to beat down the prejudices of Protestants on the one side, and to meet the attacks of Roman Catholicism on the other. For this reason, they often say of themselves that they are "Catholics, but not Roman Catholics," and this is the title of a pamphlet by Dr. Littledale. The earlier disciples of Newman, Pusey, Keble, and Froude, the later scholars of Carter, Mackonochie, Denison, Bennett, and Liddon, entrench themselves behind the Catholicity both of their doctrines and of their practices as behind a wall which may defy all assaults and repel all attacks.

These men desire to be, and assert that they are, real Catholics. The catholicity of a doctrine, or of a practice, becomes their leading principle, their touchstone, and the directing rule of their conduct. It is by means of the well-known formula, given to us by St. Vincent de Lerins: *Quod ubique, quod semper, quod ab omnibus*,[1] that they hope to avoid all the difficulties which result from their religious eclecticism. They accept, assert, and claim this principle, and even boast of being the only men who declare it openly to the world. The Hon. Charles L. Wood, President of the English Church Union, has lately affirmed :—

> "For those who cannot reconcile the papal pretensions with their submission to the Church, for those who believe that faith must be always the same, for those who *ex animo* accept this definition of Catholic truth and this definition alone: *Quod semper, quod ubique, quod ab omnibus*, can there be anything more important than to present to the world in unmistakable characters the fact so grievously misunderstood, that Catholicity is not identical with the pretensions of Rome? If there ever was a time when it was needful to assert this truth, it is now, when on the one side we see the Church in communion with Rome admit a theory of infallibility which changes the infallible testimony of the Catholic Church with respect to the faith once delivered to the saints into an authority infallible in its institution of fresh dogmas; and on the other side we hear it openly asserted that there is neither a revelation, nor a church entrusted with its preservation. Our cause is among the most sacred committed to man; for we do not strive for this or that political party, we do not defend the witnesses of a charter, our efforts are not limited to our fellow-countrymen or to our race; our interests are more sacred and more exalted, since they are the interests of the Church of Jesus Christ Himself." ("Church Review," Dec. 1875.)

---

[1] This maxim of St. Vincent of Lerins, which is so frequently quoted by Ritualistic Writers or speakers, is often distorted, and used in a sense which is not warranted by the context. The intention of St. Vincent is this: He wishes to assert the Catholic principle for arriving at the certain knowledge of *Apostolical Doctrine*; that is, to the decision of absolute *antiquity*. And he formulates these two rules: 1, the *present* unanimous consent of the Church; 2, the consent of the Church *before* the rise of controversy. If these two rules do not apply, then he allows of an appeal to the Holy Scriptures.

IV. It cannot be denied that this is a grand principle ; and there can be no better proof of it than the use made by Catholics in all times of this celebrated maxim of St. Vincent de Lerins. Universal consent has always been regarded as the most solid proof and satisfactory warrant of truth. In philosophy it is sometimes the final criterion ; and it was natural that this argument should also find a place in religion. It is in fact impossible that a truth or a practice, in which all Christian people are agreed, can be wrong. Reason alone tells us so, without appealing to faith ; and St. Vincent has only impressed the seal of genius on a philosophical and rational thought, when he defined Catholic doctrine, in the words of a maxim : *Quod semper, quod ubique, quod ab omnibus.*

The whole question consists in ascertaining whether this proposition is as true in its *negative* as in its *affirmative* sense ; viz., if a truth can only be such on the condition that it has been believed everywhere, always, and by all. This question is important ; but, it would perhaps take us too far from our subject to solve it here, though we may possibly return to it.

The simple statement just made will, we think, suffice to show the form which, from the doctrinal point of view, the Anglo-Catholic movement has taken. The universal consent of Christianity on any point of doctrine or of ritual is certainly a strong citadel ; and although Protestantism has affected a great disdain for tradition, it is impossible to remain insensible to an obstacle which it cannot easily evade. Reason is convincing on this point, and superior to Rationalism.

There is, therefore, a firm foundation for Ritualism, both with respect to doctrine and practice ; and yet, it must be admitted, that this is not the way in which Ritualism has become a power in the world, has exercised influence on the people, and has advanced into the heart of the English nation—making progress which has perhaps been slow, but is continual and apparent. Although doctrines undoubtedly play a great part in the lives of men and of peoples, there is something which speaks more clearly to the masses, and which is more convincing than doctrines—and that is, good works; since works are the touchstone of doctrines. Reason itself confirms the great principle of Jesus Christ—"By their fruits ye shall know them." Systems may be known by the practical consequences to which they give birth, by their results, and the fruits which they produce.

Now, Protestantism is condemned from this point of view. We do not wish to speak here of its intellectual results, which touch too closely on the province of doctrine. We rather propose to point out the moral effect of Protestantism on the religious life of men and of peoples. Nowhere are they so apparent, so palpable, and so tangible as in England.

It was one of the visions of Protestantism to spiritualise human worship, but it has done more than spiritualise—it has rarefied, suppressed, destroyed it. From the moment precise dogmas were set aside, belief became vague, and practices became uncertain, and finally, the people who by nature are the most religious in the world, as they are the gravest and most earnest, have ceased to regard religion as anything more than an intellectual act. Religion has for a long while consisted, as it still consists for many Anglicans, in reading the Bible or in hearing a sermon. The Bible is much used in England; there is generally one in every room of a respectable house; it is often to be found in hotels, and even at some railway stations. And although family reading of the Bible has ceased in many places, there are still copies of the Bible which contain records of all the memorable events connected with the house to which they belong. The religion of England was once summed up in the reading of the Bible; and it was at that time that the Evangelical party was at the height of its power. The

English Church was never more powerful from the merely human point of view; the union between Church and State was never more intimate; and the Church was never more wealthy, than in those days. She never possessed a more able and learned ministry; and yet, in spite of all this, the action of the clergy was never so powerless and sterile. They finally contented themselves with a life of learned leisure; and the day at length came when the temple committed to their care was closed, because there were no more worshippers.

Let us seek for the cause of this state of things. The inquiry is interesting, and will repay the trouble of consideration.

We have already said that the questions of doctrine are, from one point of view, of secondary importance, and this is strictly true so far as the mass of the people are concerned. The people judge of doctrines by the works which they produce. Works are in their eyes the proof, whether the doctrine be good or evil.

If those whose office it is to teach lead a life which is morally unproductive; if their acts show none of the spirit which we call zeal and devotion—it is easy for the people to see that the doctrine is bad. This was precisely the result of the Established Religion in England. Its ministers were well-born and well-educated, and they often presented a perfect type of what was called a perfect gentleman. But, they were far from resembling any other Christian clergy in their education, in their habits, in their tastes, and in their mode of life; and they were, in general, not conspicuous for the apostolic spirit which appertains to the holy ministry. They rarely possessed anything of the sacerdotal character, and in type they resembled the professors of a French Lycée rather than the members of the French clergy.

Neo-Anglicanism has attempted to fill up this void, and has to some extent succeeded in so doing. It has regained some Catholic doctrines; and with the doctrines, it has recovered the spirit which they represent, the zeal to which they give birth, the devotion which they impose, and the sacrifice which they involve; and so, instead of a purely intellectual life, we now see a life which may be indeed called a religious and spiritual. The minister is no longer only a man of letters; he has become a shepherd once more, and a shepherd of souls. He takes an interest in the moral and religious welfare of his flock; he looks after the sheep who err and go astray; he finds his way to the shop, the cottage, and the hovel, to the lodging-house, to the refuge, and to the prison. Good works of all kinds have been established; schools have been founded for the poor and ignorant; and where torpor and stagnation formerly prevailed, we note the signs of energy and of life.

Anglicanism has, in this way also, made itself Catholic; and it is chiefly by this means that it is regaining a portion of its empire over the masses and over the poor. The people have understood that the clergy were working for them, and the poor have no longer felt that they were alone. The artisan has recognised a feeling of goodwill towards him; and all classes have been drawn towards the religion which they formerly ignored.

The apostolic spirit is the great power of Ritualism. To that spirit, wherever it is known and well represented, its popularity is due. When the people have a consoling sense of the devoted and self-sacrificing efforts which are made for them, they need nothing more, and say with the sure instinct with which God has endowed the heart of man: there is "the way, the truth, and the life."

The enemies of Ritualism cannot refuse to admit that it is distinguished by this apostolic spirit, by zeal, by devotion, and by self-sacrifice. The bishops who most dislike the Ritualists have repeatedly accorded this homage to them; and when Ritualists are prosecuted, their opponents are not ashamed to say that, from a moral point of view, their ministry is not only irreproachable, but is even worthy of admiration and of praise.[1]

If Ritualism is advancing, if the good works which it organises and inspires are diffused in every direction, it is due to the apostolic spirit which it has reinfused into the Anglican schism. There is in it, perhaps, only an incomplete life; but life is really there, a life full of thoughts of God and the soul; a life which understands that faith without works is dead, that to believe without devotion and self-sacrifice is neither meritorious nor enduring—this is, we repeat, the principle of the success of Anglo-Catholicism. If the English people are drawn in this direction, and are in this way brought back to holy religion, it is because they find in it some vitality, while, elsewhere, Protestantism has nothing to show but the coldness of death and the stillness of the tomb.

V. It is intelligible, after what we have said, why the Anglo-Catholic movement—we willingly accept this term, since it characterises the origin and the tendencies of the religious transformation of contemporary Anglicanism—should have made progress, in spite of all the opposition it encounters, and in spite of all the obstacles, legal or otherwise, placed in its way. It is because it contains in reality a considerable

[1] Not long ago the Bishop of London wrote to the parishioners of St. Alban's, Holborn, about the Rev. A. H. Mackonochie as follows:—"I am not surprised at the warm feelings of respect and affection which you and so many of your fellow-parishioners entertain towards Mr. Mackonochie. It would be strange if it were otherwise. I myself appreciate highly and admire the unwearied zeal and devotion with which he and those who have been helping him have been labouring among you for more than seventeen years, and the many useful and helpful works which they have established and maintained. I only regret the more that all this was not done, as I believe it might have been done just as well, without the disregard of the laws and customs of the Church of England and disobedience to lawful authority, which have caused so much disquiet and disunion in the Church, so much trouble to yourselves, and to me so much anxiety and sorrow."

portion[1] of Christian truth, and a strong tide of spiritual life. Admitting that it is imperfect and rudimentary, yet, an evil course has been forsaken by it for a good one. The movement has taken a right direction: turning its back on Protestantism, it advances, if we consider the matter only from an external point of view, with rapid strides towards Catholicism, although it still remains very far off in its cardinal principles and doctrines.

It is consequently easy to explain the opposition offered by Protestants of the Low Church, and of the Broad Church schools of thought, when they see Catholic practices revived in the bosom of the High Church parties. They consider themselves not only forsaken, but betrayed. The Ritualists are not merely deserters who forsake their cause and refuse to take up arms to defend it; they are traitors, who seek to pass over with arms and baggage to the enemy, in order to fight against their former friends with all the animosity and energy which are derived from a truth achieved at the cost of sacrifices, sometimes at the cost of tears, of blood, even of life. The ranks of Protestantism are thinned, and its ramparts lack defenders; while the forces opposed to it are re-doubled by the power which they receive from these new recruits. It is still more exasperating to Protestants to note that, with few exceptions, it is their best men who forsake them. When there is a pastor zealous for the salvation of souls, a minister who loves the poor, a clergyman steeped in the learning of Christian antiquity, an enlightened mind, an upright character, a brave heart—such men swell the ranks of the High Church party, in order to become Ritualists, and oftentimes from being Ritualists, to end in becoming true Catholics.

Nothing can give Frenchmen an idea of the acri-

---

[1] This assertion, of course, is only true of Ritualism taken in general; for it is very difficult to say what any given Ritualist believes, and practises. Ritualism is a comprehensive and vague term.

mony which exists between the two extreme sections which flourish and develop beneath the shadow of that singular institution which is called the Church of England. Our political parties in France show no tenderness for each other; yet, till the last few years, they were far from the bitterness which divides Protestants of the Low Church party from the Ritualists.

Roman Catholics are not in good repute with some of the religious and political parties in England. Although great progress has been made in subduing passion, there are still many prejudices to destroy; and it would be a mistake to suppose that there was no more to be done, because there have been illustrious and numerous conversions. As a nation England is still Protestant to the backbone, and very Protestant. A few years ago it was sufficient to call up before her the spectre of Romanism, in order to break all her political bonds, and to animate her against what she regarded as a fresh Papal aggression. Men speak as if the conversion of England were already accomplished. But, this is an error: the transformation has indeed begun, and there is every reason to believe that its progress will eventually be rapid; though that day is still far off.

Of whatever suspicions Catholics may be the object, they are now less unpopular to ordinary English Protestants than the Ritualists; and this fact is easily explained. A speaker (the Rev. G. Weldon, reported in the "Rock," May, 1875) has said:—

"The most vital doctrines of Romanism are openly taught by clergymen of the Church of England: some of the books containing these doctrines have been published by dignitaries of the Church, and contain prefaces written by bishops. It is this which makes Ritualism more dangerous than the Papal religion itself, for while some people are deceived, others carry out the deliberate purpose of Catholicising, or rather of Romanising, the Church of England."

Again, an anti-Ritualist journal, the "Rock," has said: " Our controversy against Ritualism is essentially a controversy against Rome." We must add, that the controversy against Ritualism is even more. It costs more to oppose those who once were friends or allies. The conflict, then, becomes more serious; since, in addition to the moral weakness involved in every desertion, it throws discredit on the cause, by revealing its weak points, and exposing its wounds and injuries. In a controversy with Roman Catholics, it is enough to say: "You represent a corrupt Church; you are sons of the harlot of the Apocalypse; you are the followers of Antichrist." But, what is to be urged against those who, only yesterday, were ranked among the adversaries of Rome, and who to-day support her cause, at any rate indirectly, by adopting her doctrines and by using her practices? Such reproaches might be met by the following reply: "You attack us because we have deserted your flag; but, we know this flag as well as that of Rome, and we know what it represents. It represents only the sectarian spirit: the spirit of error instead of doctrine, and the spirit of impotence instead of action. We lived in your midst, we have seen your works, we have judged by your fruits as our Master has commanded, and those fruits are not those of the Tree of Life. We know your prejudices, sympathies, and tastes; and we are certain that when you have to choose, you will prefer vice to virtue, error to truth. You will always be in favour of impiety rather than religion, of rebellion rather than obedience. We know your system and its weapons, and we do not fear them."

Such is the reply which the Ritualists now make; and with it they will continue to repel the Evangelical attack. We believe that it is a valid and unanswerable answer. If there be an adversary against which Ritualism must prevail, it is Protestantism. The reply is not merely a reproach constantly directed against the well-known Reformers of the sixteenth century; it is a protest against their work, and a condemnation of their memory. English Protestants feel that it is so. Ritualism casts its spears into their flanks, piercing them to the quick, and causing blood to flow from wounds which are never healed. For this reason, Protestantism, irritated by suffering and torture, and provoked by its own impotence, makes the air resound with loud cries of anger and of vengeance. It abhors Ritualism even more than Catholicism, and wishes to make an end of it at any cost. It is a question whether Protestantism will ever succeed in so doing, and the future only can reply.

VI. We have now to ask: why Catholics are also opposed to Ritualism; and why they dislike a party which was not in its origin their enemy; and whose cause is almost identical with their own? It is the right, and almost the duty, of Protestants to hate the Ritualists, whom they regard as traitors and conspirators. Nor have we any difficulty in explaining why Ritualists detest Protestants. It is their part to do so; they know Protestantism, its passions, and its prejudices. They have been deceived by Protestantism; and when the veil fell from their eyes, they were at once filled with a feeling of hatred against the teaching which misled them, and which threatened to wreck their lives. We repeat, that this mutual dislike between Protestants and Ritualists is easily understood; but, until very lately, it was more difficult to see why some Catholics should attack the Ritualists.

It is impossible to deny, that Ritualists have not always been treated by some Catholic writers as they seemed to deserve. On the other hand, the Ritualists have not acted fairly in their dealings with Catholics. Words of bitterness and blame, of ill-nature and derision, have escaped them on various occasions, especially of late. But, it would be strange if it were otherwise. There are reminiscences of the past which they are endeavouring to extinguish; and we must not be surprised if they are sometimes wanting in fairness and goodwill. Nevertheless, the tone of the great majority of the Protestant press and of Ritualistic literature, at least outside their newspapers, is polite and courteous.[1] We are sometimes astonished to find in Anglo-Catholic books and newspapers passages which force us to ask if they were really penned by Protestants. Why are the Ritualists sometimes ill-treated by Catholic writers?

We are far from accepting as incontestable, or at any rate as widely true, the assertion of a writer in the "Church Review" that "it is certain that the Ritualists are more disliked by Roman Catholics than are all the other parties in the Anglican Church, and that they will rejoice when the Church Regulation Act is put in force." (Church Review, Dec. 1875.) This assertion is exaggerated, if not wholly false; and we do not hesitate to say why we are convinced of the contrary. If it were true, as the writer asserts, that the Ritualists are so much disliked by Catholics, this

---

[1] Our exception, of course, specially applies to the "Church Times," whose tone and language are extremely offensive to all honest readers. Many writers also do not act as courteous opponents ought to do. In this volume we shall give too many proofs of the unbecoming language used by Ritualistic controversialists. We are sorry to be obliged to name Dr. Littledale as the chief transgressor of common courtesy. Every Christian man must deplore the absence of charity and politeness which characterise the Ritualistic press. In fact, Anglicans themselves protest against the tone of some papers; and we find this letter—which is one amongst others that might be quoted—in the "Church Review" of 1879, page 175, col. 3:—"Will you pardon a very sincere wellwisher of the 'Church Review' for venturing to remonstrate with you on the tone you have of recent years assumed towards the Roman Catholic Church? One is not surprised at whatever such a paper as the 'Church Times' may be pleased to say about Roman Catholicism, or any other subject; but I confess I do expect better things of the 'Church Review.' Of course, I do not either wish or expect you to defend what you believe to be wrong in Romanism; and I fully admit that, in controversy with Roman Catholics, it is frequently necessary to show that you are aware of the fact that their shield has a reverse side as well as our own. But what I complain of is, the carping sarcastic tone you too often adopt in writing of Rome, and the avidity with which you appear to seize upon any point which, you think, tells against her. That you may plead the evil example of Roman journals as an excuse I fully admit; but why follow a bad example? Surely, if we are the true Catholic Church in England, we can calmly look down upon the abuse which springs from envy and jealousy! But, I was pleased to notice a few months ago, when I last had an opportunity of seeing the 'Tablet,' that that extremely well-written paper had adopted a much more charitable tone towards us than had been the case a year before when I had last seen it."

would suffice to conciliate the toleration, if not the affection, of the other parties of the English Church. But this is not the case. Ritualists are deeply hated by Protestants of the old school, and cannot therefore, we may suppose, be equally hated, as it is asserted, by Catholics.

But are this writer's assertions altogether unfounded? Every allowance may be made for exaggerations. It is quite true that some words have been spoken by certain members of the Catholic Church, which ought not to have been spoken. We could quote newspaper articles of a nature which must be wounding to those who have retained throughout their controversies a feeling of courtesy and delicacy; and we do not hesitate to say that a tone of bitterness and contempt is neither Christian nor politic. When men come to us with hasty steps, after they have shaken off a mountain of prejudices, removed obstacles most difficult to overcome, broken the closest bonds of fellowship for the sake of opinions, and endured to be censured as cowards, traitors, and conspirators, they ought to be treated with respect and charity, even if they do not act as true Catholics. They are often men of culture; warm-hearted and upright men; men whose ideal has been, and is, to remove the barriers which separate them from the Catholic Church. When therefore they display a flag of truce, they ought not to be still treated as enemies.

The Catholic Church, as a Church, has never acted thus. It has condemned errors, while displaying pity and gentleness towards men, because she knows that souls are won by charity rather than by arguments; and the controversy which now agitates England concerns nothing less than the loss or the salvation of souls.

Moreover, we must consider that such conduct is impolitic, since Ritualism is partially accomplishing a work which Catholicism alone could accomplish, if at of a legislative assembly—have thought it strange that the privilege which they deny to many should be accorded to a single individual.[1] Infallibility, imperfectly explained or misunderstood, could not fail to be a stumbling-block to many serious minds and loyal hearts. Yet, we do not believe that this will, for any length of time, prove to be the reason of a Protestant reaction in England. For, when convinced of the truth that the Church is a divine society, it is not difficult to understand that infallibility is necessary to it. Reason herself tells us so; and she adds, that God finds it as easy to make one man infallible, as to make it impossible for the many to be deceived, or to deceive themselves or others. The hand of Providence is ever extended over the Church; and the infallibility of the Head of this Church is a necessary corollary of all the other privileges which are involved in the existence of the inheritor and guardian of divine truth.

But, in any case, if Protestants of the Low and the Broad Church schools find some difficulty in becoming Catholic after the definition of Infallibility, the same cannot be said of High Churchmen and of Ritualists. What is there in the doctrine of Infallibility which can long withhold them? An infallible Pope! Those among themselves whom they deem infallible may be counted by hundreds.

"Mr. Mackonochie is infallible; so are Mr. Bennett, Dr. Lee, Dr. Pusey: all the Ritualists are infallible, in spite of the difficulties which divide them. Each priest is a pope to himself and to his congregation."

Thus the "Rock" declared six years ago (Dec. 1874), and that newspaper added—

"Consequently there is no dogma to which the Ritualist clergy are so resolutely opposed as to the idea of submission to Rome; for, this would oblige them to receive a lesson of humility, and no longer to assume an air of independence."

---

[1] See a portion of the speech cited before, by the Hon. Charles L. Wood, p. 32.

If it may be admitted that some individuals of the Ritualist party are influenced by the considerations imputed to them by the " Rock," it is not so with the mass; and we cannot believe that the definition of Infallibility is the sole cause for the slackening of the impulse given to Protestantism in the direction of Catholicity forty years ago. A more general cause must be sought for the explanation of this fact.

It has been asserted that Ritualism is the real cause of the fact to which we allude; and this is stated by two classes of people, who are opposed to each other as they ought not to be, at all events, not after the present fashion—Ritualists and Catholics. If the Ritualists alone maintained this assertion, which looks like a paradox, and is, we believe, a paradox, we should perhaps refuse to believe it, and we should mistrust their testimony, fearing that it was an illusion, or a *ruse de guerre* on their part. We understand, indeed, their satisfaction in boasting of this fact, and how it would serve to repel the attacks of Protestants. It is an excellent mode of defence to be able to say to Evangelicals: "You accuse us of leading Anglicans to Rome, and say that for this reason you persecute us. Facts speak for themselves, and they are exactly opposed to your words. Since the rise of our party, conversions have everywhere diminished, and where Ritualism takes root, where souls can find, together with a doctrinal system which is more compact, sustained, developed, and catholic, a more ornate ritual, which interprets belief more exactly in speaking to the eye and the heart, there we find that the progress of secession to Rome is at once arrested. Cease therefore to accuse us. We are better defenders of the Anglican Church than you are; and you ought to aid us, instead of persecuting us."

Such language would come naturally from the lips of Ritualists, if it were true that Ritualism had retarded their return to the Church of Rome; and we could understand its use by Ritualists, since it would be their best defence. But, precisely because this language might be a weapon of Ritualism, we regard it with suspicion, although some Catholics accept all these assertions, and find in this false neo-Catholicism the most important hindrance to conversions. Yet, since Ritualists and Catholics assert a fact which provokes enthusiasm on the one side and anxiety on the other, we must submit to evidence, and confess that it is partially true, and true under some aspects of the case.

Some Catholics ask, Why should we leave the Ritualists in peace? why should we treat them with indulgence, charity, and goodwill, and fail to see the mischief they are doing? They assert that Ritualists arrest a multitude of souls half-way, which, without them and their imitation of Catholic worship, would attain to truth and the Catholic Church. They think Ritualism more dangerous than Protestantism, since it is more illusive, and more apt to mislead the masses. "It should therefore," they say, "be attacked and harassed without truce or respite, so that its adherents may be driven either to advance or to retreat. That they should advance is the object of our wishes, hopes, and prayers; and to this end we would give the last drop of our blood, nay, our very lives. But, it is certain that if the Ritualists will not advance, it is better that they should retreat and fall back into Protestantism." Such are the reasons which inspired the late attack on Ritualism, as it has been made by the press and by some Catholic writers. Let us inquire into the truth or falsehood of this view, its exact appreciation of the situation, and what our conduct should be with respect to it.

Before we proceed, it is perhaps expedient to ask ourselves if Ritualism is the only cause of this check or retreat, and if some Catholics have not in some degree contributed towards it. There are truths which, set forth inaccurately and without clearness, have wounded to the quick a people which are loyal and just, but jealous, susceptible, and imbued with many prejudices against Catholic doctrine, Catholic practice, and Catholic ritual. It is always a duty for Catholics to be wise, prudent, charitable; but this obligation is never more pressing than in a country where the Church is watched and surrounded by enemies. Every Catholic, then, represents Catholicism, and must be careful of his words, as well as of his acts. The innovations in ritual which have been brought forward may have been neither judicious nor discreet; and prudence would have enjoined reticence in religious manifestations which, good in themselves and excellent for other nations, astonish, alarm, and irritate a nation unaccustomed to their use for the last three centuries. It might, perhaps, have been possible to proceed more slowly, to make essentials the first object, and to advance by degrees, leaving it to time and reflection to prepare minds and hearts to welcome more varied and complete forms of worship. Before casting a stone at the Ritualists, it is well for us to examine our consciences, and to see if we have nothing with which to reproach ourselves. These questions are not out of place, and may provoke more than one reflection salutary to the good of the Church and the salvation of souls; for we must remember, that the good fame of Catholicism depends, to some extent, upon every one of us.

Perhaps we should not have had to complain of a momentary check in conversions, if Catholics had always followed the line of conduct marked out with a clear intuition and firm hand by the late Cardinal Wiseman, of revered memory; and if all Catholics knew how to listen to the teaching and to imitate the examples of those eminent men who, endowed with the purple, the mitre, or the crosier, or in the ranks of the priesthood, or the retirement of the cloister, are devoting themselves to the interests of God and the Church. Unhappily, this is not always the case, and this may be one of the reasons which suspend for a time the return of Protestants to the Fold; if, indeed, it be true that in reality there has been a certain falling off in the number of conversions to Rome.

We say, *if it be true*, for we are not convinced by the evidence before us, that there exists a real falling off, or, in any case, an unexpected falling off. It is not easy to find in a nation many generations as that of the Tractarians; and we cannot expect that we shall receive every year into the Catholic Church men like Cardinal Newman, Cardinal Manning, Canon Oakeley, Father Faber, Mr. Wilberforce, Mr. Wm. Palmer, Mr. Allies, and many more. If the new converts do not equal in literary fame the earlier Tractarians, it is simply because the Anglican Church herself does not contain men of repute so numerous as forty and fifty years ago. She still possesses, of course, a learned clergy; but we do not find in her many men who may be classed in the first rank of intellectual power. It is then easy to explain a certain falling off in conversions to the Catholic Church; but, this falling off consists rather in the *lustre* than in the *number* of the persons converted. We have reason to believe that, if we had official returns of the conversions, the truth would be precisely the reverse of what is said by Ritualists, and sometimes also by Catholics.[1]

---

[1] It is indeed denied by Low Churchmen and even by Catholics. Lately, in the "Rock" (1880, p. 148, col. 2), appeared the following letter:—
"Having once been a member of the congregation of St. Alban's, Holborn, although I left in 1868 to join the 'Church of Rome,' I have read with much amazement the statement of Mr. Craik, that the teaching of that establishment does not lead people to Rome. I am able from my own personal knowledge to give a flat denial to this statement, as I entered St. Alban's for the first time on the last Sunday of November 1866, a Protestant, and left there in July 1868, so indoctrinated with Catholicism, that on my presenting myself to the Catholic priest who received me, he remarked that I was thoroughly acquainted with every Catholic doctrine. During the time that I was at St. Alban's, I attended confirmation classes held by Mr. Mackonochie, and also went to confession to him and to Mr. Stanton, who on the last occasion of my going to him was good enough to excommunicate me for a month. I regret to say, I do not remember why. I also

But, admitting that the number of conversions is less than in former times, and that Ritualism is the true and principal cause of this grievous phenomenon, are there not various lines of conduct to be pursued, and might not the same object be attained without discouraging the earnest and pious souls which seek for truth, sometimes at the cost of their fortunes and of their lives?

We can understand the grief and impatience which possess some minds, when they see others faint or fall so near to the haven. But, we should not consider only the souls, which, at the present day, are lost to the visible Church; we should also consider those souls which, in the future, shall enter in the true and one Fold, under the influence, it is true, of the divine grace and by the mercy of God; but also, after having been prepared to accept the full truth of Catholicism, even through the mutilated dogmas of Ritualism. While, then, to these Ritualism is fulfilling a providential mission, is it not more correct to say, even of others who are less happy, that Ritualism brought them only half the way, than that it arrested their onward course?

The conversion of England in the mass is sometimes spoken of in France; but this is a chimæra, an illusion which three days' journey on the other side of the Channel suffices to dissipate. If England as a whole were now converted, it would be the greatest and most evident miracle the world has yet seen. Yet, if Ritualism continues to spread, as it now does; if it penetrates the whole of society, and effects the slow but great revolution which insensibly transforms English society; then, and then alone, when minds have been enlightened, and hearts have been subdued,

recollect that shortly before I left St. Alban's, I had a discussion with another member of the congregation on the number who had left for Rome; we were able to recall the names of over a hundred. If we could do this in 1868, may I ask for the numbers now? It would be a breach of confidence to give the names of private individuals, although I could easily do so."

the conversion of England *as a nation* will become possible, and may even actually take place. Until that good time arrives, we can only hope for isolated conversions, and, one by one, for many chosen souls. Many Catholics do not wish it to be otherwise.

Ritualism is helping the Catholic cause, even although at times it may seem to paralyse it. We must never forget that it is working for Catholicism; and if the sight of souls which lag behind draws tears from our eyes, the sight of many souls which shall one day be converted, ought to console us and make us patient. Let us never forget that God has His own times and seasons.

For this reason, perhaps, it might be better and more profitable for English Catholics to keep silence. At any rate, silence would compromise neither the present nor the future. It would not involve the Church in any given course; and if it may be thought undignified to stand by with crossed arms and closed lips, while the religious parties of the Anglican Church are in conflict; yet, there is no doubt that it would be advantageous to reserve our strength for the propitious hour. Which side soever is triumphant, whether the Evangelical or the Ritualists, it is Catholicism which will profit by disasters on the one side and by victories on the other. When the souls which are wearied by the spectacle of these struggles begin to sigh for peace and light, Catholicism need only stretch forth its hands, and they will fall into them like ripe fruit, which the slightest shock suffices to detach from the branch which nourished it. To keep silence, to stand by—not as indifferent spectators of conflicts which have long lasted, and will still last long in England—but as sympathetic and watchful spectators, such a line of conduct is, we think, neither undignified nor useless. The combatants will respect this reserve; and sooner or later Catholics will reap the fruits of it.

Supposing, however, that it is necessary to break

silence—and we can understand how some people think it their duty to do so—nothing can be more injurious to the cause of Catholicism than a tone of ridicule or bitterness. Certainly the Church is not responsible for the errors of her children; but those errors may compromise her in many ways, since men are not always able to distinguish between persons, and the cause which they defend. It is in all cases necessary to remember this truth, and it specially concerns English Catholics to remember it.

VII. We must ask, moreover, what there is to fear in Ritualism? and if it is, or is ever likely to be, a real source of danger for the Catholic Church? Surely not.

If Ritualism has any power, it is against Protestantism. It has nothing but weakness in its relations to Catholicism; and its weakness is that of Protestantism, with some additions peculiar to itself. For instance, it contains the fundamental error of the Protestant system in relying altogether on the right of private judgment. In whose name are all these achievements of doctrine and ritual effected? In whose name do Mr. Mackonochie, Dr. Pusey, Dr. Lee, Mr. Ridsdale, Archdeacon Denison, and others, carry out their reforms, and impose their opinions on their people? If in their own names, are they infallible? And, if not, from whom does their teaching derive its authority? Not from their bishops, who disavow and condemn them. They themselves admit that they are at open strife with the episcopate. Nowhere else in Christendom, whether Catholic or Protestant, do we find the portentous spectacle of the inferior clergy being in absolute and open revolt against their ecclesiastical superiors.

If the Ritualists entrench themselves behind the Anglican Church, we must ask—if that Church is really with them, are they in accordance with the bishops, the convocations, the clergy, and the faithful laity? We might go further, and ask if the Anglican Church has any real existence; if the State has ever recognised such a church; and if it be not simply by a moral fiction that the union of the dioceses of England are held to form one and the same society? There is not, and there never has been, what can properly be termed a Church of England; there are Anglican churches, not an Anglican Church.

We must ask, also, the meaning of their loud assertion of Catholic privileges; and if the mere acceptance of certain dogmas and practices is enough to enable them to attain the truth, and to work out their own salvation? Questions of discipline, of hierarchy, of submission to authority, of jurisdiction, all have a place in the Catholic creed; and if these are set at nought, what becomes of the principle of Catholicity?

Ritualists may make the most careful historical researches without finding at any time, or in any age, a position resembling their own. If belief in a creed is all that is necessary for salvation, the most degraded savage of Oceania, and the rudest colonist of the "Far West," might be saved without the aid of a Church or a missionary; he need only glance at the catechisms of the four or five great Christian Churches of the world.

Ritualism, like old-fashioned Anglicanism, is deficient in logic. It contains fair and excellent doctrines, noble and salutary practices; but, the whole forms an aggregate of fragments, collected together without relation to each other, or any real bond of union. This fact is so apparent, that it is necessary to be an Anglican not to be immediately struck by it; and it is this which must prevent Ritualism from being dangerous in the future, since the time must come when the people will begin to think and reason for themselves, and when that day comes in England, Ritualism will cease to exist. It must either advance as far as Catholicism, or relapse into Protestantism—that is, into Rationalism and Infidelity. Catholicism and Rationalism are intelligible; but all intermediate systems are illogical, and consequently are doomed to perish.

It is perhaps as well to point out the weaker points of Ritualism, in order that souls may not be lulled to sleep in a deceitful security. It is well to declare that Ritualism is not logical, even according to its own principles, and that it has only an arbitrary existence. It is well to hold up before Ritualists the lamp of truth, which enlightens the road by which they have to travel; and this may be done with the calmness which befits the Church, with the charity which is a precious jewel of Catholicism, and with the amenity of language which goes direct to the heart, since it shows that everything is prompted by an inspired love of truth, and with the sole object of working out the salvation of that which is only less precious than God Himself —the salvation of an immortal soul.

THE INCONSISTENCIES OF RITUALISM.

WE have said that one of the chief reasons why Catholic writers have sometimes disparaged Anglican Ritualism and Ritualists, is the supreme inconsistency of their system taken in its entirety—in its doctrine, ritual, and practice.

This is, indeed, a fact so manifest to every Roman Catholic that we are at a loss, when we perceive how men can reconcile good faith with tenets so glaringly illogical. Of course, we admit that the Ritualists, as a body, adhere to the system called "Ritualism" with an upright intention and a pure conscience; but, finding this moral problem difficult to solve, we, Catholics, sometimes speak of them as if we do not believe in the honesty of Anglican-Ritualists. Their language and method are not to be approved; but their intentions are not to be blamed. The latter are good and charitable, although the former may be incorrect or even bad.

The subject is extremely wide, but the matter is so important that we will endeavour to show, by some examples, how Ritualism is full of inconsistencies, and how Catholic writers may be excused if they speak sometimes slightingly of it.

I. Before we enumerate what we call the inconsistencies of Ritualism and the Ritualists, it may be as well to define what we mean by inconsistencies. We mean that want of logic which causes a man to admit two sets of propositions totally contradictory to each other: inasmuch as, on the one hand, he is forced to recognise facts which are evident, palpable, tangible, and directly before his eyes; and, on the other, he has not the resolution to break with prejudices or to resist passions which necessarily imply the negation of those facts. We call it inconsistency to admit certain principles, or to acknowledge the truth of certain facts from which certain conclusions are necessarily, naturally, and directly deducible, and then to neglect to draw those conclusions, to deny them, or to adopt other conclusions entirely opposed to them. And when we speak here of conclusions or consequences, we do not mean remote conclusions which are connected with the principles by a complicated chain of deductions; but those immediate consequences which are manifestly involved in certain principles, and of which the necessity is at once visible.

It is an inconsistency, for instance, in the physical order, to lay down premisses in which it is presupposed that it is night; and in the conclusion to say either that it is not night or that it is day. And it is an inconsistency in the moral order to affirm, in the major or minor premiss, that this or that kind of act is bad; and to maintain in the conclusion that those same acts are good or indifferent. It is an inconsistency again, in the religious, Christian, and supernatural order, to attribute to God the foundation of certain institutions, and afterwards to represent these institutions as essentially bad, or defective to that degree, that there is in them nothing that is divine. It is, lastly, an inconsistency to recognise in certain systems the presence of grave defects, and to refer them nevertheless to God as their author, even in their actually evil condition.

Now, Ritualism and the literature and life of the Ritualists present inconsistencies of this kind, and inconsistencies so numerous and so striking that one is tempted to ask: how any one can remain permanently in such an intellectual position. One can just understand that an individual may pass through this system in one of those phases, the aggregate of which make up the moral life of man. But, what one cannot conceive without difficulty, what one cannot understand at all, is that enlightened intelligencies should remain fixed in a system which is, in its nature, essentially transitory.

To tell the truth, it is one of those things which seem to us the most curious among the phenomena of Ritualism. We admire, as we have said already, the intellectual vigour, the activity, the zeal, the devotion of this party in the Establishment. And yet, what astonishes us the most, and seems to us the most worthy of attention in all this movement, is to see how the Ritualists justify the position they have taken up, and how they reconcile themselves to a line of conduct which is, to the highest degree, illogical and inconsistent.

In the purely philosophical and moral order there is here matter for a curious psychological study; for the phenomenon thus presented to us must be susceptible of some explanation other than bad faith or madness. It is not simply because Ritualists are afraid of the consequences, and still less because they are in bad faith, that they remain contentedly in their system.

Taken as a whole, the Ritualist section of the Anglican clergy is certainly one of the best. As far as intelligence, zeal, activity, and devotion are concerned, it furnishes in the spiritual world some of the finest specimens of the vigorous Anglo-Saxon race.

How, then, can we explain their attitude towards the Anglican Establishment and the Roman Church? Besides the very natural explanations, suggested by the habits of thought and action engendered by their education, and by the prejudices of race, of insularity and belief, there is, to our thinking, another way of accounting for it, which, however, the present writer would have had some hesitation in mentioning, had he not found in English authors an acknowledgment of what may be termed, an intellectual infirmity of their nation. It might not have been becoming in a foreigner to remark, that the English people are wanting in a certain rigour of logic, and are thus led at times to admit principles without accepting their consequences; and he would risk the violation of the laws of courtesy, and of due regard to the feelings of his neighbours, were this remark to originate with him. The English themselves, however, readily admit the defect, and he may therefore venture to refer to it.

In fact, it has always appeared to us, that this was one of the most striking defects of the English nation: and in tracing their history, and studying the events which are taking place before our eyes, we have often asked ourselves, how a part of that people could reconcile their action with logical consistency; and more particularly does this question occur to us, when engaged in the examination of Ritualism and in the study of the Ritualists.

How can the Ritualists logically defend their conduct and their principles? How can they reconcile the one with the other? This, we repeat, has always passed our comprehension. We have indeed heard reasons brought forward, and apologies proffered, but neither the reasons, nor the apologies, appear to us to be satisfactory. We will proceed to illustrate our argument by the Ritualistic theory of the Church.

II. It is needless to observe that errors and inconsistencies upon this point are of the gravest character. This is evident to all. The error of an individual in conduct, or even in belief, entails no general consequences; but, if a considerable number admit, in the very basis of the society of which they are members, principles that tend to mutual annihilation, and which manifestly contradict each other, it may well astonish the unbiassed spectator who, not wholly indifferent to the struggle, can yet look on in a spirit of calm impartiality. Now, we say it candidly, the manner in which the Ritualists speak of the Church appears to us to be extremely inconsistent, inconsistent both in detail, and in its general outline. It were an endless task to deal with this subject in all its phases, or to attempt to reconcile, compare, or refute the inconsistencies of each individual, or even those of the most prominent writers upon Ritualism.

We will, for the present, content ourselves with a consideration of the principles generally admitted by the more moderate members of the party, and a review of the question as a whole.

The first instance of the inconsistencies of the Ritualists to which we shall draw attention is this: Every one knows that they have an exalted conception of the Church, its constitution, its powers, its mission, and its destiny. They feel for "the Church," not only the greatest reverence, but also an ardent affection, a love of such intensity that they would sacrifice all for her: and this is a sentiment which it is impossible not to admire. Having the rights of the Church so much at heart, her name is ever on their lips, both in their words and writings. Sometimes indeed this entity which they call the Church is turned to a practical use, and made to form a buckler behind which they seek refuge to defend what in reality are but their individual opinions. For a period of many years the name of the Church was but seldom heard in the controversies of the English nation; and hence, when, by the influence of the Ritualists, the word is again introduced, it is received with some degree of surprise, and people sometimes derisively call the Ritualists *the Church*.

They have no reason to blush at this designation applied to them in jest, for they have done well in teaching their countrymen, that side by side with the

State which would be everything, there is also a divine institution, which, although it seeks not to be everything, must yet be something; a divine institution, which desires "to render unto Cæsar the things that are Cæsar's," but also to "render unto God the things which are of God."

But the inconsistency of the Ritualists appears most strikingly, when we consider that although they entertain the most exalted sentiments respecting the *divine origin* of the Church, they yet seek to reconcile those sentiments with a different theory as to *her destiny*. Thus, according to them, Jesus Christ, the founder of the Church, is, in truth, the Son of God made Man: whereas, He is no longer so considered by such writers as the author of "Ecce Homo" and "Philo-Christus." In the eyes of the Ritualists, Jesus Christ is true God; the Church is a divine work; the Church is the continuation of the Incarnation; she has Jesus Christ in her midst, for many personally present in the Blessed Eucharist, for all present at least by grace, by Providence, by His Divine assistance. The Church is a work divine in its institution, and its divine nature may be so clearly recognised, that to enter its bosom is an obligation binding upon all mankind.

III. Such, in general outline, is the theory of the Church which has been adopted by the majority of Ritualists and High Churchmen. So far we have no objection to make. But how does all this agree with that other theory of Ritualists and High Churchmen, according to which all controversies of the day should be definitely decided by an appeal to the tribunal of primitive antiquity? Can it be that the Church of Jesus Christ only lasted until the fifth or sixth century? And if this be so, what of the divinity of Jesus Christ, and of the divine character of His work? Has Jesus Christ laboured for the first five or six centuries of Christianity only? Has He been content to preserve the integrity of His work for five hundred years, and then to abandon it to the fate of all merely human institutions? Did Jesus Christ want the power, or the will, to watch over His Church for more than five hundred years? If He has been unable to bestow upon her an infallible existence for more than five hundred years, where is His divine power? If He has been only willing to guarantee a regular and perfect discharge of her functions for five hundred years, where are His wisdom, His goodness, His mercy? In either case, how is it possible to believe that He is truly God?

We can perfectly well conceive, that a man may deny the divinity of Jesus Christ, and rate Him merely as a sage or a philosopher; and for such an one the Anglican theories on the supreme authority of primitive antiquity, the purity or corruption of doctrine, and similar matters, present a meaning and significance, because they refer to the work and teaching of a man. In such a case, these theories are intelligible because, no doubt, in human affairs, the ideas of a man are best understood by those who have been upon intimate terms with him, or have lived in times nearest to his own. But, when we speak of a divine work, such as is the Church according to the Ritualists, time counts for nothing. It is as easy for God to maintain the infallibility of His Church after five hundred years as after so many days, at the end of fifteen centuries as at the end of two.

We must be consistent. If the Church is, and must ever remain, a divine work; if she teaches, and must continue to teach in the name of God; if she enjoys, and must ever enjoy, the protection of her Divine Founder; if she endures, and must endure for ever—then, we must not take from her with one hand what we present with the other; we must not limit her to five or six hundred years. We must always recognise in the Church divine attributes; we must form a logical and consistent theory; and, to express our meaning in a simple and intelligible form, we must not proclaim Jesus Christ to be God and at the same time attribute to Him conduct unworthy of God. But, this is precisely what is done by those who, while they affirm His divinity, assert that He has taken no precaution to insure the permanence of a society which He has made the depository of His truth, of His grace, and of His Sacraments.

And then, by what authority is primitive antiquity limited to the first five or six centuries? It appears to be so limited in order to save the theory of the "undivided Church," and to give some colouring of reason to the admission, that an infallibility existed in the primitive Church, which is denied to the Church of the following centuries. But, did this "undivided Church" exist during five centuries in the sense in which the Ritualists understand the term, Church? Was not the Church divided, in the fifth, the fourth, the third, the second, even in the first century, even in the Apostolic times, by theories at least equally legitimate with those of later ages, as those, for instance, of the Broad Church or the Low Church divisions of Anglicanism? How many Sabellians, Arians, or Nestorians are there not among the laity, the clergy, perhaps among the highest dignitaries of the Established Church of England? And yet, not only do the Ritualists tolerate the presence among them of men who they well know teach these errors; but, they persistently declare that nothing would induce them to expel such men from the Anglican Church. These diversities are termed "schools of thought;" and they consider it a happy characteristic of their Church to be so comprehensive as to receive to her bosom and gather under one roof so many dissimilar and contradictory systems. The Ritualists sanction and applaud this wide toleration. While their adversaries seek to expel them, they, on the contrary, although maintaining a lofty ideal of the

Church, of her unity, her holiness, her divine origin, yet show themselves tolerant in the extreme, and declare to the world that they will exclude from their Church no individual and no system. The leaders of their party, and their organs in the press, incessantly make this declaration. We find it in an article which has come into our hands as we write these lines. "We do not ourselves see," says the "Church Times," of the 24th May, 1878; "we have never seen, why there should not be ample room in the Church of England, within reasonable limits, for the three great schools which are now found within its pale. We certainly do not want to drive any one of them out, and are content to make our proselytes by fair argument."

It must be acknowledged that the Ritualists do not treat their adversaries with severity. But what becomes of their theories of the divinity of Jesus Christ, and the divine teaching of the Church, if they admit into the bosom of Christianity those who disbelieve these fundamental doctrines, and deny their necessary and logical consequences?

Up to the fourth century, the divisions among Christians were not so conspicuous as in later times; because their numbers were smaller, and they did not play so important a part in the affairs of the world. But, in reality, the divisions were perhaps even greater than they have been since. A Sabellian was no more a member of the Church than a Unitarian. An Arian or a Nestorian was not more to be excluded from the "undivided Church," than an Anglican Broad Churchman or a Greek Schismatic. We repeat, that in all these fine-spun theories of the Ritualists about the Church there is a want of unity, of logic, of consistency, which betrays their birthplace and their origin.

There is but one Church which has never claimed infallibility, except perhaps on a single occasion; and which then only made use of infallibility to point out, as has been wittily observed, the fallibility of the

Church in general and even of the Œcumenical Councils. And that Church, is the Established Church of England.

Do Ritualists admit the Twenty-first Article? If they do, what becomes of the authority derived from the primitive antiquity of the first six General Councils, and even of that "living voice" of which they have now so much to say? If they admit it, in what is their Church more divine than any other human institution, inasmuch as God is in one sense the author of all things? If they admit it, what can we call them but semi-Rationalists; and what need have they of an ecclesiastical authority which has never existed in the form of their conceptions, and which in any case, according to them, has never spoken without risk of falling into error? If, on the other hand, they do *not* admit it, upon what reasoning can they seriously rely when they limit to the first five centuries the period of time during which the Church has spoken infallibly in the name of God and of Jesus Christ?[1]

The truth is, that either there has been in the Church of God a living voice, speaking in the name of God, after the fifth century as well as before it; or this living voice has never existed. For, *after* as well as *before* that epoch, we find an authority claiming to speak in the name of God, while some men accept its teaching and others reject it.

---

[1] We may perhaps quote the explanation of this inconsistency as given by Dr. Littledale: "There is in Scripture no promise of infallibility to the Church at any given time.... The Church of one generation may err, and that grievously; but there will be always enough truth mixed with the error to bring things right again. That is to say, the Church is *indefectible* in the long run, though the teaching voice may be fallible at any given time. General Councils are adjustments only, and valid just as they discharge honestly the office of attesting the continuous historical belief and practice of the Church, checked by incessant appeal to Holy Writ" (Plain Reasons, &c., pp. 132, 133). We should have much to observe on this theory of Dr. Littledale, but we doubt very much if indeed all the Ritualists endorse his opinions as stated in the quoted passage. For what purpose a Church, which may and does err, and which is not *infallible*, but only *indefectible*, and that in the *long run?* For what purpose the Christian revelation, the Sacraments, and the like? It was better for God to leave us alone with our natural reason and conscience.

It must be confessed that this theory of a Church, which may be designated by the title of a celebrated work published more than thirty years since, "the Ideal of a Christian Church," scarcely harmonises with what the Ritualists tell us of the Church as it existed during the first five centuries.

This is one instance of a want of logical consistency, but it is only the prelude to many others.

IV. The Ritualistic ideal of the Church of Christ, of its origin and its divine mission, does not accord, as we have seen, with the other theories of the Ritualists —as that of the duration and vitality of the same Church. Having characterised the Church as an institution divine in its inception, and in the first centuries of its existence, they maintain that, in the succeeding ages, it became but too human in its imperfection. Having admitted that Jesus Christ, true God and true Man, watched over the infancy of His Church, and promised to watch over her for ever, they proceed to assert that the Church has *not* received the promised assistance, and has nowhere entirely escaped the contagion of error. This, in the case of the Oriental sects, the Copts, the Syrians, and the schismatic Greeks, has been long acknowledged, notwithstanding the attempts made in latter times by prominent Ritualists to enter into communion with them, as is testified by the Bonn Conferences, the petition to the Canterbury Convocation, and the celebrated visit of Dr. Liddon, and Mr. MacColl and others to Bulgaria. Nor is the Latin Church, the great Western Communion, as it is sometimes called, considered spotless, although upon the whole the Ritualists would probably have felt more sympathy for her than for any other Christian community, if the Latin, or Roman, Church either would or could have met the advances which have often been made to her.

It is true, indeed, that a change has taken place

in the manner in which some of the Ritualists and a portion of the Anglican press speak of the Roman Church, her head, her Bishops, her practices. These matters are no longer treated with the courteous, the kindly, the charitable tone which prevailed some years back. We remark with no little regret that the tone of certain Ritualistic journals is no longer, we will not say what it has been, but what it ought to be, even in the interest of the cause which they advocate. It is not by unseemly jests, by verbal quibbles, by coarse expressions, by want of charity, that a cause is the best defended. Rather, is it damaged by such weapons as these.

Notwithstanding this degeneracy in the tone ot the Ritualistic press, we gladly believe that the real sympathies of the party are still with the Roman rather than with the Greek Church. The Ritualists had hoped that their advances would have been met by concessions on the part of Rome. No such concessions have been made, no such concessions as they seek could have been made. And hence have arisen irritation and the use of unseemly language prompted by annoyance and disappointment. A deeper study of the history of the Holy Roman Church would have forbidden these ill-placed hopes and prevented this self-pleasing delusion.[1]

As to the Anglican Church, it is evident that, according to the Ritualists, she has not for the last fifty years harmonised with their ideal of the Church

[1] The Ritualists should suffer at least to be taught by their friends. "For my own part," says one of them, "I believe that, where Rome gains one 'vert by the arguments of her adherents, she gains a dozen by what is said and done by Anglican bishops, priests, and newspapers. I am sure that I am never so anti-Roman as after a friendly argument with a Roman Catholic friend, and never so inclined to Rome as after reading or hearing harsh and sometimes unjust attacks on her. Take, for example, Mr. Ingle's letter in the last 'Church Times,' a letter that I was surprised that even that not over-particular periodical condescended to publish, especially as it was written by a gentleman who some years ago wrote an indignant letter to a newspaper denying that he had assisted in celebrating the Popish festival of Corpus Christi!" ("Church Review," March 1879). The letter of Mr. Ingle's referred to, was relative to one of our essays published in the " Contemporary Review," and was somewhat inconsiderate in tone and in argument.

of Christ, and does not do so now. And in this we see another inconsistency into which Ritualists have fallen.

In fact, if there is anything universally acknowledged at the present day, it is that for the last three hundred years a wrong road has been taken. The proof, or rather the discovery of this fact, has been slow, painful, and laborious; but, it has been worked out, and is put forward by all the writers of the day. It is met with in the pages of every Ritualistic publication; and in the midst of the controversies of the hour there is no journal which does not over and over again revert to this unhappy issue. If we speak of dogma, of morals, of public and exterior worship, or of private and interior devotion, the Ritualists, with more or less unanimity, will tell us, that in respect of all these things, they have retrograded from true religion. They will repeat, in terms more or less forcible and direct, that the Anglican Church has gone astray in all these matters. And they will use language expressive of an irritation which, it must be confessed, is not without cause. For, though we may treat with indulgence a difference of opinion in the matter of the use of candles, and flowers, and church ornaments, and chants, and sacred music, it is not easy to meet with the same composure the denial of important dogmas, such as baptismal regeneration, the supernatural efficacy of the Sacraments, the Real Presence, the necessity of confession, the Sacrament of Holy Orders, the reality of the Apostolic succession, the communion of saints and prayers for the dead, the reverence due to the cross and holy images, the eternity of the pains of hell, the divine origin of the Church, and its independence of the civil power. All these questions are not of like importance, nor are they the only ones upon which there is division in the Anglican Church; and there are indeed many others which we might have mentioned, in addition to those already enumerated.

But, it is as clear as day, and no Ritualist denies it, that all these important Christian doctrines have been, and still are, unrecognised, disputed, denied by a large part of the Anglican Church, and that many of the dignified clergy in particular admit scarcely any of them.

We have but to open the " Rock," the " Record," or the " Christian World ; " we have but to listen to the sermons of Dean Stanley, of Lord A. Hervey, of Bishop Ryle ; we have but to read the charges of Archbishop Tait, of Bishop Ellicott, of Bishop Jackson ; we have but to note the speeches delivered at meetings and in Parliament itself, to be convinced that, upon all these important questions, the Anglican Church is, at the present day, in a state of chaos. What is believed by the Ritualists is denied by Broad Churchmen, is abhorred and anathematised by the Low Church party. The eternity of the pains of hell is a doctrine of no secondary importance ; and yet for years back, reviews and journals have been filled with articles in which, under such signatures as " Eternal Hope," " Restitutionism," or " Universalism," this doctrine is discredited, disputed, minimised, denied. We are even now not very far from the controversy which Canon Farrar's book has provoked on both sides of the Atlantic.

But, to pass from this consideration, we would ask leave to address a simple question to sincere Ritualists, and especially to those who cherish a high ideal of the mission of the Church, and who, with St. Paul, consider her to be the column and the support of truth in this world. We would ask if they seriously believe that a Church—we use the word, improper as it is in this sense, to conform with established usage—if a Church which, for a considerable period, has let these important truths escape from it, has any title to be considered the Spouse of Jesus Christ ?

Do they even believe that such a Church can be a

part of the Church of Jesus Christ? of that Church which Holy Scripture describes to us as unspotted and unstained? Can they, in fine, believe—can any one believe—that a Church in which such important truths are actually denied by a great number, if not by the majority of her adherents, can be the true Church?

We think that, if they would but compare the ideal which is before their eyes when they study the New Testament, and the Church of the first centuries, with the reality which they see and form a part of, they would realise that the two Churches no more resemble each other than night resembles day.

V. It is true that the Ritualists do not consider themselves beaten, and that if at times this painful comparison presents itself before their minds, they console themselves by saying that in time they will succeed in regaining all these truths, and in making them reach the mass of the people—even those amongst them who are at present hostile. Very different are they from the partisans of the Broad and of the Low Church schools; they do not aim at the persecution of their adversaries—and on this we can but congratulate them, for they set a good example of moderation and of Christian patience, an example which is to our judgment worthy of a better cause, and one which we fervently trust that God will not leave unrewarded.

"Only give us time," say they; "only give us a hearing, and you shall see if we do not make progress —whether that which we maintain and defend will not prove to be the truth. In less than thirty years we shall have renewed the face of England." Such is frequently the language of the leaders of the Ritualistic party, or at least of the organs which represent their ideas. We take pleasure in acknowledging that their language is founded on truth; and, in fact, that, if Ritualism continues to advance as it has done for the last twenty years, the Anglican Church will no longer be recognisable. If a person who died at the beginning of this century were to come to life again now, he would hardly know where he was—he would find himself completely bewildered, so much so that he would inquire whether he were not rather in the Roman Church than in the Anglican. But what does all this prove? Does it prove the Anglican Church to be the true one, or that, if she had ceased to be the true Church, she has re-entered the true Church? By no means.

We must be allowed to dwell a little longer on this side of the Ritualistic question—which appears to us to be so much the more necessary, because there is something about it calculated to deceive earnest minds and souls of a generous character. Perhaps, it is on this account that so many virtuous and holy English Catholics fear and condemn Ritualism. They find the system most dangerous to souls, and that it is likely to cause a great number to stop short, so to speak, on the very threshold of the truth. However, when we get to the bottom of these facts, at first sight so capable of deceiving, what is it that we find? We only find contradiction, inconsistency, and chaos. We find such evident and clear proofs that Ritualism, with all its apparent beauty, is tainted with vice in its origin of which it will never cure itself, except by making itself Roman Catholic, that is to say, by ceasing to be Anglican.

The better to make clear this point of view, which appears to us to be very important, we must be permitted to have recourse to a supposition. Supposing that some man, whoever it may be, not being a Christian, but knowing and admiring the Catholic Church, should set himself to copy her exactly, to reproduce her faith, her morals, her worship, in short to form a society, externally quite similar to the

Catholic Church—would he then have another, a second Catholic Church? No such thing. There might be a copy, a resemblance, a photograph, if you will, but he would never have the true Church, the living Church, or—what makes it living—the Church of Jesus Christ. And wherefore should this be so?

For the one reason, that it may be in man's power to imitate the works of God up to a certain point; but it is not in his power to give them life. God has reserved to Himself, or to His representatives, the privilege of giving life. This Church then, in appearance so perfect and so similar to the other, cannot be more than the work of man, which must always remain merely human, since God has never breathed upon it the breath of life to make it divine.

We have called this a supposition; but, the supposition is really a fact, and one that occurred only quite recently, as it has occurred many times since the commencement of the Christian era. Not long ago the Bishop of St. Albans protested against a new sect calling itself the "Reformed Episcopal Church of England," a sect which it appeared to him was making progress, and was likely to lead the people into error by its external forms.

Why did this Bishop protest? Was it simply through jealousy and professional rivalry? Was it because this sect has no creed? Perhaps, it has the same beliefs as the Anglican Church; it imitates its rites, baptism, confirmation; it divides the country into dioceses and parishes. In the name of whom and what is the sect to be condemned? The Bishop would, without doubt, reply that it is because the chiefs of that sect, supposing that they have received episcopal consecration such as the Anglican Church gives, have not therefore received authority or mission; and he would indeed, in a certain sense, be in the right. When one goes to the bottom of all religious controversies, they resolve themselves into a question of authority. The question is, in whose name such or such a thing is restored or destroyed, added or suppressed. That which is done with the approbation and sanction of legitimate authority is always good. That which is done without the concurrence and *à fortiori* against the will of this authority, is evil, and is affected with a radical taint of which no success can heal it. The Bishop of St. Albans can condemn, up to a certain point, the Reformed Episcopal Church of England, because he can say that this Church has not the sanction of Convocation nor that of the Government—two things which to an Anglican represent all that can be honoured with the name of legitimate authority.

We have no wish, then, to examine if Drs. Gregg and Cumming might not have something to reply to the Bishop of St. Albans, and might not ask him who authorised *his* predecessors of the sixteenth century to rebel against the Pontifical authority. If indeed the partisans of these gentlemen are in fact schismatics, why are not the Anglicans, considered as a body, schismatics likewise?

But, if the Bishop of St. Albans had grounds for condemning the Reformed Episcopal Church of England, what have the Ritualists to say? Nothing. They can but be silent; for Dr. Gregg would be able to reply to them thus: " Gentlemen, between you and me there is but one essential difference. It is this. I do not like the way in which things go on in the Anglican Church, nor have I the vocation to reform the Church. But, at all events, I have the courage to leave the Anglican Church with the emoluments and the benefices which she offers me, to act as a reformer at my risk and peril. Now, you want to reform the Anglican Church which will have none of your reforms, and that not only without the concurrence but against the will of your Bishops. You wish to reform the Anglican Church, and you partially do reform it. But you wish not to reform it at your risk and peril, and therefore you take good care to retain your benefices. Acknowledge, gentlemen, that if there be any difference between us, it is all to my advantage. At least, I cannot be accused of conspiring against the Church which maintains me."

It is evident that the Reformed Episcopal Church of England might address this language to Ritualism, and we cannot well see what reply Ritualism could make. If, indeed, there is a contradiction, and a striking inconsistency in Ritualism, it is this—that while it exalts the authority of the Church, the divine character of the Episcopate, and the Apostolic succession, it takes no account of them or scarcely any, in practice. You are quite willing, that the Bishops should be the representatives of Jesus Christ. You admit, that without them nothing can be done. But, why then treat them as you do? A single day does not pass without your dragging them in the dirt, without your covering them with ridicule, with abuse, and with contempt; and you pretend to venerate them, you pretend that they are your fathers. There is a mystery here which ought to be explained. How comes it that your theory and your practice are so opposed to each other? This is a serious question which we have here asked, and it deserves a candid consideration.

VI. That the ordinary attitude of the Anglican episcopate in the present religious controversies is extremely displeasing to us, we frankly confess. It seems to us, in short, in no way conformable to what is required by natural equity, being always or generally spoiled by partiality. For, whilst the bishops forgive everything, even heresy, to a portion of their adherents—the very portion who would, if they were allowed, have destroyed both the episcopate and even the Anglican Church itself—they excuse nothing in those who show themselves the most zealous for the salvation of souls, and for the defence of their Church. But, this avowal once made, we plainly declare that we are more than astonished, we are scandalised beyond expression, by the manner in which Ritualists treat the Anglican episcopate. For, even in a country where liberty of speech knows no limits, as is the case in England, it appears strange that they cannot set bounds to their license of expression. That the partisans of the Low Church school should treat the bishops lawlessly may at all events be expected; because they ridicule both the episcopate and episcopal ordination. But, that High Churchmen, that the Ritualists as a body, should speak as they do, is what surprises us, scandalises us, and grieves us so profoundly.[1]

We understand, doubtless, that the Ritualists can hardly be satisfied with their bishops; for there is not one amongst them who is really and truly on their side—but what would they have? There is not and has never been a single bishop who looked on things exactly from their point of view, excepting perhaps at one time, during a short period in the seventeenth century. The present episcopate are certainly above the average level of Anglican bishops. And if the present bishops do not come up to the type proposed to himself by the Ritualist, that is not the bishop's fault—but that of the English Church herself. The Anglican communion is but the shadow of a Church; therefore, there neither is, there never will be any more than the shadow of an episcopate in the Anglican Church.

[1] These are the admissions generally current in Ritualistic circles. You say, writes one of this party in the "Church Review" (1880, p. 135, col. 2): "You say as regards the Wife's Sister Bill, 'It matters nothing to Churchmen how the two archbishops may vote.' This is of course sadly true thus far, that no true Churchman would ever think of following the lead of the archbishops. The public, however, believes that the bench of bishops represents the Church in the House of Lords. I venture, therefore, to say that it is a matter of importance that the Church should not be betrayed by those popularly supposed to represent her, whether the act be from cowardice or perversity."

Instead, therefore, of waging war with their episcopate, as they do; instead of repudiating by their daily acts their theoretical respect for their bishops—the Ritualists had better by far allow their own eyes to open and at last to see that, having but the appearance of bishops, they can have but the appearance of a Church. The mere appearance of a Church can by no possibility have more than an appearance of an episcopate; and a mere shadowy episcopate can be the foundation only of an imaginary Church.

It is true, that the Ritualists hope to reform both their episcopate and their Church. But, at this they labour in vain. They will only succeed in making an imaginary difference, in causing it to appear a little less repulsive, a degree less removed from the ideal they had formed to themselves; but, in fact, they will still have no more than a nominal Church. And wherefore? Because the authority to make a Church and a real episcopate is wanting to them.

It is of no use to dig a magnificent canal, unless you open the sluice which places it in communication with the spring or reservoir; and this God has reserved to Himself to do. Looking beneath the surface, we see that all resolves itself into a question of authority. And precisely because this is wanting to the Ritualists, they are obliged, in spite of themselves, practically to fight against the authority claimed by the bishops and by the Church, which in theory they exalt. And so much the better for them; for this position of theirs, so essentially illogical and inconsistent, is sufficient to open the eyes of a great number, allowing them to arrive at length at the real truth. Indeed, we are persuaded that it costs them much to write and speak as they do about their bishops and their Church; and yet, they feel constrained to do so, because on the one hand they believe their own theory to be right, and on the other they find this theory continually contradicted by facts. This contradiction compels them either to abandon their theory, or else to protest against the practice. They have either to give up their ideal of the Church, or to confess candidly that this ideal is just opposite to the reality of Anglicanism. This consideration has of itself opened the eyes of a large number amongst them; and will, we hope, do the same to many more. There is logical consistency in the truth alone. Outside the truth there is no possibility of anything but inconsistency.

We are not ignorant that this authority which we demand from the Ritualists, they pretend to have found in that maxim of St. Vincent of Lerins, so well known and generally esteemed—*Quod ubique, quod semper, quod ab omnibus,* what is held everywhere, always, and by all. The proverb or maxim is not only ancient, but it is good; and it may serve for some good purpose.

For the present, we content ourselves with bringing to light the sophistry which hides itself beneath the use made by the Ritualists of this maxim, and with dissipating an illusion which perhaps it tends to maintain in them. When, for instance, we say to some one of their number: "Why do you believe that? Why, in the present age, do you believe in confession, in baptismal regeneration, in the supernatural efficacy of the Sacraments? You plainly see that all these things are either condemned, or treated with silence, or positively disapproved by your Articles of Religion. Then, you are going against your Church and against your episcopate? You act, and you believe, without authority. In reality, you are but modified Rationalists, what one might call Christian Rationalists. It is not, in fact, from the authority and teaching of your Church that you derive your faith. It is from your own reason, and from your own understanding."

To this the Ritualists make answer: "It may be true that we have on our side neither our episcopate nor our Church, though there may be this or that text in our favour or against us, though this or that bishop may have taught this or that truth. But, if our Church and our episcopate have for us no authority, we have at least the authority of the Universal Church." And here again at once comes the *quod ubique, quod semper, quod ab omnibus;* and they make haste to exhibit it to all who present themselves. But to what does all this amount? It amounts, in truth, to a mere sophism and a mere illusion.

If, in order to form a part of the Church of Jesus Christ, it is sufficient to have some articles of faith and practice, and certain rites in common, then truly one may understand the language of Ritualists. They would be right in saying to their opponents: "We have more than you demand of us. We have not, it is true, the authority of our prelates; but we have the authority of the Christian world." Only, in this case, the word authority would be synonymous with witness, and not with jurisdiction, with sanction, with approbation. However, it is with all these that we have to do as necessary and not simply with a witness.

The Church, really, is a living society. In this society there are beliefs, it is true; but, there is also a government, an authority, a jurisdiction, which legitimises, governs, administers. And in order that all things may be done validly, or at all events lawfully, there needs an express or virtual mission from this authority. If a man acts contrary to this authority, not only does he sin, but often what he does is without any worth. It is this authority which is the guardian of faith, of the Sacraments, of discipline. And if there be any who ought not to go against this authority, it is above all the Ritualist; for he alone of all in the Anglican Church has held this belief. For Ritualists alone is the Church a living society, perfect and complete; for them alone unlimited inquiry is a false and destructive principle; for them alone the authority of the Church is a reality, and something distinct from

Scripture or from the State. How then does it happen that, after they have acknowledged, proclaimed, exalted this authority as divine, they practically come at last to reduce it to nothing? It is not sufficient to say that they also confess, that they believe in the communion of saints, that they also pray for the dead. The layman or the priest, who in France, or Germany, or Russia, prays for the dead, communicates and hears confessions, or himself goes to confession, this layman or this priest does these things by the authority of the bishop or of the Church; whilst in England, the Ritualists do all that in spite of the authority of their bishops and of their communion.

Evidently, there is no comparison, nothing in common, between the two cases. Well, it may be asked: Who gives to the Ritualists the power of doing all they do? No one: must be the answer. If they do not give themselves the power, certainly neither their Church, nor their bishops give it to them; no more does the Universal Church.

The Ritualists cannot be ignorant that some facts done without commission are not only irregular, they are likewise invalid. Then, what are they doing when they pretend to administer the Sacrament of Penance? Supposing their ordination to be valid, which, to say the least, is doubtful, they do but distribute shadows of pardon, and simulate the effects of the Sacrament. For, the bishops who protest against confession did not understand when they ordained them, or instituted them to their benefices, that they thereby gave them the power of hearing confessions.

The Ritualists are too forgetful that all religious questions are as much a question of authority as of faith. It is in vain for them to hide themselves behind St. Vincent of Lerins. His axiom does not confer upon them the authority that is wanting to them, and does not redeem their acts from the character of illegality, of which they are accused. His axiom does not really save them from eclecticism, or from being as insular in their practice as they are in their belief. It is, in fact, their individual reason that guides them throughout and at all times, rather than the authority of the Church; or rather, the authority of the Church, this "living voice," about which nowadays they say so much, does not really exist. At all events, for some centuries, it has been reduced to silence, if it be not condemned to silence for ever.

We see now how little agreement appears between the principle and the practice of Ritualists. And at this we cannot be surprised. Ritualism is, in fact, only a reaction from the Protestant negations, a reaction which leads to the resumption, one by one, of all the divine treasures that have been rejected by Protestantism. Traditions were buried in the bosom of the Anglican communion to such an extent, that at this day it is only at the cost of much study, and of varied efforts and inquiries, that they can succeed in restoring a part of that which has been buried. But, even when they succeed, they must not always take for granted that it is a restoration. It is often rather a new creation, and indeed a mere human creation. There is nothing divine, in the true sense of the word, in the restorations piecemeal and on private judgment, of Anglican High Churchmen; and, for this reason, we Catholics do not feel any respect towards Ritualism as a system, even if we feel some commiseration for or some sympathy towards Ritualists as a result of the system.

THE CHURCH, THE STATE, AND THE RITUALISTS.

WE have tried to show how the ideas of Ritualists on the Church are inconsistent one with another; but we have not exhausted the subject, and we may now proceed to examine it under a new aspect. It is, in fact, well worthy of lengthened consideration, for among the interesting facts which Anglicanism presents to outsiders, the nature of the relations which exist between the Church and the State is, from our point of view, the most worthy to attract the notice of thoughtful minds, and to call for the attention of politicians.

This assertion will perhaps be received with surprise, and may be contradicted by some of our readers. "What! (it will be said) you undertake to teach us some new thing on a subject as old as the hills! But, we know all that can be said about the relations of the Church, or of other Communions, with the State. The several systems of relations which it is possible to imagine, or to establish between Church and State have each, at some time or other, formed part of our experience. We have seen the State oppress and persecute the Chuch. Then, the Church has governed and directed the State. At a later period, the Church and the State have entered into an agreement to regulate the relations which ought to exist between them. We have even seen, and may still see in more than one country, Church and State living side by side, disconnected, and feeling no concern for each other. What, then, is left for us to learn, and what, at this time, remains for us to observe?"—We have to contemplate, we may reply, a national Church struggling to recover her liberty. Nothing of the kind has been witnessed before; and such a spectacle is now afforded by the Established Church of England—a spectacle which we frankly declare to be one of the most interesting and instructive which have hitherto been brought under our notice. Our readers may perhaps require an explanation of the grounds for this assertion.

I. It is undoubtedly a fact, obvious to every attentive observer, that the relations between Church and State in England cannot long continue in their present condition. The State and the Church tend towards a separation in this country, as in most other European states; but, in this case, the separation offers certain peculiarities which are not to be found elsewhere. We repeat, that this is a positive and obvious fact, and it is generally admitted. It is a fact repeated and proclaimed alike by friends and foes, by members of the Establishment and by Nonconformists, by statesmen and churchmen, by politicians and public men. All admit that the days of the Established Church are numbered.

A large number of publications on the subject, in the form of pamphlets or articles in reviews and newspapers, have appeared in the course of the last few years. We might instance dozens of such essays, emanating from all the religious sects which divide the population of England. In 1875, a distinguished person, sometimes honoured with the title of "Protestant Pope," said that the evil was irremediable; and, so far from retracting this assertion, he has since confirmed it repeatedly in his public speeches. While some people are lamenting over the fall of the Establishment, which they regard as possible, probable, certain, and even imminent; while the "Protestant

Pope," of whom we have spoken, did not believe in 1875 that the Established Church had ten years more to live, and the "Liberation Society" only gave her four years of existence, others rejoice and triumph in the presence of a future to them so full of hope. But, it is strange and significant that this satisfaction should be in some degree felt by members of the Establishment. In any case, if they do not go so far as to rejoice, they accept the fact and do not appear to regret it.

"We have (said the 'Church Times' of January 1, 1875) always regarded the Establishment as an encumbrance. The honours and emoluments, the dignities and offices which belong to a State Church, are not for us; and yet, although we have built our churches at our own cost, we are told every day that we make use of our endowments, and of the prestige which belongs to a national church, for our private ends. For us, disestablishment has no terrors; we should hardly consider it an evil at all, and, the moment it comes, at least nine-tenths of the calumnies, misrepresentations, and mistakes against which we have to struggle would melt into air. If we do not take it up now, it is from pure unselfishness, and a desire to shield our bitter enemies from the tribulation and woe that Mr. Miall would bring upon them."

This is strange language; and although we believe, with a distinguished leader of the Anglican Church, that there is some exaggeration in it, yet we cannot agree with Bishop Ellicott (of Gloucester and Bristol) in maintaining that the action of the Ritualist party can have no influence on the future of the Church of England. We hold, indeed, a directly contrary opinion. We believe that, if a considerable section of the Established Church declared itself in favour of disestablishment, the severance would be accelerated by some years. The expressions we have quoted above are not, therefore, destitute of aim and meaning. Indeed it has since been confirmed by facts; and an active, if not a numerous, section of the Ritualist party has declared itself in favour of disestablishment. Some Ritualists go further. Disestablishment is not enough for them; they also profess to wish for disendowment. We are aware that these ideas are not shared by many of the clergy; but, it is not less remarkable, that they should be put forward and discussed at the meetings of the English Church Union.

It is equally remarkable that the Conservative party, which by inclination and tradition is a friend of the Establishment and an advocate of State Churches, has done more to compromise the State Church than the body of clergy of whom we have just spoken. This fact has been noted, with some surprise, by the Low Church party.

"It seems strange (said the 'Rock,' in 1875) that, notwithstanding an overwhelming majority of supposed good Churchmen in power, the danger of disestablishment was never felt to be so great as at the present time. One of the Tory High Church papers is appalled, when it admits that there is palpably a veering round to the Miallite view. Another Liberal paper of the same school now boldly advocates it. Of course, all the secular journals that formerly advocated disestablishment and disendowment do so still, and with additional zest, inasmuch as, with Mr. Gladstone leading the charge, it affords them the only chance of resuming office within a reasonable time. . . . That we have not mistaken nor exaggerated the danger will now be conceded by all who have studied the present attitude of Dissent, but it may be well to give one example—*ex uno disce omne*—that has just come to us from India, and which is taken from the report of a very able lecture delivered by the Rev. Isaac Allen, and reported in the 'Indian Daily News.' 'The disestablishment of the Churches of England and Scotland is,' Mr. Allen observes, 'in all probability, but a matter of a few years. . . . But of course the bishops do not intend to disestablish the Church of which they are the overseers: neither did Napoleon the Third intend to disestablish the Empire in France.'"

Such an admission on the part of the Evangelicals certainly gives matter for reflection; and it is still more striking that mere spectators of the controversy, even those who are hostile either to the Conservative Ministry or to the Establishment, also allow that the Tory party has compromised the future of the English Church. A reviewer writes:—

"The hope of disestablishment is so far from being extinguished, that it is, on the contrary, more cherished than it has ever been. And, moreover, it is felt by all those who are clear sighted enough to look below the surface of events and beyond the present moment, and who are too independent to be blinded by party feeling, that the Conservative Ministry has done much to hasten its fulfilment. It was, indeed, an adverse critic, though an earnest Churchman, who said that they had done more to weaken and imperil the Establishment in five months than their predecessors had done in five years; but there is a widespread conviction, shared by a large number of Conservatives, that Mr. Goschen was right."

When we study the events of the last seven years, we are forced to recognise the justice of these admissions and complaints. The party favourable to disestablishment in the last Liberal Parliament had seen their numbers decrease from year to year. After obtaining eighty-nine votes in 1871 and ninety-four in 1872, there were only sixty-one in 1873. This falling-off boded ill for the enemies of the Church, and was very favourable to the partisans of the Establishment. Mr. Gladstone, therefore, one of those men of whom the "British Quarterly Review" spoke as "clear-sighted enough to look below the surface of events and beyond the present moment"—Mr. Gladstone, in his reply to Messrs. Miall and Maclaren in the session of 1873, said to them, with a slight touch of irony, which appeared to be almost prophetic: "I do not think that my honourable friend would maintain that the minority in this House would be increased in number, if it were in our power to take the judgment of the country on this great subject." And in fact Mr. Gladstone's prediction was fulfilled. In the ensuing elections, those who wished to disestablish the Church of England were disestablished of their seats in Parliament. This fact was significant.

What is now the case? In spite of the favour and protection accorded to the Establishment by the Conservative party, we might say, with one of the principal Nonconformist organs, that if the Church of

England has never been stronger as a Church, it has never been weaker as an Establishment. Since the elections of 1874, the question of disestablishment has been discussed more frequently than it ever was before, and every event which has taken place has tended to hasten this solution. Men speak and argue as if this great event were on the eve of accomplishment. Some newspapers and private persons have even proposed to organise a movement from within having this object in view, and all advise the Church to prepare herself for the final crisis. The most moderate section of the High Church party does not yet see the necessity of preparing for this issue: they even hope to avert the blow which threatens the Establishment, fearing, from more than one point of view, to sever the bonds between Church and State. The Dean of Manchester, in a speech in Convocation, reported by the "Church Times" (1878), said that "he had a perfect horror of disestablishment, chiefly as a citizen."

While this is passing in the bosom of the Church, an analogous movement is taking place in the political world. Mr. Gladstone, who in 1873 regarded disestablishment as still far off, subsequently broached the grave question: "Is the Church of England worth preserving?" And the newspapers have taken care to show how this question threatens the future of the Church.

Mr. Miall's motions have not been brought forward in the late Conservative Parliament, but Mr. Osborne Morgan's famous Church Burials Bill, which involves nothing less than the disestablishment of churchyards, has been presented repeatedly; and for three or four years successively. It has only been rejected by a majority of from fourteen to eighteen votes. Formerly, moreover, the Bill was passed by the Commons, and rejected by the House of Lords; and in the year 1877-78, the Bill, with Lord Harrowby's amendment, was accepted by the House of Peers, including some of the bishops and the two archbishops. In the Commons it was only thrown out by a majority of fifteen votes. The Dissenting newspapers were justified in regarding this defeat as almost equivalent to a victory.

This appears to us the time to recall the words which appeared five years ago in one of the most advanced organs of Ritualism, after an almost similar vote on Mr. Osborne Morgan's Burials Bill :— .

"The moral is, how excessively precarious the existence of that Establishment will become, the moment Churchmen cease to stand shoulder to shoulder upon the question. With their usual want of wisdom, certain prelates have scoffed at the idea of a disestablishment movement springing up within the pale of the Church as the result of their own blundering; but, with a majority of only fourteen votes against the disestablishment of our churchyards, the danger can be regarded as by no means visionary or even distant." ("Church Times," April 1875.)

A general election has lately been held, and should the overwhelming majority on the Liberal benches of the House of Commons feel disposed or feel able to combine in favour of disestablishment, under the leadership of the eminent statesman now at the head of the State, the days of the Established Church are numbered.

We are certainly far from desiring the immediate fall of the Establishment, since it would be, from more than one point of view, a great misfortune for England. Yet, this fall appears absolutely inevitable, and perhaps not far distant. Mr. Gladstone has more than once been entreated to take up the cause; and although up to this time he has hesitated to do so, the day may come when he will feel himself compelled to go forward. When that day comes, if we may judge from the case of Ireland, his action will be at once prompt and vigorous. The noble words which he addressed to Parliament in 1873, in his reply to Mr. Miall, are still present to our memory. We understand the difficulties which surround the colossal enterprise of disestablishment in England, if it is to be accomplished with equity and justice and not in a revolutionary manner; and we think too well of the English people to suppose that they will, like the continental Radicals, cease to respect vested rights.

It seems to us, moreover, that Mr. Gladstone is less positive on the subject than he was seven years ago. His character as a churchman and a statesman must make him hesitate. We have only to see whether events will not force his hand; and we believe, that if the Church of England is to be subjected to many such cases as those of Messrs. Tooth, Dale, and Ridsdale, Ward, Carter, Randall, Edwards, Green, Mackonochie, &c., a change from without must be made, willingly or unwillingly.

In 1874, it was declared to be "extremely doubtful whether the Public Worship Regulation Act would realise the expectation of Protestants;" but it was asserted with confidence "that it had shaken the Establishment to its base." ("British Quarterly Review.") And again, "that the idea of disestablishment was suggested to every one, and gained strength from day to day, as much by means of the friends as of the enemies of disestablishment." (*Ibid.*)

II. It is interesting to place on record facts like those we have noticed, since such facts really compose the moral history of nations. But, it is not enough to collect testimony, admissions, and complaints, as we have just done; and the philosophic minds so numerous in England will, as we believe, agree with us in this opinion. The causes which produce situations analogous to those we have described afford a more interesting and instructive study. If, as we have said above, the religious movement now taking place in England is so attractive and full of teaching, it is chiefly because it reveals certain phases of the moral and religious nature of humanity with which we are imperfectly acquainted.

Whence, then, comes the opposition to the Establishment which is now felt by a large portion, perhaps by a majority of the English nation? The English people, who were formerly proud of their Established Church, have gradually lost their attachment, and discontinued the praise of which they were so prodigal. Has the Church ceased to deserve well of the nation? Is she no longer the *via media*, of which we have heard so much, which avoided the corruptions and excesses of Rome on the one side, and the shortcomings and errors of Geneva on the other? Is she no longer the Alma Mater which moulded this noble Anglo-Saxon race, the most active and self-controlled people in the world? Has she alienated from her the sympathies of the powerful aristocracy which remained standing alone, or almost alone, when all the other aristocracies of Europe were declining? Has she lost the secret of maintaining her sway over the youth of the upper orders and of the upper-middle class, whom she trained in the knowledge of science, or in the culture of literature and the fine arts? Has she entirely forfeited her position of friend and mother with the poor and the labouring classes, specially of the agricultural districts?

We have but one answer to give to all these inquiries, namely, that the Established Church has never been more brilliant, zealous, and fruitful than she is in our days. We believe that we may look in vain in the history of the last three centuries for an epoch to be compared with the present. The eighteenth century, generally stigmatised as the Georgian or Hanoverian age, cannot maintain a shadow of comparison with modern times. If there be a gloomy period in the life of the Anglican Church, it is in that age. The seventeenth century, again, is certainly inferior to the nineteenth.

The episcopate, taken as a whole, was never more

worthy of respect, composed as it is of men of capacity and worth. It is, indeed (from many quarters), the object of ceaseless attack; and we allow that some reproaches are not undeserved. But, we are not the less convinced that the Anglican episcopate of to-day, is superior to the same episcopate of preceding ages. It may include no men of the highest excellence or talent; but such men are always rare, and the age is fortunate which sees two or three such stars shining in its firmament. The English bishops of to-day respond to the expectations aroused by their position and character; they nearly all rise above the average, as it may be termed, of the Anglican episcopate.

What we say of the episcopate may be said with still greater justice of the clergy. We doubt whether the Anglican communion has ever possessed a body of men endowed with equal culture and piety, with such good breeding and zeal for the salvation of souls, combined, as we find in the clergy of our day. The Anglican clergy form a race apart from clerical bodies in other parts of the world. They are a class of picked men, often learned, sometimes scientific, and generally well-educated. If England has still retained, among the nations of Europe, a numerous public with a taste for literature; if in that country books, reviews, and newspapers succeed better than elsewhere; if every scientific work is sure to find readers, to whatever category it belongs, whether it be in the domain of philosophy, of history, of archæology, of classics, or of patristic learning; if, finally, there be in England an elevation of tone, a cultivation and a refinement of manners which contrast favourably with the democratic habits of the Continent, we readily admit that the English people owe these advantages to a large extent to the Anglican clergy.

We are therefore far from denying that there is something great and noble in the history of the Established Church. The history of England during the last three centuries cannot be understood without the previous study of the history of the Anglican communion. We do not, however, go so far as to consider the organisation of the Anglican clergy in the seventeenth century as a " blessing to England," as it has been sometimes called. The clergy was a benefit to English society : but, it was a benefit not so much as a clergy, but rather as a learned, social and moral corporation ; and we do not doubt that any other corporation might have rendered the same, or almost the same services, without having the privileges and distinctions attached to the character of the clergy. It was, in fact, impossible that a body of men, richly endowed with wealth and leisure, should have been placed at the heads of colleges and schools, or dispersed through the towns and villages, without forming a species of intellectual aristocracy which must give the tone to those who surrounded it. This was the necessary result of the retention of the system of rich benefices. The men who obtained them had only to occupy themselves with the study of literature, and the exercise of an enlightened philanthropy, in order to constitute a select body, capable of directing society, of refining manners, of preserving healthy traditions, and of producing a good tone.

The Anglican clergy of our time maintains the traditions of its predecessors ; and we do not believe that there is anywhere a more learned and studious body, producing so many and such meritorious works in the province of religious literature, and still more, it must be added, however incongruous the fact may be thought, of secular literature. Historians, Hellenists, philologists, orientalists, mathematicians, astronomers, and naturalists may be freely numbered among the Anglican clergy. If the Universities of Oxford and Cambridge are unrivalled in England, it is precisely because they are stamped with the mark of the Anglican clergy.

All this we admit and appreciate; yet, we do not hesitate to say, that if the clergy had no other claim to the gratitude of England, they would be unworthy of their name. They would perhaps be a distinguished, and even an extremely useful academical body; but, they would not be a body of priests in the strict and rigorous sense of the word. However important the culture of science and letters may be, it is, after all, a secondary matter : it should never be the sole, exclusive, or even the principal occupation of the clergy, taken as a whole.

From this point of view it may be asked, whether the Anglican clergy did not in some degree fail in past times—if, in other words, they did not lose too much of their clerical character in order to become an academic and learned body. And if the question were now put in England, every one would reply in the affirmative, since it is generally admitted that, by devoting themselves to the study of literature, the English clergy ended in forgetfulness of their first and chief mission, the cure of souls; and it is therefore indirectly allowed that the former influence of the Anglican clergy has not always been a blessing to the country. The clergy deserve gratitude as an academic body, but not as a clerical body. They forgot that there were souls to be saved; and they made men forget that they were only placed in the world in order that they might work out their salvation.

Let us hasten to recognise that the Anglican clergy have now admitted their mistake; and, without losing any of their high culture, many have once more become apostles. They have returned into the right path. In the course of the last forty years a great renovation has been accomplished in England, and in the most distant of her colonies. Bishoprics have been founded; missions have been opened; great works have been undertaken, leading to a happy issue. Zeal, ardour, self-abnegation, and generosity have been manifested.

Thousands of churches have been built or restored; a religious and sacerdotal life has been resumed; associations, the press, newspapers, temperance societies, institutes, schools, and education have become objects of interest. Not a single detail of religious and social life but has beheld the dawn of youth and vigour, where formerly reigned neglect, indifference, torpor, and the silence of death. The Anglican Church of to-day bears scarcely any resemblance to that of eighty years ago. The fiercest opponents of the Establishment admit and proclaim this fact, while the Nonconformists, finding the Established Church too active and vigorous, and alarmed at her recovery, would rejoice to see her decline; and even those who do not believe in Christianity watch her with interest.

"The Church of England (says the 'Pall Mall Gazette,' January 3, 1878) has undergone a transformation which may be described by saying that it has become interesting. Pretty much the reverse of this characterised it thirty or forty years ago, and the Church may be said to have prided itself on being unattractive. 'Next to a sound rule of faith,' says the preface to the most famous Anglican book published in this century, 'there is nothing of so much consequence as a sober standard of feeling in practical religion;' and then the writer of the 'Christian Year' proceeds to use language which sounds very like an apology for publishing the religious poetry which became afterwards so celebrated. The Church was, in fact, grave, sober, learned, respectable, but profoundly uninteresting. But the Whig statesmen who reformed it, and the Oxford Tract writers who fired it with mysticism, have changed it into a body that has almost nothing in common with the Establishment of half a century since. It is full of activity and life, even if the activity be something feverish, and the life occasionally breaks out in morbid growths. For good or for evil, it now interests men, and particularly young men. The attractiveness of Dissenting bodies in former days lay in their including both a secular and religious organisation; but the Church of England is now the centre of a religious and secular organisation on the largest scale. It is quite clear that this new vigour of the Establishment is telling injuriously on the Nonconformist sects. A young man may have been born into them, but if not why should he join them? These are not the days in which anybody would embrace any one of their narrow creeds in the spirit of a convert, and by uniting himself to them he would gain nothing intellectually, and lose a great deal socially. It is plainly a matter of life or death to them to get rid of a competitor which has enormous advantages on its side."

We find little to gainsay in this estimate of a journal which has in general but little sympathy with the Establishment, or indeed with any form of religion. It finds the Anglican Church interesting. We find in her a sense of fervour and zeal which she never before possessed. For this reason we readily agree with an acute observer that, as a Church, she was never stronger; but, we must add with him, that she was never weaker as an Establishment. These propositions may appear to contradict each other, but they are both true, rigorously true.

It must be confessed that it is strange that, at the moment when the Anglican Church is more full of life than she has ever been, she should threaten to perish as an Establishment. This problem deserves examination, and its solution is by no means difficult to find.

III. There was a time when the sixteenth century, the century of the English Reformation, was, by all Englishmen except the small body of Roman Catholics who had escaped the rigours of persecution, held to be a sort of golden age, such as the world had never before witnessed, nor was likely to see again. The majority of English churchmen believed as firmly in the inspiration of Cranmer and his associates as in that of St. Peter and St. Paul. They spoke with respectful admiration of the martyr-saints of Oxford, and regarded them as almost the equals of San Carlo Borromeo, St. Augustine, and St. John Chrysostom. Princes and peoples, men and things, beliefs and practices were all surrounded with a divine halo which gave them a supernatural appearance. Henry the Eighth, Edward the Sixth, and Elizabeth were not merely able and successful rulers, they became the equals of the righteous kings of which the Bible tells us; and since these righteous kings exercised a great influence over the direction of religious affairs, the same rights were accorded to the sovereigns of England. All these principles and ideas led to the debasement of the Anglican Church as a religious community, but to its vitality as an Establishment, a vitality which no society has elsewhere enjoyed. Insensibly and by degrees the Anglican body became, in less than a century and a half, what was once termed in Parliament, "a scandal to Christianity."

It would be useless to insist on this side of the religious question in England. For, if there be a subject which often recurs in modern controversy, it is this very debasement which characterised the Established Church at the beginning of the present century. Friends and enemies alike admit that the Church, as a religious body, was a disgrace to the nation and a scandal to Christianity. Volumes might be filled with the admissions made by the most distinguished Englishmen, both among the clergy and laity, who belong to every party in the Establishment.

Happily for herself, the Anglican Church has issued from this condition, and day by day she does so more fully. We assert the fact with pleasure and without reserve, although we are far from feeling unqualified approval, or from forming any expectation of miracles in this religious movement. But, at what cost has the Anglican Church reconquered all that she had forgotten, forsaken, and lost? It is only by denying her traditions of the last three centuries, by rejecting the principles, the men, and the laws which created her. It is only by condemning the authors of her existence, and by disowning her origin. It is by shaking off those chains of gold with which she was decked, and which she found to be bonds and fetters. It is by destroying all which she had adored, and by adoring all which she had destroyed. It is, in a word which has been frequently used during the last thirty years, by effecting a counter-Reformation diametrically opposed to the first.

The subject is so vast that a volume would be needed to point out the aims accomplished, and the results attained by the present religious movement.

All these secondary questions, which are the subject of so much litigation, excite only a languid interest in foreigners, who see the concerns of the Anglican Church and English nation from the outside, and rather as a whole than in detail. To us, Catholics born and bred, it seems simply puerile for members of a "church" to dispute, complain, and appeal to the civil tribunals on the question whether the priest shall stand at the north or the west side of the communion-table, whether he may turn his back to the people, whether he may light the altar candles, swing a censer, or put up a reredos or a crucifix. We cannot understand the hot and eager controversy about such trifles. If we attach any importance to such matters, it is merely as symbols. We cannot understand why the English should fight so fiercely for the outworks. We would rather see them go straight to the heart of the controversy, and when they have distinctly formulated their respective claims, the final conflict for victory should be fought out. Instead of taking the "bull by the horns," to use a familiar expression, they seize him by the tail, and for this reason the religious controversy, by being begun at the wrong end, may be prolonged indefinitely, unless other causes precipitate the inevitable conclusion.

All this seems strange to the looker-on and the foreigner, but it is in perfect agreement with the Anglican system. Since this system is essentially a compromise, a definite judgment on all vital questions has been avoided; and hence, men do not yet know what they are bound to believe on the most fundamental points. Take, for example, the Real Presence. You will find some Anglicans who deny, and other Anglicans who confess it. A confraternity of the Holy Sacrament has been instituted, which includes about one thousand of the clergy among its members. Take Apostolical Succession. One man will tell you that it is a myth, another that it is a reality, a third that you may believe or disbelieve it as you please. And yet volumes have been written on the validity of English orders, although it is certain that for at least a century not one person out of a thousand had ever thought of ordination as a sacrament which gave a certain character and intrinsic power to perform sacred functions. Take the Royal Supremacy. One man will tell you that Her Majesty Queen Victoria, the successor of the godly princes mentioned in the Bible, referred to in the Articles, has absolute power over ecclesiastical persons and things—that she is, *de jure* and *de facto*, the supreme governor of the Church. Another, on the contrary, will distinguish between power exercised for *correction* and for *direction*, will discuss the meanings of *head* and *governor*, and try to reduce the Royal Supremacy to a purely honorary title. These attempts are obviously unsuccessful; and, in spite of all distinctions, the Royal Supremacy still continues to bear hardly on the Established Church.

Such vagueness and contradictions are admirably adapted to a "Church of compromise" and to an "Establishment," but they are not adapted to a strongly defined religious system, nor to a powerful and energetic Church. But, an attentive observer of the Anglican Church must be struck by the fact that it now contains an active, busy party, which is already numerous, and of which the number is increasing, whose object is nothing less than to transform the Establishment into a Church. This, moreover, is the name which the party has assumed. It has taken, or at least is accused of having taken, the name of "the Church." Let us consider the characteristic features of this party.

To those who regard the matter from without, three characteristic features of the movement are apparent. 1. This party regard the Reformation as "a monstrous failure" and "an unmitigated disaster." They do not perhaps go so far as to treat the Reformers of the sixteenth century as though they were, without distinction, "a set of miscreants" or "a ribald party," but the mildest expression they use with respect to them is that these Reformers are no more entitled to be called martyrs than Dr. Dodd. 2. This party has an exalted idea of the spiritual and moral life. It has returned to a sense of, and a belief in, the supernatural, and consequently it admits or claims for the clergy the character, privileges, and the honours of the priesthood. Hence, it tries to infuse into the clergy a sacerdotal air in their priestly functions. This fact appears in a thousand ways, and it becomes daily more apparent in England. Everything in the High Church party bears the impress of "Sacerdotalism," their worship, the education of their clergy, their mode of life and deportment. Even their dress betrays this tendency. As the table has once more become an "altar," so the minister has become a "priest." 3. The last characteristic trait of the contemporary religious movement in England is, as it seems to us, a profound and humiliating sense of the faults committed by the Established Church. In consequence of the study of primitive Christianity, of historical research, and a comparison of different systems of Christianity, the Anglican clergy have developed a sense of humiliation at the sight of the degradation of the Established Church, and this feeling of humiliation has been sometimes evinced by language of extreme bitterness and violence, so that it is difficult to understand how men, with such an idea as these Anglicans hold of the Church, can remain within the pale of the Establishment. Volumes might be filled with a collection of contemporary sayings on this subject. The impression made a few years ago by the pamphlet called "Christianity or Erastianism," by "Presbyter Anglicanus," cannot be forgotten. It was ill received in the English Church; and a protest was immediately drawn up against its author—although this protest did not hinder those who signed it from the frequent use of the same expressions. We should have no difficulty in giving written proofs of this assertion; they are so abundant that the only difficulty would be in choosing which to adduce.

This is not all. Search has been made for the origin of the evil which is admitted to exist in the Anglican body of our day as well as of days gone by, and what is the result of these researches? The primary cause of all these evils is discovered to be the Royal Supremacy—that euphemism which was adopted in England in order to disguise the utter and degraded subjection of the Church to the State.

Modern controversy is wholly concentrated on this main question: Is the Anglican Church subject, or ought she to be subject, to the State? To us, Catholics and outsiders, who have nothing to do with the Establishment and have no personal interest in its existence or decay, it seems astonishing that thoughtful and religious men should have taken so long to discover, first, that the whole evil is due to the subjection of the Church to the State, and, secondly, that this subjection exists in England.

It is indeed true that the nature of civil government is ill adapted for the preservation and propagation of Christian doctrine. It is not the duty of States to recognise and maintain orthodoxy. In our days they concern themselves little, nor were they ever greatly concerned, with the spiritual, supernatural, or moral perfection. They may be, as we have sometimes observed, willing indirectly to recognise these things, but it is not their mission to bring them about. All that they require is a respect for morality and social laws, and that no embarrassing cases should occur.

They have, in general, little taste for men of decided doctrines and principles rigorously defined; they require no apostles. The English nation has long displayed this tendency of governments in the Anglican Establishment and in Scotch Presbyterianism; and the Queen, against whom complaints are more than whispered from time to time by the organs of the High Church party, shows her fidelity to the English constitution by appearing as a Presbyterian in Scotland, as an Anglican in England, and, if newspaper reports may be trusted, as a Lutheran on the Continent—it has even been said, to the extent of receiving the communion. Such conduct does not perhaps fulfil the Christian ideal; but from the English constitutional point of view it is at all events perfectly correct.

It is possible, nay, it is necessary to criticise the system; but, given the system, its consequences must be accepted. And besides, High Churchmen who tolerate the members of the Low and Broad Church parties in the comprehensive system of Anglicanism, and even apologise for it, are scarcely justified in complaining of such conduct. We do not see any real difference between the ideas, principles, and theories of these three sects, Anglicanism, Presbyterianism, and Lutheranism. If the Anglican compromise, which includes Rome and Geneva within the same fold, is considered as a benefit, there is no justification for rigid intolerance.

But, the astonishment of those who are, like ourselves, merely spectators of the disputes by which England is agitated, reaches its height when it is gravely asserted, that the Anglican Church did not begin with Henry the Eighth in the sixteenth century, and above all when it is actually denied that she has abdicated in favour of the State. Nothing has appeared to us more curious than the attempts which have been made for the last forty or fifty years to prove these two positions. We are well acquainted with modern theories on the subject, and admire the learning and subtlety which they display in the pursuit of this object; but, we must again express our astonishment that such attempts should be made. It appears to us a mere play upon words; and, in these subtle theories, there is no trace of the "plain-spokenness" of which England boasts.

If indeed there be two facts in history which are fully established, they are the following : namely, that England has broken with the centre of Catholicism ; and consequently, that in denying the fundamental principle of the Catholic system, she has adopted a new constitution; secondly, that the Anglican Church only received that portion of liberty which the State has been pleased to accord to her. Exception may be made in details; but, when examined as a whole, these two facts may be deduced from the history of the last three centuries.

We can understand those who regard the subjection of the Church to the State as an ideal or a necessity, and from this point of view the Low Church and Broad Church parties appear to us far more logical than High Churchmen. Their fundamental principle is open to criticism ; but, at all events, they are consistent. But, the High Church party, who attempt to show that there is no discontinuity between their Reformed Church (or deformed, as some have called it), and the Church before the Reformation, appear to us only to play with words. And when they assert that the Reformation only restored to the Church of England the rights usurped by the Pope—and when they add that the Anglican Church after the Reformation yielded certain rights to the Crown in consideration of certain privileges—it is impossible to repress a smile.

It becomes every day more apparent that the Royal Supremacy was only an euphemism for the complete subjection of the Church to the State. Here, again, we can adduce the admissions and evidence of the High Church party, the only one of the three schools which, to maintain its consistency, is interested in disputing the fact. The following are two passages, taken at random from among many others:—

> The Tudors (we are told) restored to the crown of England those ancient prerogatives which had been for a time usurped by the Pope. This is the lawyer's theory. But every one who has taken the least trouble to learn the truth knows perfectly well that this theory is a mere fiction, without even a plausible basis of fact. . . . The establishment of the Church—that is, in plain terms, the subjugation of the Church to royal authority—was simply an act of absolute and irrepressible power; Henry VIII. and Elizabeth could plead the same justification for their acts towards the Church, as the Norman William could for his conduct towards the State—the right of conquest, and no other."—("Church Review," 1876.)

In the same journal of the year before we find these words:—

> "The so-called Reformation of the sixteenth century was in reality no reformation at all. When Henry VIII. kicked out the Pope, he made himself Pope, and something more. The Tudor system was only Popery Erastianised. The great object of the Reformation was the confiscation of Church property. The removal of abuses, the restoration of Church rights, were not thought of then, nor have they been cared for since. The civil government has gone even further than the Roman curia in usurping the rights and restricting the just liberties of the Church."—(*Ibid.* 1875.)

Men's minds have been gradually enlightened. The ready-made opinions which were accepted at school or college have been set aside. They have been replaced by others, and these later opinions are diametrically opposed to the former. Insensibly, the chief cause of all the failures of the Established Church has been admitted, and they are ascribed to her subjection to the State. Thenceforward, we have seen the aspirations of High Churchmen—clerical or sacerdotal aspirations as they may be called—culminate in the assertion of the liberty of the Church, in opposition to the oppression of the State.

Such is the form which the religious controversy

has finally taken; and such is the form which it now retains. Towards this central point converge all aspirations, prayers, efforts, and resistance.

These aspirations, which, a few years ago, were those of a small number, are now held by many. They make their way everywhere in spite of opposition; and an Anglican journal was justified in the assertion "that it is not too much to say, that there is a large and rapidly increasing number of High Churchmen, firmly believing in the God-given authority of the Church, and resolutely determined to vindicate her honour and their own rights and liberty, even, if need be, at the expense of a total severance of the Church from the State" (*Ibid.* 1876). We can adduce two recent facts as symptoms of the progress made by these ideas. 1st. The manifesto of the Church of England Working Men's Society, which contains these words:—

"Why should it (the Anglican Church) not be as free and unfettered as the General Assembly of the Church of Scotland? If the Establishment on the north side of the border can be trusted with the administration of its own affairs, it is an insult to the prelates and clergy of the Established Church on the south side, if they cannot be entrusted with a like liberty."—(*Ibid.* Jan. 19, 1878.)

2nd. We may also quote the debates in Convocation of late years. The Bishop of Carlisle, when reintroducing the scheme of a bill proposed by the Bishop of London in 1874, claimed for convocation a real, if very limited, right of legislation. We see from this that the episcopate, naturally more favourable to the Establishment than to the Church, has joined the crusade in favour of the liberty of the Church which was initiated by the Ritualist party.

IV. We believe that we have clearly shown that the Established Church was never stronger as a Church than now. She has never approached more closely to the constitution of the Church of Jesus Christ. Her high standard is manifest; and there is, at the same time, a sense of spirituality, a love of souls, a zeal for the conversion of men, which is unprecedented in any other epoch of her history. The common people, who are perhaps more competent judges on this point than the higher classes of society, appreciate the fact, as appears from the manifesto of the Church of England Working Men's Society, in which we find these noble words:—

"We defend those clergy who have been, and still are, so cruelly ill-used, because we know them to be earnest and devoted to their duties; and many of us have been led by them from darkness into light, and learned of them the way of life. While they have been ill-used and abused, we have been drawn closer to them, because we know and admire their holy, earnest lives."—("Church Review," Jan. 19, 1878.)

The enemies of the Ritualists, bishops or others, within the fold of the Establishment, publicly proclaim the honesty and virtue of this section of the High Church; and whenever they are mentioned by those Nonconformists who are not carried away by their prejudices, the word which instinctively comes to their lips as a characteristic expression is "zeal." One among them did not shrink from saying, in the Assembly of United Presbyterians in Scotland, that the formation of the High Church party was one of the most remarkable events of our day.

Yet, if the conquests achieved by High Churchmen and even by the Established Church constitute its strength as a religious body, they are a source of weakness as an Establishment. This is a singular and overwhelming truth. The Establishment destroyed the Church, and the Church is now about to destroy the Establishment. Those who speak of the Establishment do in fact mean more than a union or *concordat* with the State: they mean submission and subordination to the State. Established Churches, as the word is understood in England, are National

Churches. And National Churches are enthralled, and consequently dead Churches.

Hitherto one Church alone has resisted the terrible ordeal of the union of Church and State—that is, the Roman Catholic Church. She also has suffered more than once from too close a union with the State. But, her sufferings have only been local and temporary; and the time came for her to cast aside her bonds and fetters, even when they were of gold, that she might find herself once more strong and free. She alone, the only real Church, has resisted the encroachments of the civil power, because she has always been able to adhere to the noble motto: *Potius mori quam fœdari*. Of this England knows something: she has heard the saying in former times, as Germany, France, and Switzerland hear it now.

The Anglican Church, when she became established, resigned herself to become only a National Church, that is to say, to remain in a state of civil subjection. She lost no time in becoming a moribund Church. She is now coming to life; or, as we may say, the restoration is half accomplished. She has almost become not merely a National, but a Catholic Church: although, of course, almost is not the same as altogether. Such, at least, is her ambition, hope, and desire. She wishes to be Catholic, only retaining the distinction of calling herself Anglo-Catholic. Hence, it is easy to infer the consequence, that, as an establishment, the Church of England must cease to exist.

The dilemma may be stated in these terms. Illusion is no longer possible. If the ideas and principles which animate the advanced section of High Churchmen, the Anglo-Catholics or Ritualists, continue to spread as they have done in the last ten years, the end of the Establishment is certain. If, on the other hand, the ideas and principles on which the Anglican Establishment depends recover strength and life, the Church of England herself must perish. The fiction of Anglo-

Catholicism must disappear, and sacerdotal pretensions and tendencies must be destroyed. No middle course is possible. It is on these terms that the battle must be fought: on them, indeed, it has already begun.

V. From this point of view, the religious strife now taking place in England presents an instructive spectacle to an attentive and disinterested observer. It furnishes matter for an interesting psychological and moral study, and leads unconsciously to singular coincidences. Who, for instance, that contemplates what is now occurring in England, is not reminded of the famous quarrel of the investitures? His thoughts must carry him back to the eleventh century, that maligned and misunderstood age, in which the Empire meditated the formation of an establishment like that in England, and the idea might have been realised, had it not been met by Leo IX. and Gregory VII., two great men supported by the authority of the Catholic Church.

Every one is acquainted, at any rate superficially, with the primary cause of this memorable conflict, and the phases through which it passed. No one is ignorant that the Empire meditated instituting something similar to the *congé d'élire*. Although not going quite so far, there was a strong tendency in that direction. The Empire felt a wish to nominate the Popes and the Bishops. In its character of temporal governor, it granted the investiture of benefices, and desired that when its choice had been made it should be irrevocable, even if the subjects on which it fell were unworthy. Although this was not practically the same as the *congé d'élire*, it approximated in principle to it; and the resemblance would soon have been complete, if the Papacy had not existed to oppose the designs of the Empire.

The Papacy, exalted in the person of Gregory VII., took up the cause of the offended consciences of Christians; and, proud of a just cause as conscious of its duty, it boldly opposed the enemy, relying on the support of Europe, which responded to the appeal. Henry IV., vanquished and humiliated, was constrained to come to Canossa, and to implore pardon at the feet of the Pontiff.

We now see a conflict reproduced close to us, which is, to an extent, analogous to that of the Middle Ages. The theatre is not so vast nor so extended as it was at that time, since it no longer concerns Europe and the Catholic Church. It merely concerns England and the Anglican communion; but, the motive for strife is the same, perhaps, in one sense even more serious, since the Catholic Church has never been subjected in a regular way to the *congé d'élire*. She has never seen a Privy Council composed of laymen, Jews, and unbelievers, appointed to interpret laws of doctrine and ritual. She has never had recourse to a secular Parliament to pronounce her laws, without previously taking the trouble to draw them up for herself, nor yet to sanction and publish them. If the Church and the Empire have sometimes issued the same decrees, this was not due to any confusion of authority, but in virtue of an understanding formulated in the legal maxim: " That the Catholic Church approves and accepts in the civil laws whatever is not contrary to her own edicts."

From many points of view, therefore, the causes which have excited the present conflict are more weighty in England at this time than they were throughout Europe in the eleventh century; but, in other respects, there are essential differences between the two situations.

In England, for example, we do not see the Church represented by its legitimate head, since that head does not exist, and has never existed, except in the person of the Sovereign. The State has been jealously careful to deprive the Church of all the individual or collective authority which might have been claimed for it. Nor is even the whole Established Church enlisted in the cause, but only a section of it, an increasing section, we admit, but as yet only a minority. This section is ready to call itself "the Church;" yet it does not include even the larger part of the Establishment.

On the other hand, when the Papacy, represented by Leo IX., and Gregory VII., took up the cause of the Catholic Church, it was supported by Christian Europe, including Germany itself, so that it possessed at once material and moral strength. In England, again, there is no longer a sovereign or chief minister, standing more or less alone, like Henry IV., but a government, which represents the majority of the nation, hostile to the Church, and "to sacerdotal ideas and ecclesiastical pretensions;" and on the side of the government, there are not only the Dissenters, but a considerable part of the Established Church, probably a large majority. The government may at any rate rely on the support of nearly all the members of the Anglican episcopate.

If, therefore, there are certain analogies, there are also numerous differences between the two situations; and both must be taken into account, if we wish to form a true idea of the importance of the growing conflict, and of its probable results. The differences as well as the analogies form data for the problem which we have to solve.

There is no room for the demand, as we believe, whether the English government or the state will go to Canossa. The Established Church of England is not the Catholic Church; the Anglican Primate of Canterbury is not Gregory VII.; Mr. Gladstone is not Henry IV.; and we are no longer in the eleventh century.

VI. Since such are the facts, it appears to us that

there are only three possible hypotheses as to the future. There will be expulsion, or disruption, or separation. We say nothing of reconciliation; since it is now admitted by all that this is an impossible solution. Things may go on as they are for a few years, but they cannot be prolonged indefinitely. We are constrained to give this opinion, which is painful to us from more than one point of view.

It is unnecessary to accumulate evidence in order to prove a fact which is accepted and proclaimed by all, since time and trouble would be thrown away. On the one hand, Catholic ideas, which are termed Sacerdotalism in England, are too widely diffused to be extinguished; and, on the other hand, the English nation, as a nation, is resolved not to tolerate such an intrusion of Sacerdotalism into the Establishment. This is declared in all newspapers, reviews, and other organs of the press, and it is affirmed by Parliament. We could quote several facts in confirmation of this resolution which have happened in the course of the last few years; and it was more especially displayed in 1874, during the discussion on the Public Worship Regulation Bill.

Clerical ideas and pretensions have long been denounced. Lord Sandon protested against them, in 1867, at the Congress at Wolverhampton; and similar protests continue to echo through the legal tribunals, at public meetings, in the press, and even on the hustings. Yet, neither the protestations of Lord Sandon, nor those of Lord Shaftesbury, nor the persecutions of the Church Association, have arrested the progress of Sacerdotalism. Friends and foes alike have been carried away by the movement. Even the Evangelical party and the bishops have somewhat advanced in this direction. A review, justly famed for the acuteness of its remarks, observed not long ago, with truth, that there is more of the Churchman than of the Evangelical in the modern Low Church party.

The union of the Church and State is therefore destined to perish, and that probably within a few years. It will come to an end at the moment when, if not before, the Ritualists are expelled from the Establishment; but, we believe this expulsion to be impossible. It is no doubt easy to declare from the tribunal, or from a seat in Parliament, that "Ritualism must be put down." This sentence, pronounced with boldness, may cause the speaker to be applauded, or gain for him a few votes. Yet, when all is done, it must be a source of embarrassment to him; and it is doubtful whether the threat would again escape from Lord Beaconsfield's lips if he had to propose another Public Worship Regulation Bill. After six years' controversy and actions at law, Ritualism is not overthrown: nor is final success yet certain. The victories obtained by the enemies of Ritualism in the courts of law have been lost in public opinion, and they have moreover provoked contempt and ridicule.

Admitting, however, this expulsion to be possible, can we suppose that it would save the Establishment? Surely not. Ritualism is at present rather like Samson. If it be cast out by violent means, it will lay hold of the columns of the temple, causing them to totter on their foundations, and will perish, crushing beneath the ruins its bitterest opponents. This is not an assertion only, it is admitted by all. The enactment of such a law as the Public Worship Regulation Bill was enough to shake the Establishment to its foundations. If other laws of the same kind should be made, if there were many trials like those of Messrs. Tooth, Carter, and Mackonochie, the question would not only be asked, "Is the Church of England worth preserving?" but it would be asked, "Whether the Anglican Church should be maintained." Expulsion is therefore impossible; nor, if it were possible, would it save the Establishment. We must therefore inquire whether we may expect a Disruption, or a Secession.

VII. We frankly admit that nine-tenths of the principles accepted by Ritualism have their logical issue in this direction. Since the Reformation is declared to be "a monstrous failure," and "an unmitigated disaster;" since the Reformers, Cranmer, Henry VIII., Cromwell, and others, are regarded as "a set of miscreants;" since the Anglican Church is admitted to be in captivity and servitude, labouring in chains, and only a shadow of the true kingdom of Jesus Christ; since Ritualists teach that the Articles are the product of an anti-Catholic age, that the doctrine and ritual of the Roman Church have preserved all which Anglicanism has allowed to perish, and that the sacramental system practised by Rome is the only true one; since the Reformers are hated, and it is proposed to go in a sense directly opposed to the Reformation; since St. Thomas à Becket is esteemed a martyr, Gregory VII., a man of unparalleled holiness, and both as lights of the Church of the Middle Ages; finally, since the isolation of the Anglican Church is deplored, and men sigh for union with the true Church of Jesus Christ—it appears to us that men who hold these opinions have something else to do than to eat the bread of an Establishment which has always rejected them.

We sincerely declare that our sympathies are with the so-called Anglo-Catholics. We admire their zeal, their activity, their self-denial and devotion to parochial work. We believe that they are labouring in a right direction, that they have found the good way, and have turned their eyes towards the true haven. But, we must also express our surprise at their conduct, which is almost a scandal to us, and we have much difficulty in understanding how they can, either from a logical or moral point of view, justify their conduct and defend their relations with the Establishment. This, indeed, exceeds our comprehension.

Although we have no sympathy with the partisans

of the Low and Broad Church Schools, yet the conduct of both these sections of the Anglican Church appears to us more regular, and capable of defence. These two parties may be mistaken. In our opinion they are much more mistaken than the High Church party; but, at any rate, their conduct is in tolerable agreement with their principles, and it is logical and consistent. When the Pope is regarded as Antichrist, and Rome as the harlot of the Apocalypse, it is only consistent to pursue with implacable enmity whatever leads to Romanism.

It appears to us, therefore, that a Disruption, such as took place in 1843 in the Presbyterian Establishment of Scotland, would be the natural consequence of the attitude generally adopted by the Anglo-Catholic party. This, if principles are pressed to their natural and legitimate consequences, must be the end. And yet, this is by no means the probable result of the present conflict.

The Ritualists openly declare that they will not leave the Establishment. They claim to represent the true tendencies of Anglicanism; they loudly assert their pretension to reform and convert it in accordance with their ideas; and they do, in fact, constantly gain ground. Just as they do not wish to be reunited to Rome as individuals, but in a body; so, also, they do not wish to sever their relations with the State individually, but collectively and as a Church.

It may be asked, whether they are influenced by a want of honesty, of logic, or of courage; whether they refuse to leave the Establishment because they shrink from the consequences involved in such a resolution; and whether, finally, they are only held back by a dread of the material and financial difficulties which Disruption or Secession would produce. We think that these motives have some influence on the conduct of Anglo-Catholics, and that some of them may be arrested half-way by purely earthly and human considerations. All men are not of the stuff of which heroes and martyrs are made. The clerical father of a family, and even a clergyman who leads a celibate life, may tremble, hesitate, and draw back from the prospect of humiliation and poverty. Conscience cannot approve of such conduct, and certainly cannot propose it as an example to be followed; but charity and justice prescribe indulgence for this weakness of poor human nature.

Yet, it is difficult to believe that such a motive generally influences the Ritualists. We rather suppose that their conduct is due to prejudices of education and to a deficiency in logic. Since they have been accustomed to doubt and to criticise everything—since they have painfully regained, one by one, truths and practices which help to form Catholicism, it is difficult for them to conceive the principles of rigorous and methodical deduction which are the distinctive features of Catholicism. In fact, we have often asked ourselves how Anglicanism is to be reconciled with logic, and we confess that this has always appeared to us one of the most curious psychological problems for study or solution. We can understand both Rationalism and Catholicism; but we cannot understand the position which Anglican-Ritualism seeks to maintain between these two extremes.

We must also say, with the same sincerity, that if Anglicanism contains a school which appears to us illogical, it is the school of which we are speaking. There are innumerable instances of its inconsequence. Take the Book of Common Prayer, the Palladium of Ritualism, the rampart behind which it entrenches itself, the weapon of offence and defence which it presents to its opponents. Yet, the Book of Common Prayer was compiled by men whom the Ritualists regard as vile and impious unbelievers, under a commission composed of infamous persons, and by a Parliament whose intervention in religious affairs is odious to them. It must be admitted that there is in the principles and practices of Ritualism, in its estimate of men and things, a mixture of good and evil, of the helpful and the harmful, of beauty and unsightliness—of everything, in short, except order, harmony, consistency, and logic.

These defects are so visible and palpable that the Ritualists are treated with too much severity, and addressed with harsh and offensive words. We shall be careful not to have recourse to such terms of reproach, since we fail to see how contemptuous language, used in regard of men whose zeal and honesty are beyond suspicion, can serve the cause of truth. We think it more equitable and satisfactory to lay aside all offensive expressions, which can only jeopardise the salvation of souls. We must not, moreover, forget that the Ritualists do not see things from our point of view, and we cannot be just towards them unless we try to understand their ideas. Indeed, it appears that the Ritualists can, in a certain sense, defend their line of conduct.

Since they have not yet the same idea of the Church and its essential oneness as Catholics possess, they recognise the differences which exist between different Christian sects, and claim for themselves a certain liberty of action; they think it is their duty to remain in the Established Church; and they trust, with time and patience, to fashion out of it a Church of fair appearance. Thus they calculate on preparing the way for the future union which they desire. We do not now estimate or decide on what there may be of substance or of chimæra in such hopes. We are content to give the general features of the system, and to seek an explanation of the reason why Ritualists do not desire a disruption or secession.

It is possible that there is no self-deception here, and that they are aware that if they were to leave the Established Church without joining the Church of

Rome, they would only form a sect without object, or influence, or future. They and their system would come to a speedy end. For these and other reasons a disruption or secession is impossible, or at least improbable. It would perhaps rejoice the Evangelical party. It would certainly lead to the fall of the Establishment.

VIII. What possible issue then remains? Only a prospect which includes all the systems which can be termed a separation, although the word indicates a voluntary rather than an enforced fact. If the Anglo-Catholic party could go on working for another twenty years in peace and tranquillity, it would perhaps succeed in infusing its ideas and clerical tendencies into a large portion of the Established Church. The mass of the clergy and laity would probably become High Churchmen. Now, it is evident that under such conditions the result of the conflict would assume a very different aspect from that in which it presents itself at the present day. A State which had to meet a compact body, such as the Established Church might then be, would think twice before engaging in the strife, and at any rate would consider whether it might not be obliged to go to Canossa in order to restore, willingly or unwillingly, the independence of the Church. But, for this supreme struggle the Anglo-Catholics require a Gregory VII. or a Thomas à Becket; and so far, Anglicanism has certainly not prepared us to expect men of this stamp. Such a surmise is therefore highly improbable. It is more likely that the conflict will go on for some time, in the midst of unworthy disputes which produce irritation and decide nothing, until the nation, both Church and State alike, are weary of discord, and resolve to sever a union which cannot continue without endangering the peace of civil and religious society. Before reaching this extremity, no doubt various expedients will be tried; a certain liberty will be accorded to the Church, or her dependence on the State will be made more close. But, it is already evident that such measures cannot avert the final crisis; they can at the most retard it.

What, then, will be the nature of this definitive solution? Will it be a true separation, a divorce arranged on both sides, a voluntary and determined act? Strictly speaking, this is one of many possible hypotheses. It is not difficult to imagine that the Church and the State, weary of their mutual opposition, may say to each other:—" Let us each resume our liberty; let us live and work side by side, without encroaching on the proper sphere of the other; let us each remain in our own domain. To one the cure of souls, to the other the care of bodies; to the one the articles of Christian faith and dogma, to the other the regulation of temporal affairs."

But this Platonic solution will never be made, for the bitterness of the conflict is now too great. Before passing the Act for the Regulation of Public Worship, a little tact, sincerity, and discretion might have made it possible. Now the die is cast, and a battle is inevitable: that is to say, there must be a victor and a vanquished. The Anglo-Catholics are keenly sensible of their false position. They set forth their real and serious wrongs with too much violence and bitterness to allow their opponents to come to terms with them, and to discuss on common ground the basis of a final treaty. The war has begun, and it can only end in a catastrophe in which conquerors and conquered will find it possible to satisfy their personal rancour. Any one who reads the daily papers, or who turns over the pamphlets and periodicals of the day, can see that the crisis has reached a degree of acrimony which must shortly end in one way or the other. There is nothing in the future to calm this irritation of mind. If the language now in use amazes and often offends us by its virulence, what will it become when it is necessary to fight for the maintenance of interests most justly dear to the human conscience, interests which are spiritual and eternal? We may expect a want of moderation in act and speech, and perhaps actual violence.

A simple separation is therefore not likely to take place. The State, which dislikes Hildebrands, and jealously guards its authority, as some newspapers have lately remarked—the State, which claims, and justly claims the honour of having created the Church of England, whatever Ritualists may think and say— the English State knows how to be master at home, and has more than once signified its intention of finding means to enforce the obedience of its rebellious and intractable subjects. Nor will the separation be merely a dismissal. The master will choose his own servants; and the State will repudiate the Church as a husband turns away a disobedient or unfaithful wife, and may even take to itself another.

In any case, the separation cannot fail to be accompanied by a certain amount of spoliation. England is jealous of ecclesiastical authority, and has taken all sorts of precautions to obviate or prevent encroachment on the civil power. She will not see without uneasiness an independent power formed in her midst, which may dispose of immense resources. Political men, even those most favourably disposed towards the Church, have declared that a disendowment must be expected. There is nothing surprising in this warning; and we are equally prepared to see the English nation proceed from speech to action, restoring indeed the liberty of the Church, but qualifying this liberty by a redistribution of Church property on a grand scale.

The greatest difficulty of the present conflict consists in this inevitable, perhaps this necessary redistribution; and for this reason men hesitate to approach the question of disestablishment in a practical spirit.

IX. We have said nothing of another solution, since it appears to us morally impossible—that is, the humble submission of the Ritualist party. Many difficulties would be temporarily removed if that party would heartily accept the decisions of its own bishops, the judgments of Lord Penzance, or the decrees of the Privy Council. We should no longer witness the religious scandal of ministers of peace who accuse, condemn, and quarrel with each other on questions of posture and vesture, of lights, wafers, or incense. But no one will expect to see this surmise realised who is acquainted with the extent of the evil, the number of the combatants, or the ardour of the strife. The Church Association and the English Church Union will not so easily come to terms; the Ritualists and the Low Churchmen cannot lay down their arms.

The points at issue are too serious, the interests at stake are too considerable, the animosity is too great, and the strife has been carried too far to make it possible for the Anglo-Catholics to submit to the Evangelicals, or the Evangelicals to the Anglo-Catholics. Those who are acquainted with the movement, and with the comments of the press for many years past, are aware that such a dream cannot be realised. Since each side has spoken out; since bishops, clergy, and societies have publicly pledged themselves and bound their consciences; since we have read the expressions used at meetings or in pamphlets; since the secular arm has been invoked on the one side, and its intervention rejected on the other; since the proceedings at a *congé d'élire* have been termed a mockery and a farce; since imprisonment has been tried, and men have elected to endure all rather than yield, convinced that the future of souls and of the Church lay in the issue of the conflict; submission becomes impossible, for it involves the loss of honour and of consistency, and it is not to be expected from either side. An organ of the more moderate Ritualists has said :—

"Whatever difficulty the press may find in understanding what is meant by the liberty of the Church, and however much our opponents and some of our bishops may dread this liberty, the Anglo-Catholic party will redouble their efforts to obtain it. We must regain the liberty of the Church : we have laid aside for ever the dread of overthrowing the Establishment in struggling to assert this liberty. We desire to avoid such an evil, yet we are ready to submit to it if our spiritual liberty is involved."

We could quote endless articles, speeches, and letters of which the tone is equally resolute and decisive, which represent the opposing parties. On either side submission is only possible at the expense of conscience—that is, of a sacrifice which would ruin any cause, however just and honest. The war-cry is "No surrender!"—a cry impelled by events even more than by men. The die is cast. The final crisis cannot be averted or even much longer delayed. The Establishment has destroyed the Church of England ; and the Anglican Church will destroy the Established Religion.

X. This fact is great and interesting enough in itself to make it worth while to concentrate upon it the attention of philosophers and politicians. Yet, we confess that it is its novelty, we might almost say its singularity, which allures us, since we have no direct interest in the matter.

For the first time a National Church is attempting on a grand scale to break its fetters, and the attempt is made solely to vindicate liberty of conscience and the independence of all that is greatest upon earth— the independence of souls, of belief, of truth.

The contemplation of the religious world can afford

nothing newer or more attractive. Whatever may be the result of the present strife, Christianity in England is certain to attract the attention of serious and thoughtful observers, and especially since the religious question is complicated by a political question. We saw, not many years ago, the attitude of the Anglican clergy with reference to the Turco-Russian war. The Anglo-Catholics and the Ritualists, represented by Pusey, Liddon, MacColl, Mackonochie, Denison, and others, took part with the Christians, and consequently, more or less, with the Russians.

While we take a lively interest in the strifes of the Established Church and the phases through which they pass, it must not be thought that we already welcome the day when that Church will assume the position only of a Christian sect, and we should be sorry to find that our readers share such an impression. We look forward to the final solution with mingled feelings; for, if we believe that the Anglican Church has been, as a religious communion, only a "monstrous failure," an "unmitigated disaster"—to adopt the words of the Ritualists—yet, we must admit that, as an Establishment, it has rendered great services to society and to the English nation. We should be grieved for the English people, whom we hold to be the first in the world, if the Establishment were to disappear without leaving anything but ruins, and without being replaced by institutions capable of gathering up all that it has effected of good, of nobility, and of greatness.

Yet, we are without anxiety on this point. We believe that the English nation is destined by Providence to continue to play a great part in the world, and that, at the given moment, the necessary institution will be formed. If, by the absorption of that which is false, the Establishment perish, it is only that the true Church may be revivified; and the Catholic Church, which has been the honour and glory of England in past times, will find in its inexhaustible devotion fitting means to become its glory and happiness in the future.

If England has any fears about her future—and how should she not have them?—let her turn her eyes on Oxford and Cambridge, let her contemplate those glorious foundations of faith and knowledge, and she will see that the Catholic Church, whenever she has been left to act freely, has been able, while occupying herself about heavenly and spiritual things, to attend to the things which make nations great, and has not neglected matters of science and art.

WHY DO NOT RITUALISTS BECOME CATHOLICS?

WHEN we see the beliefs and practices of an advanced section of the Anglican communion approaching more and more nearly to those of the Roman Catholic body; when we find in use books of devotion of which it would be hard to say whether the source was Protestant or Catholic; when the resemblances become so many and so close that eye, ear, and intellect fail to distinguish between the two communities, there is a question which forcibly suggests itself: Why do not all the members of this advanced section of the Anglican Church become Roman Catholics? Why do they remain in communion with a Church to which, so to speak, they no longer belong? What is it which thus makes them pause on the threshold of true Catholicism?

This appears to us a most natural question; but it is also, we readily admit, a momentous religious question of the present day. Our aim now is to answer it as clearly and as completely as possible. The subject seems to us worthy of the attention of all interested in the good of souls, and specially of those who, as a means to that end, seek in the first place their own proper good. We therefore repeat the question: What is it which prevents English Ritualists from becoming Roman Catholics?

I. Before commencing our inquiry, we will make one observation. From a study of the theory of Protestantism, we are led to ask ourselves, how can there be a *bonâ fide* Protestant who is not at the same time more or less a Rationalist? We refer, of course, to enlightened Protestants, men who think, reason, and reflect, and then render to themselves an account of their beliefs and of the position they have taken up. The thing seems so anomalous when we examine it thus in the abstract, that we can hardly conceive it possible that there can be any enlightened Protestants who are thoroughly sincere in their convictions; and yet, as a matter of fact, it is unquestionable that there are such, and many such.

There are degrees, however, both in good and bad faith. There is a faith which has not the shadow of a doubt as to the rightness of the position it holds. And there is a faith which is doubtful, nay, suspicious of its own attitude; which perceives that it is not in the truth, but fears to acknowledge it; and which refuses to look more closely into things lest it should be constrained to take some decisive step. Now, in this dubious, wavering state of mind, how many degrees do we see to be possible, how many we find actually existing. Just as there is a degree of doubt which permits of no further hesitation without positive bad faith, so there is a degree of doubt so slight, so vague, so largely counterbalanced, that the soul may silence it without doing any real violence to conscience. Now, if there is reason to believe that the number of enlightened Protestants who remain such from honest and thorough conviction is extremely small, the case is very different with those whom we may call half-believers. One who knew Anglicanism well, once wrote the following words, which are singularly appropriate to our subject:—

"What young man or woman is there who has not at some time doubted as to whether the Church in which they have been brought up is the true Church of Christ? I had my doubts as to the truth of the Anglican Church being of God, and for God, and in God; whether she was part of the Catholic Church; whether her teaching was holy and true; whether she was what she represents herself as being."

The number of enlightened Protestants in the

Anglican Church or elsewhere, who are living in absolute good faith, in that good faith which excludes every doubt, every suspicion, and all anxiety, is, as we believe, small; and the grounds on which we have come to this conclusion are the following.

There is always going on in the mind of man a process of comparison between his own belief and the opinions of others. This process, which is universal and continual, and often unwittingly carried on, becomes still more active when circumstances bring us into contact with those who differ from us in opinion and in religion. It is enough for us to know that opinions and beliefs opposed to our own exist in the world. Knowing this, we are at once brought under the necessity, whether we will it or not, to subject our faith to the test of examination, and, by a comparison of it with other beliefs, to satisfy ourselves that it rests upon a basis that cannot be shaken. This comparison, we repeat, we make instinctively, sometimes even involuntarily, for, in order to preserve our inward calm and peace, we must be able to say, "I am in the truth." And if we cannot always be assured that we have arrived at absolute truth, we must at least be able to say, that we have apprehended as much of the truth as others, and more. Without this assurance, our mind becomes troubled, our hearts are restless, and we know no peace, because we can never escape from the voice within which says, "Are you sure you are in the truth? You are not; then up and seek it." This comparison between various beliefs is always going on in thoughtful minds. But there are times when it is more active than at others. For example, when the intercourse between nations becomes more close and frequent; when commercial, scientific, literary labour receives some new impulse; when, lastly, through the advance of civilisation, various creeds are brought closer together, as those who profess them meet and jostle one another daily on the highways of life. In times like these, men's minds and consciences are kept on the alert. They observe, examine, compare, pronounce, judge. And, therefore, these are always periods of intellectual and moral unrest. A sore travail seizes all noble minds; they toss about, and cannot be quiet; and the more generous and high-minded they are, the more bitter are their pangs. They must find certitude, or in default of certitude, at least a high degree of probability, that they are in the right, while those who differ from them are in the wrong.

That we are passing through such an epoch at the present time, is a fact which must be admitted by every impartial observer; and the further we advance, the more strongly shall we find the age marked by the characteristics we have just described. In the days in which we live, nations are, in fact, no longer isolated, entrenched, as it were, behind their own defences. There is a constant interchange of communication of every sort between one nation and another A press, vast in extent, and marvellous in the number and variety of its instruments, carries daily to the ends of the earth the knowledge of all systems new and old. No one, therefore, has any pretext for ignorance. It needs only an effort of the will to keep oneself acquainted with everything that is thought or wrought under the sun.

What has been the consequence of this advance in civilisation? What has been the result of the creation of the telegraph, the invention of railways, the application of steam power, the development of the press? One result has been to give an immense impulse to religious discussion. Religion, which was sometimes said and thought to be dead, has sprung up into new life; and, with an energy such as it had never shown before, has resumed or is resuming over society its sway. Everywhere men have begun to study, to compare, to discuss, to criticise religious questions.

There is no flagging in the spirit of inquiry, and everything indicates that we are only at the earliest stage of the religious movement. A glance over the face of Europe suffices to show that there is widespread agitation and convulsion, especially in. Protestant countries.

The first result of this close contact, we might say, of this friction of religions and of creeds, has been a tendency towards Catholicism; and nowhere has this tendency been more marked than in once Catholic England. For the last century, and especially for the last fifty years, there has been a movement, perhaps even unconscious to itself, of all that was best in the Anglican communion towards Catholicism. Much which Anglicanism had retained of Catholicism has been developing, extending, and assuming larger proportions. Much which it had lost of Catholicism has, to a large extent, been regained, in spite of all the barriers of custom and prejudice, of articles of religion and formularies; so that the illusion, if not complete, is at least so great as to mislead any but practised eyes.

The second result of the religious agitation we have described, has been an increased tendency towards Rationalism under one form or another. When once the moorings are loosened by which, after its deliverance from the yoke of ecclesiastical authority, man's spirit is held in natural and wholesome restraint, it is like a disabled ship in the midst of a stormy sea, carried hither and thither by every wind of passion or by the inclination of the moment, and dashing itself against all systems of unbelief. The tendency towards Catholicism, on the one hand, has had its counterpart in the dissolution of orthodox Protestantism. Rationalism prevails to-day among the Protestants both of France and Germany. In England it is not so advanced; but it is gaining ground every day among Dissenters and even in the Church of England. This is a fact recognised and avowed on all hands.

We need only note that which has lately taken place among the Presbyterians in Scotland and among the Congregationalists in England. Indeed, we need only follow the controversies of the day to be convinced that such is the case. What is the offence with which Professor Robertson Smith and the Rev. Fergus Ferguson are charged? It is Rationalism. What is the evil which is spreading so rapidly among the Independent and the Congregationalist bodies generally? It is Rationalism. What is the great subject of complaint with the Anglican bishops? It is Rationalism. What is it we hear repeated perpetually in meetings of High Churchmen and Low Churchmen, in the pulpits of Anglican cathedrals and of the universities? It is, again, invectives against Rationalism.

Rationalism on the one hand, and Catholicism on the other—these are the two systems on which seems to devolve the religious future of our race. Already there is an evident movement among the masses. The waters are dividing; and the currents are setting in towards Catholicism on the one hand and towards Rationalism on the other.

Midway between Roman Catholicism and Rationalism stands Ritualism—that hybrid and inexplicable creature which is neither the one nor the other; which belongs to no recognised species; which aims to find, and deems that it has perfectly succeeded in finding, the *via media* of time-honoured religious fame in England.

We return, then, again from these preliminary observations to our first question: What hinders the Ritualists from becoming Catholics, pure and simple?

II. This question, like all moral questions, is evidently a complex one. It requires much careful observation, and much discernment, to reply to it. Moral difficulties cannot be cut like the Gordian knot; and to disentangle their complicated meshes demands patience and forbearance. Men rarely decide for one simple reason. They are habitually influenced by a combination of concurrent causes.

We must go even further. It is not enough to analyse the reasons by which men may be moved to a certain course. We must also take account of the obstacles in their way. Obstacles, it is true, do not act in the same way as reasons; but they do exercise, nevertheless, a real influence upon all our movements, intellectual, moral, and physical. Reasons determine; obstacles arrest. Reasons strike the judgment and act upon the will. Obstacles paralyse the will or the judgment; oftentimes they paralyse both; sometimes they even prevent reasons from suggesting themselves at all to the mind, or at least from taking such a hold of it as to produce an impression.

Now, there is not the slightest doubt that beside the reasons which determine the Ritualists not to join the Roman Church, there are also obstacles which prevent them from seeing clearly the motives that might influence them to leave the Anglican body. These obstacles may be summed up in a single word—education; or in what Cardinal Newman has so justly described as the "great Protestant tradition."

There has been such a travesty of the Roman Catholic system, of its ideas, its facts, and its principles, current among Protestants generally, and even among Anglicans, that it is difficult for them to discern at all the true beauty and grandeur of the Roman Catholic Church. What, in fact, has been, and still is, the conception of Holy Church entertained by the majority of Anglicans? It is regarded as a tissue of iniquity and error, of vice and falsehood, from which every well-regulated mind, every honest heart, must recoil. So much has been written and said against Rome; it has so often been represented as the Scarlet Woman of the Apocalypse; it has been so generally accused of having perverted Christian doctrine and Christian morality, both in theory and in practice, and the prejudice against it

Why do not Ritualists become Catholics? 129

has taken such a firm hold of the public mind, that it is scarcely possible for an ordinary Protestant of to-day to overcome all the obstacles in his way unless by a sort of miracle.

It may be said, that there is not a single question bearing on the Catholic Church which has not been so travestied for a long course of years, that there has grown up a public opinion, a sort of "tradition," as Cardinal Newman calls it, against which no Anglican thinks of protesting, and in relation to which any protest that might be made would probably be useless. Opinion on this matter is so formed, fixed, widespread, that the possibility of establishing a contrary view would hardly occur to any one. Popery is, in a religious point of view, the synonym for corruption, falsehood, and error; from a political standpoint, it means slavery, tyranny, oppression, the Massacre of St. Bartholomew, the Dragonades, the Inquisition, mock trials, False Decretals, and much more to the like effect. These are the typical themes which have furnished the arguments for popular declamation, and which represent in the eyes of most Protestants the whole of the Catholic system. There is no remembrance of all that the Church has suffered from Protestants and heretics; there is no consideration that the Catholic Church is not responsible for the faults committed by her children; there is no intimation that she has disavowed all the crimes perpetrated in her name, that she has denounced every abuse of things sacred, and that no protest has been more emphatic than hers against the confusion of the spiritual and the temporal powers. Sustained by the evil instincts of humanity, favoured by natural preference for a certain order of opinion, and aided most of all by the habit of cherishing illusions which please and flatter us, and of allowing the unchecked indulgence of our passions—these prejudices have gained ground, and so effectually that it was at one time held as an incontestable axiom, that to be a Catholic and an honest man were impossible. The term Romanist, or Papist, became almost an equivalent for rogue, liar, thief, assassin, or for a man without character and without honour. To be a Catholic and a gentleman seemed no longer possible. Under this aspect, English literature has presented a curious study for the last three hundred years. If in a stage play, or a novel, there occurs the part of a rascal, it is sure to be given to a Catholic. If, on the contrary, the character to be represented is noble, high-minded, generous, a Catholic is ineligible. There is a striking example of this in one of England's most popular novelists.

Such being the moral attitude of Englishmen towards the Catholic faith, it will be readily conceived that the return to that faith has been, and must still be, greatly retarded. Men will not even entertain the idea of returning to a system which they neither admire nor esteem, and which they have been taught to regard as dangerous and false. Such a system scarcely receives consideration or study from them. Between it and human reason there is a wall great and high which obstructs the view, a thick cloud which wholly obliterates it. Before any approach will be even attempted, this cloud must vanish, this wall must fall. Now this is the work of time, of centuries, rather than of men. Men may certainly do some thing; but, it is not in a day that the thoughts and habits of a nation can be changed.

Time is needed to accomplish such a moral revolution, and therefore the return of England to Catholicism can only be the work of a long series of years. We know well that there are those who, guided rather by their desires than by their experience, by hope rather than by fact, think otherwise. But we ourselves are convinced that, humanly speaking, generations will elapse before the nation and people of England will be restored to the bosom of Christ's Holy Church.

It must be said, however, that there are many signs of a change already perceptible. Catholicism is better known, and Catholics exert an influence over English society out of all proportion to their numbers. The whole situation is changing. Ideas are expanding; prejudices are softening, melting, and vanishing away; facts are regarded with a calmer, and therefore with a clearer, eye; the judgment is less influenced by passion, and therefore is more equitable. In a word, obstacles are beginning to disappear; and they will disappear more and more rapidly as time advances, till at length there will remain only reasons against becoming a Catholic. The issue will then be greatly simplified; it will be merely a question between truth and error. Is Catholicism true—more true than Anglicanism? Much will have already been gained for Catholicism, when it can be thus placed on the same level with Anglicanism; and to this point, we are free to avow with candour, the English nation has been brought mainly by the Ritualists. These men have made Christian antiquity a special study; they have examined more closely Rome and Catholicism; they have arrested the floods of prejudice which were increasing daily; they have turned back the course of the current, and have almost proved that it is possible to be a Roman Catholic and yet not a villain. This is unquestionably a great service rendered; and when we know the point from which they started, and see the point to which they have come, hope is largely renewed. Many obstacles to the conversion of souls have disappeared, and the rest will soon follow. The sun of Catholic truth is beginning to shine more brightly on the horizon of Protestant England. We can feel already its lightening, its warming, and its quickening rays.

III. The way is not yet clear, however, for the conversion of England; and the Ritualists themselves who come so near to Catholicism do not, as a fact, cross the line. They remain, and they desire to remain, Anglicans. They are anxious indeed to repudiate, as an injurious libel, the name of Protestant which is sometimes given to them. They are willing to call themselves Anglo-Catholics, but they shun the name of Catholic alone, in the sense of Roman Catholic.

It is curious to analyse this moral and intellectual attitude, and to ask why these Anglo-Catholics hesitate to leave a communion with which they have lost sympathy, and to join another which they esteem and with which they ardently desire fellowship.

The Ritualists, indeed, made no mystery of their desires and hopes; and though it cannot be said that all share the views of the "Association for Promoting the Unity of Christendom," yet all perceive more or less clearly the ultimate issues of the religious revival known as the Oxford Movement. When, therefore, the Rev. H. N. Oxenham not long ago proposed, at a meeting held at Oxford, the following resolution:— "That the ultimate aim and solution of the Oxford Movement of 1833 must be sought in the Restoration of the corporate Union of Christendom"—he was only giving expression to a desire felt more or less by all hearts not only among Catholics, but also among Ritualists. Hence, the satisfaction with which the election of His Holiness, Pope Leo XIII., was hailed. The Ritualists, no doubt, like the rest of the world, were struck with the simplicity, rapidity, and, above all, the unanimity, with which this election was accomplished—an election which, even from a simply human point of view, invests a man with the highest authority in the world. The Ritualists think also that they have more to hope from the present Pope than they had from the late Pontiff. Possibly this is an illusion; but why deprive them of it, since it may do them good? Pius IX., like Leo XIII., would have been happy to welcome them into the Church. Pius IX. would as willingly have given his life for the salvation of their souls, as for the conversion of their country; but he could not purchase their return by compromising or denying the truth ; and Leo XIII. will abandon, as the last Pontiff did, the joy of seeing England restored to the bosom of the Church, if he can only secure it by failing in his duty. The case has not, however, yet advanced so far; and our hopes must be still limited to partial returns, and to isolated and personal conversions.

It is, nevertheless, true that Ritualists, as a body, desire to draw closer to the Roman Catholic Church, and would like to be in communion with her.[1] What hinders them? Why do they not go further? Why, instead of advancing, have they for some time been even drawing back? These questions suggest themselves naturally to every mind, and we shall attempt to reply to them.

The reasons which hinder Ritualists from entering the Roman Church may be arranged under three classes. There are what may be called (1) interested, (2) sentimental, and (3) intellectual reasons. It is not our intention to enter fully into all these in the present paper. We shall, however, offer a few words about each of them, laying particular stress upon the last.

IV. That there are reasons which may be called those of worldly interest[2] must be obvious to all.

---

[1] This is somewhat changed now; the old dream and struggle for Reunion is fast giving way to a wretched determination to keep isolated from all Catholics who do not happen to belong to the Church of England. (See "Church Review," 1880, p. 135, col. 3.)

[2] I suppose that Dr. Littledale alludes to this paragraph when he speaks of "motives more or less ignoble," which I attributed to Ritualists. I have disclaimed in the preface all intention of wounding the feelings of any one, and said what was my scope in treating this subject. I could quote many testimonies on this. There is one recently published by a convert from St. Alban's Church:—
"My own opinion is that any person who has studied the elements of logic, and is not held back *as many are* by family and worldly reasons, could not rest content with the evasions which pass current in Ritualistic circles. Although I do not agree with the views expressed in your journal, I write this letter to you in the interests of truth." ("Rock," 1880, p. 148, col. 3.)

A clergyman, for example, holding one of those valuable benefices which the Church of England allots to her dignitaries—a bishop, a canon, a rector, a rich vicar—must necessarily think twice before renouncing such a position, one acquired, perhaps, by costly sacrifices of time and labour, to enter a communion in which possibly only suffering, poverty, misery, and humiliation may await him, with no other compensation but a sense of duty done. Even for a young and unmarried man, who is still under the spell of those illusions and of that enthusiasm to which sacrifice seems gain and labour ease, the loss of a position already achieved, the abandonment of a brilliant future, are burdens not easy for human nature to bear. But, what do not such sacrifices become when they are required of men who have passed the meridian of life, upon whom old age is creeping, and who see dependent upon them a wife and family, whose position would be utterly changed by such a step; and who, if the head of the house declared himself a convert to Catholicism, would be cast from a domestic life, humanly speaking one of the happiest, into poverty and distress? If duty demands it, to forget oneself, and to sacrifice oneself, this is possible, at any age, though perhaps not without the help of God; still, we do see every day noble instances of abnegation and of self-devotion. But, to sacrifice with oneself those whom one loves better than self, to change their lot from happiness to misery by word or deed of ours—this is hard indeed; and we can well conceive how the heart stands still, the hand trembles, and the tongue refuses utterance, before the step can be taken which is to produce these consequences.

Such sacrifices are, indeed, eloquent arguments in favour of the religion that can inspire them, for conscience must speak in a voice not to be mistaken, and truth must appear very clear, before a man can thus lay on the altar all that nature has taught him to regard as sacred and precious.

Why do not Ritualists become Catholics? 135

Without going back to the times when not to attend the communion in the Church of England was a crime punishable by exile or the confiscation of goods, we call to mind many instances of such lofty heroism. There is to-day in England more than one convert from Anglicanism who can say to his former brethren in the faith, "I have become a Catholic, and my Catholicism has cost me all that I possessed, all that I loved in the world;" while there is not a single Protestant convert, or reconvert to Anglicanism, who can say any such thing, or anything comparable to it.[1]

This is a simple fact; but, it may suffice as a test of the value of the system which we are considering.

There can be no disputing the force of these interested reasons, no denying the influence they exert on the decisions open to a man. It is easy to talk of devotedness, of heroism, and of self-sacrifice by the chimney-corner, comfortably seated in an armchair, and with our feet on the fender. But, the scene is suddenly changed when we find ourselves face to face with stern, severe, and pitiless duty. It is easy to brand as cowards those who linger, hesitate, draw back on the verge of a great decision. But, hard words do not argue much knowledge of the human heart, much experience of the realities of life, or much exercise of Christian charity. Assuredly, those who draw back when conscience speaks, when it speaks clearly and positively, have no right to be called

[1] Nobody ignores what material losses have been sustained by many converts to the Catholic Church. They have left riches and honours to follow the dictates of their conscience. None can deny this, and that is a proof of sincerity which no convert to Anglicanism is able to proffer. Even Dr. Littledale admits this in his "Reply to the Abbé Martin," p. 15: "Although there have been, at the lowest computation, proportionably as many Evangelical clergymen in our time whose sympathies were entirely with Dissent, and Broad Churchmen who preferred Unitarianism and Deism, as High Churchmen who leant towards Rome, it is only the last-named who have had to any practical extent the courage of their opinions, and readiness to make great sacrifices in order to follow their consciences. I am unable, speaking under correction, to name ten men in either of the two former schools who have abandoned their clerical position under circumstances involving them in poverty, but those of the third section who went out to begin life over again with no settled prospects can be counted by the hundred."

heroes. They know it well, and confess it to themselves; but it is not given to every one to be a hero in this world. Those who know something of life, understand what conflicts may be all the while rending the soul in its lowest depths; and if they do not always excuse those who fall, they speak of them without bitterness and with charity.

But is it, in fact, these interested reasons, of whatever nature, which prevent many Ritualists from becoming Catholics? This is a secret between God and the conscience. Judging by human appearances, these are not the reasons which most frequently negative the decision that might otherwise be taken. It would rather seem that these reasons prevent the truth from being seen in its clearness. They paralyse, by anticipation, the efforts which but for them might be made to discover the truth. Men dare not see. They shrink instinctively from inquiring. They know too much not to feel some doubt; but they do not know enough for conscience to say, "You must act;" and therefore they rest in that state of half-belief which is not altogether to be condemned, but, on the other hand, is not wholly justifiable. If they do not hang a veil over their eyes that they may not see, they at least make no effort to see, because they feel instinctively that if they saw and were convinced of certain things, they would be constrained to go further. Behind the light they discern the sacrifice, and so they remain in the shadow, in that state in which, without being untrue to conscience, they can say with Keble, "Nothing could justify one's quitting one's own communion except a strong, deliberate, unwilling conviction, found in one's heart and conscience, as well as intellect, that it [the Church of England] has fallen from being a Church."

Is it often thus? Is it true that these interested reasons are often a hindrance to the inquiries which would lead to conversion? We have been told that this is no rare case ; and we believe it will become more and more common as the increasing internal divisions of the Anglican body suggest with growing force the question, whether it has, or has not, the right to regard itself as the true Church.

We love to deceive ourselves when our own interest is concerned, and we are adepts in finding excuses for our conduct. Hence, when reasons of interest have already shaken the will, reasons of feeling are not slow to come to their aid, in postponing the grave decision which would compromise us. Reasons of feeling do undoubtedly exercise a real and deep influence over the course that each one of us takes in life.

V. What may be these reasons of feeling, the sentimental reasons which prevent Ritualists from becoming Catholics ? They are many and various, according to individual character ; but they can all be reduced to three heads—vanity, self-love, affection.

A man is playing, perhaps, an influential part in the religious world and in English society. He is at the head of a large church or parish ; he is looked up to by a large congregation whom, perhaps, he has drawn together ; and he feels instinctively that a change of faith on his part would put an end to his influence, and would throw him into the shade ; that he would be ignored, perhaps misjudged, and certainly condemned by those who are to-day his more than admirers, his devoted adherents. Human vanity shrinks from all this ; and, anxious to escape the sacrifice, it endeavours not to see the duty, or to see it other than it is.

Self-love interposes also, and represents as a disgrace a step which involves a painful avowal—the avowal, namely, that a man has been mistaken during thirty, forty, fifty years of his life, and that he has been helping to mislead others. Obviously, motives like these for retaining the *status quo* are not avowed even to the man himself, but they exist nevertheless in the depths of his soul, and unconsciously influence his conduct. Conversion is a great and noble thing. It is the evidence of uprightness of will and force of character; but it is accompanied by many pains and humiliations. Hence, it is difficult to pass from one religion to another, especially when the step is dictated by conscience, not by passion; by reason, not by interest.

But of all the sentimental reasons which influence Ritualists in the present day, the most powerful is unquestionably their affection for their friends and for their Church.

It must be confessed that it is not common to find in the world in which we live such noble friendships as may be found in England. The traditions of domestic and social life are preserved in that country as they are nowhere else; and it is not rare to meet with friendships which, begun in childhood, are prolonged through life, and outlast all the vicissitudes of the most chequered career.

The education received by candidates for the Anglican ministry, the social atmosphere in which they live, the upper-middle and higher classes to which they belong, the family relations which enrich their favoured lot, and especially the results of their University life—all these circumstances combine to form ties which are only strengthened by years, and which it is not easy to break unless duty and conscience speak in no uncertain tones. And when we remember that the marriage of the Anglican clergy multiplies all these ties indefinitely, it will be easily understood how difficult it is for them to take the final step of conversion.

In how many souls this position gives rise to painful and constant struggles, only those who are familiar with the inner life of English society, especially in its higher circles, can at all divine. We get some glimpses of it in such books as the "Life of Keble;"

and this is only one of many examples that might be taken from English life in the present day. We see there how deeply wounded ·Keble was by the conversion of Newman; and Newman in his "Apologia" tells us what distress of heart his conversion cost him.

It is impossible to break the bonds of friendship and family affection without trembling, and we can well conceive that the man who sees such trials before him may find his eye grow so dim with sorrow, that the path of duty seems obscured. In view of sacrifices which are certain, and results which are uncertain, he hesitates and draws back; and finally, in the struggle between the heart and the conscience, the heart is victorious, especially when the, conscience is not thoroughly enlightened and convinced. To this feeling, which exerts a great influence over the decisions that men may take in controversies of the day, we must add the attachment felt by the Ritualists for the Church of England. They recognise its defects. They do not cloak its imperfections, blemishes, and errors. They are the first to own that it has not fulfilled their expectations. Sometimes, they speak with even excessive severity of its shortcomings. Nevertheless, they love it with all their hearts, and their very life seems bound up in it. To them the Church of England represents all that is beautiful, noble, grand, and true in their country. That communion has produced so many great writers, has formed so many noble characters, and is so blended with the whole national life of the people, that it has become, as it were, the living embodiment of every high and holy thought, memory, purpose, hope. An English Churchman (not long ago we might have said simply an Englishman) sees everything through the medium of his Church. The memories of his childhood, the occupations of riper years, the history of his travels round the world, all bring him back to the same starting-point—his Church.

There he finds his home. It blessed his cradle.

Its influences at school and college moulded his young life. In riper years it appealed to his generosity and to his heart, to aid in ameliorating and reforming society. The English Church, in short, is to many an Englishman a mother and bosom friend. Hence, it costs him much to forsake her, even when he sees that she is not the true Church of Jesus Christ; and the sacrifice seems impossible so long as he is only doubtful of the legitimacy of her claims. Ritualists have the same weakness for their Church that Englishmen have for their nation. They are somewhat insular, and it is not easy for Catholicism to triumph over insular prejudices. They love their Church, as an Englishman loves England, as the dearest of fatherlands; and they greatly fear failing in gratitude and affection towards an institution to which they owe much, if not everything. This fear they cannot shake off, even when they have discovered that the Church they had regarded as a mother, had been after all but a stepmother. They try, therefore, to deceive themselves, and create imaginary duties in order to avoid so painful a rupture. They ask themselves, whether it is not their duty to remain in the Church of England, to reform it by degrees, and cautiously to prepare the way for its reabsorption into the Church Catholic; and they succeed in convincing themselves that they ought not to forsake a communion on which, in these latter days, Providence has seemed to pour down blessings. They invent theories of the "primitive and undivided Church," of "branches of the Church," of the origin of Christianity in England, of the character of the Reformation in England, of the relations theoretical and practical of the Church to the State; and they spend an untold amount of effort, time, money, and learning in propping up systems which have no foundation in fact, and are perpetually contradicted by history. They talk to us of "no secession, but incorporation with the Catholic (not the Roman Catholic) body."

But, what is generally the meaning of all this? Simply, that Ritualists desire to remain where they are, in order to avoid painful sacrifices, and to quiet the voice of conscience which remonstrates, protests, threatens. They say to themselves, that they will do where they are (as Anglicans) the same work which they would do if they went where duty bids them depart, viz., to the Catholic Church.[1]

In a word, Ritualists allow themselves to be guided by sentiment rather than by reason; and then they try to make excuses for themselves, or to find pretexts, to justify the course which they are pursuing.

There is something extremely dangerous in this position. It is so easy to deceive oneself in matters of duty involving sacrifice, that the truest soul sometimes falls into the snare, and those who would be utterly ashamed of themselves if they saw clearly that they had yielded to self-interest, admire and applaud themselves when they think they have made a surrender of it. So subtle are the devices of the human heart that, unless we are on our guard, we fall into its snares.

But reasons of sentiment rarely stand alone; they are almost always accompanied and sustained by other arguments.

VI. Ritualism, in reality, only continues the traditions of Anglicanism under a more subtle and dangerous guise. It is on this account, no doubt, that it has

---

[1] We may hear, for instance, Dr. Littledale in his "Reply to the Abbé Martin," p. 55:—"Now a Christian can explain an unparalleled (?) and varied movement like this only on the hypothesis of Divine grace. . . . That grace, as theologians agree, may be ordinary or extraordinary in its channels and manifestations. If it be ordinary here in England, then it must prove that the Church of England is a true Catholic body, drawing grace from valid orders and sacraments, to abandon which would be schism. If it be extraordinary, then God is dealing with us by miracle, and under a special dispensation, as when He sent Elijah and Elisha to minister in the northern kingdom of Israel, with no hint in their teaching that its citizens were bound to go south and be reconciled to the High Priest in Jerusalem; and it is our duty to wait God's pleasure, so long as He is plainly working amongst us, nay, with us as His instruments; and not to go elsewhere, with, to say the least, small prospect of finding the like tokens of spiritual revival; and none at all of being allowed to undertake like reforms of evils."

been sometimes attacked with vigour and even with a violence, which might be mistaken for passion, if we did not know the aggressors sufficiently well to be assured that their one motive was a great zeal for the salvation of souls. One who, after many years of labour and struggle, had reached the goal of Catholicism, said, long after his conversion, "I still feel myself haunted and troubled by this theory." There is, indeed, something very seductive in the representation it gives of the Church as a federation of patriarchates, and in its recognition of Catholicity as the basis of all true doctrine. But, are these not specious and delusive semblances, mirages, so to speak? When we come to examine them in detail, and to see how they will work practically, do we not find them contrary to the Gospel, to the practice of primitive ages, nay, contrary even to reason and good sense? What, in fact, has this theory produced?[1] It has produced the Eastern Churches, almost all of them dead or dying for the last many centuries. It has produced the Church of England, which is to-day that which it has been often described in language not more severe than just, as "a monstrous anomaly," a "monstrous failure," "a stupendous self-contradiction," "a practical failure," a scene of "utter disorder." The most devoted members of the English Church can never say of their ecclesiastical system, as Englishmen do of their political constitution, "It works well; do not touch it; let it alone!" They are bound,

---

[1] Dr. Littledale has taken objection to this passage in the "Contemporary Review," November 1878, p. 125:—"What he (Abbé Martin) means by the Anglican theory (which to his mind must imply a post-Reformation date) having produced the Eastern Churches, which are older than Rome itself, I confess I do not understand." Of course, when I speak of an Anglican theory as Anglican, I allude to the post-Reformation; but when I speak of a Federation of Patriarchates, I do not speak of anything which may not be anterior to the English Church. The English Church has adopted the theory of Federation; and this system may thus be called the Anglican theory. But, as a fact, I must observe that I have never said that the "Anglican theory (meaning by this the Federation of Patriarchates) has produced the Eastern Church." This mode of rendering a statement, perfectly just in itself, should be avoided in controversy. It is one of many cases of misquotation which unhappily disfigure Dr. Littledale's pages.

on the contrary, to admit that it works badly; and that it works never more badly than when it puts forth fresh life and vigour.

Thus, there is no party in the Anglican Church which is not anxious for some change in its constitution, only desiring that its own peculiar tenets and views may be respected. For three hundred years the cry has gone up on all hands to the bishops, to " set their house in order." But the bishops have never yet proved equal to the task, as is shown by the history of the past fifty years, and by the present crisis in the Church of England. That Church has never enjoyed quietness, peace, and order, except when the civil power which holds it in check has so tightened the reins, that it has been unable to make the slightest movement. When the sovereign, exercising his legal supremacy in religious no less than in civil causes, has reduced bishops and Convocation to silence; when he has asserted over all his own supreme will and pleasure, then there is an interval of order and peace: but, it is the peace of inanition and of death. There has never been made an attempt to infuse new life into the Anglican Church which has not produced schisms and convulsions, by which it has a hundred times narrowly escaped collapse. And if, at the present moment, its existence as an Establishment is gravely endangered, this result is to be traced simply to the efforts made by Ritualists in the direction of Catholicism. Nothing can show more conclusively how hopeless those efforts are, than the unanimity with which they are condemned. Friends, enemies, neutrals, all recognise the zeal of the Ritualists, praise their intentions, admire their self-denial, activity, and devotedness; and yet—all disapprove of their endeavours. And why? Because Ritualists are working against the system of Anglicanism, and indeed against their own system; for, as was justly observed in the " Daily News " in reference to Mr. Mackonochie, " an example of private judgment of an audacious sort is set continually by men who pretend to detest private judgment."

This is so evident that we ask ourselves how it is possible for Ritualists to justify, first the position taken by the Anglican Church, and then their own attitude as members of that Church?

This appears all the more incomprehensible, because Ritualists hold a high idea of the Church, of its origin, its mission, and its claims; because they nominally repudiate private judgment; and because they emphatically appeal not only to the interpretation of Scripture according to primitive antiquity, but to what they call the "living voice" of the Church.

These being their avowed beliefs and principles, the question naturally arises, Why do Ritualists remain in the Anglican communion, and what hinders them from becoming Catholics? We have spoken of the reasons of interest and of sentiment; we shall now say a few words on the intellectual reasons.

VII. It must be borne in mind at the outset, that Ritualists, having been educated in the principles of Anglicanism, have a host of prejudices to overcome, and of things both to learn and to unlearn. Their intellectual and moral nature needs to be recast in a new mould; and even when they seem to have reached outwardly the borders of Catholicism, there is still a wide intervening, and almost impassable gulf.

They approach Catholicism by what we may, perhaps, call an analytical method. They examine every point in detail. They do not look at the system as a connected and harmonious whole, but they take each part separately, without relation to the rest; and hence it is, that out of the many who start in the right direction, so few really arrive at the goal of the Church. To us Catholics, who are accustomed from our childhood to take an elevated view of our system, to regard it as a whole, in its harmonious unity, the conduct of Ritualists appears unreasonable and in many ways inexplicable. Ample excuse, however, may be found for them in the manner in which they approach the study of Catholicism. They rarely look at the question in the outset thus: " Here is a system, at least the rival of Anglicanism, which claims to be the truth—what is it as a whole? What do reason and experience say of it? Taken as a whole, is it or is it not more true than Anglicanism? Is it better adapted to the needs of man, to the ignorant, the vicious, and the poor? Has it produced, on the whole, good results?"

If the English Ritualists took this course, we do not doubt that large numbers would become Catholics. They could not but be struck with the vast superiority of Catholicism, in its adaptation to the needs of the common people, in its dealing with sinners, and in its training souls ; with its admirable unity, its organisation, and its calm, steady advance in dignified order ; with its respect for authority, and its invincible firmness, blended, however, with kindness and gentleness. When once the mind had thus been enlightened by such a view of Catholicism, as a whole, it might then descend, and apply itself to details, and examine each part separately without the danger of stumbling and falling at every step. Seekers after truth would have grasped, in fact, principles which would show them clearly that things are not as they had imagined them in their minds, or as they had read of them in books. They would receive with caution the statements of controversialists ; and instead of simply taking the word of the historian, would demand proof, would search for it themselves, and would arrive most frequently at the conviction that the asserted facts were either false, or mistaken, or distorted. If, sometimes, they met with things little in harmony with the divine theory of the Church, they would remember that institutions cannot be made responsible for the faults of individuals ; and when all the shortcomings of the Catholic Church had

K

been fully recognised, they would still find that it is far superior in its operation to any other Christian community. Not only would they feel bound to confess "it works well," but they would own that "it is the only system that works well."

Unhappily Ritualists do not proceed in this way. Instead of beginning from above and working downwards, they try to mount up from below, and hence so few of them ever reach the summit. They stop by the way, tired, deceived, disappointed; and they find it easier to turn back than to proceed.

Most frequently, Ritualists are led to study Catholicism by some isolated dogma or fact which comes under their notice or attracts their attention. At one time it may be confession and its use, or works of charity among the poor, the aged, or the young; at another, their thoughts may be drawn to the catechisms in use among Catholics, and to their teaching, or to Catholic missions, religious orders, and seminaries. These things strike them; they look into them, find they are not so bad as they have been represented, and are forced to admit, to their own astonishment, that there is something good, nay, much good, in Roman Catholicism. From one inquiry they go on to another, till at length the conviction takes firm hold of their minds, that the Roman Catholic Church is really the true Church.

But at what an expenditure of time and effort is such a conclusion reached! It is not merely that the inquiry is long, but that at each step it is beset with difficulty and the danger of mistake. There is not a single fact or institution of Catholicism in connection with which there has not accumulated a mass of Protestant prejudice and error. How are these errors to be discovered, and these prejudices to be removed? Mere reading will not do it. Most frequently the only books that come into the hands of inquirers are works written in a partial and sectarian spirit; and even if they have access to sources of information, men have not always the leisure and the patience to use them. Take, for example, the history of the Inquisition, of St. Bartholomew's Day, of the False Decretals, of Pope Honorius, of the Roman Congregations, of the power of the Pope in the first centuries; the causes which in some towns give a greater proportion of criminals among Catholics than among Protestants; the history of the Reformation in England and in Germany—and see what an amount of inquiry and sifting will be required in order to arrive at a just idea of any single fact, or any single dogma.

What, then, often happens? The Ritualist pauses half-way and remains where he is. He is deterred from going further either by misconception of certain facts or truths, or is daunted by the vast expenditure of time and labour and thought required.

Hitherto, the mode of proceeding we have described has been the one most commonly adopted; and it must be said, that it is in accordance with the genius of the English people to fix their attention upon facts, and only slowly to rise from facts to principles, or to deduce results. Other nations generalise and come to more rapid conclusions. The Englishman prefers to dwell upon details. He is a minute and careful observer.

We believe, however, that in the end Anglican Ritualists will find themselves driven to adopt other methods, and to consider these grave questions rather in their general bearings. We believe that the controversies of the day will have no small influence in bringing about this change, by making manifest the grave imperfections and the fundamental vices of the Anglican system. Instead of discussing isolated facts, such as those above named, they will turn their attention to the main questions at issue. They will take first a comprehensive view of the two systems—the Roman Catholic and the Anglican—and they will only descend to details after having reached general conclusions.

VIII. We have now shown why so many Ritualists do not really cross the boundaries of Catholicism, though externally they seem so close to them. They lose themselves in details, are perplexed by countless difficulties, and feel the necessity of recommencing their religious education from the beginning. But, in attempting this task they are constantly misled by the prejudices imbibed with their mothers' milk; they fall into involuntary misconceptions, because they lack a guiding rule. Having no tradition to direct them, they often, as they themselves confess, lose much time in fruitless search; and when they succeed in reconstituting what they call the "Catholic system," it is but an incomplete and partial representation. Take, for example, any one point of doctrine—the practice of the Sacrament of Penance, the celebration of the Mass, or any other—and it will be seen that in every case the chain of tradition has been broken, and that Ritualists are invariably constrained to have recourse to Roman Catholic authority, whether books or priests. This was made evident recently when Dr. Pusey translated Gaume's "Manual for Confessors."[1] Why

---

[1] Dr. Littledale has replied ("Contemporary," p. 817) to this observation of mine by this objection : " No fact is better established than the scantiness, poverty, and ineffectiveness of Roman Catholic apologetic literature or efforts against Rationalism and infidelity. If the Abbé Martin cite Dr. Pusey's version of Mgr. Gaume's manual on confession, as showing how England is forced to borrow from Rome, I would refer him in turn to the 'Démonstrations Évangéliques' of the Abbé Migne, where he will find the Anglican names of Locke, Burnet, Leslie, Clarke, Stanhope, Tillotson, Warburton, Bentley, Lyttelton, Butler, Porteus, Milner, Paley, and Buckland, to cite no more, in the list of authors included, and remind him, further, that at the epoch of the great Deistical assault on Christianity in the last century, it was England, not Rome, which routed the assailants; while if there be any eminent and successful Roman apologists for Christianity against the newer forms of unbelief living now, I am not fortunate enough to be acquainted with their names."

To this I must reply: 1. That there is no parity at all in the two cases. When a question so important as that of confession is agitated in the bosom of a Christian church, it is really strange that this church has not, I do not say a book of first rank, but any single manual at all. And I feel bound to ask, How do the Anglican confessors fulfil their delicate mission? Dr. Littledale has overshot the

did Dr. Pusey translate this manual? Because he had more confidence in that which had been said by a man who had an experimental and life-long acquaintance with confession, than in any words of his own.

While, therefore, books or men furnish much useful aid, they can never take the place of experience and of the traditional knowledge of a system. This experience and tradition are utterly wanting in the Anglican Church; hence, everything in that Church is in a state of chaos. Every one adopts and introduces that which seems good to himself; and although in detail the choice may be good and the intention may be praiseworthy, still it must be allowed that, as a whole, Ritualism bears no small resemblance to the Tower of Babel.

Having shown how the theoretic errors of Ritualists arise, it would seem needless to take up and refute each misconception separately, a task which would indeed be endless. Think, for example, of such questions as the prerogatives of St. Peter, his primacy and the permanency of that primacy, and the infallibility of the Pope; think of the influence, real or pretended, of Protestantism on the prosperity of nations; think, finally, of the questions relating to the Reformation generally and the English Reformation in particular—and it will be at once obvious that it would require volumes rather than a paper like the present to discuss any of these subjects.

We must confine ourselves to a few general observations, adding one special remark on the theories held in relation to the Reformation in England. Nothing could show more clearly the unsatisfactoriness of the

---

mark. 2. As to Deism and Deistic literature, the Catholic Church is not so devoid of special books as Dr. Littledale believes. Even in the "Démonstrations Evangéliques" he may ascertain this fact. In our days more than one Catholic writer has treated this subject with arguments proper for our time. Nevertheless, it is true that the English Church has produced many books against Deism, but the reason is easy to be found; it is because infidelity was, for a time, the plague of England, and because many of her clergy were no more than Deists. Lastly, it may be doubted if the anti-Deistic literature has ever made a Christian.

method adopted by Anglicans in religious controversy than these theories.

Starting from the position that the Anglican body is a part of the true Church of Jesus Christ, it was incumbent on Ritualists to justify the Reformation, and to invent a system which could be adapted to this conception of the Church. Hence, have arisen all the theories of the Church and its branches, of the origin of Christianity in England and its development, of the Reformation and its causes. All these theories are in contradiction with facts; and sometimes the contradiction is so glaring that certain Ritualist writers have felt bound to admit it.

And yet, in spite of all this, when it comes to deducing the general principle from the facts, most Ritualists stop short; they quibble, discuss, analyse, and deny the conclusion. Whence comes all this? Undoubtedly from the prejudices of education, from the habitual attitude of the mind, from the affection that gives the one system the preference over the other, from the desire (perhaps unconsciously cherished) to justify their own position and to avoid the painful acknowledgment of having lived until now in error.

It must now be easy to understand why Ritualists find it so difficult to receive Catholicism. If we consider, further, that their system of education develops in them a certain lack of habits of strict logical deduction, it will be still more evident why the work of conversion to the Church goes on so slowly.

IX. There is yet more to be said. If from an intellectual point of view we find that Anglicans and Ritualists are hindered by logical difficulties, it is equally true that, on moral and disciplinary questions, they are staggered by the Catholic doctrine of authority.

Accustomed by their political and social education to govern themselves, they dispute any authority that fetters and embarrasses them, and take, with their ecclesiastical superiors, liberties for which they would scarcely find precedents in the "undivided and primitive Church," and which in any case the Catholic Church would not for an instant tolerate. Nothing shows more clearly the theoretical and practical unsoundness of the Church of England than its absolute impotence in all matters of discipline. This brings out also most forcibly its subjection to the civil power.

Ritualists are struck by the unity of the Catholic Church both in doctrine and discipline; and yet, while admiring the effect, they criticise the cause. They are afraid of ecclesiastical authority. They feel that it is contrary to that liberty which they have loved and exercised all their life. And they understand clearly, that in becoming Catholics they must, in religious matters, make an entire surrender of their personal liberty and of their own will.

Such a sacrifice is not easy to men of any race. It is supremely hard to men of Anglo-Saxon blood. An act of episcopal authority putting an end to a difficult and scandalous situation; such words as were spoken by Cardinal Bonnechose in full French Senate—" My clergy is a regiment; when I say *march*, it marches;" a summary decision of the Pope; or the condemnation of a Roman Congregation;—things like these offend and alarm them. It is more than a dozen years since Cardinal Bonnechose used those famous words; and the English Protestant journals are speaking of them still.

The fact is, that the disciplinary system of the Catholic Church is not lax and powerless like that of the Church of England. In six months, nay, in as many days, the Catholic Church would have solved the problem of Ritualism; or, rather, Ritualism would never have sprung up in its midst.

We understand perfectly the astonishment and alarm

that such a system must inspire in the minds of Ritualists. They see only its objectionable side—that which makes them regard Catholicism as a despotic system, tyrannical and oppressive to the consciences of men. This is in exact accordance with the traditional idea they have received of the Papacy. But, in thus judging, they show themselves to be but superficial and prejudiced observers. If they would study more deeply the subject of Catholic discipline, they would see with what scrupulous care the interests of individuals are watched; how the weak are protected against the strong; what barriers are raised against oppression; and how those accused of crimes have the means placed at their disposal to secure an equitable and even a lenient judgment. Nowhere is so much consideration and forbearance shown to penitent criminals as in the Catholic Church. The one thing that cannot be forgiven or tolerated is persistent rebellion against constituted authority. A priest who thinks himself wronged and ill-treated by his bishop, has the right to appeal from his tribunal to that of the metropolitan, and from the metropolitan to the Court of Rome. We do not pretend to say that there may not be here and there abuses, and that these abuses are not sometimes hard to redress; but what conclusion can be drawn from such an admission? Is there anything in the world that escapes human imperfections? Is any institution faultless? The thing we want to ascertain is, what is the system which works the best, first for society, and then for the individual? We place the individual second, because it is just that private interests should be subservient to the general good. If sometimes an individual finds cause of complaint, he ought to bear it in silence, where the common weal is involved. The fundamental principle of Catholic discipline is respect for authority; and this principle is wholly absent from Protestantism.

We can easily conceive that Ritualists may find it

hard to submit to discipline like this. Their religious and political training has in no way fitted them for it; and they regard it as the cause of the humiliation of the Catholic clergy in many countries; as, for example, in France. It seems to them that the clergy are bound hand and foot to the episcopate, and that a bishop can do with his priests exactly what he likes.

We do not deny that there may have been, or still are, abuses of this kind. Abuses are inevitable in all human institutions; but in the Catholic Church they are certainly not so frequent nor so flagrant as they have been represented; and we may make two observations in regard to them:

1st. The situation of the Catholic Church in France is not a normal one; it is not the ideal of the Catholic system. Ecclesiastical law is there but little known and seldom applied, not so much through the fault of the Church, as through the revolutionary conditions of the times.

If the Church were left free to act, this situation would soon be changed, and the regulations of Canon Law touching the collation of benefices and the irremovability of the beneficiaries would soon be again put in force. As a matter of fact, the only laws protective of their individual rights which the Anglican clergy possess, came to them as a legacy from the Catholic Church. At the time of the Reformation, the Church of England did not repudiate these as it did so many articles of dogma and of morals; and thus its code of laws is to a great extent identical in form, though of course not in application, with that of the Church of Rome.

But we shall be asked: "How is it then the Catholic Church in France cannot act freely? Why has it been the victim of the Revolution? Is not this a proof that the nation is hostile to it, while there is no such hostility, or, at all events, hostility to a much less degree, felt in England towards the National Establishment?"

To this question the reply is easy, and the facts themselves speak eloquently. If the Catholic Church is persecuted by the Revolutionists, if they despoil and mutilate it when they have the opportunity, it is because they know that the Church will make no compromise with them, that rather than surrender one iota of its independence in essential points, it will freely pour out its blood. It has done so more than once in the past, and its spirit is the same to-day. Now, the powers of the earth do not like to feel that there is side by side with them, a power equal or superior to their own. This feeling is as old as Christianity itself, and will endure so long as the world lasts. It is more than sixteen hundred years since a Cæsar said he would rather see a tyrant arise in any part of his empire than hear that a Pope had been elected in Rome.[1]

It is true that the English nation has loved its Church, and loves it still; but at what a cost has not that Church purchased this affection and goodwill? Is the English Church free? Can it make the smallest change, even in its rubrics, without an Act of Parliament? Can it assemble in Convocation without the sanction of the Crown? Who elects its bishops? Who gives them jurisdiction? The civil power, through a Minister who may be anything, even an Atheist. Has the

---

[1] Here Dr. Littledale has reminded me (1) that the French clergy blessed the Man of December; (2) that this was "a bargain as to the occupation of Rome entered into with certain bishops who put thus the screw on their subordinates;" (3) that "it is still believed that the disastrous war of 1870 was prompted by clerical intrigue far more than by dynastic motives." To the first I reply that only a part of the French clergy did, not bless, but accept the Man of December; that another part blamed this conduct—for instance, Father Lacordaire; and that when civic disorder has attained its supreme height, every dictator is welcomed as a saviour. I begin to conceive, by what is going on now, how men, otherwise liberal, submit to despotism. As to the second and third assertions, I simply deny the statements. Such petty gossip is unworthy of consideration by serious men. I marvel that Dr. Littledale has not spoken of the 16th of May as prompted by the clergy, and of the now famous Seventh Clause of the Ferry Bill as introduced by the Jesuits to ruin the Republic! Such illustrations would adorn his "Reply to the Abbé Martin," and "His Plain Reasons against joining the Church of Rome." I hope that Dr. Littledale will take notice of these two facts in the next issue of his pamphlets; they will embellish them.

Church of England a shadow of independence? Not the slightest. And whenever it has shown any desire for liberty, the State has roughly made it feel that such conduct could not long be tolerated. Look for example at Convocation, which had its sessions suspended for more than a hundred and fifty years, without any other cause or motive than the will and pleasure of the Government for the time being.

This is our first observation. Our second is as follows:—

2nd. If the Catholic Church in France has not a highly cultured, polished, and distinguished body of men in its clergy, the cause is to be found in the social conditions of the country at the present day. French society is, in fact, becoming more and more democratic and radical; and such is indeed the general tendency of European society in this age. Democracy is in the rising, aristocracy is in the falling scale. If, then, it be true that noblemen and even gentlemen (in the old English acceptation of the word) are rare among the Catholic clergy of France, it is not less true that they are also rare in the nation at large.

This may be a cause of regret. We may lament over the lowering of tone and of manners. We may weep over the ruins which the past has handed down to us, or which are being made in the present. But, *bon gré mal gré*, we must accept the position.[1]

This being granted, it must be admitted that the French clergy are in harmony with their surroundings; that they are adapted both in mind and heart for the work they have to do. This is all that can be required

---

[1] On this subject see a paper at the end of this volume on the "Present Position of the Church of France," reprinted from the "Nineteenth Century," Dec. 1879. Dr. Littledale says (1) that in France we have 150,000 ecclesiastics and 60,000 priests; (2) that there are not ten (priests or ecclesiastics) from the higher social grades, outside the Jesuit body; (3) that 3000 benefices and 3000 parishes have neither priests nor churches. All these statements are perfectly untrue. They show that Dr. Littledale has not the faintest idea of our social state in France. But it would be too long to expound the facts as they are. (See also two letters by the present writer, on this topic, in the "Guardian," 1880, 1. pp. 85, 151.)

of them or of the Church. The Church was not founded to make gentlemen, but to save souls.

Moreover, may it not be fairly asked whether the English clergy, by becoming pre-eminently a class of cultivated gentlemen, have not lost something which it would have been well for them had they carefully preserved? In becoming men of letters, have they not ceased in some degree to be shepherds of souls? Have they not forgotten that their first duty was to seek the salvation of men, and that this end is not to be accomplished merely by writing books, or even by reading the Bible and preaching manuscript sermons?

We do not wish to carry these questions further, because our aim is to show the true situation, to give hints and suggest reflections, rather than to say things which may anger and irritate. Our desire is only to enlighten, to attract, to bring together, to unite. We do not deny that there are imperfections and blemishes in Catholic society; still less do we deny that the Anglican communion produces fine characters. But, both these facts may be naturally explained. In both we must take account of the man himself, and of the atmosphere in which he lives. What we do deny is, first, that the imperfections and blemishes of Catholic society destroy the divine character of the Roman Catholic Church; and next, that the noble natures developed in the Church of England prove its divine origin.

X. We will not continue our inquiry into the intellectual difficulties which Anglicans encounter in their movement towards Catholicism. The subject is inexhaustible. There is scarcely a practice, a doctrine, an historical fact, which may not furnish matter of controversy. Such controversies, carried on as they are with warmth on both sides, rarely lead to any beneficial result. These are subjects which need to be considered with calmness, goodwill, and good faith.

We are not surprised that Anglicans should find many points doubtful and obscure in the life of the Roman Catholic Church. That Church has passed through so much, it has occupied so large a sphere in the world's history, that it would be a marvel if there were not found something to animadvert on in its various movements. But this proves absolutely nothing, and can furnish no ground for controversy. Great institutions, like great buildings, ought to be judged by their broad outlines; they are meant to be seen from afar, at a glance and by all. They should be such as all men can recognise, appreciate, and use. The criticism of details may be left to men who have time and leisure for small things. We shall not, therefore, enter more fully into those intellectual difficulties, which have something specious in them, but which are, perhaps, too often in reality only excuses and pretexts sought by uneasy consciences that would fain be left in peace. Many a time, indeed, it happens that the heart has a presentiment of the truth, and the mind a dim vision of it; but, arrested and alarmed by what we have already described as considerations of interest and of sentiment, men search for something which may silence the importunate voice within, and justify them in remaining where they are. And they find precisely what they seek, not in a broad, general, elevated view of Catholicism as a whole, but in petty, captious, and mistaken criticism of the Catholic Church.

If they took what is commonly called a "bird's-eye view" of the two systems—the Roman Catholic and the Anglican—it would not, as it seems to us, be possible to hesitate for a moment, so vastly does the one surpass the other in grandeur, in power, in dignity, and in consistency. Weaknesses there may doubtless be in the Roman system, failures in detail and in application; but no blemishes which would not be still more apparent in the Anglican system. This Ritualists themselves freely allow. On the other hand, there are in Catholicism beauties so exalted and sublime, that all eyes are involuntarily drawn to them, and even its bitterest enemies are forced to exclaim, like the prophet on whose lips the curse was turned into a blessing: "How goodly are thy tents, O Jacob, and thy tabernacles, O Israel!" How often have we not noted with surprise expressions like these in the books of Ritualists, or in the writings of their party!

It is idle, in this age, for them to declaim against the infallibility of the Pope, to complain of the omnipotence of the Roman pontiffs, and to assert that the authority of the bishops is tyrannical and oppressive; for at heart the Ritualists feel the need of this infallibility, and would only be too glad if their Church was governed on like principles with the Catholic Church. Therefore, when we hear them thus crying and lamenting, they remind us of children singing at the pitch of their voices to drown other sounds and to keep themselves from being frightened. They are compelled to stifle, at any cost, the voice which in their better moments makes itself heard in the depths of their consciences, and which if it does not say—"Leave thy father's house, and come into a land which I will show thee;" does at least say—"Look, consider, inquire, study, and prove that which is good."

And this will be increasingly the case as we advance. All those legal proceedings in relation to Ritualism which are at present agitating public opinion in England, are like so many thunder-claps arousing dormant consciences, and scarcely allowing them time to slumber again. Is it possible to observe all that is happening, without asking: "But what then is this system on which no two persons are agreed, in which all parties are ready to eat and devour one another, while there is no authoritative voice that can command obedience? What is this system in which the religious authority is *nil*, and in which even such a simple matter as a prescription relating to the lighting of a wax taper or the wearing of a vestment must be referred to a Parliament which is anything but Anglican, or even Christian ?"[1]

Where there remains in the soul any vestige of faith in Christianity, in religion, in the supernatural, such an anomaly as this must surely prompt to reflection and inquiry.

The times of good faith, of full, simple, absolute assurance, seem to us to be gone by for men of intelligence, of culture, and of thoughtfulness in England. Soon it will have to be said that Ritualists are deterred rather by considerations of interest and sentiment, than by reasons derived from logic or history, from joining the Catholic Church. The convulsions of Anglicanism give so complete a vindication to Catholicism, that intellectual difficulties about its claims must, almost of necessity, vanish.

If then, hitherto, historical, theological, scientific, or moral difficulties have all combined to keep back Ritualists from the truth, it would seem that henceforward reasons of sentiment and of interest can alone retain much power. May we not hope that these, too, will soon lose their influence, and that the day may come when we may welcome back our brethren of England into the one Faith, and the one Fold, and with united voices sing the old song, " Quam bonum et jucundum habitare fratres in unum "?

[1] There are, amongst others, the charges brought against the bishops by Dr. Littledale, in his "Reply to the Abbé Martin," p. 43, that is, in his very defence of the English Church : "Now, not only did no bishop attempt to rebut the false accusation, but several of them repeated it, knowing well, as they could not help knowing, its entire falsehood. And lastly in this category, the complaint is often heard that Ritualism, which is at the worst a devout and earnest movement, erring if you please, but ardently Christian and missionary, is the *only* kind of clerical action with which a bishop will interfere penally. Open depravation of Christianity itself in the pulpit, personal immorality of life, daring nonconformity in public worship, gross neglect of pastoral duties, illegally exacted fees for gratuitous offices, deliberate sordidness and irreverence in the ministration of sacraments ; all these I have myself known to have been laid before bishop after bishop, with no result whatever save a snubbing to the complainant, while the slightest hint of Ritualism was sure to meet with immediate attention and expression of readiness to suppress and punish it if possible. That sort of thing sends men over to Rome." (And, of course, no wonder.)

CATHOLICISM AND RITUALISM COMPARED.

In the month of August 1878, we contributed to the "Contemporary Review" an article entitled "What hinders Ritualists from becoming Roman Catholics?" It was an epitome of a series of personal observations made with a view of finding some explanation of a situation deserving the attention of all students of the social life, and especially of the Christian social life, of our day. It was not our idea in the first instance to present our thoughts under the form of a question—which implies an exhaustive reply—but rather as a meditation on the difficulties in the way of Ritualists becoming Roman Catholics. The title finally adopted, however, had the advantage of bringing the subject at once to a definite issue, of arresting attention, and provoking all thoughtful minds to give their own reply to the question thus raised.

Such a response to our appeal was in truth readily given; and the readers of the "Contemporary" have had two solutions offered them, the first from the pen of Mr. Gladstone, the second from that of Dr. Littledale.

Before entering on the remarks which a careful study of both papers suggested to us, we must first thank both writers for the readiness shown by them to discuss a problem of such vital interest to all; and, widely as we differ from many of the sentiments expressed in their articles, we are yet glad to recognize that on more than one point we are in agreement, and that we are all prepared to say, with the old philosopher, "Humani nihil a me alienum puto."

We are greatly indebted to both these eminent writers for the service they have done to the cause of truth in thus drawing public attention widely to this important question. It is a question which deserves to be pondered and answered by a large number of those who accept the designation of Ritualists. To many of these it is a matter of life and death, for it is one involving their moral rectitude. The Church and the moral sense join in testifying that there can be no salvation, no right-doing, nor virtuous practice, no conduct, in fact, worthy of eternal life, where there is not genuine good faith. And the Catholic Church, when she says that outside her pale there is no salvation, is always careful to call attention to the fact that she claims as belonging to her, as her children in spirit, even persons living in error, if they hold their errors in good faith. Good faith, absolute and entire, is then an essential condition of salvation. And it is because this good faith seems to us all but impossible for those who are lingering, like the Ritualists, at the very gates of light, that we challenge them to vindicate and to make good their present position. The efforts they have already made to return to Catholic doctrines and Catholic practices render it incumbent on them to explain clearly, why they have gone so far and no further.

There are undoubtedly conditions in life which render absolute good faith a matter of extreme difficulty. It requires no long experience of men or things to discover that there are certain truths from which human nature shrinks, with an intuition of danger lurking in their hidden depths. To such studies men need to be urged and impelled, and it is sometimes the greatest service that can be rendered to compel timid souls to quit, as it were, the branch to which they have been clinging, and to stretch their wings towards regions of a higher and purer atmosphere.

These brief explanations are intended to meet the criticism of those writers who have imagined they could trace in a previous article from our pen "a veiled censure on the policy and language of the Ultramontane faction now dominant in the Church of France," and who see in our last article "a quasi-retractation of the earlier essay" ("Contemporary Review," Nov. 1878, pp. 792, 793). We may perhaps be allowed to say briefly that we have written simply on our own personal responsibility, that we have consulted no one, and that our sentiments with regard to that portion of the Anglican Church known as Ritualist *are* unchanged, or rather, to be quite exact, *were*, when these words were first written, unchanged. In the one paper we dwelt on the nobler aspects of the movement; in the other we pointed out what appeared to us to be its illogical, incomplete, unsatisfactory aspect. Every medal has its reverse. All we want to ascertain is which impression is the more powerful. We do not hesitate to avow our admiration and esteem for the Ritualist party, for its zeal, its devotedness, its activity, its energy, its enterprise, and its success. It is the very strength of our sympathy which leads us to say to these men, who have striven so hard to come near to Catholicism: "Are you quite sure that you have reached the end at which you are aiming? Have you not some reason to think that you have halted half-way? Carefully consider this question, and then act as conscience dictates."

It is from no desire to break a lance with the English Church or its representatives that we have taken up this subject. We write in the interests of truth, not from any love of controversy, which, conducted as it too often is with bitterness, virulence, and mutual recrimination, never yet made a convert.

I. After these preliminary remarks, we shall proceed at once to take up what seem to us the main points in the articles of Mr. Gladstone and Dr. Littledale. We cannot in a single paper attempt anything like an adequate reply. All we can do is to make some general observations, and lay down some leading principles which may help in the solution of the question as a whole.

We would observe, first, that Mr. Gladstone avowedly sets aside the question before us. He says : " Into any of the specialties attaching to the name of Ritualist, or the name of Protestant, we will not enter. We pass by the men, and go to the case. The appeal which we wish to recognise is really a broader one, on more open ground, in fresher air" ("Contemporary Review," Oct., p. 428).

Mr. Gladstone has given us a study of the Reformation, and while admitting that in many instances it overshot the mark, while condemning some of the means employed, and while pleading "guilty" under many heads to the charges against it, he yet concludes that as a whole it has been productive of more good than evil. Mr. Gladstone himself warns us that we must not expect to "receive on all hands the benefit of such admissions as have here been made. Many among us will demur to them on their merits, many more out of deference to tradition ; *videlicet*, the current popular tradition. Some will probably go so far as to censure any writer by whom they are made" (Ibid., pp. 436, 437). We thank Mr. Gladstone for his candour, though we scarcely needed to be assured that the popular tradition is still too strong in England for any condemnation of the Reformation to be generally tolerated. He modifies, in the same way, another passage in his article in which he seemed to admit that the prejudices against Roman Catholics have almost disappeared. Nor are these the only instances in these pages in which he furnishes an illustration of the fact, that "it is a serious matter to shake any tradition established with regard to religion." Difficult, however, as it is to ascertain the precise views of Ritualists on this subject, since there is no authentic organ of their opinions, we imagine that the great majority of them would readily subscribe to what Mr. Gladstone has written. There are many, unquestionably, who would go, and do go, much farther, as all must be aware who have read the writings of Dr. Littledale, the Rev. Malcolm MacColl, and the Hon. C. L. Wood, President of the English Church Union, not to speak of the writers who have gone thoroughly into the subject in treating the history of the period. We doubt very much whether the great body of Ritualists regard the Reformation, in England or elsewhere, as "a great and immortal performance." And, if some members of this party still speak of the performers as "signal public benefactors," others do not shrink from applying to them such epithets as "thieves," "liars," "adulterers," "murderers," "scoffers," "scoundrels," "miscreants," and "unredeemed villains."

Compared with the expressions constantly recurring in Ritualistic books and journals edited by men otherwise moderate, the admissions made by Mr. Gladstone are slight indeed. Dr. Littledale, in a letter to the "Guardian," brought out very forcibly the wide divergences of view that might subsist with regard to the Reformation and the Reformers. He said :—

"It is quite possible for men to take very widely different views as to the Reformation itself in its character and results. Some may look on it as a Pentecost: I look on it as a Flood, an act of Divine vengeance, not of Divine grace; a merited chastisement, not a fresh revelation. . . . I gravely assert it to be absolutely impossible for any just, educated, and religious men, who have read the history of the time in genuine sources, to hold two opinions about the Reformers. They were such utterly unredeemed villains, for the most part, that the only parallel I know for the way in which half-educated people speak of them amongst us is the appearance of Pontius Pilate among the saints in the Abyssinian Calendar." ("Guardian," May 16, 1868.)

By setting aside the direct subject of our remarks, Mr. Gladstone has not, indeed, deprived it of all interest, but he has placed it at a great disadvantage. The study of the sixteenth century is unquestionably one well worthy of the close attention of thinkers and philosophers; for the whole order of things in the midst of which we live dates from that epoch. But it will be long yet before an estimate can be given of it which will be generally accepted.

We should not have attempted to prove to English Protestants that the Reformation, as it was carried out in the sixteenth century, deserves the reprobation of all right-minded people, if we had had to address ourselves only to Dissenters — Baptists, Presbyterians, Methodists, Congregationalists—or even to adherents of the Broad or the Low Church "schools of thought." We know too well that it would be labour lost to discuss the point with any of these. We are too far removed from one another to catch each other's meaning.[1] We see everything under a different aspect, and our points of view are directly opposite. With Ritualists it is not so; and indeed, it may be fairly said, that for the last fifty years this advanced section of the Anglican Church has been constantly returning to the old paths, and effecting what has been called in high quarters a counter-Reformation.

All the force and all the interest of the question proposed by us in August last hinges, as will be readily seen, on the word *Ritualist*. It can be no ground for surprise that Protestants, holding the views of their

[1] The organs of the Dissenting press have shown, by their criticisms on Mr. Gladstone's article, how vain it would be to discuss with them the question of the merit and demerit of the Reformation of the sixteenth century. They complain that he has attached too much importance to Christian organization generally, to the primacy of St. Peter, to the Apostolic College and Council, to prayers for the dead, to confession, to the Church, and to tradition. If Mr. Gladstone is too Catholic for the Dissenters, how must they regard Ritualists, and, most of all, Roman Catholics? It would be obviously fighting the air to propose a question of this sort: "What hinders Protestants, Rationalists, Dissenters, Broad and Low Churchmen from becoming Roman Catholics?" With Ritualists the case is different.

communion or of Nonconformity, should not think of becoming Roman Catholics; but how is it that Ritualists pause half-way?

We are well aware of the difficulty there is in giving such a definition of the principles, beliefs, and aims of Ritualists as shall be accepted by all. Their party bears, in this respect, the true image of the Church from which it springs, and much "comprehension" is necessary in order to include under one and the same designation all the individual varieties of Ritualism. The scale which extends from the High Church, pure and simple, to extreme Ritualism, contains many notes, and presents gradations of tone very difficult to distinguish. It may perhaps be said, within the limits of truth, that the Ritualists accept *all* the beliefs and *all* the practices of the Roman Catholic Church, with very rare exceptions.[1] It is certainly far easier to enumerate the things which they *do not* receive than those which they *do;* as, for example, the Immaculate Conception and the supreme jurisdiction and infallibility of the Pope in his capacity as Head of the Church. If we are not greatly mistaken, these are the grave *doctrinal* difficulties at which Ritualists stumble, and which hinder them from becoming Roman Catholics. On almost all other points they are in agreement with us. They acknowledge the Church as a divine institution. They would easily be brought to declare it infallible, though this is not quite in accordance with the Anglican Article XXI. The only difficulty is to determine when and how this infallibility comes into operation. With regard to

[1] A recent convert has propounded the same view in the "Tablet" (1880, page 300, col. 2). He says:—"I would, however, descend to particulars. I would take a thoroughgoing Ritualist, and would ascertain in what relation he stands towards Catholic belief and Catholic practice. And I say by anticipation, that to a certain extent he believes the same truths, but on a different authority; or he believes similar truths, but to a different extent. The like may be said of his practice. But, as a rule, in no case does he believe any truth or employ any practice *avowedly* at issue and on different lines with the use or faith of the Catholic Church."

prayers for the dead, the adoration of the saints, of the Virgin, and other points, Ritualists have long cast away, and taught others to cast away, their Protestant prejudices. The actions against Mr. Ridsdale and Mr. Mackonochie have given sufficient proof of the length to which Ritualists have gone in this direction.

We know that "popular tradition," and even sometimes the tradition of "men thoughtful and trained," still speaks of Romish superstitions, and charges the Catholic Church with having made unwarrantable additions to its worship. In the papers of both Mr. Gladstone and Dr. Littledale we catch an echo of these old accusations.[1] It must be obvious to them, however, that the common people cannot be reached in the same way as thoughtful and educated men; and experience must have shown them that it is not by a dry, colourless, purely intellectual service, such as to a great extent the Protestant service has become, that the masses of the people are moved and governed. In this respect, the English Ritualism which Mr. Gladstone and Dr. Littledale defend so well serves as an admirable illustration. If Anglicanism has recovered some hold upon the masses, it has been by

[1] A Ritualist has lately shown the injustice of these accusations and the inconsistency of his co-religionists. "Why," says he, "why will Anglicans persist in asserting that the Roman doctrine of Transubstantiation is a different doctrine to their own of the Real Presence? Why is Purgatory so scouted by people who pray for the dead? Why are so many so strong in condemning the Roman cultus of our Lady and the saints who never hesitate to say an *Ave Maria* or *Ora pro nobis* themselves? Why will people who surround sacred images with lights and flowers persist in calling Romans 'idolaters' for doing the same thing? Even granting that foreign Catholics do seem somewhat extravagant in their devotion to the saints, I think we have enough to do to mend our own way before we attack theirs. What is the use of 'Anglo-Catholics' talking of their belief in the power of the keys if they never use the sacrament of penance? What is the use of talking about 'Church law' while days of fasting and abstinence are passed over quite unrecognized, and feasts of obligation allowed to go by without an attempt to hear Mass? Is it not a little strange that those who are so ardent in condemning the Mariolatry of foreign Catholics never think of doing what these people who are said to neglect Jesus for Mary never fail to do?—I mean frequent the daily Mass. No, Sir, I am convinced that it would be far better for England's Church if 'moderate Catholics' (whatever that may mean—I presume those who have a moderate grasp of the truth) would leave off airing their anti-Roman crotchets" ("Church Review," 1880, p. 135, col. 3).

abandoning the dry, bald traditions introduced into England by the Puritans, and still adhered to by Low-Church Evangelicals.

To return, however, to that point from which we started. When we find men who believe and practise well-nigh all that is practised and believed in the Roman Catholic Church, and who each year are adopting some fresh belief or some fresh practice from the same source, may we not fairly say to them : Why do you remain at all where you are? Why do you not become Roman Catholics[1] at once? Consider, in fact, what your position is. A little more than three hundred years ago, you formed part of the Roman Catholic Church. You received its dogmas, its laws, its envoys; you were members of that great community. Then one day, by no fault of yours, it is true, but by the fault of the times, of your grasping aristocracy, and most of all of your wicked king, you broke with Rome, and accepted that Reformation which one of your own organs brands in the following terms :—

"The so-called Reformation of the sixteenth century was in reality no Reformation at all. When Henry VIII. kicked out the Pope, he made himself Pope, and something more. The Tudor system was only Popery Erastianised. The great object of the Reformers was the confiscation of Church property. The removal of abuses, the restoration of Church rights, were not thought of then ; nor have they been cared for since. The civil government has gone even further than the Roman Curia in usurping the rights and restricting the just liberties of the Church. The incapacity and folly of the Privy Council, which may be fitly described as the ' Papacy in Commission,' have brought matters to a crisis, and some change must be speedily made. But what is to be the nature of that change? The necessities of the present time, the tenor of legislation from Magna Charta down to the Tudor period, the principles of the Reformation, the divinely ordered constitution of the Church,

---

[1] I said in a former paper that Ritualists reject the name of Catholics simply. I have been told, and to an extent with justice, that this is not true. But when Ritualists call themselves *Catholics*, they do not take the word in its ordinary, common meaning. This is so much the case, that if in England a person was spoken of as a Catholic, no one would imagine for a moment, without a previous explanation, that an Anglican was meant.

all point in one direction—the State must concede to the Church her inalienable right of managing her own affairs. Establishment, if we mean by this term the subjection of the Church to State control, must become a thing of the past. The Oxford movement, from which such great and lasting benefits have already resulted, necessarily involves this, and must be either nullified or result in it." ("Church Review," 1875, p. 459, col. 3.)

Nor is it one journal alone which speaks thus of the Reformation in a single passage : the writers and speakers may be counted by scores who refer to this subject uniformly in the same tone :—

"In sober truth the English Reformation was an unmitigated disaster. It was simply a hypocritical pretence to veil an insurrection of lust and avarice against religion; it corrected no evil whatever." ("Church Times," May 14, 1868.)

Again : "On the whole, there is no reason whatever to suppose that there is any larger proportion of really God-fearing persons now than there was before the Reformation of religion was taken in hand by a conspiracy of Adulterers, Murderers, and Thieves!" (Oxonius: "Facts and Testimonies touching Ritualism," 2nd ed. p. 72.)

It is true, that these are not recent testimonies. Lest, therefore, we should be accused of being ten years in arrear, we will quote another witness, and this time not from the ranks of what might be called the *enfans perdus* of Ritualism. We cite from the address of the President of the English Church Union, delivered only a few months ago. He says :—

"However necessary that which was popularly called the Reformation may have been to clear the air, it was impossible to sympathise fully either with those who carried it out, or with much that they did. No doubt it was exceedingly difficult to place ourselves in their position, and for many things they could not be accounted responsible; nevertheless, the fact remained, that while they got rid of many abuses, in so far as they hoped to restore primitive faith and practice to the nation at large, they signally failed of success. The position the Holy Eucharist had occupied amongst us in these later times was a proof of this assertion. The instance was a crucial one. The Reformers, like the Council of Trent, wished to get rid of solitary Masses, and to bring back frequent communion. The motive was excellent, but how was it carried out? By acts on the part of individuals, such as the destruction of altars, of which they could never think without shame, and by alterations in the Liturgy which had the practical effect both of obscuring in popular estimation the great Christian doctrine of the Eucharistic Sacrifice, and giving to the Church of England the unenviable distinction of celebrating the Holy Communion less frequently than any other portion of the Christian Church. This practical neglect of the Sacramental system, and all that it involved, accounted for the failure of the Church of England hitherto to get hold of the people generally, notably in such districts as Wales and Cornwall, which, like Brittany, ought naturally to be the strongholds of the Church. Her altars, too long empty of all that made them precious, had been abandoned for the emotional excitement of Protestant Dissent. And yet, strange to say, in the sight of such facts, if the members of the Church of England had been marked out by one characteristic more than another, it had been by the assertion of the absolute perfection of that portion of the Church to which they belonged. These words were not uttered in any feeling of discontent; they did not betoken, as the Bishop of Gloucester and Bristol might perhaps suggest, that the real home of their affections was elsewhere." ("Church Times," Jan. 25, 1878, p. 52, col. 1.)

We do not, of course, lose sight of the fact that it is often fair and needful to distinguish between the actors and their acts. The actors may be bad and their acts may be good and praiseworthy. We should not, however, be prepared to go so far as to say that "it is one of the characteristic marks of God's providential intervention in the affairs of men that He sometimes uses bad or worthless instruments to achieve His purposes." (Rev. M. MacColl on "The Principles of the Reformation" in the "Church Review," 1876, p. 227, col. 3.) Doubtless the "sometimes" corrects to some extent the "characteristic;" but we have too high an idea of the goodness of God to admit that it may be one of His providential *laws* to choose "bad" instruments to do excellent works.

But do all Ritualists thus distinguish between the Reformers and the Reformation?

We know that on this point there is less unanimity than on the preceding. Many, when they speak of the Reformation in general, defend and approve it, and recognize it as necessary; though when they come to details they invariably withdraw all their encomiums. But a very large proportion do not hesitate to condemn it *in toto*. We have already quoted passages which are very conclusive on this point, and it would be easy to multiply such quotations from very recent writings.

In fact, for the last fifty years the religious movement has been entirely retrograde, and might be fairly characterised by the words *Vestigia retrorsum*, which were used not long since, in a journal not of the extreme school, as the heading of an article which gave a description of the inevitable consequences of this retrograde movement, if carried on without the support of the Church. The "Church Review" said :—

"In ordinary cases, if a man has lost his way, the best thing he can do is to retrace his footsteps. If he tries to take a short cut, or to travel across an unknown country, the chances are that he makes bad worse, or that at the most he wastes further time and strength. Now we have nothing to do with the Reformers; but one clear outcome of their handiwork is this—that, until the Catholic revival, we had as a people lost our way in the matter of worship. The Mass had vanished as the central act of Christian worship. This was admittedly the state of things which the Catholic revival found when it commenced, and with this abuse it has been one of its foremost duties to grapple, for no man can be said to understand the Catholic faith who does not make the Holy Eucharist the centre and channel of his worship, and no priest can hope to Catholicise his flock unless he makes for this point. As to this we are all agreed. But when we look around us, we fail to see any *consensus* as to the means to be employed in attaining to this end. In many cases short cuts are taken, and with the usual result. In other cases priests try new ways, suggested by their own originality of invention, the result of which is certainly not more satisfactory." ("Church Review," 1878, p. 31, col. 3.)

Here, then, is a series of acknowledged facts:—
1. The English Reformation was not the result of religious, Christian, and supernatural influences at work in the minds of men. 2. The Reformers, having little personal claim to respect, are unworthy of the name. 3. The consequences of the Reformation have been

deplorable, alike from a religious, moral, and social point of view. 4. The only course open to Anglicans is to retrace their steps, and to repudiate the Reformation, the Reformers, and their principles. 5. Hitherto this retrograde movement has been made in an arbitrary, erratic, almost chaotic fashion.[1]

Yet further it is admitted :—1. That the Church is in its origin divine. 2. That it is divine in its life. 3. That it does not depend on men; that it is a separate power independent of the State. 4. That it has and ought to have a "living voice," laws, and tribunals of its own.

In addition to this, it is admitted that the Roman Catholic Church has formed, and still forms, part of the Church of Jesus Christ. A few years ago English Churchmen went even further, and spoke of the Roman Catholic Church only with respect and love, and with a manifest and earnest desire to be reunited to it.

When we come in contact with a body of men holding the opinions of Ritualists, does it not seem natural to say to them : "What is it that hinders you from going to the head of the Catholic Church and saying to him

[1] Note how a Ritualist speaks of the Anglican Church, after nearly fifty years of effort and triumph on the part of High Churchmen. I should not have dared myself to use language so bold :—

"The numerous awful scandals which make our unhappy Church almost 'a hold for every unclean beast, and a cage for every unclean bird'—to wit, the 'marriage' of 'divorced' persons by priests of our Church ; the 'marriage' in our churches by our priests of Christians (so called) with Jews, infidels, and heretics ; the incessantly recurring burials, with our Burial Office, and by our priests, of suicides, upon the mere strength of the transparent verdict 'while of unsound mind,' many of them dying simply because mad with drink—that curse of our nation ; burials of open infidels and known evil-livers of all sorts ; the utter want of any legal questioning by the priest in baptism, in marriage, in confirmation, in Eucharist, or in burial—that is, questioning of a nature to ensure some safeguard from the profanations of each and all these rites, which occur continually ; the fearful evils and rottenness of the whole Divorce Court system ; the *utter* want of any real discipline, rule, or order, throughout the whole Anglican Church, wherein literally 'every man doeth that which is right in his own eyes' (save and except alone those who really strive only to obey the Church too much, and to be too reverent) ; and last, but not least, the profane and ridiculous insult of the State's last attempt at meddling with the things of God, the Court of Lord Penzance, and its parent the Public Worship Regulation Act (of a Parliament of all beliefs and none)," &c. . . .

So the enumeration continues. I may refer any reader who wishes to follow it further to the "Church Review," August 10, 1878, p. 578, cols. 2, 3.

frankly, 'We have been misled; we acknowledge the error of *our fathers*,[1] and we return to you'? You condemn almost everything in the Reformation, except the rebellion against him who was head of the Church. Are you very sure that you have gone as far as you are obliged to go? Are you certain that you ought not, in order to be consistent, to make your submission to the Supreme Pontiff?"

It seems to us that there is special reason to urge on men in the position of the Ritualists this question, which would have no force if addressed to Evangelicals or Dissenters, to Greeks or Russians. The Ritualists "do not truly belong to the Church of England," for they strain the limits of that Church in one direction to a degree incompatible with its formularies, and hence their enemies charge them with being Romanists in disguise, or Romanisers. Some even go so far as to brand them as "traitors" and "conspirators," which is in no sense true according to the strict and proper meaning of those words.

From another point of view, however, it may be said that "Ritualists continue the traditions of Anglicanism under a rather more subtle and dangerous guise." Anglicanism, in fact, is a combination of all the doctrines and practices ranging from the borders of Roman Catholicism to pure Deism. It appears as though this system had been framed with a view to retain within its bosom all descriptions of Christians excepting pure Roman Catholics and pure Deists. To fulfil its design, therefore, it ought to embrace at one extreme all the affirmations of Catholicism *minus* Catholicism, and at the other all the negations of Rationalism *minus* Rationalism pure and simple. In this respect it may

[1] The first reason which Dr. Littledale gives in explanation of the conduct of Ritualists is, that a man must not forsake the religion of his *fathers*. But, to this it may be replied, that Ritualists, in becoming Roman Catholics, are only returning to the religion of their *grandfathers*. We are reminded of the reply of the French Ambassador, who, being asked if it did not grieve him to be buried in England, in Protestant ground, replied, humorously: "Why should it grieve me? Let them only go a few feet deeper, and I shall find myself in Catholic ground."

be said that never, even in the seventeenth century, was Anglicanism so perfect. To-day the Broad Church party are vying on some points with the Rationalists of Germany, and Catholics might sometimes take lessons from the Ritualists. The Broad Church party retain those who are inclining to Rationalism; the Ritualists stop the way of those who were in full march for Rome, or beguile them by their incantations into remaining where they are. They thus play the part of the sirens in the fable; and in this sense it is only just to acknowledge that they do "continue the traditions of Anglicanism under a rather more subtle and dangerous guise."

II. We think we have now shown that there is ground for addressing to Ritualists the question, which to others would be impertinent: "What hinders you from becoming Roman Catholics?" They are in fact far nearer to Rome in their belief, their practices, their worship, and their aims, than the other sections of the Anglican Church, and notably than the Nonconformist sects.

Mr. Gladstone has replied, first, by an argument *a pari*, which he expresses thus ("Contemporary Review," Oct., p. 427):—

"The Abbé must be aware not only of the admitted nearness of the Easterns to the Roman pattern, but also of the fact that nothing is so rare as a theological or ecclesiastical conversion from among them to the Latin communion. He may, then, do well to take the beam of the non-conversion of Greeks and Russians out of his eye, before he troubles himself so seriously with the mote of the non-conversion of Ritualists."[1]

To this objection it may be replied that the position

---

[1] Mr. Gladstone has taken my remarks on the "dead or dying Christianity of the East" as an insult to the misfortunes of Christians oppressed by the Turks. I would reply, in the first place, that I had no intention of speaking slightingly of Christians who have a claim on our interest and sympathy. And next, I would draw Mr. Gladstone's attention to the fact, that there are in the East seventy millions of Christians, not subject to the Turks, who have never shown any great signs of life.

of Ritualists is in no way parallel with that of the Orthodox Greeks; and it is for this reason that the Greeks have so coldly received the advances repeatedly made to them of late years by the Church of England. As regards the Greeks and Eastern Christians, the question is almost entirely one of schism. Except on the point of the primacy and of the jurisdiction of St. Peter and of his successors, the Orientals are in all but· complete accord with the Latin Church. Sacraments, ecclesiastical orders, the hierarchy, the regularity of episcopal succession, all these have been retained as they were before the schism of the ninth and eleventh centuries. The conferences held at Bonn between the Old Catholics, Anglicans, Protestants, and the Greeks, had this good result, that they brought the Greeks and Russians to recognise that on the fundamental doctrine of the procession of the Holy Spirit there was not, properly speaking, any difference between the Eastern and the Latin Church.

In this respect the doctrinal and theological position of the Greeks and Russians is incomparably better than that of any Protestant sect, including Anglican Ritualists. The Russians and the Greeks may even, though in a very restricted sense, adopt the motto *semper eadem*. But for Anglican Ritualists what can be said and what is said? It must be confessed that, from the time of the rupture up to the beginning of the present century, the moral and spiritual decadence in England was such that even the capital truths of Christianity, viz., those relating to baptismal regeneration, to the number, order, and character of the sacraments, to the Real Presence, to the sacrifice of the Mass, to prayers for the dead, to the worship of the Virgin and of the saints, to Apostolic succession, to the origin, nature, and permanence of the Church—all were contested, denied, explained away, and repudiated by a large proportion, if not by the great body of the Anglican Church. It must be owned that the

Anglican orders, condemned by many from the first as null, and regarded practically for more than a century as merely ceremonial, have become in our day still more dubious from the laxity with which for a long time the ordinance of baptism has been administered.[1] Who does not call to mind the clamour raised in Ritualistic journals, like the "Church Times" and the "Church Review," by the question of the fact and validity of the baptism of the Primate of Anglicanism, the Archbishop of Canterbury? Even if it be allowed that Parker's consecration was valid—a point much in dispute—it remains none the less doubtful whether the orders received by the Anglicans of to-day are valid. This fact is, indeed, so patent that of late years we have heard of Anglican priests who have sought ordination elsewhere.

Now, if this be granted—and on this subject the testimonies of Ritualists are abundant and uniform—what course of conduct is incumbent on men who believe in the Church as a divine institution, in Apostolic succession, in the necessity of the sacraments and of the religious orders, and who regard heresy and schism as crimes condemned by Holy Scripture, and still more clearly and emphatically condemned by the constant practice of that "primitive and undivided

---

[1] All fair-minded Anglicans acknowledge that *practically* the Catholic Church has never admitted the validity of the Anglican orders. One of them wrote, as follows, in the "Church Review," March 29, 1879:—"I cannot see what change the Vatican Council has made in the treatment of the Roman Curia towards us. It was nearly twenty years before the Vatican Council that the Curia professed to plant a new Church in England; for more than half a century before then Anglo-Roman priests had been ordered to give conditional Baptism to Anglican 'verts under ordinary circumstances. I believe, ever since the final schism, the Roman authorities have ignored the sacraments of confirmation and orders as ministered in the English Church; and certainly from the days of Parker there was always a Roman 'mission' in England. It is true that there have always been some Roman Catholics who admitted the validity of our orders *theoretically*, but I doubt whether there is an authentic case which can be cited to show that they have even been *practically* admitted. Dr. Lee, in his 'Validity of Anglican Orders,' certainly does mention the case of one priestly 'vert, who for a long time said Mass on the strength of his Anglican orders; but when this attracted the attention of the authorities in Rome he was forced to submit to conditional reordination as a compromise."

Church" to which they so often appeal? What did they do in the early ages with those who were guilty of heresy or schism? They put in practice the counsel of St. Paul: "*Cum ejusmodi nec cibum sumere*" (1 Cor. v. 11).

The course of conduct becoming men who hold the principles just described is clear and plain. There is not a philosophical or theological treatise which does not say, when it is a *question of things necessary to salvation*, then a *probable* opinion will not suffice, there must be *certitude*. And this course of conduct, which must commend itself to every reasonable man, is especially incumbent on those who do not hesitate boldly to criticise the Holy See for having recently bestowed the title of Doctor of the Church on St. Liguori, a man who, they say, has espoused the unauthorized theories of *Probabilism*. But, even if this be so (for we forbear to enter on the much-vexed question), St. Liguori would never have embraced principles which could justify the conduct of the Ritualists.

What, in fact, are the Ritualists doing? They are living in daily contact with men whom they know to be heretics, and whom they consider as such. They content themselves with orders which they know are regarded as dubious, which some of them believe to be so; or they go elsewhere, seeking contraband orders from they know not what bishops or what sect. Is conduct like this logical? Is it consistent with principles which they hold, at least theoretically? Is it in harmony with practices which they adopt, at least partially?

When we calmly observe the course of events as it is passing before our eyes, we can but ask for a decided and definite answer to this question: What is it which, in the view of Anglican Ritualists, constitutes heresy or schism?

Not long ago a religious journal, well known for its advanced Evangelical opinions, inserted a letter containing a series of questions, at the head of which appeared the following :—

"1. Assuming the Church of England to be a true Church, is it so (*a*) because it is episcopal, or (*b*) because it is established, or (*c*) because it is Protestant?

"2. Would our Church cease to be a true Church if (*a*) for any reason it dispensed with episcopacy, or (*b*) if it were disestablished, or (*c*) if it ceased to be Protestant?

"3. Are the Dissenting Churches in England—as Ritualists, so-called High Churchmen, and even some Evangelical Protestant Churchmen assert—'schismatical' communities; and, in that case, are they to be so regarded because they are non-episcopal, or because they are non-established?" ("Rock," May 31, 1878, p. 485, col. 2.—No reply has been given to this letter, which well deserved to be answered.)

Still more recently, another journal inserted a correspondence, in which the following admission was made :—

"Would not the 'Church Review' be rendering good service to the Church of England if its influence were used to prevail upon the clergy generally to speak out more strongly with respect to the terrible sin of schism? Surely the making light of the rending of the mystical body of Christ is a sin, not merely of our nation, but virtually, indeed, of our Church, or at least of the majority of her members. Often enough do we hear this sin condemned in general terms; but then the terms are so general, the condemnation so very mildly expressed, the allowances to be made so numerous, the exhortations to charity so touching, the warnings not to judge others so appalling, that if the ambiguous teaching leaves any impression at all, it is but a confused kind of notion that it is quite right to be Church, but the Dissenters are not such bad folk after all, and that 'we are all aiming for the same place.'" ("Church Review," 1878, p. 463, col. 1.)

How is it possible to raise the cry against heresy and schism when, in the first place, men like Dr. Littledale can speak of the grave divergences which exist in the English Church on the most important truths, as a benefit, nay, almost as a mark of the true Church (see the "Church Quarterly Review," July 1878); and when, secondly, they plead for the union of all the sects which believe in Jesus Christ and in the Trinity? (*Ibid.*, "Home Reunion.") So long as there is to be such toleration of differences on fundamental points as the Ritualists approve of in their own Church, it follows inevitably that schism and heresy must not be so much as named, or, if they are, it must be with bated breath—"very mildly," as, for example, when the President of the English Church Union recently said—

"If in such matters there is toleration of error amongst us, the only excuse that can be made for it is the hope we entertain that such toleration may, in the long run, win back to the faith those who reject any portion of it." ("Church Times," Oct. 4, 1878, p. 546, col. 3.)

In the same tone the "Church Review," when criticising Dr. Littledale's article on "The Dogmatic Position of the Church of England," remarks:—

"The article is suggestive, and will lead the thoughtful reader to the consideration of many subjects which do not lie on the surface. Having said this, we feel free to confess that we rise from the study of it with a sense of imperfect satisfaction. We are tempted to suggest that a better title for it would have been, 'An Apology for Disunion in Teaching,' or, to use the author's terminology, for the want of homogeneous teaching in the Church of England. We do not say that there is no room for such an apology, nor that it cannot be successfully made, but we doubt whether it can be so completely palliated, and even shown to be an advantage, as the reviewer seems to think. We are not sure that the line which ultimately leads to the better moral result is not that which frankly confesses the practical uncertainty of teaching amongst us, openly deplores it, probes its latent immorality, and shows how it is a departure from the dogmatic basis laid down, and interpreted by the quotation from Bramhall and the canon." ("Church Review," Aug. 24, 1878, p. 403, col. 2.)

The changes in the past and the conflicting opinions existing at present in the Anglican Church altogether preclude any parallel between Anglican Ritualists and the Orientals. The fixity of ground among the latter may help to mislead them as to their true position; while, on the other hand, the repudiation of so many doctrines in the past, and their readmission in the present, ought to open the eyes of the blind. What, indeed, is the True Church, if not the guardian of the trust of Revelation? and what becomes of its character as a true Church when it has scattered to the four winds of heaven the treasure of truth committed to it? It ceases to be the Church.

III. But it may be said: If the English Church has lost the trust of revelation committed to it, if it has debased Christian worship and has allowed Catholic discipline to grow lax, the Anglican Ritualists are doing their utmost to repair all these breaches, and to rebuild the ecclesiastical edifice, gathering together all the scattered stones. Only wait, and you will soon see that "Rome has literally nothing to offer them which they do not possess, or are on the point of acquiring in a much better form. Why then should you urge them to become Roman Catholics? They are not such simpletons." ("Church Times," Aug. 9, 1878, p. 447, cols. 3, 4.)

We do not question that Ritualists have made and are daily making a certain amount of progress; nor that they are daily recovering more and more of Catholic belief and practice, taking as the rule of their faith the celebrated maxim of St. Vincent de Lerins: "Quod ubique, quod semper, quod ab omnibus."

On the pretext that every Christian ought to be able to render an account of his faith, some Ritualists go so far as to imply by their conduct, that each individual may form a creed of his own, by interpreting in his own way the *quod ubique*, and by pursuing unaided his own study of Christian antiquity "in the primitive and undivided Church." But what becomes then of the Church, and of its mission as a teacher?[1] Do

---

[1] Dr. Littledale has endeavoured to prove, by the Council of Trent, that "Catholicity of doctrine" is the basis of "Christian solidarity." What is the precise meaning of the words Christian solidarity, as used by Dr. Littledale, I do not profess to understand. But in any case, it seems to me that he is wrong in going back to the Council of Trent to establish his theories against the unity of the Church, for it is not possible to cast a shadow of a doubt on the part which the Fathers of Trent assigned to the Pope. Their words cannot then bear the meaning attached to them by Dr. Littledale.

they count for anything or as nothing? Theoretically they are recognized; but practically they are ignored.

The principle of Catholicity, or the maxim of St. Vincent, cannot be taken in an absolute sense; for, if it was so, there could be no creed, since there is no truth which has not been contested, and generally widely contested. If then the authority of the Church is suppressed, there is no means of knowing whether any particular truth is or is not truly Catholic, even in the sense in which the Ritualists understand the word Catholic.

And, after all, is the Catholic religion only a thing of dogma? Has it not also authority and a commission? Is it enough to have valid Sacraments? Is it not necessary also, that Sacraments should be lawfully administered, that is to say, with the approbation and sanction of the Church? But if a commission is necessary, if authority is required for the due and lawful administration of the Sacraments, if the authority of the Church, in short, is a real thing, how can Anglican Ritualists defend their position?

Who gave Parker his commission? Queen Elizabeth. Who in the present day gives the bishops their jurisdiction? The Crown through the Prime Minister, by the will of the popular Assembly, the House of Commons. Is such a commission valid?[1] Many Ritualists would find it difficult at this moment to acknowledge the Sovereign as the source and fountain of all jurisdiction, when they are waging war to the death against the Royal Supremacy. Ritualists cannot carry with them in their restorations and innovations either the English nation, or the Anglican episcopate, or the majority of the Anglican Church. They are playing the part of a parliamentary opposition, with no assurance, as yet, of attaining to power.

[1] I see, with pleasure, that the grave question of a valid commission is beginning to be agitated among the Ritualists. (See the "Church Review," June 8, 1878, p. 269.)

Nothing that they do or teach comes with any authority. We repeat, therefore, what we have already said elsewhere, that—

"Nowhere else do we find the spectacle of a clergy in absolute revolt against its superiors. We must ask the meaning of their loud assertions of Catholic principles, and if the acceptance of certain dogmas and practices is enough to enable us to attain to the truth, and to work out our salvation. Questions of discipline, of hierarchy, of submission to authority, have all a place in the creed; and if these are set at nought, what becomes of the principle of Catholicity? Ritualists may make the most careful research without finding at any time or in any age a position resembling their own. If belief in a creed is all that is necessary for salvation, the most degraded savage of Oceania, and the rudest colonist of the Far West, might be saved without the aid of a Church or of a missionary : he need only glance at the catechisms of the four or five great Christian Churches of the world !"

We would ask Ritualists to weigh carefully these words, and to determine whether there is truth in them. From a study of their past and present conduct, we might be led to think that they reverse the Catholic adage *Nil sine episcopo*, and that their tenet is that everything must be done either without or against the bishops. The Archbishop of York made this observation at the Sheffield Congress, and with but too much reason.[1]

With their principle of Catholicity, the Ritualists then

---

[1] Here is the language used by Dr. Littledale in his "Reply to the Abbé Martin," pp. 41-43, that is, in a pamphlet written in defence of the Anglican Church and of the Ritualist party :—"Chief of all the sentimental reasons, however, is disgust at the almost unbroken and unvaried misconduct of the collective English bishops; their lack of moral courage, their servility to the civil power, nay, even to popular opinion, however crude, ignorant, and even openly irreligious; and, above all, their uniform failure to regard themselves and to act as the natural heads, and therefore as the natural leaders, champions, and protectors, of the clerical body, as the Judges do for the Bar, and the Horse Guards do for the army. . . . They never come forward to correct any popular misapprehension, to allay any wild panic, of which the clergy are the objects, but themselves swell the chorus of vituperation at the top of their voices, lest they should incur any share of the passing unpopularity. This was notably the case quite lately when the storm was raised about the 'Priest in Absolution.' Not one bishop had the boldness to say plainly that the Church of England teaches auricular confession in its Prayer Book, and that clergymen who were simply carrying out its directions, were more honest, loyal, and consistent, than those who not merely neglected but reviled the practice, and ought accordingly to be let alone."

may set up something which shall bear some apparent and external resemblance to another episcopal Church, but it will not be the true Church, the Church of Jesus Christ. It will be their own Church, a Ritualistic Church, for it will be their workmanship, not God's. And sooner or later the day will come, when they will see clearly that it is but an invention of man, if indeed they, or some of them, do not see it already.

That Ritualists regard their triumphs past and present as manifestations of Divine grace, we do not for a moment call in question. We know that wherever there is genuine good faith, the Spirit of God works in the souls of men. For this reason, far from bewailing the appearance of Ritualism, we rather rejoice in it, as a palpable sign of aspiration towards a higher order of life than the "earth to earth" of Nonconformity and Evangelicalism. We feel, indeed, that Ritualism is fraught with danger, and that it may arrest some souls who, without its intervention, would have at once embraced Catholicism; but, we hope God may yet be pleased, in His own good time, to transform that which is at present a hindrance into a means of conversion.

There must inevitably come a time when the illogical and inconsistent attitude adopted by Ritualists will be no longer tenable, at least by men of intelligence and of good faith. It will be seen that there must be either a further advance, or a decided relapse into that vague Christianity without any defined outlines which constitutes the creed of the majority of Protestant sects at the present day, and which finds its ideal in Congregationalism, as that is represented in the "Christian World." It is possible for an Orthodox Greek to remain where he is, for he has a clearly defined cultus, something in which the mind and the senses may find satisfaction; but the Anglican Ritualist cannot remain where he is. Ritualism is either simply a return to the past, or a mere arbitrary reaction from Protestantism, which, as such, can have nothing permanent in it. It is not we alone who feel this; Ritualists themselves acknowledge it :—

> "It has been frequently said that it is a good thing for the Anglo-Catholic movement that it has had no recognised leaders, and no policy. I have always doubted the truth of that assertion myself, and I think what is now going on amongst us justifies my opinion to a very considerable degree. We now find priests who are credited with being very 'advanced men' indeed, openly throwing themselves into the arms of the Essayists and Reviewers, as regards the doctrine of eternal punishment, to the great scandal of old-fashioned Catholics like myself, as well as of Evangelical Protestants. I had thought that the day was not far off when the Evangelicals, seeing the indefensibility of their own position, would have added what is wanting to their faith, and made common cause with us in maintaining historical Christianity against the phantom Christianity of the Rationalists and the Agnosticism of philosophers, falsely so called. But if 'Ritualism' is to be a mere eclectic 'ism,' which picks and chooses such portions of Catholic belief and ritual as commend themselves to individual members, we must bid farewell to all hope of winning over our Evangelical friends, and we must be prepared to see them, as well as large numbers of so-called Ritualists, seeking elsewhere for the faith once for all delivered."
> ("Church Review," 1878, p. 242, col. 2.)

IV. We have only been able to touch slightly on the great question of the Catholicity of the Anglican Church, which might alone occupy an entire article.

One of the most interesting points in Mr. Gladstone's paper—a point on which Dr. Littledale has also cursorily touched—is his discussion of the

> "Method which bends submissively to all historic evidence, which handles that evidence in the domain of Church history on the same principles as in any other domain, and which has for its aim nothing else than this—to come at the clear and entire truth, without fear or favour." ("Contemporary Review," Oct., p. 431.)

This is what is generally called the appeal to history, that "historic Christianity" treated of in the passage already quoted, that recourse to experience behind which the Anglican Church shelters itself, under the name of an appeal to the "primitive and undivided Church."

Mr. Gladstone and many Anglicans distinguish between this historic method and what the Catholics call tradition, setting the one in opposition to the other. In their view, tradition consists chiefly of facts distorted by prejudice and passion, or coloured by prepossessions, while history "is formed upon facts alone, . . . and looks at the face of things as they are in themselves." ("Contemporary Review," Oct., p. 431.) That Protestants — Anglicans and others — should attach supreme importance to the historical method is easily conceivable, since they recognise no divine Church, no Church with a divinely sustained existence and authority, a divine indwelling, and a divine infallibility. It is a matter of necessity, therefore, that they should have some means of judging of Christianity; and, having rejected the divine and infallible authority of the Catholic Church, they are fain to have recourse to their own reason, and consequently to human history.

For a Catholic it is otherwise. Being fully convinced of the divinity of the Church, of its divine origin, preservation, and operation, he finds in its authority the supreme rule of his judgment, and the final appeal on all dubious points. Not indeed that the Catholic has recourse to the Church to know what he is to think at all times and on all subjects. But he always cherishes this mental reservation, "Salvo ecclesiæ judicio"—that is to say, in all cases in which his views incur the reprobation of the Church, the Catholic must be ready to submit, to offer any explanation that may be demanded, and, if needful, to retract his own opinions. In other words (for it is important to be very clear in a matter on which prejudice is so strong), the supreme rule for the judgment of the Catholic is not his own historical studies, aided or unaided by other men, but the authority of the Church.

All is coherent and consecutive in the Catholic system. The divine origin of the Church, its infallibility, and as a consequence the submission of its children in the last resort to its authority, whether it instructs, or commands, or condemns—this is, in substance, what we Catholics often describe by the name of Tradition, especially when we speak of it in connection with Holy Scripture.

It is of course open to any to dispute the bases of such a system. But the system itself cannot be charged with want of logical coherence. The premises being granted, the consequences follow in rigid sequence.

This is not the place in which to offer a complete apology for the Catholic system. But, since we desire to give explanations frankly and fairly, we may be allowed a word in its defence. When we as Catholics appeal to the judgment and authority of the Church, is it supposed that we reject history, archæology, patrology, and all other sciences? We answer: Not in the least. We simply subordinate all these to the authority of the Church. As formerly it was said of science that it was "ancilla theologiæ," so we say now that it is "ancilla ecclesiæ." And since science and the Church both proceed from God, we do not allow that there can be any *real* contradiction between them. But there may be *apparent* contradiction, and when this is the case, we surrender the ever fallible teaching of history to adhere to the teaching of the Church, which is always infallible.

A Catholic who, instead of submitting to the judgment of the Church (which he confesses to be divine), should adhere to the testimony of human history when it appears to contradict the Church, and who should do this deliberately and knowingly, would cease to belong to the Church. He would be no longer a Catholic; for he would be guilty, not merely of treason and heresy, but of apostasy.[1]

---

[1] It can be scarcely needful, I imagine, to observe that in controversy with non-Catholics, Catholics *do* accept the appeal to history, and *do not* invoke the testimony of the Church.

Catholicism and Ritualism compared. 187

It was in this sense, no doubt, that Cardinal Manning used the two words which are often quoted against him in Protestant journals. Exception should be taken (if at all) not to the expressions used by his Eminence, but to the very foundations of the Catholic system, namely, to the divine origin and infallible authority of the Church.[1]

Two reasons may be briefly given why Catholics, while they do not neglect the careful study of his-

---

[1] When this rejoinder to the papers of Mr. Gladstone and Dr. Littledale was published in the "Contemporary Review," I did not know the exact words employed by his Eminence, Cardinal Manning; but it was, of course, not difficult for me to understand in what sense they had been spoken or written. My readers, I hope, will be gratified to read the very words of the Cardinal, explained by their eminent author more than once; and they will judge, by this remarkable example, how prompt Protestants are to distort and misconstruct the sayings of Catholic writers, however clear and simple they may be, and how slow they are in their retractations.

The original words of Cardinal Manning were as follows : "The appeal to antiquity is both a treason and a heresy. It is treason, because it rejects the Divine voice of the Church at this hour; and a heresy, because it denies that voice to be Divine." ("Temporal Mission of the Holy Ghost," p. 226, 2d edit., Longmans, 1866.)

These words are very clear and easy to be understood. But here is the sense which has been appended to them, by Dr. Littledale, in his original paper in the "Contemporary Review," Nov. 1878, p. 812: "I do not forget that Cardinal Manning, who is probably more familiar than any man living with the art of proselytism, has denounced the 'appeal to history' in questions of religion as 'heresy and treason'—a tolerably sufficient proof as to the sort of evidence he thinks discoverable by that process."

Every one may judge for himself if Dr. Littledale correctly interprets the words of Cardinal Manning. But, as if it was not enough to have misconstructed in this wise so clear an assertion of the eminent writer, Dr. Littledale has, in a reproduction of his former essay in a pamphlet form, joined the following rider, as a fit commentary on the above text : "And by history here is meant Church history, Church documents, liturgies, creeds, canons, and the like. It is not an appeal to something external, against the Church, but an appeal to the Church herself, as to whether she really does teach what is tendered now as her true doctrine." ("Reply to the Abbé Martin," p. 38.)

I ask myself, and all unprejudiced readers : Has Dr. Littledale ever read the exact words used originally by his Eminence with the explanation sent to the "Daily Telegraph" of Oct. 6, 1878 ; or, has he never read them? For, whichever alternative he may choose, he appears rash in his assertions and unjust in his imputations. If he *has not* read them, how has he been able to impute such strange opinions to a man not less eminent by his abilities than exalted by his rank in the Church? If he *has* read them, I think that there is every reason to ask if the present is not an example of "the constantly recurring proofs of bad faith in nearly all Roman controversy, garbled quotations, incorrect renderings, &c." ("Reply," p. 61), but, of course, *not* in the sense asserted by Dr. Littledale.

Although this exposure has been for some months made in the public papers, Dr. Littledale has not yet apologized for his untrue statement, nor has the English Church Union yet repudiated Dr. Littledale.

tory, yet defer ultimately to the judgment of the Church.

The first is, that it is only by means of a teaching body invested with authority, that the knowledge of truth can be brought within the grasp of the masses, especially of the most ignorant.

The second is, that all science, and pre-eminently the science of history, is liable to mistake. Mr. Gladstone seems to think that history is above human passions and prejudices. Would that it were so, and that men, divided on all other subjects, could at least meet on this common ground! But this is far from being the case; and it needs no reflection to show that if there be a science on which the influences of education and of national and party prejudice may make themselves felt, it is assuredly the science of history. The readers of the "Contemporary Review" have had more than one illustration of this before their eyes; and it is scarcely needful to ask whether Mr. Froude and Mr. Freeman would severally give the same version of the facts of history, say of the history of St. Thomas à Becket?

What, then, is the value of these appeals to human history? What weight can they have with ninety-nine hundredths of the human race? Is it actually possible to write, or even to read, history without prejudice? Where is the ordinary reader who can to-day re-construct the true history of the sixteenth century? The late learned Dr. Maitland, Dr. Littledale, Mr. Blunt, and still more lately, Dr. F. G. Lee, and many others, have already told us what we must think of the history of the period written by such men as Foxe and Burnet. We need not perhaps do more than remind Mr. Gladstone and Dr. Littledale of the vigorous language (to use no stronger adjective) in which the latter has himself characterized the Reformers. Thank God, the age is advancing, and to-day the heirs of the English Reformation are beginning to recognize that even in relation to the facts of the sixteenth century, Roman Catholic writers are more worthy of confidence than the Puritan or Protestant historians. Men's views are gradually veering round, and justice is being done at last to men, facts, and things. If any authors might be excused for writing with passion, they would be the English Catholics of the second half of the sixteenth century. As a rule, however, they have not done so, but have treated their persecutors with remarkable moderation. Attention was drawn to this fact, a short time ago, in one of the Ritualist journals. Speaking of the Records of the English Province of the Society of Jesus, the "Church Review" says:—

"There are minor matters scattered up and down amidst the story of hairbreadth escapes, tortures, executions, ministrations, and religious consolations, and of conversion, when conversion meant at the least confiscation of goods and imprisonment. The Marian persecutions had their counterpart in the Elizabethan; Foxe's 'Book of Martyrs' tells nothing of the one that is not surpassed by these records of the other—*with this great difference, however, between them, that the virulent defamation and scurrilous abuse of the one never appears in the other.* Contrast, for example, the mention of Queen Elizabeth in the freedom of intimate letters such as those of F. Rivers, from which we have quoted, and their 'thanks be to God' for her Majesty's good health and frolicsome humour, with the terms in which Foxe speaks of Queen Mary, and which indeed have been followed down to our own days and latest writers. Hallam, whose accuracy no one questions, and who was calm and even cold, as well as accurate, tells us that 'intolerance and persecution was the original sin in which the Reformed Churches were cradled,' *and he might have added evil speaking, lying, and slandering, which nourished and exasperated that intolerance and persecution.* The worth of this volume of records is that they are genuine, made at the time, not for the purpose of proving anything, simply 'records' of what happened." ("Church Review," 1878, p. 86, col. 3; p. 87, col. 1.)

Mr. Gladstone tells us that the "great Protestant tradition" is extinct. Nevertheless, he himself applies elsewhere the title of "Bloody" to Queen Mary, in contrast, no doubt, to the leniency shown by "good Queen Bess" and her royal father towards Catholics.

Happily Dr. Littledale is not afraid to correct this one-sided testimony by assuring us that

"Sir Thomas More, Cardinal Fisher, Bishop Gardiner, Queen Mary, and Cardinal Pole, whatever their errors and sins may have been, were *angels of light* compared with the Protector Seymour, with Bishop Cranmer, Bishop Poynet, Queen Elizabeth, and Bishop Bale." (Dr. Littledale, "On the Reformers," p. 6.)

The great Protestant tradition is not dead in the heart of the common people of England, and if in the minds of lettered and cultivated men it is less bitter than among the populace, it still lives on with much of its old intensity. We note more than one trace of this in Mr. Gladstone's "Study of the Reformation," and many traces of it in Dr. Littledale's article.

It is because we are convinced that it is "well-nigh impossible for ordinary readers to get at the facts" (*Ibid.* p. 20), that we have pointed out, as one of the great hindrances to the progress of Ritualism towards Catholicism, the manner in which many Englishmen take up the study of religion. We have dwelt especially on the dangers of the historic method, so strongly recommended by Mr. Gladstone—a method which, to quote only one example in passing, leads him to represent Cranmer as dying "on the heights of heroism," while Dr. Littledale assigns to him the coward's death (Dr. Littledale, "On the Reformers," pp. 15, 16, and 43; No. 29 of the note "On Cranmer"), and adds, "Lord Macaulay may well say that Cranmer was no more a martyr than Dr. Dodd." So fraught with peril and with paradox is this long and arduous method, which to be pursued aright demands an elevation of character, an uprightness of will, a purity of intention, together with a power of work such as are rarely to be found; nor is all this enough, unless the circumstances of time and place are also favourable. How can a man who breathes an atmosphere charged with prejudices against Catholicism, and who has within his reach documents conceived and framed only with an anti-Catholic bias, attain to a just perception of things as they are? Humanly speaking, it is not possible. Hence we said: "There is not a single fact or institution of Catholicism in connection with which there has not accumulated a mass of prejudice and error. . . . Take, for example, the history of the Inquisition, of St. Bartholomew, of the False Decretals," &c. ("Contemporary Review," Aug., p. 128.) We quoted these as examples that would require volumes for their fair and adequate discussion. We abstained from expressing any opinion of our own; and we are not ashamed to say that we have not studied all these subjects — as our critics appear to have done—so thoroughly as to venture to express an independent opinion upon them. What we meant to say was, that on all these points and many more there is a great divergence of view and this statement is fully borne out by the two papers of Mr. Gladstone and Dr. Littledale. Both agree, however, in condemning the Papacy for the rejoicings in Rome and for the medals struck on the occasion of the St. Bartholomew Massacre (*Ibid.*, Oct., p. 439; Nov., p. 795).

Into a discussion of these facts we cannot attempt to enter here. We can simply make a few brief observations upon some of them.

It is not our business to explain or to excuse the massacre of the Protestants. Dr. Littledale has said: " Few know that the atrocities which the Protestants themselves ten years before had committed at Beaugency, Montauban, Nismes, Montpellier, Grenoble, and Lyons, *equalled, if they did not exceed, that terrible crime.*" (Dr. Littledale: "On the Reformers," p. 19.) We might add to this that the provinces of the west and south of France are still covered with ruins which date not from "ten years before" St. Bartholomew, but from the year 1568. The Huguenots were not simply men who fought for liberty of conscience. They were the Communists of the age, rebels who laid waste provinces, and, by their frequent plottings with the foreigner, kept the State in perpetual danger. They were public enemies. That it was justifiable on this account to kill them like dogs or to shoot them down from behind hedges, as if they were wolves, be it far from us to maintain. But we repeat it; the question is not, Was the massacre of St. Bartholomew right? but, Did the Pope order rejoicings over the event *as a massacre*, and did he have medals struck to perpetuate the memory of so ignoble a victory? Everything depends on the light in which the Massacre of St. Bartholomew was presented to Gregory XIII. It is evident that, if the St. Bartholomew reprisal was represented as the triumph of order over disorder, of conservatism over revolution, of honest men over rogues; then, the rejoicings which are made such a reproach to Pope Gregory were as natural as the congratulations addressed to a sovereign or to a nation on the escape from some great peril. Now, historians tell us that the events *were* thus represented to the Pope, and the statement is verified by the fact that afterwards, when Gregory became better acquainted with what had passed, he disapproved of the massacre of St. Bartholomew.

It is obviously impossible for us to enter here into a full discussion of this subject, nor can we hope readily to shake the rooted opinion of Protestants on the point. But the divergence of sentiment, not only between Catholics and Protestants, but between writers of the same body, is sufficient proof of the futility of the appeal to history as a final test of truth. There is not a single fact involved in any amount of obscurity about which any two writers are perfectly agreed, unless they have copied each from the other.

We have mentioned also the False Decretals. Dr. Littledale, referring to this subject, says, "that a large portion of the Roman Canon Law and of the Papal claims have absolutely no other basis whatever."

("Contemporary Review," Nov., p. 796). This is a very serious and grave assertion. For, the Popes exercised the authority and enjoyed the privileges of the Papacy *long before* the False Decretals were put in circulation; and these False Decretals themselves would not have been accepted if they had not been in harmony with the ideas commonly received at the time of their appearance. We are reduced, then, to one of two alternatives: either the Decretals ran counter to the ideas and practices of the age, or they were in perfect harmony with them.

If the first hypothesis be the true one, how was it that, among so many persons whose interest it was to protest, not one lifted up his voice to denounce the imposture and the usurpation? Were the men of the ninth and tenth centuries not men of like passions with ourselves? Had they not the same independence, the same love of liberty? Why, again we ask, did no one protest?

If, on the other hand, the second hypothesis be true, then the comparison which Dr. Littledale institutes between the Papacy and a proprietor in possession of an estate gained by a false title, altogether fails. It was not, Decretals in hand, that the Popes took possession of the government of the Catholic world. It was, because the Popes were already the rulers of the Catholic world that the Decretals were at once accepted, without a too close inquiry into their origin and titles. The fact that the Popes, or the lawyers who edited the Canon Law, accepted them as a fitting embodiment of their ideas, lends them a value which intrinsically they did not possess; just as a false title becomes valid and genuine if the seller and the buyer both consent to subscribe their names to it.

V. Our two honourable opponents lay stress on the social superiority of England, as compared with the nations of the Continent, especially with France, Italy, and Spain. Mr. Gladstone, in particular, has given great prominence to this fact; but the same tone runs through all the pages of Dr. Littledale's paper, and becomes very marked towards its close. This superiority is shown, firstly, by the little influence which the Paganism of the Renaissance has exerted upon English society and literature, while it has struck to the core Italy and France. Secondly, by the hold which Christianity has retained, till our own times, on the upper and middle classes of English society; while elsewhere, in France and Italy for example, these classes are either indifferent or positively hostile to the Church. Thirdly, by the ease with which the ranks of the ministry are recruited, the classes from which the clergy are drawn, the measure of education which they receive and retain, the position which they occupy in society, and the part assigned to them in public life.

It would be easy to enumerate other evidences of this social superiority of England over the Catholic nations of the Continent; but, the three points already named seem to suffice for the purpose.

We would observe, first, that the order of things indicated by these words, "superiority" and "social superiority," is a very comprehensive one, and that it is not easy to say always to what cause they are to be assigned, or to distinguish, among many co-operating causes, that which has the largest share.

We are perhaps more disposed than many to recognize the relative social superiority of England. But we are not convinced that Protestantism, the Reformation, and Anglicanism are the principal causes of this superiority. And, even if these systems could vindicate their claim to the character assigned to them, we should not be prepared to allow that therefore they were divine.

England occupies a position unique in the world. A girdle of seas encircles her, and isolates her from all

other nations. Her cold and severe climate, while it
repels strangers, accustoms her children to lead that
manly, austere life, full of activity and energy, which
prepares them so well to play their noble part in the
history of the world. To this isolation, combined with
the consciousness of power characteristic of the English
nation, is to be traced that British pride which has preserved, and will perhaps long preserve, England from
the false doctrines and corrupt practices of the Continent. The English people is an "imperial people;"
it knows and feels its own worth, and its lawful self-
esteem is perhaps not unmixed with a tinge of contempt
for others. A study of the English character recalls
involuntarily the noble lines of the poet—

"Tu regere imperio populos, Romane, memento;
Hæ tibi erunt artes, pacisque imponere morem,
Parcere subjectis, et debellare superbos."
—VIRGIL, *Æn.* vi. 852-854.

The English nation, moreover, is a nation relatively
young as compared with the French and the Italians.
These have passed through many stages in life; they
are on the verge of old age, some say of decrepitude
and decline. France and Italy have been trampled for
centuries by the feet of the stranger, who left to them
his vices while he borrowed not always from their
virtues. They are open countries, accessible to all
invasions of new ideas; and they suffer, at least by
reaction, from all the political convulsions of their
neighbours. No true comparison can be instituted,
therefore, between them and the English nation.

But, to pass from such general considerations to
the three points brought forward by Mr. Gladstone
and Dr. Littledale. Even if it be a fact that
Paganism has cast its roots so deeply and widely, as
they assert, in France and Italy, this would argue
nothing in favour of the Reformation, unless it can be
shown (and this has not yet been attempted) that it
was the Reformation which repelled from England the

invasion of Paganism. The countries into which the Renaissance has introduced most largely the languages of Paganism, are first Italy, and next France; and this is naturally explained by the ancient, prolonged, and frequent relations of Italians and French with Eastern countries. At the time when the treasures of Greek and Pagan antiquity were introduced into the West, first by the decadence and then by the fall of the Greek Empire, when the great families were driven by the approach of the Turk into Italy—at this time, we say, there was a sort of infatuation abroad about the antique. People raved about the ancients, and emulated their speech. The admiration for them passed all bounds. But the people still remained Christian, while borrowing the language of the Pagan. It was pre-eminently a literary Paganism; and there are generations of men still living, who have watched it pass away.

The same causes have produced the same effects from another point of view. England has been and will be slower than the nations of the Continent in becoming un-Christianised. There may still be persons who, scarcely knowing what Christianity is, yet glory in being Christians. But Protestantism cannot claim the credit of this. The majority of the nation was still Catholic in belief and practice, long after the Reformation. Some writers go so far as to say that at the death of Henry VIII., eleven-twelfths of the English people—obviously not of the nobility—were Catholics in heart and conviction. What wonder is it, then, if the higher classes have retained a certain Christianity corresponding closely in character with what is called Evangelicalism? Here also, however, the current ideas of the age are spreading, and there is every probability that in thirty years from this time, the religion of the upper classes will have greatly changed its character.

If Catholicism is at the present moment somewhat

forsaken by the middle class and by the men generally, it must be admitted, first, that it is making progress, and next that it retains its hold at least on the poorer classes, the common people. This Protestants themselves admit. Let any one enter, on any Sunday, a church in the poorer quarters of Paris, and he will see there more working people, men and women, than in all the churches of London put together, those of Ritualists included. The like remark may be made of the early and late services in the Catholic churches of London, in comparison with the churches of the Establishment. As the "Church Review" lately said :—

"Sacrament Sunday has lost us 'the common people.' This is a phenomenon unique in religious history, including under that phrase the history of false religions as well as true, of Paganism as well as Christianity. No one was ever so independent of the forms and observances of his national faith, being at the same time not a professed infidel, as the ordinary uneducated Englishman. We do not speak of a failure to produce the highest results, but of a failure to produce any tie, to exact any adherence, to make religion a familiar thing in its external observances, as a necessary aspect of life, or an outward surrounding and profession. The anomaly is not merely that piety languishes, that Christian virtues decay, that the flesh is too strong for the lower classes, just as the world and the devil are too strong for the higher, but that for the lower classes the Church and her system should be remote and unrecognised objects, taken for granted by them as not being for them, and in which they recognise no claims and no beauties that answer to something in their individual mental history." ("Church Review," 1878, p. 467. See also p. 395, cols. 1, 2.)

If, then, we may accept as any "test" of the divinity or superiority of a system the social class upon which it takes most hold, it seems to us that Catholicism must have more of the divine in it than Anglican Ritualism; for Jesus Christ never said, "Divitibus," but He did say, "Pauperibus evangelizare misit me" (Luke iv. 18). St. Paul himself observed, in his day, that not many rich nor great ones were seen among the Christians: "Non multi potentes, non multi nobiles" (1 Cor. i. 26). We may even go further, and say that if there is one system which suits the rich, but is ill adapted for the poor—and this was true of Anglicanism before the rise of Ritualism—there is some reason to think that such a system is not so much divine, as "worldly and devilish."

And why? Because the higher classes of society are something like the Governments which they form and lead; they do not like a popular religion, one that preaches self-denial, sacrifice, devotedness, and equality. They want a religion of silk and velvet, in which dogmas occupy but a small space, and irksome duties still less, which amounts, in fact, to a moral anodyne, colourless and vague, a feeble, philanthropic philter.

The higher and the middle classes of society, those who are described in England as "well-to-do people," have but little sympathy with clericalism and sacerdotalism. Ritualists have been made to feel this. They are hated and persecuted because they make some pretensions to the priestly and clerical character. Now Evangelicals, Broad Churchmen, Dissenters, and men of the world do not like clerics or clericalism. And yet, strange to say, it is since Ritualism has restored clerical or sacerdotal customs and claims, since the Anglican clergy has returned to the Mass, to confession, and to the use of retreats and missions, since it has begun to lead a more earnest, retired, and austere life, that it has regained to some extent its hold upon the masses of the people. It will, at least, be admitted, that there is a strange coincidence between these two facts, if the one may not be allowed to be the cause of the other.

When we consider the situation of the world in which we live, the various aspirations by which it is stirred, we cannot fail to recognize the same conflict of principles which has left its mark on the past ages. In truth, we are taking our part to-day in one more struggle between the priestly and the imperial power, with this difference, however, that the empire is not represented simply by an individual, but by the multitude. It is a new phase of a conflict which is as old as Christianity itself, the conflict between the natural and supernatural, between earth, as represented by the laity, and heaven, as represented by the priesthood. Upon the Continent the battle has long been waging. In England the clerical pretensions of Ritualists have first awakened the clash of arms.

But why, we ask next, does the Anglican clergy represent a higher social class than the Catholic clergy in France? The condition of society in the two countries offers sufficient explanation; and, moreover, the same proportions being kept, the Catholic clergy of France does occupy a position as elevated in relation to the population around, as does the Anglican clergy in relation to the English people. French society is on the descending scale; under the present testamentary law in France it is impossible for families to maintain their position unimpaired for more than three generations. And with the great families perish the traditions which form the strength of the country. When whole classes are thus sinking to a lower social grade, the individual is carried along with them.

The priesthood in France has little to expect but self-sacrifice. It cannot, therefore, be deemed strange that those who embrace that calling in the age of fervour and of illusions, should sometimes look back regretfully and falter, or even retire before they are irretrievably engaged, finding the burden too heavy to be borne. This is the explanation of the defections of which Dr. Littledale speaks, and for which he reproaches the Catholic clergy of France, with, as we think, undue severity.[1] God forbid that we should make heroes or models of these deserters! But let us not, on the other hand, be without consideration, sympathy, or mercy.

Dr. Littledale dwells upon the literary culture of the

[1] On this point the reader is requested to consult the next essay, page 247.

Anglican clergy, to which we also pay full and willing homage. But, he reproaches the clergy of France with falling behind in this respect. Is this just? Is it possible that a clergy, despoiled as the French clergy has been, without leisure and without means, paid on an average at the rate of £60 per annum,[1] should devote itself like the clergy of England to letters and science? Surely, this is asking what is impossible. We must be fair to all, and judge of men by what it is possible for them to do, under circumstances in which their lot is cast.

To us it seems rather matter for surprise, that the clergy of France attain such a high degree of culture as is generally to be found among their members; and in any case, one thing is certain, that they are far better instructed in the proper duties of their priestly order than other clergy more favoured by fortune. And it is, after all, by the knowledge and the virtues of their profession that the true work of the clergy is done. This Dr. Littledale has admitted and owned, as has many a Ritualist: "Talking, and writing, and arguing against atheism is not much use. Never was more of these things done than in England a hundred years ago, when the Church was all but dead. Praying and working are the true weapons." ("On the Reformers," p. 27.)

Moreover, since the above lines were published in the "Contemporary Review," Dr. Littledale has made certain important confessions, of which the following extracts may be taken as a fair summary. In a paper on "*The Professional Studies of the English Clergy*," inserted in the "Contemporary" of April 1879, he recognizes as plain and evident facts—

I. In regard to the Catholic clergy, and especially to the French clergy—1. That "they know what they have been meant to learn, and that they seldom forget it, . . . that they are thoroughly versed

---

[1] In this figure, £60, is included not only the salaries paid by the Government in lieu of the property it has appropriated, but also all incidental sources of income.

Catholicism and Ritualism compared. 201

in the ordinary routine of parish duties" (p. 10). 2. That "the Roman seminaries are very careful in teaching their students how to recite their office, to perform Divine service, and to celebrate the sacraments correctly" (p. 22). 3. That " there is no question at all that the young priest is turned out a fairly serviceable implement for the kind of work he is to have intrusted to him" (p. 10).

These avowals are, of course, somewhat meagre, and they are conveyed in words calculated to show that they are reluctantly made. But, if we look to another side of the picture, perhaps we shall arrive at a just conclusion. Dr. Littledale confesses, indeed—

II. Relating to the Anglican Church and the Anglican clergy, even the Ritualistic clergy.—1. That " the professional training of the clergy has been quite inadequate " (p. 4). 2. That "there is no systematic, complete, and logical teaching of theology, rites, preaching, moral theology, casuistry, church history. In other words, that the Anglican clergy are taught everything save what it is their duty and business to know." Consequently, Dr. Littledale proclaims— 3. That "the net result is, that the ordinary clergyman of average intelligence and acquirements *practically knows almost nothing of theology, and literally cannot tell what the teaching of the Church of England is* on almost any question whatever, even if it be in regard to some point not in dispute amongst the competing schools" (p. 25). 4. That the university course "fails signally to meet the daily needs of a parochial clergy" (p. 12). 5. That at the time of the deaths of Keble, Williams, Neale, "*not fewer than thirteen* Episcopal sees, including at least four out of the five principal ones, were occupied by prelates *whom not flattery itself could credit with even a superficial acquaintance with the primer of theology*, and that the whole Bench of Bishops did not attain *a respectable level*" (p. 7). 6. That "the net result was, that *the clergy of the English Church, alone of all important Christian bodies* having a stated ministry, began their professional education without having any instruction to acquaint them, even imperfectly, with the sacred ministry " (pp. 1, 2).

These are, indeed, very strong admissions considered in themselves; but they appear even more so, when we see them made by so prejudiced an opponent as Dr. Littledale. They do not, however, preclude the eminent controversialist from disparaging the French clergy and from exalting his Ritualist friends.

Mr. Gladstone and Dr. Littledale think it strange

that the Catholic clergy should live so isolated as they do from the world. They would have them enter more generally into the current of social life, and take a greater part in public affairs.

It is indeed to be desired that the influence of the clergy should be more felt in secular life. And at one time, when Europe was Christian and Catholic, they did notably occupy positions of influence. But, to-day all is changed. The general tendency is towards the separation of the Church from the State, of the spiritual from the temporal; priests are not supposed to be wanted in the Councils of State; there are some who would even go so far as to shut them up within their sacristies.

In such a position of things, is not the Church justified in giving her clergy such a special training as may best prepare them for entire self-devotion and self-sacrifice? Is it not the same feeling, or at any rate the recognition of a like necessity, which has led the English Church to found her theological colleges, and Anglicans to found their Keble College?

VI. But we must hasten on. One of the great objections raised by Mr. Gladstone against the Catholic system (and in this he is seconded by Dr. Littledale) is that Catholicism, being a religion of authority, is incompatible with liberty. Both look upon it as one of the great benefits of the Reformation, that it brought to the surface this "gigantic question, namely, whether freedom is one of the vital and normal coefficients for all healthy life and action of the human soul." ("Contemporary Review," Oct., p. 446.)

This objection we have met with several times in Mr. Gladstone's writings, but, we must confess, without being fully able to understand it. Does Mr. Gladstone mean, that every one has the right and the liberty to think, say, and do whatever he will on all subjects, and on all occasions? If this is what he means, then surely it must be allowed that the Reformation brought in no such liberty. Mr. Gladstone himself admitted this in reference to the English Reformers, at least to the early Reformers ; and experience teaches us that never, at any time, in any place, under any system, whether political or religious, has such liberty been tolerated. Count Bismarck refused liberty to the Catholics some years ago, as at the present time he is refusing it to the Socialist democrats ? The Swiss Protestants have followed Bismarck's example. They have proscribed and compromised the Catholics, who were far from claiming liberty to think and to say everything ; who were perfectly willing to submit to strict and equitable laws ; who asked nothing, in fact, but what was the common right of all.

The truth is that absolute liberty is not possible anywhere, either in politics or in religion. The liberty of man is restricted, firstly, by reason ; secondly, by his natural conscience ; thirdly, by his supernatural conscience or faith.

When a man thinks and speaks freely against his reason, he is held to be mad, and is put under restraint. This is the common verdict on liberty of thinking and speaking without regard to the first authority—the authority which is placed by God within us, and which we call reason.

When a man thinks and speaks in defiance of natural conscience, he is called a dishonest man, a rogue, a dangerous person ; and the law lays its hand upon him as a noxious and unsafe member of society.

Upon these two points there is not in general any divergence of opinion among men. But when it comes to a question of thinking and speaking against the Christian faith, against the Holy Gospel and tradition, as both represented by the Church, there is a difference of opinion at once. Mr. Gladstone and Dr. Littledale regard it as a desirable thing that men should be allowed to think, say, or do anything they please. "For the spirit of the Christian religion," says Mr. Gladstone, "such as we profess it, is undoubtedly a spirit of examination;" while "the spirit inculcated, and generally prevailing, in the Latin communion is a spirit of acquiescence." (*Ibid.*, p. 430.)

It seems to us that in this objection against the Catholic Church, which recurs several times in Mr. Gladstone's pamphlet, there is a great confusion of ideas, a great want of clearness and precision. If Mr. Gladstone had analysed his ideas, pen in hand, perhaps he would have been led to express in a less vague manner this his great grievance against the Catholic Church.

We would call the attention of Mr. Gladstone and Dr. Littledale first to the fact that the English Church itself does not tolerate liberty of thought, speech, and action under all conditions. The Book of Common Prayer and the Thirty-nine Articles impose restrictions on and define limitations to this liberty. Ritualists are finding out, at this moment, by experience, that, if they enjoy a somewhat larger liberty in the Anglican than they would in the Catholic Church, it is only on condition that they use this liberty in the direction of Protestantism, Rationalism, or Deism. They may deny, they may not affirm. They may violate the rubric of the Common Prayer Book, they may not observe it. Are we not stating plain facts? What do Mr. Gladstone and Dr. Littledale say to these things?

We maintain, then, that if there be a difference between Anglicanism and Catholicism in this respect, it is a difference of degree, not of kind. And we hold that the difference is entirely in favour of Catholicism.

What, in fact, does the Catholic Church say? She says: "I do not forbid you to study, to examine, to think for yourselves, provided only that you do all this in submission to my authority, because that is an infallible authority. I have received a commission to teach. Anything, therefore, which I have taught, or may teach, you are not at liberty to deny or contradict, under pain of ceasing to belong to me. If you desire to study the Scriptures, follow the unanimous tradition of the Fathers, and never forsake it, or you will fall into error. Do you desire to speculate? do you form schemes and plan theories? Think, speculate, speak, and write. But if one day I say to you: Beware, you are in error; what you are saying is not true, or is dangerous—you must be ready to submit at once."

This then is the practice of the Church. Is it unreasonable? Does Mr. Gladstone think that the license to think, speak, and write granted by Protestantism has produced good results on the social and spiritual life? In Germany it has killed religion. In England it has given birth to one hundred and fifty sects, and it will one day kill religion there, if Catholicism does not save it. This Ritualists are nearly as ready to avow as ourselves:—

"The reflection that on the continent of Europe there is no refuge from Romanism even in its Vatican form, ought to reconcile us to our lot as members of the Church of England. Nearly everywhere on the continent now Romanism is honeycombed with infidelity, and flings back men who wish to be Christians on a harsh though disagreeable alternative. Scepticism progresses in the Prussian Church, which is at this moment agitated by the fact that of thirty thousand parishioners, nine hundred have protested against a pastor who 'denies' the supernatural, and, therefore, cannot believe in Christ. Similar revelations crop up in the Protestant Church of Holland, where the difference between the Low and the High among ourselves become a difference between believers and nonbelievers in the Nicene creed. Protestantism on the continent is helpless as a defence of the fundamental verities of Christianity" ("Church Review," 1878, p. 1, col. 2).

But is there, then, nothing latent beneath the complaints of Mr. Gladstone and Dr. Littledale? There is something. These honourable controversialists cannot understand how such truths, for example, as the Immaculate Conception[1] and the Infallibility of the Pope—truths which up to 1854 and 1870 might be denied by good Catholics—are since that time made obligatory on all members of the Catholic Church.

The case, however, is very simple. These two truths, formerly denied, or, to speak more correctly, disputed by some few, but affirmed by the great majority of Catholics, have been defined, as fourteen or fifteen centuries ago the Consubstantiality of the Word was defined at the Council of Nice, as the Divinity of the Spirit was defined at the Council of Constantinople, as the Unity of Person in Jesus Christ and the Maternity of the Virgin were defined at the Council of Ephesus, and as the Duality of Natures was defined at the Council of Chalcedon.

We can perfectly understand that the basis of the Catholic system, which is the infallible and divine authority of the Church to teach, may be called in question. But if this authority be once admitted, its consequences cannot be disputed. If Christianity speaks of *rationabile obsequium*, it speaks also of submission to and respect for authority. "Docebit vos omnem veritatem—Ecclesia columna et firmamentum veritatis." To a Catholic, this is the compendium of faith.

We know, unhappily too well, that the mind of man rebels sometimes, for reasons more or less openly avowed, against the authority of the Church. Revolt is natural to humanity; calm, unhesitating submission is not so. We know too, however, that men at

---

[1] Speaking of the Immaculate Conception, Dr. Littledale ventures to say that the definition of 1854 "*contradicts the well-nigh unanimous testimony of ancient Christendom*" ("Contemporary Review" for Nov., p. 822). This assertion, which I should have read without surprise in a Protestant newspaper, astonished me as coming from the pen of Dr. Littledale. If he would be prepared to ensure the insertion of an article on this subject in the pages, say, of the "Church Quarterly Review," I should be prepared to prove to him, on grave and ancient authority, that even outside the Latin Church, the dogma of the Immaculate Conception has been received. (This challenge, uttered many months ago, has received no answer.)

least the equals of Döllinger and Hyacinthe do accept unquestioningly the precepts and teachings of the Catholic Church.

Dr. Littledale cannot see the justice and reasonableness of Cardinal Bonnechose's words: "My clergy is a regiment; I say 'March,' and it marches." We confess that we do not like the word, because it may give offence; but it does, nevertheless, bring out very forcibly one strong aspect of the Catholic Church—the discipline which constitutes its strength, because its unity. Since the French Revolution, the Church in France has been poor; but, it is powerful nevertheless, for it is united. And it is united, because the Concordat, while it deprived it some years ago of some of its rights, constrained it to draw closer to the Holy See. That Concordat was not of its own making; it was not even the complete triumph of the See of Rome. The Holy See and the Church of France had each to make many sacrifices in the interests of souls, and they went as far as they could go in the path of concession without failing in duty. Their part was mainly passive. We ask ourselves, therefore, what account of the negotiations which issued in the Concordat Dr. Littledale can have read, that has rashly induced him to characterise it as "a plot of Pius VII. with Napoleon I."? ("Contemporary Review," Nov., p. 810.) If Dr. Littledale will read on this subject the Memoirs of Cardinal Pacca and Cardinal Consalvi, still better the History of M. d'Haussonville—who is not, we believe, a Catholic—he will probably form quite another idea of the part taken in this matter by Pope Pius VII., and will not again dare to apply to it the word "plot."[1]

[1] In the same place ("Contemporary Review," Nov., p. 810), Dr. Littledale says that "the same policy is being carried out more and more in the Anglo-Roman body, where the State does not meddle at all;" and that "the bishops in Belgium extort bonds of resignation from the beneficed clergy." What is going on in England I do not know; but I suppose that things are much the same as in France. So long as the *true* benefices of the Church are not restored, and she lives a precarious life, the rules of the canon law cannot be observed in

VII. We must, however, draw these explanations to a close, thoroughly inadequate as we feel them to be to the complete treatment of the many questions raised in the two articles before us.

Of the reasons which Dr. Littledale gives, why Ritualists do not become Catholics, we have found none which may not be brought under one of the three heads described by us as "interested, sentimental, or intellectual motives." He brings out more forcibly some of the points we have touched on; but he says absolutely nothing which does not confirm our view of the situation.

We can thoroughly appreciate the delicacy of the position of this religious party, which, conscious of its own strength, and of the good which it is doing or would do, yet finds itself under a constant cross-fire of attack on every hand. It needs some courage for men thus to expose themselves to the charge of being traitors, cowards, deserters, while they are conscious of intentions so widely different. We should, therefore, keenly reproach ourselves if we had said the least word which could wound the feelings of any such. Nothing that we have advanced has been prompted by any feeling of hostility to the party of Anglican Ritualists. On the contrary, our one desire is, that God may make clear to them the truth, and that they

all their rigour. They apply to a state of things which has been completely changed.

With reference to Dr. Littledale's statement about Belgium—a statement which has appeared also in English newspapers—we give it a categorical denial, if it is intended to describe a general practice. If it refers only to *an isolated fact*, it cannot be used as an argument. It is an illegality, neither more nor less, for which neither Catholicism nor the Holy See can be responsible.—I spoke thus, when this paper was published in the "Contemporary" of Dec. 1878. Dr. Littledale when printing his "Reply to the Abbé Martin," under the auspices of the English Church Union, appended this note to the passage: "The Abbé Martin says that if this be true at all of Belgium, it is only an isolated fact, and not the usual practice. He offers *no disproof*, and I therefore simply record his protest." I ask every unprejudiced reader if Dr. Littledale has rightly interpreted my note, and truly recorded my *categorical denial?* I have published official letters on this matter in the "Nineteenth Century" of Dec. 1879, p. 1112. See also the last essay in the present volume, "On the Present State of the Church in France" (p. 281). When will Dr. Littledale and the Ritualistic press apologize for this and for other untrue statements?

may have the courage to embrace it. It is solely with this view that we have urged and re-urged upon them this question : "What hinders Ritualists from becoming Catholics?" We beseech them to weigh it calmly, and in doing so to guard against that impatience and irritability which too often characterize their writings. One of them recently wrote as follows :—

"It would be a good thing, I think, if some of our friends would read what was written in past times by Tractarians, Puseyites, Reunionists, and then ask themselves what was the object of the movement, whither it tended, and whether they really belong to it? Are they tending towards the same direction? I think they are not. The object of the Catholic Movement, as I understood it, was to raise the Church of England out of the stupor into which she had fallen, and then to bring her into full communion with the other branches of the one Vine. The new policy, on the other hand, is only likely to stereotype her insular character, and to prevent her sister Churches recognizing her legitimacy. From ten to twenty years ago the desire for corporate reunion was expressed by every one who called himself an Anglo-Catholic. Year by year we heard of the wonderful increase of members of the A. P. U. C. [*i.e.*, the Association for Promoting the Unity of Christendom] : now one hears next to nothing of that excellent society ; I doubt if it maintains its former numbers, much more that they are increasing ; while abuse of Rome and Roman authorities has taken the place of a perhaps too deferential tone towards them. It seems to me that there is something wrong somewhere, and I end as I began by asking, Whither are we drifting?" ("Church Review," 1878, p. 242, col. 2.)

There is no worse counsellor than passion. It may be, that some Catholics have occasionally been unjust to the Ritualists ; but we are certain, that even those who have erred the most in this respect would willingly give their lives to lead Anglicans into Catholic truth.

RITUALISTIC PREJUDICES AND MISCONCEPTIONS.

SUBSEQUENTLY to the appearance of a portion of the foregoing pages in the "Contemporary Review" of December 1878, Dr. Littledale published, in the form of a pamphlet, with a few additional notes, and some slight modifications of various passages, his answer to the fifth paper in the present volume. A society which exercises a certain amount of influence over the Anglican religious world, viz., the "English Church Union," gave the sanction of its authority to the publication of the pamphlet in question, up to the moment when, in deference to remonstrances which might have been readily anticipated, it felt bound to withdraw Dr. Littledale's work from circulation.[1]

Since then, Dr. Littledale has brought out a small volume, at a moderate price, purporting to give the reasons best calculated to keep Anglicans from entering the Roman Church. The substance of these reasons had already appeared, first, in Dr. Littledale's organ of opinion, the "Church Times," then in the "Contemporary Review," and afterwards in the pamphlet published under the auspices of the "English Church Union."

Having thought it well to collect in one volume the chief portion of our essays on the Anglican Church, we believe also, that the reflections which have suggested themselves to us in glancing through Dr. Littledale's latest work, may be of service to some of

[1] See the series of letters on this subject by Mr. Orby Shipley, which appeared in the "Tablet" under the heading "Truthfulness and Ritualism," and which have now been published by Messrs. Burns & Oates.

our readers. His " Plain Reasons against Joining the Church of Rome " is a book which deserves notice, not at all from its intrinsic merits, but because we find it a brief, though very complete epitome of all ⸱ prejudices, the false views, the misconceptions, and the inaccurate notions on the subject of the Catholic Church, which the Protestant spirit has fostered in a body otherwise religiously disposed. Moreover, the book is worthy of our attention from another point of view.

If it were the production of an avowed free-thinker, of an acknowledged Dissenter, or of a member of the Broad or Low Church parties, there would be little need for us to concern ourselves about this work. We are, of course, well aware of the opinion which those who hold the above-named tenets entertain, respecting the Catholic Church and those who belong to her. From ultra-Protestants, or from infidels, the Church and her members expect neither impartial treatment nor a fair hearing. Protestants and free-thinkers are alike imbued with prejudices against Catholics, against the Church, and against her history, her dogmas, and her practices—prejudices which are hastily conceived on insufficient grounds, frequently as the result of much superficial reading of anonymous pamphlets : prejudices which it would be idle to attempt to combat, since we should only come into collision with a dead wall of preconceived ideas.[1]

The work quoted above, "Plain Reasons against

---

[1] As an instance of these preconceived notions, and of the foolish and unreasoning hatred which leads men to receive with avidity and to swallow without hesitation the most absurd gossip against the Catholic Church and Clergy, I may quote the Rev. Horatius Bonar's "The White Fields of France." Anything more shameless than the falsehoods it contains I do not remember to have seen. I am told that this book has attained considerable popularity in England. For the credit of the English people I must take leave to doubt this; else I must despair of their common sense. The exaggerations and untruthfulness of every page are patent. See the following specimens :—1. The priests do not believe, pp. 11, 12, 30. 2. The priests are immoral, p. 36. 3. The priests live in luxury, whilst the poor are starving, pp. 7, 8, 34, 36, 97.—Every one may judge for himself of the amount of luxury attainable on stipends of from 1200 to 1500 frs. (£48 to £60) per annum.

Joining the Church of Rome," is not the production of a free-thinker, nor of a Dissenter. Dr. Littledale is a Ritualist clergyman of the most advanced type. He possesses a quick intelligence, cultivated by an extensive, though not, perhaps, a very systematic course of reading, assisted by the powers of a memory which is seldom strictly accurate, but which always to a certain extent responds to the calls made upon it. His pen is ready, almost too energetic; and it runs on freely, at need, and sometimes further than is necessary. It is only common justice to say that Dr. Littledale is a man of a certain mark in the advanced ranks of Ritualism. We are much mistaken if the organs of that party, more especially the "Church Times," are not often, perhaps are constantly, indebted to him for their inspirations. There is such a strong family likeness between many articles in the "Church Times," and the "Reply to the Abbé Martin," and the "Plain Reasons against Joining the Church of Rome;" there is so much similarity in the tone of thought, in the style and in the metaphors, that, although the articles are unsigned, their authorship is unmistakable. To give only one instance: no reader can fail to recognize the pen of the author of "Plain Reasons" in the series of articles entitled "Anglican Advantages," which appeared recently in the "Church Times."

Catholics may gather from the perusal of "Plain Reasons," in what estimation they are held by Ritualists; and Ritualists will be able to judge of the distance they have travelled from Rome, after having made so much progress towards her, and after having so long dreamed of a reunion as to which Catholics, so far as we know, have never encouraged any illusions, but, on the contrary, have always declared it to be impossible from the Ritualistic stand-point. The alternative of "submission or resignation" has not been placed before the Ritualists in so many words; but they have been told plainly enough that, in the presence of the Catholic Church, only one attitude—that of unreserved submission—is fitting for sincere Christians who believe in her divine prerogative.

The time for "Eirenicons" has gone by. War has now been declared, and the contest appears likely to be a bitter one. And already it has ceased to be chivalrous.

Are all visions of reunion to end thus, in attacks which we should stigmatize as false and calumnious, if we did not know that their author has, possibly, been misled, but that he is, doubtless, in good faith?

We must own that we have felt much and deeply pained in reading Dr. Littledale's "Plain Reasons;" and we think that those Ritualists who, having read the work, are willing to glance over these pages, will acknowledge that we have good cause to point out to them the danger of their position, whether regarded from the moral or the religious point of view.

We have no intention of writing an exhaustive answer to "Plain Reasons." Were we to attempt a rectification of all the uncertified anecdotes, the inaccurate quotations, the passages carelessly read and only half understood, the misrepresented premises and the unwarranted conclusions contained in that book, we should fill several volumes. Nor have we sufficient leisure for such an undertaking. We can only devote a few pages to the subject; but we trust that they will serve to convince all who are in good faith, that Dr. Littledale's assertions, so far from deserving implicit belief, require to be rigorously sifted.

Leaving to those Catholics who have more time at their disposal the task of answering Dr. Littledale at length, we shall proceed to make a few observations on "Plain Reasons"—firstly, on the shape in which it has appeared; secondly, on the authorities quoted in it; and, lastly, on the author's thesis, and on the arguments employed by him in his demonstration.

I. Hitherto, we have always considered that religious questions, affecting the salvation of souls, should be treated with a sobriety and earnestness proportioned to the importance of the subject under discussion, and with a due sense of the influence which every syllable written on such topics may have upon individual souls. Now, what at first especially attracted us towards England, and disposed us to examine the singular religious phenomenon which that country presents to our observation, was the tone of dignified courtesy still preserved there in the conduct of religious controversies. This, which we may call the English method, differed widely from continental countries, where the growth of democratic ideas and manners has introduced an extraordinary license of language as regards religion and morality; where every calumnious insinuation is eagerly welcomed; and where every weapon, every stratagem is considered lawful, provided only it be used against the Church. Whilst, then, we observed these tendencies generally throughout the continent, and, notably, amongst the irreligious portion of the French press, it seemed to us that English Protestant controversialists, particularly those of the High Church school, were remarkable for a loftiness of thought, a purity of views, a courtesy of language, and a dignity of tone, which did honour to their communion, to their literature, to their country, and to themselves. Whenever an uncalled-for attack was made upon the Catholic Church, whenever uncourteous expressions were used regarding her, it was by Dissenters, or by writers belonging to that portion of the English Church which is most closely allied to Dissent. The members of the High Church party, those especially belonging to the "English Church Union," and the "Association for Promoting the Unity of Christendom," spoke and wrote of the Catholic Church always in terms of courtesy, sometimes in those of praise and admiration, often in those of respect and affection. Now, for some time past, this state of affairs has altered much, and the alteration is particularly observable in the case of certain writers, amongst whom Dr. Littledale, unhappily, stands pre-eminently foremost.

We can hardly venture to say how offensive his controversial style appears to us, vulgarized and degraded as it is by comparisons with matters which have no real analogy—comparisons of the impalpable workings of the soul and conscience, the secret dealings of the creature with the Creator, to the material and even gross gratification of our bodily needs. Dr. Littledale has not scrupled to aver that many converts have entered the Church because they had a taste for Catholicism, precisely as they might have a liking for "oysters and pastry" ("Reply to the Abbé Martin," p. 39); or again because Gothic architecture inspired them with devotional feelings. Such are the facetiæ in which the reverend author indulges, not to speak of lower motives, which it pleases him to ascribe to men whose moral character is above suspicion.

In his new work, Dr. Littledale carries this style of argument to a wearisome excess. He compares conversion to emigration (p. 1), and Catholic controversialists to "interested emigration agents" (p. 2). When we seek to learn the designs of God in our behalf, "we are as likely to go wrong in our guess as a dog is in guessing what we think about and mean to do" (p. 60). This principle covers a wide space; if accepted, it would condemn three-fourths of the writings of the Fathers, of the School-men, and perhaps even those of Dr. Littledale himself. Elsewhere, he compares Our Blessed Lady to the Duchess of Kent, who was placed in the background by her daughter's accession to the throne (pp. 61, 62). The devotional practices of the Catholic Church are sneered at as charms and spells, resembling the fetichism and idol-worship of savages and heathens. Devotion to St. Joseph is characterized as a "huge tumour." The

Church praying for the souls in Purgatory is compared to the staff of a railway company which, in the event of a collision, should make great exertions to save the first and second class passengers, leaving the occupants of the third class carriages—that is to say, the poor, the miserable, the forsaken ones of this world—to their fate!

Is this a true representation of the Catholic Church? Is this fair or honest? Can any one assert that this faithfully portrays the action of that great body which, as all unprejudiced persons must acknowledge, is absorbed, to an extent approached by no other society upon earth, in furthering the spiritual and physical welfare of the poor? It is the Catholic Church which succours and consoles every known form of suffering. It is the Catholic Church which not only relieves the wants of the poor, but which preserves their self-respect, and makes them objects of reverence to their benefactors. It is the Catholic Church which has thrown such a halo of sanctity round poverty, as to make the rich strip themselves of their wealth and become beggars for the love of Christ's poor. It is not Anglicanism, not Ritualism, that could have achieved this. It is not to them that we owe the Mendicant Orders, the voluntary adoption of poverty by the rich in order to elevate the poor. It is not amongst them that homes for the aged, orphan asylums, and refuges for penitents have originated. The Catholic Church has not borrowed from Anglicanism or Ritualism her admirable machinery of charity, her Sisters of St. Vincent de Paul, her Brothers of the Christian Schools—for whom John Keble, of venerated memory, cherished such deep respect—her Little Sisters of the Poor, and innumerable institutions of the like character. Nor can any one seriously believe, that the Church which cares so tenderly for the poor during their earthly existence, forgets them when they have passed beyond the veil. This subject is treated by Dr. Littledale in a tone at once of levity and scepticism, which makes one fear that he is incapable of approaching it with the delicacy so necessary in touching upon what relates to the spiritual life. He writes, indeed, in a manner which goes far to prove that he utterly misunderstands the Catholic Church ; that he does not even know the A B C of her belief, her practice, or her laws. He is, evidently, in a state of mind in which he reads everything backwards, and interprets everything in a contrary sense to the reality.

II. We cannot, however, be much surprised that Dr. Littledale should be so completely mistaken on all points relating to the Catholic Church, when we inquire into the sources from whence he derives his information, and the authorities whom he has consulted. This is the second consideration which the perusal of his latest work has suggested to us.

The whole tone of the book, the discourtesy of the language employed, the vulgar levity with which serious charges are brought forward, the bitterness of the attacks, the severity and harshness of the expressions —all are characteristic of Dr. Littledale. His style is well known—too well known to be disguised. He evidently thinks that the hardest hitter must always be in the right, and consequently, he has a paradox always ready to hand. Exaggeration also suits his turn of mind. There are some kinds of argument which ought, so to say, to be put in quarantine, and which should never be admitted into religious discussions. Dr. Littledale's book is full of such arguments. Scandalous charges against men and things are scattered broadcast throughout the work ; and Dr. Littledale appears to take intense pleasure in recording them and giving them the sanction of his *imprimatur*. He would, nevertheless, we venture to think, be considerably puzzled if he was obliged to give any trustworthy authority in support of these charges. If Catholics were to write in a similar strain about Anglicans and

Ritualists, how indignantly would Dr. Littledale denounce them in his own special language, as liars and slanderers!

The authorities upon whom Dr. Littledale relies for proof of his accusations may be classed under three heads: he quotes (1) Protestant writers, (2) apostate Catholics, and (3) Catholic authors, both dead and living. We will say a few words respecting each class.

In the first place, respecting Protestant writers, Anglican or otherwise, we have little to remark. We shall not impugn their character in general terms. We readily admit that many of them are exceedingly candid, fair, and unprejudiced. Generally speaking, those who are most candid and unprejudiced, approach nearest to Catholicism; and not a few of these end by embracing the faith. Whatever Dr. Littledale may have said to the contrary in his "Reply to the Abbé Martin," he knows perfectly well that, during the last half-century, the Catholic Church has had the consolation of receiving into her fold hundreds of men and writers of this class.

Can he give us, in return, the names, not of a hundred, but of ten Catholic writers of distinction who have become Anglicans? If Anglicanism has occasionally received a few recruits from the Catholic ranks, we do not think that it has much reason to be proud of them. Not long since, a man, who had attained a certain celebrity, wished to attach himself to the Anglican communion: he tried his utmost to find some loop-hole through which he could creep into that Church. But Anglicanism would have none of him: it kept him at arm's length, and declined the honour which this deserter from the Catholic Church proposed to confer upon it. We are far from finding fault with the behaviour of the Anglicans in this conjuncture. On the contrary, we think they did well to show how perfectly they divined that some coalitions cannot fail to be harmful. Dr. Littledale has but to glance at the "Church Review," at the "Guardian," or even at his own organ of opinion, the "Church Times," to enter into what we have just said. He will there see that Anglicans and Catholics are tolerably well agreed in their opinion of Père Hyacinthe.

Having made this remark by the way, we now proceed to observe that, generally speaking, Protestant writers are by no means trustworthy guides as to the *belief* or the *practice* of Catholics.

If this is true in general, it is more especially true with regard to particular periods, particular facts, and particular persons. Hardly any Protestant author seems capable of giving an impartial account of such periods, facts, and persons. We do not mean to say that they intentionally pervert the truth; but, the mental atmosphere in which they live, and the prejudices which have been instilled into them, make it impossible for them to view fairly or judge calmly such persons and facts. Occasionally, indeed, Protestant writers have knowingly misrepresented occurrences, and slandered the Catholic religion. This is not a gratuitous assertion on our part; it is made by Dr. Littledale's own friends. We could quote numerous contemporary, or all but contemporary, authors who make this admission, from Hallam to Green, including Macaulay, Maitland, Froude, Pocock, J. H. Blunt, Dixon, besides many less celebrated writers, not to mention newspaper articles, and pamphlets.[1]

But it will be more to the purpose to quote Dr. Littledale himself. He says:—

"Two mendacious partisans, the infamous Foxe, and the not

---

[1] Even the "Church Times," the leading Ritualist journal, which is not over-particular when Catholicism is concerned, avows the one-sidedness of Protestant writers, when narrating the history of the English Reformation. I will quote only the beginning of an article on this subject ("Church Times," 1878, p. 595, col. 3): "No fact is more hopeful for the future of the Church of England and for the stability of the Catholic reforms of the last forty years, than the gradual vindication of the true history of the Tudor Reformation from the misrepresentations, *at first deliberate*, as with Foxe, and *afterwards traditional*, as with Strype and his followers, which had made its real nature and progress mere matter of mythical legend for all but a small minority of scholars."

much more respectable Burnet, have so overlaid all the history of the Reformation with falsehood, that it has been well-nigh impossible for ordinary readers to get at the facts; and prejudice has done its work, for an amiable clergyman of our own day, the Rev. F. C. Massingberd, Chancellor of Lincoln Cathedral, has, in all sincerity of heart, I doubt not, written a book which he calls 'The English Reformation,' which is about as trustworthy and accurate as the 'History of the Seven Champions of Christendom.'" ("Innovations," London, Mowbray, pp. 16, 17.)

We have but to change the name of the author and the title of his work, and we may then say with truth that—not an amiable, but—a very respectable clergyman belonging to the advanced Ritualistic section of the English Church, has written an account of Catholic dogma and Catholic practice about as truthful as the "History of the Seven Champions of Christendom."

Although Dr. Littledale is perfectly well aware of the untrustworthiness of the records left by the English and German Reformers in all matters relating to the Catholic Church, yet he does not scruple to refer to these very records when he sits in judgment upon Leo X. and on the acts of the Council of Trent. For instance: the forty-first paragraph of "Plain Reasons" is taken from the "Hundred Grievances of the German Nation;" and, not satisfied with quoting the said document in this portion of his work, he recurs to it several times (see pp. 171, 172). It is from Protestant sources, too, that he derives his criticisms upon the careers of Popes, the histories of Councils, the accounts of the Inquisition, of the Massacre of St. Bartholomew, and of the False Decretals.

He forgets that all these matters are, of their own nature, very obscure and very involved, and that they have been still further complicated by the ignorance or the wilful prejudices of the narrators; so much so, indeed, that, to use Dr. Littledale's own words, "it has been well-nigh impossible for ordinary readers to get at the facts." Keeping this just remark in mind, we must observe that these disputed facts of controversial history ought in no sense to influence intending converts. If people, before entering the Church, are to insist upon having every circumstance cleared up which appears to tell against Catholicism, it will be long, if ever, before they become Catholics. We are far from saying that the study of history may not be a means of bringing souls into the Church. Many, and some recent instances might be adduced to show that conversions are not unfrequently the result of such study. But this is not, and ought not to be the path trodden by ordinary men. In so saying, we merely give utterance to a common-sense proposition. Ordinary men cannot safely or speedily investigate such historical problems as the Massacre of St. Bartholomew, the False Decretals, the condition of the Papacy in the tenth, fourteenth, and sixteenth centuries. With respect to these matters we can but say again and again, " It is well-nigh impossible for ordinary readers to get at the facts."

Dr. Littledale perfectly realises the truth of this axiom; for, not only has he himself laid it down, and applied it to the events of the English reformation, but he especially mentions the Massacre of St. Bartholomew, in reference to which he says, " Everybody knows that there was a horrible massacre of the French Protestants on St. Bartholomew's Day, 1572, but few know that the atrocities which the Protestants themselves, ten years before, had committed at Beaugency, Montauban, Nismes, Montpellier, Grenoble, and Lyons, equalled, if they did not exceed, that terrible crime." ("Innovations," p. 19, and notes, p. 33.)

Moreover, Dr. Littledale has said elsewhere in the "Contemporary," 1877, ii., p. 113 :—

"Unlike those English Roman Catholics who rallied round Elizabeth Tudor when the tidings of the Armada came, and who were so ill requited for their loyalty, the Huguenot leaders from the first made common cause with the enemies of France, and from the revolt of Guyenne, under Henry II., in 1548, till the peace of Alais, under Louis XIII., in 1629, they were a constant element of national insecurity; while, in particular, their exploits during their brief tide of success in 1562 amply account for, though they do not excuse, the St. Bartholomew ten years later, and help to explain the slightness of the impression which their creed has produced on their nation."

It is strange that Dr. Littledale, under this conviction, should not have written more guardedly; and that he should, in spite of it, have persisted in laying this misdeed, with divers others, at the door of the Catholic Church.

We must take exception to the means employed by Catherine de Medicis and Charles IX. to rid themselves of Coligny and the Huguenot party; indeed, all must unite in the condemnation of assassination in itself. Those who wish to know the true cause of the Massacre of St. Bartholomew may be referred to what Dr. Littledale himself has said of the German Protestants :—

"Men had seen the horrible excesses which some of the so-called Reformers, such as Thomas Muncer and John Boccold of Leyden, the Anabaptist leaders at Munster, and Theodore the Adamite at Amsterdam, had committed, and it was not strange if they thought that the only way was to deal with the peril as we did with the Sepoy Mutiny, and with the cattle plague." ("Innovations," pp. 18, 19.)

If Dr. Littledale will but apply his own description of the German Protestants to their French brethren, he will see that it completely explains the Massacre of St. Bartholomew. The Huguenots had burned and pillaged large tracts of country: the ruins scattered throughout France still bear witness of the fact. Catherine de Medicis treated them—to quote Dr. Littledale's own words—as we treat "a cattle plague." That the Huguenots were deserving of chastisement is beyond a doubt. But the form, however, in which it was inflicted upon them was, and must always be considered as criminal in the highest degree. But the crime must be placed to the account of Catherine de Medicis, and of the regal power. It can in no sense be laid at the door of the Catholic Church, which had, absolutely, no share whatsoever in the business.[1]

III. The second class of authorities on which Dr. Littledale relies, is composed of those persons whom we have styled deserters from Catholicism ; men who would have been cast out by the Church, unless they had previously taken the precaution of quitting her of their own accord ; writers whose works may usually be found on the " Index," whose words breathe rancour and spread infection. Let not Dr. Littledale accuse us of slandering these authors. We will give a list of the so-called Catholic writers quoted by him, whom we have ranked in the second category: Van Espen (p. 37), and Oswald (p. 46), and Scipio di Ricci (p. 99), and Janus (pp. 104, 106, 146), and the Abbé Michaud (p. 164), and Liverani (p. 174),[2] &c. If we add to this list the names of Pomponio Leto and Paul Parfait, we shall have a tolerably complete catalogue of all the writers who have broken, to a greater or lesser degree, with the Catholic Church. Several of these authors are already on the " Index Expurgatorius," and all of them deserve to be there. It is an established principle that the fact of a work being on the "Index " adds much to its value in Protestant eyes; and this, no doubt, is the reason why Dr. Littledale thinks so highly of the above-named writers. But, in common fairness, he ought not to quote as Catholics, men whom the Catholic Church has rejected from her fold, or who have themselves deserted from her ranks. It does not surprise us that Dr. Littledale and his Ritualistic friends should have a great affection and esteem for Van Espen. So unsound and rash a canonist could not fail to enlist their sympathies. This is quite in keeping with the taste of the

[1] I hope some day to make public convincing proofs of the truth of this statement.
[2] I had inserted the name of Père Gratry, but have now erased it, remembering how nobly he has atoned for his momentary aberration.

day for what may be called morbid apotheoses. It is a time of sunshine for doubtful reputations. When excuses are found for Judas Iscariot, Van Espen surely may be treated with indulgence. Only, it would be as well if Dr. Littledale, when bringing out his next edition of "Plain Reasons," would not persist in calling Van Espen a "candid Roman Catholic," for in writing thus he gives us reason to think that the "candour" of his own simplicity is far greater than his acquaintance with his subject. In point of fact, every Catholic knows, or ought to know, (1) that all Van Espen's works are on the "Index;" (2) that Van Espen was under sentence of excommunication at the time of his death; (3) that he was a Jansenist; and (4) that his reputation is wholly and solely due to the Jansenists, who exalted him at the expense of Père Petau, from whom Van Espen borrowed many of his ideas—and that, without "candid" acknowledgment.

In short, Dr. Littledale's work is chiefly made up from pamphlets. It is an edition of Janus, adapted for the use of the Anglican Church in general, and of Ritualists in particular. But, can Dr. Littledale think this proceeding a justifiable one? Does he really, seriously, believe that these pamphleteers can be relied upon to speak the truth respecting the Catholic Church? Does he imagine that he will learn to know the Catholic Church more intimately through the utterances of Père Hyacinthe—that modern Prodigal Son, as much to be pitied as blamed, to whom the English Church half opened her doors, whilst taking good care to prevent him from crossing her threshold. Does he think that the ex-Père Hyacinthe, the Abbé Michaud, and the score or two of apostate priests who have disgraced the very name of Old Catholicism by adopting it, can teach him what the Catholic Church really is. The very idea presupposes a more than childlike simplicity of mind, and those who pin their faith on such authorities do.

not give very convincing proof of their discriminative powers.

Perhaps, however, Dr. Littledale may retort upon us Catholics, that we mete out precisely the same measure to Anglicans and Ritualists, and that he is therefore only giving us, in vulgar phrase, "a Rowland for our Oliver." Not so. We do not form our opinion of the Anglican and Ritualistic bodies from the individuals who pass from thence to the Catholic Church.

Even, if we did so, the two cases would not be parallel. Whatever Dr. Littledale may say, there is a vast difference between deserters from the Catholic Church, and fugitives from Anglicanism and Ritualism who take refuge within her fold. Dr. Littledale has written some passages on this subject, which are quite unworthy of his position. We feel certain that when he reads them over again, unbiassed by controversial prejudices, and unheated by polemical strife, he will bitterly regret having ever spoken in such terms of the Catholics of England. There are certain charges which a Christian, a just man, a gentleman can never bring himself to make against his opponents, unless he is forced thereto by a sense of duty; in which case he makes it a point of conscience to support his charges by such undeniable proofs as place the matter beyond question. Dr. Littledale has drawn down upon himself, and justly so, a shower of indignant protestations from friends and foes alike, to which we, reluctantly, unite our own. We, nevertheless, gladly accept his test: and, whenever he wishes us to do so, we will take, at random, a hundred names from the list of "Rome's Recruits," and the same number from amongst those who have left the Catholic Church to embrace Anglicanism, if indeed so many can be found. We have not the slightest fear of the result; the contrast between the two sets of men will be so marked, that even Dr. Littledale himself will be forced to recognize the difference. True, there are converts and converts: and, therefore, we have already said that we do not, after Dr. Littledale's fashion, take every convert to be a typical specimen of the communion which he has left. He judges the Catholic Church from the writings, literally overrunning with hatred and malice, of men like Janus. So far as we know, no English convert has ever produced any work in the style of Janus, any pamphlet or publication, against Anglicanism to which he dare not affix his name. We should never appraise Anglicanism at the valuation of a Protestant Janus or of an English Pomponio Leto. No, we judge Anglicans and Ritualists out of their own mouths, and from their own words written.

If Dr. Littledale would care to put this to the test, we can only say that we are quite prepared to form an estimate of Anglicanism and Ritualism from his own writings since the year 1860. He shall be his own judge, his own historian, his own theologian, his own critic—in short, whatever he pleases. Let him send us all the pamphlets he has written, all the tracts he has published, all the speeches he has made, and, above all, all the anonymous articles he has printed. From these we will undertake to extract a mass of doctrines, practices, laws, and rules, which may fairly represent to us the Anglican Church; and, when we have classified our extracts under the two heads of dogma and discipline, we shall ask him whether he himself believes that such a doctrinal and disciplinary Babel can possibly claim to be the Church of God, such as she is described to us by the holy Evangelists, and as she showed herself during the first five centuries. If Dr. Littledale believes that the Anglican communion can make good such claim, his idea of the Church must be a peculiar one. We cannot help hoping that, on reflection, he will own that Anglicanism and Ritualism, *as drawn by himself*, are very singular phenomena indeed; that they are of the earth, earthly, having about them nothing whatsoever of the divine.

IV. Lastly, Dr. Littledale quotes Fathers of the Church, theologians, Acts of Councils, writers of unimpeachable orthodoxy, prayer-books, and devotional works. Dr. Littledale's course of reading has been extensive rather than judicious. He either reads very carelessly, or he wholly mistakes his authors' meanings. Sometimes, indeed, the mistakes are of such a character as to make us suspect, with no breach of charity, that they are *not* purely accidental.

The catalogue of errors to be rectified in "Plain Reasons" is so lengthy that several volumes would hardly suffice to contain the corrections if supported by quotations and proofs. Many have already been pointed out; but the list is far from being exhausted. The more closely his quotations and statements are examined, the greater appears the need of such correction. Not having ourselves the leisure necessary for a thorough revision of the book, we will take only some of the more salient examples.

Dr. Littledale seems to have devoted a portion of his time to the perusal of the Fathers, and of the Acts of the Councils. But, much of this knowledge exists in his mind in an imperfect state, and seems to have been frequently acquired at second hand. In short, Dr. Littledale's reading has been too wide to be solid. He ought to have devoted several years to the preparation of this work, to which he has, probably, and from internal evidence, only given a few months. We may be thought too severe in our remarks, but it is not fair to write as Dr. Littledale has written, and to bring forward such serious charges against the Church of God and her members, without being fully prepared to substantiate every adopted statement, without having studied the subject dispassionately and exhaustively.

If there be one single point on which we should have expected strict accuracy from Dr. Littledale, it is on what relates to St. Peter as Head of the Church; for he has written several articles upon the "Petrine Claims" in the "Church Quarterly Review."

Now let us see his comments upon the text from St. Matthew's Gospel, xvi. 18. He says that the Catholic assertion as to St. Peter's claim to be considered the foundation stone of the Church is "contrary to the *unanimous* consent of the Fathers" ("Plain Reasons," p. 15), since the following Fathers explain—

"The Rock to be Christ, or faith in Christ, and not St. Peter: Origen; St. Hilary, Doctor; St. Chrysostom, Doctor; St. Isidore of Pelusium; St. Augustine, Doctor; St. Cyril of Alexandria, Doctor; St. Leo the Great, Pope and Doctor; St. Gregory the Great, Pope and Doctor; Venerable Bede, *Doctor;* St. Gregory VII., Pope. Whilst St. Epiphanius, Doctor, St. Basil the Great, St. Ambrose, and St. Jerome, Doctors, take it in both ways, leaning, however, more to the view that Christ is the Rock." ("Plain Reasons," p. 16.)

If we were to argue this question as thoroughly as it deserves, we should find that the Fathers interpret the word Rock as signifying (1) Christ Himself; (2) the Faith and the Confession thereof; (3) St. Peter. But these three interpretations given by the Fathers do not contradict or clash with one another. On the contrary, they are co-ordinate. Christ our Lord is Himself the chief foundation stone.[1] Then, faith and the confession thereof, in union with our Lord, forms, in a certain sense, the foundation of the Church. Lastly, St. Peter the Apostle, by his faith and confession of that faith, became one with Christ, who appointed him to a special office—that of representing the foundation stone of the Church upon earth. It is very evident that here there are no opposing or contradictory claims. It is the same idea viewed in different lights, and developed by the Fathers according to the subjects they were discussing or the texts they

---

[1] This is precisely what St. Leo says: "For thou art Peter; that is, whereas I am the inviolable rock, I, the corner stone who made both one; I, the foundation besides which no one can lay other; yet *Thou also art a Rock*, because thou art consolidated by My might, that what things are Mine alone by My power may be common to thee, by participation with Me." (See Mr. C. Allnatt, "Cathedra Petri," second edition, p. 25.)

were commenting. When they proclaim St. Peter to be the Rock on which the Church is built, they do not thereby deny that our Lord, that faith, is of the foundation—this they take for granted, even where they do not expressly affirm it. Similarly, when they speak of our Lord as the foundation stone of the Church, they do not exclude the claim of the Apostle to that title, although in a different and secondary sense.

Besides, the Fathers often give the three interpretations side by side—a clear proof that they do not consider either one of the three as nullifying the two others. Also, the very Fathers referred to by Dr. Littledale, teach that St. Peter *is* the Rock on which the Church is built, and apply the text from St. Matthew in the literal sense. These passages are quoted by Mr. C. Allnatt, in his most valuable work, entitled "Cathedra Petri" (Second edition, pp. 15-30). Origen does so in eight passages, St. Hilary in four, St. Chrysostom in five, St. Augustine once, St. Cyril of Alexandria and St. Leo the Great, each three times, St. Epiphanius and St. Basil the Great, each twice, St. Ambrose seven times, St. Jerome thrice.

In studying the writings of the Fathers we see plainly that all, or nearly all of them, understood the above-quoted text, as relating to St. Peter, in the literal sense. If they have applied it, occasionally, to our Lord, or to the faith and confession of St. Peter, it has been as a necessary and self-evident sequence. Not *one* Father of any weight has ever asserted that St. Peter *was not the Rock* on which the Church was founded by Christ Himself. Let Dr. Littledale contradict this statement, upon evidence, *if he can*. We now see how much or how little importance we are to attach to Dr. Littledale's statement that the interpretation given by Catholics to this text is contrary either to the "unanimous consent" or to the "great majority" of the Fathers. If we consult the Fathers quoted by him, we find that the greater number support the

Catholic view. The only quotation from St. Gregory the Great having any reference to the text, is usually considered as of doubtful authenticity. As for St. Gregory the Seventh, he has scarcely left any writings whatsoever. But we hardly think that Dr. Littledale would care to call him into court as a witness against St. Peter; for, if there ever existed a Pope prepared to claim and to exercise the prerogatives of St. Peter to the fullest extent, that Pope was Gregory the Seventh. And as regards the Venerable Bede, we know not if he be a Doctor of the Church in the Ritualistic Calendar—as may be inferred from Dr. Littledale's description above quoted; but, he certainly has not yet been raised to that rank in the Catholic Church. (See the "Tablet," 1880, i. p. 236.)

Here, then, we have Dr. Littledale contending that the Fathers, in calling our Lord, or faith, the foundation stone of the Church, thereby deprive St. Peter of all claim to that title. We have disproved Dr. Littledale's statements, and we most emphatically deny his conclusions.

We may, we trust, be dispensed from entering upon the discussion of the other Petrine texts—those of St. Luke[1] and of St. John, since full explanations of these will be found in all but the most elementary manuals of Catholic theology.

To proceed: one of the fundamental rules of criticism is, to interpret obscure passages by parallel passages which throw light upon them, or by their context. If we examine the passages quoted by Dr. Littledale in conformity with this rule, we shall find

---

[1] Dr. Littledale says, "*No Father whatever* explains it in the modern Ultramontane fashion" (p. 17). He proceeds to state that Bellarmine was the originator of the Ultramontane interpretation, about the year 1621, since when, Dr. Littledale continues, "St. Peter was infallible, and charged with guiding the faith of the other Apostles." The statement is utterly groundless, and the assertion as to the origin of the interpretation is equally false. Hundreds of writers prior to Bellarmine explained the text from St. Luke as referring to the infallibility of St. Peter and of his successors. (See the "Tablet," 1880, i. p. 237.)

that so far from the meaning being what he supposes it to be, it is often the exact contrary.

Let us take, for example, two passages, one from St. Leo the Great, the other from Pope Gelasius the First, on the necessity of communicating under both species. Dr. Littledale goes so far as to say: "Pope Leo the Great declares that abstinence from the chalice is a Manichæan heresy." ("Plain Reasons," p. 70.) Catholics are, consequently, Manichæans, according to Dr. Littledale! We hardly think that the worthy controversialist would take so extreme a view as this; but if his observation has any meaning at all, it shows him to be not particularly well versed in Church history; for the passage quoted by him from St. Leo, instead of proving the necessity of communion under both species, in reality makes against this necessity. In point of fact, the only reason which the holy Pontiff gives for imposing such a rule is to guard against the danger of committing an act of Manichæism. St. Augustine tells us that the Manichæans drank no wine because they believed that alcohol contained the evil principle. ("Lib. de Hæresibus ad Quodvultdeum, cap. xlvi., Patrol. Latina. Migne xlii., col. 37, line 11.) During the pontificate of St. Leo, the Manichæans were still numerous. Therefore, Catholics who did not receive the chalice ran the risk of being accused of Manichæism. St. Leo, consequently, seems to have ordered them to receive communion under both kinds. ("Homily," xlii., No. 5, Patrol. Latina. Migne liv., col. 279-280), and hence sprang the canonical rule, which was inserted in the Canon Law, and preserved there down to the Middle Ages.

Dr. Littledale cannot think that there is any cause for apprehending a revival of Manichæism in the present day. In France, at all events, the danger lies quite in an opposite direction.

Further on ("Plain Reasons," p. 41) Dr. Littledale asserts that the Papacy is purely human in its origin.

This he proceeds to demonstrate by a reference to the 28th Canon of Chalcedon, which said Canon was never received by the Church, and against which St. Leo protested most energetically. Can it be true that Dr. Littledale has actually ever read the Acts of this great Council? Did not the Fathers there assembled acknowledge in St. Leo the "Head of all the Churches" (Labbe, "Sacrosancta Concilia," iii. Session 1, p. 93), "the Ruler of the Universal Church," "he by whom Peter had spoken" (*Ibid.* Session 3, p. 368), he who, under the command of Christ the Lord, was the chief pilot appointed to steer the Church's bark? Let not Dr. Littledale, and still more, let not his unhappy because misguided readers, imagine that these were mere empty phrases. What was the subject of the reproof administered to Dioscorus by the Legates of St. Leo? They rebuked him for having held a Council without the permission of the Holy See; and they added, "Such never has been, nor can it be, lawfully done." (*Ibid.* Session 1, p. 94.) Then, too, is not the letter addressed by the Fathers to St. Leo, at the close of the Council, a convincing proof of the supremacy both of precedence and of jurisdiction, which has always belonged to the See of St. Peter? It says:—

"In the person of Peter, our interpreter, you preserved the chain of faith, by the command of our Master, descending to us. Wherefore *using you as a guide*, we have signified the truth to the faithful, not by private interpretation, but by one unanimous confession. If, where two or three are gathered together in the name of Christ, He is there in the midst of them, how must He have been with five hundred and twenty ministers? Over these, *as the head over the members*, you presided by those who held your rank : we intreat you, therefore, to honour our decision by your decrees; and, as we agreed with *the Head*, so let your Eminence complete what is proper for your children." (Harduin, ii. 660. See the "Tablet," 1879, ii. 814, col. 2.)

Do these passages, in Dr. Littledale's opinion, mean nothing? Why did he not mention them, if he were already acquainted with them? If he was ignorant of them, how culpable appears his carelessness in collecting references before writing on subjects of such high importance. It is true, that we shrewdly suspect Dr. Littledale of providing himself with references at second hand. To him, the writings of Janus and his Confraternity carry "confirmation strong as words of Holy Writ." Any one, on reading page 144 of his "Plain Reasons," with the accompanying footnote, would naturally come to the conclusion that St. Gregory the Great in no wise believed himself to be the Chief Bishop, or the Head of the Church Universal, and that he, therefore, rejected this title of Œcumenical, or Universal, Bishop, as savouring of profanity, or of pride. Such is the obvious meaning of the passage to which we refer, and in which there is not a single word about the real motives which induced St. Gregory to assume the title of "Servant of the Servants of God" instead of that of "Œcumenical Patriarch."

We will briefly glance at these motives, for the sake, not of Dr. Littledale, but of his readers. The successors of St. Gregory have retained the first title, whilst also adopting the second, although Dr. Littledale insinuates that such is not the case. The history of those times puts us in possession of the true reasons by which St. Gregory was actuated. The ambition of the Patriarch of Constantinople, John the Faster, urged him to claim the title of Œcumenical Patriarch in the year 587, and this title he refused to relinquish. Although St. Gregory declined the honorary title, he did not shrink from the duties and rights which the title imposed upon him. He proved this sufficiently in the struggle which he maintained for more than ten years against the selfish ambition of John the Faster and his successor. After this fashion does Dr. Littledale pervert history.

We might say much the same with regard to the

passages to which Dr. Littledale has helped himself from the writings of St. Jerome and St. Alphonsus Liguori, two doctors of the Church to whom he deals out very unequal justice. Father Ryder has, however, already attacked Dr. Littledale, very wittily, on the coolness with which he transfers dates, forges systems of moral theology, and invents literary history, whenever his cause seems to call for the performance of such controversial feats. It is impossible to read without a smile Father Ryder's amusing observations on the "schoolboy mistakes" ("Plain Reasons," p. 194), which Dr. Littledale condescendingly attributes to St. Jerome ("Tablet," 1880, i. p. 267), and on the ingenious manner in which the Latin of the original is mistranslated, whether consciously or not, so as to convey a meaning precisely the reverse of St. Jerome's. It is to be hoped that, on reverting to this melancholy series of literary blunders, the worthy controversialist may be inspired with a modicum of wholesome self-mistrust, and that in future he may be more cautious when speaking of the Fathers and Doctors of the Church, even should it be only St. Alphonsus Liguori who is under discussion.

We sometimes feel inclined to ask what St. Alphonsus Liguori can possibly have done to Dr. Littledale, to deserve such constant and persistent ill-usage at his hands? St. Liguori lived to a great age. His whole time was spent in good works—in giving missions, in preaching, in study, in hearing confessions. Amongst the Saints of modern times, few are more worthy of our unmixed reverence. In the midst of the toils of a most laborious ministry, this great Saint found time to write many spiritual books, and his theology, in particular, is held in high estimation. Catholics know well that from a literary point of view, St. Liguori's works are by no means faultless. But much may be excused in a bishop, in a missioner, engrossed by such various duties. We cannot expect from him that accuracy of scholarship which we look for in a student who can spend his learned leisure in a library with all his authorities at hand for instant verification. Even Dr. Littledale himself, scholar, critic, censor, controversialist though he be, *sometimes* needs that the same amount of indulgent allowance should be made for him; although, as he does not appear to be officially attached to any diocese, we do not suppose that the labours of the confessional, of the pulpit, or of the parish, can make any great demands upon his time; nor are we assured that on him, as on others of his Ritualist brethren, has been surreptitiously conferred (as is reported of some) the episcopal character. We have already shown that accuracy is not the strong point of "Plain Reasons."

Dr. Littledale had already been very severe upon St. Alphonsus Liguori in the "Reply to the Abbé Martin." In his new work he goes beyond all bounds. Probably, as the Church has recently conferred the title of Doctor upon St. Alphonsus, Dr. Littledale feels it incumbent on him to accuse the Saint, in his own choice language, of "idolatry, blasphemy, and mendacity, and of having taught others to do the like." ("Plain Reasons," p. 168. See also pp. 104, 108, &c). These are hard words; and, truly, it would seem that St. Liguori must have been guilty of great enormities to draw them down on himself. Dr. Littledale professes to have read the theology of this great Doctor of the Church, but he seems to have read it in such a superficial manner as never to have arrived at the faintest notion of the system which has made the name of St. Alphonsus so famous—the system of Probabilism. On this head the worthy author has made some most marvellous discoveries, some of which have been pointed out already in the "Tablet." ("Tablet," 1880, pp. 172, 173.) There is, therefore, no need to pursue this topic any further, and we shall content ourselves with recording Dr. Littledale's extraordinary find during his cruise amongst the Catholic moralists. Here, however, we must quote our author's own words, lest we, too, be accused of the like crimes with God's saint:—

"Is *explicit* belief in the mysteries of the Trinity and the Incarnation matter of necessity? And the answer is, that opinions are divided on this head, but *the more probable one is the negative*, because a mere implicit belief sufficed before Christ's coming, and therefore ought to suffice afterwards also."

This is what the Anglican divine has found out in Gury—a work which has become classical in our seminaries, printed at Rome, indeed, at the Propaganda! Naturally, Dr. Littledale draws from his own wonderful discovery the following conclusion, that "a Roman Catholic is at liberty to believe no more than Judas Machabeus!" ("Plain Reasons," p. 61.) Poor Dr. Littledale is certainly somewhat unlucky. It seems hardly possible for any one to have understood these passages in a sense so opposed to plain reason, and to their obvious meaning. He must read Catholic writers through spectacles which distort the vision. He could not, otherwise, misinterpret them as he does.

A despised and well-abused seminarist of barely a year's standing could have solved this mighty difficulty without consulting Père Gury's work. If Dr. Littledale had simply read the context with care, if he had even observed the reason which the theologian gives in support of his negative opinion, "because a merely implicit belief sufficed before Christ's coming," he would have seen that Roman Catholics have no more concern in the question than Judas Machabeus himself.

But Dr. Littledale may perhaps inquire: "Why are theological works written in Latin? Why do they touch upon questions of this nature?" To this we reply: "Why, good Dr. Littledale, do you insist upon taking up subjects which you have not been trained to understand, on which you exhibit your incapacity and ignorance by dealing with when untrained? If you wanted to study astronomy or geometry, you would begin by

mastering the first principles of those sciences. Try to do as much for theology, and for all ecclesiastical subjects. Being a Protestant, and a very ardent one to boot, you are incapable of understanding the Church and what appertains to her. In future, when you wish to write about her, give yourself time to read about her, beforehand, and take pains to read aright."

V. If we turn from these patristic, historical, and theological authorities, under the various travesties which they have suffered at Dr. Littledale's hands, to the consideration of the thesis which he has attempted to prove from their words, we arrive at the following conclusion. This doughty controversialist, this accepted champion of Anglican Ritualists, does not affect to think that his own communion, the English Church, is much nearer perfection than the Catholic Church. In point of fact, he could hardly advance such a proposition, remembering the terms in which he and his friends have written respecting the Established Religion. He " pleads guilty," and therefore his book

" Is defensive, not aggressive, and is not addressed to born Roman Catholics, nor does it undertake to measure their responsibility or to point out their duty. . . . But it is addressed to those who have seceded, or are tempted to secession, from the Church of England to the Roman communion : that they may see what is the true nature of the accountability with which they are charging themselves in following their own private judgment, rather than the providential order of God." (" Plain Reasons," prefatory note.)

This, it will be observed, is a commentary on the motto quoted by Dr. Littledale elsewhere : "Sparta is thy lot ; adorn her."

We shall not pause to show to what lengths the maxim here enunciated would lead, if it were followed out to the letter. Why, indeed, should not Dissenters from Dr. Littledale's own communion, Baptists or Congregationalists, why should not even Infidels, Mohammedans, or Buddhists make use of exactly the same argument employed by Anglicans and Ritualists: "God has placed us here; here let us remain"?

Dr. Littledale "pleads guilty." He has but one object in view—that of supplying an antidote to the influence of the Catholic "emigration agents," by showing that, all things considered, the Catholic Church is no better than the Anglican. And how does he prove his thesis? The style of controversy adopted by him might justify us in saying that he endeavours to establish his theory by means of exaggeration, falsehood, and forgery. But, we dislike applying such terms even to a not over-scrupulous author, as is Dr. Littledale. Controversy should never stoop to use abusive language. We should think it wrong to speak thus of any one, and Dr. Littledale's failings in this respect would be no palliation of our own. We will therefore say, in simpler and more courteous phrase, that Dr. Littledale tries to prove his argument by asserting:—1. That much in the Catholic Church is as doubtful as in the Anglican Church. 2. That the Catholic Church does not encourage the study of the Holy Scriptures. 3. That she has failed everywhere. 4. That she is immoral. We have a few words to say upon each of these points.

VI. According to Dr. Littledale the Catholic Church possesses no certainty as to her dogmas, her orders, her sacraments, or her moral teaching. She has no means of rectifying this defect, since infallibility neither has been, nor can ever be, of any use in the matter. Her clergy are not united amongst themselves; the regulars hate the seculars, and the seculars cannot endure the regulars. The Catholic laity are divided into two camps, the "maximisers" and the "minimisers," who are always making war on each other. *Et cetera.*

In reading all these charges, we feel inclined to ask ourselves whether we are not under some delusion, whether we have not mistaken one word for another?

"The Catholic Church uncertain?" who will believe this on Dr. Littledale's mere testimony? Does Dr. Littledale himself believe what he says? Let him only question the first Catholic whom he may chance to meet, and he will see that in the mind of that Catholic not the shadow of hesitation exists as to where he must go for the sacraments and all the essentials of the faith. "The Catholic Church divided against herself?" Can Dr. Littledale be speaking seriously? Has he no eyes for what goes on around him? Does he never read a newspaper? Do not the events of the last ten years, do not even the incidents of the present struggle in France, supply a very telling commentary on the assertions of this Ritualistic counsel? Are the clergy, are the Catholics of France in antagonism to each other? Has Dr. Littledale heard, we will not say many dissentient voices, but even a solitary one? When facts are so patent, it is difficult to believe that educated men, not to say ministers of religion, can be found to wilfully misrepresent and distort them.

VII. "The Catholic Church neglects the study of the Holy Scriptures." We had always thought that the Ritualists, whilst setting a due value on the Holy Scriptures, did not cling, as other Protestants do, to the famous maxim of "The Bible and the Bible only." But on this point Dr. Littledale has undeceived us; for he makes texts of Scripture, interpreted—be it observed—after his own fashion, the test by which everything is to be judged, condemned, or approved. As we cannot enter upon this subject at the length which its importance deserves, we will only put the following questions to Dr. Littledale. Does he consider the work of destructive criticism current in the Church of England, which casts doubt upon every incident recorded in Holy Scripture, to be any proof of real progress? Does he think that the writings of German

Rationalists, already so much admired and studied in the Establishment, have contributed to strengthen belief in the divine authority of the Bible? We cannot think so; and we need not go beyond the Anglican territory to find more than one conspicuously placed dignitary, with whom Dr. Littledale lives in full communion, to whom the books of the Old and New Testament are purely human productions like any other writings.

The Catholic Church destroys nothing. What she believed in the sixteenth century, that she believes now. The same Bible is in her hands; she treats it with the same reverence; she explains it to her children in the same way; she recommends it as heretofore to their perusal under certain conditions and subject to certain precautions. And the fullest justification of her conduct is to be found in the inconsistencies and extravagancies which both Anglican and Rationalistic writers have fallen into in their Biblical criticisms. When once the attitude of the Catholic Church in this matter is thoroughly known and explained, an attack such as Dr. Littledale's falls helplessly to the ground.

He who writes in this strain must be predetermined to believe any calumny however self-contradictory, provided it be aimed at the Catholic Church. If Dr. Littledale had taken reasonable pains to inform himself as to what goes on amongst Catholics, he would have known that in every seminary, (1) the pupils have to attend courses of lectures upon the Holy Scriptures; (2) they read daily a prescribed portion of both the Old and New Testaments, so as to go through the whole Bible in a given period; (3) at an appointed time each day the students assemble together and read, kneeling, several verses from the New Testament; (4) seminarists and priests usually carry about them a Greek or a Latin Testament; (5) all priests are specially desired to continue through life the practices which they have begun in the seminary; and the greater number faithfully carry out this recommendation, as may be seen in the many biographies of saintly priests which, from time to time, are given to the world. It seems to us that no better plan could have been devised to ensure a thorough acquaintance with the Holy Scriptures, than this constant, assiduous, reverent perusal. Can it be true that, as Dr. Littledale asserts, Catholics are unable to study the Divine writings for want of works on the subject?

Dr. Littledale appears to rate the value of a book at its weight avoirdupois. Himself an indefatigable and voluminous writer, he thinks less of the contents of a work than of the space it will occupy on a library shelf. This is scarcely a fair mode of judging. In this case we surely ought to say, *Non numerantur sed ponderantur.* What has been the result of all the rationalistic efforts of the last three centuries? 1. They have destroyed much. 2. They have tried to build up again a portion of what has been destroyed. For example: What are the Ritualists now endeavouring to do? With infinite toil and labour, and with inadequate success, they are striving to raise once more a few scattered stones of the building which their forefathers deliberately overthrew, and which their contemporaries would rather leave lying undisturbed. Was it worth while to accomplish the widespread ruin of the Reformation, only to have, after three hundred years, the trouble of repairing the havoc that was then wrought? Here we may commend to Dr. Littledale's earnest consideration the judicious reflections addressed to him by Mr. Thomas Arnold in the "Month," and recalled to his recollection by Mr. Orby Shipley in the "Tablet." Catholics preserve instead of destroying; they correct and improve whenever the march of modern progress calls for such correction and improvement. The Catholic Church knows how to turn even the destructive works of Rationalists to account. If any fragment of truth is contained therein, she draws it forth; she takes the honey, and leaves the poison.

Did Dr. Littledale know the Catholic Church better, he would not write of her as he has written, and he would speak of her in far different terms.

VIII. The third charge against the Catholic Church is, that wherever she has set her foot she has failed. All her efforts have resulted in "conspicuous failure. . . . Its influence on a larger scale is little short of disastrous."

The Catholic Church has failed in Europe, in Asia, in America, in all countries where she has established her missions! But, if it be so, why do Dr. Littledale's friends, why do the Rationalists and the free-thinkers throughout the world, call upon the secular arm to help them in their work of crushing down the Church by stifling her under a mass of penal laws? Here, we are told, is a Church which is gradually and surely destroying herself, which, morally, intellectually, and politically, is crumbling away year by year; yet, her enemies, instead of leaving her to perish by this natural decay, rouse all the low and bad passions of human nature against her, frame special laws to coerce her, place her under the ban of modern civilisation, close her churches and schools, rob, imprison, or exile her priests, and, in the name of liberty and enlightenment, take upon themselves to play the part of bigoted persecutors. The all-powerful Bismarck cannot sleep in peace so long as Catholics inhabit the German empire. The French Republic is hardly established before it begins an anti-clerical war to the knife. And this needless task is undertaken in order to destroy a building which is falling of its own accord!

How can Dr. Littledale expect his intelligent fellow-countrymen to believe such ridiculous and self-contradictory assertions? He must surely be laughing at his readers "in his sleeve," and sardonically laughing at himself into the bargain, when he writes in this strain. How can it be alleged that the Church in France is a "conspicuous failure" when in less than eighty years, and in the face of innumerable obstacles, she has raised herself again from the ruins of the Revolution?

But, whilst we are told that the Catholic Church is a "conspicuous faillure," we are gravely informed that Ritualism is "a marvellous success, unparalleled in the world's history." ("Plain Reasons," p. 197.) We hope that Dr. Littledale really believes his own statement. But many grains of salt must be added before it is accepted, we do not say by Catholics but, by Ritualists themselves, or by one educated Englishman out of a thousand.

We do not think that we can be accused of blindness to all that is remarkable or interesting in Ritualism, nor of despising its results. But, still, we may be suspected of underrating it for controversial reasons. We have, therefore, decided upon quoting from "Notes on my Life," a late volume by the well-known Archdeacon Denison, a work which Dr. Littledale in his "Reply to the Abbé Martin," commended to our perusal. The Venerable Archdeacon thus sums up the result of fifty years' continuous efforts, in these remarkable words — remarkable, as coming from a leader of the Ritualists :—

"'The Establishment of England representing for the time the Church of England, has been overcome by the World of England, and lies prostrate at its feet. I am not forgetting here, nor am I unthankful for that Revival of Religion within the 'Establishment' which has been manifested during the above period *in individuals and in congregations*. But of the *corporate* life of the Church of England as represented by the 'Establishment'—that life by which it stands or falls—I say that it has been overcome by the life of the World of England. . . . The logic of facts is not to be overcome." ("Notes on my Life," p. 385.)

It seems to us, on taking a survey of the existing state of affairs in England, even as regards the most advanced portion of the Anglican communion, that it would be becoming in Dr. Littledale to speak with very much more diffidence of the "unparalleled" Ritualistic "revival," and with somewhat less acrimony of the Catholic "failures." The truth, perhaps, could be more nearly approached by a "candid" interchange of those phrases.

IX. The fourth general charge levelled at the Catholic Church by Dr. Littledale is that of immorality.

1. The Church is immoral in her teaching, for she teaches Probabilism and the theology of St. Alphonsus Liguori. To this charge we can only reply by recommending Dr. Littledale to resume his studies, and to try to find out the nature of Probabilism, and what St. Alphonsus Liguori's theology really is, before writing about either the one or the other.

2. The Church is immoral in her devotions, for she worships the Blessed Virgin Mary, St. Joseph, the Sacred Heart, saints, and images.

On this point so much may be said, and of that much so little would be necessary for persons in good faith, that on the whole, we think it better to pass over this imputation than to treat it superficially; particularly as a small amount of common sense, and a slight knowledge of the Catholic faith, suffice to show the injustice of the charge.

3. The Church is immoral, because, speaking generally, her clergy are corrupt themselves, and are the cause of corruption in others: those who become Catholics only do so in order to gratify without restraint their lower and baser inclinations.[1]

[1] See the "Reply to the Abbé Martin," pp. 45, 61; "Plain Reasons," p. 130. I have already said that Ritualists nowadays speak and write about the Catholic Church in precisely the same strain as the Evangelicals. There is really no difference in tone between Dr. Littledale's writings and the accompanying extract from the "Rock," 1880, 170, col. 2 :—"Romanism is error of the worst kind. Spiritually, it destroys souls; morally, it corrupts individuals; socially, it degrades and enslaves families; and politically, it would rob the nation of its independent existence. Patriotism would be extinguished, liberty

When we read these and similar accusations so frequently repeated in the "Reply to the Abbé Martin," and reappearing in "Plain Reasons," we feel compelled to ask who and what Dr. Littledale can be? We are not surprised that newspaper writers of the present century, the correspondents of the revolutionary press, the "République Française," the "Mot d'Ordre," and the like, should bring forward these shameful and degrading charges, wholly unsupported by evidence. This may grieve, but cannot astonish us. But that a man of education and position in the Establishment, a High Church clergyman, should reproduce these 'base insinuations, the mere gossipings of people as devoid of religion as of character—gossipings which, though baseless, are yet most hurtful to the reputation of worthy men—this, indeed, may well cause us to wonder, and to ask ourselves whether Dr. Littledale has ever taken to heart the commandment against bearing false witness? How can he thus wantonly attack a body of men, estimable in themselves, looked up to and trusted by their flocks? How, without either proof or provocation, can he soil his hands by casting mud at them?

His conscience does not prick him, and he does not consider himself under the slightest obligation to make reparation for the wrong he has done, because he has only attacked a body, instead of assailing individuals, God's Church instead of an unit in God's creation. What, then, can be his notion of common fairness and literary honesty, to say nothing of Christian charity?

To speak candidly, we think that Dr. Littledale should rather have cut off his right hand, than have allowed himself to write as he has done. We hope and believe that he himself would willingly retract the insults he has proffered, and that he now bitterly regrets having

annihilated, truth exiled, and national prosperity rendered impossible, if Popery were to regain its ancient ascendency in this country. It is therefore no token of bigotry or intolerance to oppose it to the utmost, but the contrary; and Christian duty, as well as regard for the best interests of man, requires a constant testimony against it."

been so far carried away by temper and prejudice. We think that he must have suffered enough already to atone for his faults, since it is not Catholics alone who blame him, but all honest men, all men of gentlemanlike feelings, specially some amongst his own friends.

If Dr. Littledale, instead of bringing vague defamatory charges against the priesthood on the authority of anonymous writers whose only object is to bring religion itself into discredit, really wishes for official statistics on this subject, we are ready and willing to meet him; and we have no hesitation in saying that there is no class of men in France superior in morality to the Catholic clergy. Quite recently, one of the worst of the many newspapers which sprang into being during our political disturbances published, under the title of "An Ecclesiastical Year," a list of the sentences passed on priests and religious of both sexes for crimes or offences. The total number of convictions amounted to eighty-three, of which not above thirty were on criminal charges; and even this number might have been further reduced upon strict examination. A newspaper which cannot be suspected of clerical proclivities, the "Figaro," made the following observations on the subject:—

"These statistics furnish a most convincing proof of the general good conduct and the high moral standard prevailing amongst the French clergy. We can demonstrate this at once by giving, from the 'République Française,' the following official report.

"According to the last census there are in France 160,000 priests and religious of both sexes.[1] If, out of this number, 83 have been sentenced for various crimes and offences, we get a percentage of 1 criminal for every 2000 priests or religious. The same census gives the whole population of France as something over 36,000,000.

---

[1] The "Figaro" is mistaken on this point: the official statistics for 1876, which essentially hold good for the present year, give the following numbers:—

Priests,	55,269
Religious men,	30,287
Religious women,	127,753
In all,	213,309

See further statistics in the Addendum, p. 288.

Out of this number, over 170,000 have been convicted of crimes and offences, giving a percentage of 9 criminals for every 2000 Frenchmen. Thus, according to the very official papers quoted by the 'République Française' to support the hypothesis of clerical immorality, we find that the morality of the clergy may be termed irreproachable, since under a government which shows them no mercy and which strikes them without a hearing, the proportion of offenders belonging to their ranks is only 1 in 2000, whilst the proportion of lay criminals is nine or ten times as great. If we compare the morality of the clergy with that of other classes, we shall not find, in any, fewer offences : whilst in those other classes, we find a large proportion of crime, and notably in the atheistic and revolutionary ranks. It is high time that the whole country should know the truth ; and it is the more necessary that it should be told in the teeth of that morbid irrational hatred which has been stirred up against the clergy. Official documents, legal statistics, scientific observations, all go to prove that, as regards morality, the clergy are the flower of the country, and that the most religious portions of the population contain the fewest criminals; whilst the criminal classes are chiefly recruited amongst the free-thinking, atheistic, and revolutionary members of society."

Since Dr. Littledale, by his unbecoming and ungentlemanlike attacks, has forced us to enter upon this extremely unpleasant subject, we may be permitted to allude to one of the most unwarranted assertions in his " Reply to the Abbé Martin." He says (p. 61) :—

"And, to touch on another side of the same topic, I learn that, (1) without counting ecclesiastics degraded or interdicted as a punishment for misconduct, (2) *at least* one hundred French priests, and (3) a *still larger* number of Italian ones, (4) abandon their clerical life yearly and retire into a lay position." (See also the "Contemporary Review," Nov. 1878, p. 823.)

We omit the remainder of this painful passage, in which Dr. Littledale proceeds to draw his own conclusions from the statement he has just made. Here we have four distinct allegations, corroborating each other, and forming, altogether, a grave and serious charge—a charge which, if true, would bear witness to a most deplorable state of affairs. Let us therefore take these allegations one by one.

Dr. Littledale perfectly understands the art of

accumulating charges until he reaches a climax in his indictment. This, however, does but add to his culpability.

1. Dr. Littledale is not referring to bad priests who have been degraded or interdicted as a punishment for misconduct. Such as these he leaves to their fate, and does not take them into account at all. He merely alludes to them so as to make it appear that they form a very large class. Thus, he indirectly blackens the reputation of the Catholic Church without openly attacking her. There is something cowardly, almost dastardly, in these covert insinuations against those who are powerless to defend themselves. If one hundred pious and virtuous priests, whom Dr. Littledale is almost ready to canonise, abandon the priesthood every year of their own free-will, how many more must there not be who are forced to quit it as a punishment for misconduct? They may, probably, be put down at one thousand, at the lowest. This being the case, who can wonder at the falling off in the number of the French clergy?

Now, is there any truth in all this? There may be, according to Dr. Littledale; but, in reality, there is not an atom of truth. If a priest, as sometimes unfortunately happens, misconducts himself, the Catholic Church has not, like the Anglican Church, been deprived of her spiritual weapons. She can punish the guilty. But, when she punishes, she tempers justice with mercy; and she strives to save the culprit, and to raise him again from the degradation into which he has fallen. She never gives him up till all hope of rescuing him is at an end.

How many priests have joined the Old Catholic body in France? Not above fifteen altogether; and out of the fifteen, not one is of unblemished character, from M. Loyson to M. Deramey. This is not a mere supposition, it is a fact, and a fact which is in itself a sufficient answer to Dr. Littledale's insinuations.

We may now see for ourselves how thoroughly he understands his subject; how accurately he states his case; and what implicit belief may be placed in his statements!

Dr. Littledale does not take into account those priests, who, worn out by the toils and struggles of their parochial ministry, retire from the active duties of their calling to devote themselves to the care of their own souls. Even if these were added to the list, Dr. Littledale's assertions would be equally groundless. But he professes to speak of priests who, wounded and irritated by the shameful treatment which they meet with from their bishops, take of their own accord a step which of all others is the most serious for a priest to take, viz., that of quitting the priesthood, and of living in the world simply as a layman. Here we have the case exactly stated. Dr. Littledale is nothing if he be not exact. But it is possible to be too exact, and so to leave oneself no available loop-hole by which to escape in the event of any mistake coming to light.

Dr. Littledale affirms that "(1) *at least one hundred French priests* (2) abandon their clerical life and retire into a lay position," and this "(3) not as a punishment for misconduct" (p. 66). This is, indeed, a most serious charge—a charge which no fair-minded man would originate, or even repeat, in a Review, or in any book written of honest purpose, unless he had convincing and authoritative proofs wherewith to confirm his assertions. Dr. Littledale has nothing to offer by way of proof or authority beyond the ominous words, "I learn." Well, we hereby challenge Dr. Littledale: (1.) To give us some proof of what he alleges—not mere hearsay, of which his pamphlets are over full but authoritative proof, such as would be admitted in an English court of law. We challenge him (2.) To give us the names, not of a hundred priests, not even of ten, but to give us the name of one only, during, let us say, each of the last ten years, of those who are said *yearly* to "abandon their clerical life and retire into a lay position," and that not as a punishment for misconduct. We challenge him, and in so doing we have little fear of his accepting the challenge.

After this, we believe that Dr. Littledale's fellow-countrymen, if not himself, will allow us to pass over the "still larger number of Italian" priests whom he allows himself to malign in a like fashion, although we could meet him on this ground likewise.

If it be true, as Dr. Littledale informs us—though we are far from believing it upon his mere *ipse dixit*—that nine or ten Anglican clergymen yearly "abandon their clerical life," &c., then the proportion of these clerical defections is nine or ten times greater in the Anglican Church than in the Church of France, for in the Church of France, defections of this kind—that is, unconnected with clerical misconduct—are absolutely unknown.

This is a specimen of the extent to which Dr. Littledale's information and statements are to be relied upon. And it may be added, that it is both improper and foolish to treat so serious a subject as religious controversy must ever be in this tone of combined levity and impertinence.

The last and crowning accusation of immorality is, that Catholics in general, and Catholic controversialists in particular, are totally unworthy of belief; that they alter texts, make use of doubtful and apocryphal writings, and that they do all this wilfully and to set purpose. ("Reply to the Abbé Martin," p. 61; "Plain Reasons," *passim*—see, more especially, pp. 99-112.)

Here Dr. Littledale makes our task an easy one. We have no wish to palliate the blunders or the carelessness of Catholic writers. But we maintain that of such blunders, none are committed designedly. No one but Dr. Littledale could entertain such an idea, nor would be capable of committing it to paper, as he has done in "Plain Reasons." We should like to ask Dr. Littledale two questions: 1. Is he quite sure that the documents quoted by Catholic writers are always of such doubtful authenticity as he supposes them to be?[1] 2. Is he quite sure that the inaccurate quotations, of which he speaks, were made purposely to deceive? We trust that he may be moved by an impulse of charity, of kind-heartedness, of candour, and that he will be less ready, in future, to impute low and bad motives to worthy men. We hope that he will not suspect dishonesty in others, unless it is so self-evident that doubt is no longer possible, and that, even then, he will be mercifully disposed towards them. This merciful spirit may most fittingly be displayed by Dr. Littledale, since he sorely needs that it should be exercised towards himself. He who so freely mutilates passages, and who so rarely takes the trouble of verifying contexts, should not presume to impute to authors opinions and sentiments the very reverse of those entertained and openly avowed by them. He should not venture to include amongst Catholic writers, men whose works have been placed upon the "Index." He should not dare to pervert his authorities before quoting them against his opponents, as in the case of these well-known lines by Father Faber, with

[1] Let me take an example: Dr. Littledale is of opinion that the Homilies upon the Blessed Virgin Mary, attributed to St. Gregory Thaumaturgus and St. Methodius, cannot be of their composition. Several Catholic critics hold the same view. Their reasoning may, however, be called in question, since the Homilies of St. Gregory were very early translated into all the Eastern tongues, and this circumstance would be difficult to account for if the writings themselves were apocryphal. Dr. Littledale undertakes to show that one of St. Methodius' homilies was not written by that saint, because it alludes to the Purification of the Blessed Virgin—this feast having only been established A.D. 542, two hundred years after the death of St. Methodius. This would appear unanswerable to those who are not well acquainted with early ecclesiastical writings. But, those who have any knowledge of the Fathers are well aware that (1) the titles of the homilies were not always given by the writers, but were often added afterwards; (2) that, long before 542, the Fathers had written commentaries on the second chapter of St. Luke; (3) that, consequently, the Fathers composed homilies on the Purification, previously to the institution of the Feast of the Purification. Therefore, it is not surprising that we should find homilies by the early Fathers on the Feast of the Purification, because the *homily* may have been written by them, though the *title* is not theirs.

the correct version of which he might have been and he ought to have been perfectly acquainted:—

> "With her Babe in *her* arms, *sure* Mary will be,
> Sweet Spouse of our Lady, *our* pleader with thee." [1]

All these inaccuracies, these mutilations, these exaggerations are indulged in by Dr. Littledale, not in one or two or ten instances, but a hundred times. His book is full of direct suppressions and subtle insinuations. Yet, all the while, he accuses his adversaries of falsehood and forgery. Let us put the matter plainly before him. Either he has made all these misrepresentations intentionally, and of full knowledge; in which case we may fairly retort upon him those charges of falsehood and forgery which he is so ready to bring against others—charges which it is unpardonable to introduce into a religious controversy. Or else, these misrepresentations have been made in ignorance, and are due chiefly to Dr. Littledale's over haste to seize upon the first weapon that came to hand; and, in this case, he must see for himself that he ought to make large allowances for those weaknesses of human nature, of which he has himself given so many and such conspicuous proofs.

X. We have now done with Dr. Littledale.

We have not said all that we might, all that we should have said, for, instead of these few pages, many volumes would have been required to correct, at length, all the inaccuracies, the mistakes, and the blunders contained in that author's "Reply to the Abbé Martin" and in his "Plain Reasons."

But we think that we have said enough to cast grave doubts upon (1) the amount of trust to be placed in Dr. Littledale's works in general, and in the

---

[1] "Plain Reasons," p. 52. Faber's words (see "Tablet," 1880, i. p. 140), are:—
"With her Babe in *my* arms, *surely* Mary will be,
Sweet spouse of our Lady, *my* pleader with thee."

two pamphlets which we are now refuting, in particular; (2) the propriety of "the distinguished patronage. which has been accorded to the 'Reply to the Abbé Martin'" by the Church Union, and to the "Plain Reasons" by the Christian Knowledge Society.

Dr. Littledale's two pamphlets sin deeply and sin repeatedly. They sin not only against historical, theological, religious, and moral truth; they sin against charity, against refinement, and against social courtesy. From this point of view we do not regret their publication. They may indeed do much harm to people who are ignorant of, and prejudiced against Catholicism; but, on the other hand, they may do an untold amount of good to the many upright, candid, pious souls by whom the Ritualistic, and more especially the High Church ranks are filled.

Dr. Littledale's pamphlets are so evidently dictated by ill-feeling and prejudice, and the rules of good breeding are so completely ignored by him, that a reader of any refinement of mind instinctively draws back from one who seems thus regardless of the first principles of Christian moderation and charity.

When once a feeling of distrust has entered the mind, it is not easily uprooted; and we think, therefore, that Dr. Littledale's writings will have an effect totally opposite to that which they were intended to produce. Many of his readers will be desirous to know more of that Church which he treats with such manifest unfairness; and they will have little difficulty in finding out for themselves the mistakes, inaccuracies and contradictions which abound in his works. These are "the sort of things which send men over to Rome."

We have written these pages without the slightest feeling of ill-will towards Anglicanism, or even towards Dr. Littledale; and if we have in any degree helped to smooth the path for some few of those many earnest souls who are seeking the truth in all singleness of heart, we can only return thanks to Him from Whom alone all good proceeds. If we have done aught to further the salvation of but one amongst them, we are rewarded far, very far indeed, beyond our deserts.[1]

[1] This book was all but printed when the Paris correspondent of the "Guardian" wrote as follows (August 25, 1880, p. 1122, col. 1 and 2) on the subject treated on pp. 238 and 245-250: "If M. Paul Bert thinks, by his distinction between 'monks' and '*curés*' to spread disunion and jealousy between the different orders of the French clergy, I apprehend he will find himself very much mistaken. He may feel assured that they are both at least aware of one thing, and that is, that, in the eyes of M. Paul Bert, six of the one are about equal to half-a-dozen of the other; and that, if he is trying now to set one against the other, it is only with the expectation and design of getting rid of both at a later period. That anything like widespread disaffection exists in the ranks of the French clergy, I, for one, do not believe. The whole body is rooted in and bound to the Roman Catholic Church, even as it is. Again and again I have repeated that they would hardly be men if it were otherwise. What other result could be expected from subjects who, after being first carefully selected, have been in training (and such training) with that very object in view, from the time they were eight years old? The branch will retain almost against every effort a bent once so firmly given to it. The question is, I admit, a difficult one to get at, and many assertions are put forward in the contrary direction. But what do they amount to, and what does the evidence put forward in support of them mainly consist of? Tittle-tattle, picked up by strangers passing through the country, at *tables d'hôte*, or in railway carriages, who meet with and hear wonderful stories of disaffection from some vicar who happens to be out of humour for the moment with his *curé*, or some *curé* with the vicar-general of his diocese, and who lets off the steam to any safe auditor, just as an English clergyman will abuse his Bishop, or—write to the 'Guardian;' neither of which the other can certainly do. But such men would scout the idea of directly breaking with their Church, if proposed to them; and very often, I believe, they take a pleasure in gulling and laughing in their sleeve at their too eager heretical interrogators. At all events, what results ever come from all that is put forth on the subject? There are absolutely none; not a man budges. What are such vague assertions, even if they could be multiplied a thousandfold, against such a single fact, for instance, as that *not one respectable member* of the French clergy, out of some forty thousand, has been found to join the well-intentioned but utterly unpractical and ill-judged movement lately inaugurated in this place? Such a fact alone speaks volumes; for it is simply impossible that, out of such a mass, the courage alone to take the step should have failed in all, had the desire to do so been present. Who followed when even a far greater man, Lamennais, led the way in revolt? And how many priests joined *la petite église?* and what has become of it and its absurdities? I was shown one of its prayer-books the other day as a curiosity, which is perhaps the only relic now left of it. *It must be remembered, too, that the conduct of the French clergy of the present day is, as a rule, exemplary.* There are no instances of gross immorality among them, as in Reformation times, either to shock the public conscience or drive the better disposed out of their ranks. This of itself is a great bond of union; and it has been shown by the way in which the entire clerical body, secular and regular, prelates, heads of congregations, *curés* and monks both, have all stuck together and made common cause against the Decrees, without a single dissentient voice or a single defalcation. M. de Freycinet's promised bill must please all, or it will be accepted by none; and M. Paul Bert may equally satisfy himself that his proposed election cry will have little effect upon the body at which it is aimed, whatever it may have upon the constituencies."

APPENDIX.

ON THE PRESENT STATE OF THE CHURCH IN FRANCE.

IN order to understand the present condition of the Church of France we must begin by going back to the year 1789. At that period, the Church, as it was represented by the clergy in the midst of the people, constituted the first order in the State.

According to the latest research, there were at that time 27,000 monks and 37,000 nuns, whilst 70,000 priests, beneficed abbés, and bishops formed the secular clergy.[1] The Church owned a fifth part of the soil, and received from her real property, or from the income assigned to her, a revenue which exceeded £9,000,000 sterling.[2]

We know what became of this revenue during the great Revolution. The State confiscated all ecclesiastical property, while granting a fixed income as compensation, which it soon ceased to pay, and became bankrupt four or five years after the appropriation of more than four milliards of francs, equal to eight or ten milliards of our money. The sacred buildings were applied to profane uses, were suffered to fall into disrepair, were sold, and in some cases were even intentionally destroyed.[3] The priests were murdered in prison, were guillotined, were drowned in the Loire or the Rhône, were exiled or transported to Cayenne. It was with difficulty that some escaped into the forests and contrived to continue to fulfil the duties of their office. The Revolution did all in its power to substitute for these men what were called constitutional priests—priests who were in general little esteemed, and who cared little for the salvation

[1] Taine, *Les Origines de la France contemporaine. L'Ancien Régime.* 3d ed. p. 530.
[2] Ibid. pp. 18, 19, 538–540.   [3] I could quote numerous instances.

of souls and for the fulfilment of apostolic duties. Even, when they possessed apparent zeal, it soon vanished before the aversion which was generally felt for their cowardly apostasy.[1]

An interval of barely ninety years divides us from those days in which religion was proscribed, and in which it was enough to hold the Catholic faith in order to be sent into exile or to the guillotine. When we remember that this violent persecution lasted for ten years, it may be asked how the Church of France was enabled to withstand such a tempest. It seems as though the Revolution must have been her grave. But it was, on the contrary, only her second cradle; and it was, doubtless, as an omen of her future destiny that God allowed her swaddling-clothes to be dyed with purple, in the precious blood poured forth by her children.

The condition of the Church in France was deplorable towards the end of these ten years, in 1800 or 1801. No ordinations had taken place, and a number of priests had died on the scaffold, in the galleys, or in exile, so that there was an immense gap in the ranks of the clergy, while no preparation had been made for filling it. The historians of the time agree in describing the situation as lamentable; and, indeed, the facts themselves speak plainly enough. If we consider the Church in her material aspect, we find that the ecclesiastical property was sold, and that the churches were destroyed or desecrated. If we look at the priesthood itself, it was decimated by age, persecution, exile and death. There were no legitimate bishops, and very few priests; their places were filled by a few apostate ministers who had sworn allegiance to the Revolution, and who, for the most part, had nothing so much at heart as the desire to prevent the re-establishment of the ancient worship.

It was in such a situation that the Concordat found Christian France. It was evident that as much courage as wisdom and discretion were required in order to bring the negotiations for the re-establishment of religion to a successful issue. The First Consul, Bonaparte, had to avail himself of all the prestige of his genius; and the Holy See also, in the person of Pius the Seventh and his ministers, were obliged to have recourse to extraordinary methods, and to

---

[1] In 1791, 148 bishops were asked to take the oath. It was refused by 141, and only accepted by seven.

push patience and moderation to their utmost limits. Seven schemes for the Concordat were drawn up; seven times the negotiations were almost broken off, always on matters of principle, on which the Holy See could not give way, since they concerned the independence and the liberty of the Church—questions on which Rome has never wavered, and never will waver, at whatever cost. For the seventh time the negotiations were resumed, and they finally produced the Concordat which we now possess. M. d'Haussonville and Father Theiner[1] have told how, at the last moment, when the signatures were about to be exchanged, the French Government officials sought to substitute a forged and altered copy for the genuine Concordat. Fortunately, this treacherous attempt was baffled, and the negotiations were brought to a conclusion in spite of it.

The Concordat was settled on the 15th of July 1801. It was ratified at Rome and Paris in the following months; and on the 18th of September, 1801, the exchange of ratifications took place at Paris. The Concordat contained seventeen articles, of which the following are the most important:—

ART. I. The Catholic, Apostolic, and Roman religion shall be freely exercised in France; its worship shall be public, in conformity with the police regulations which the Government shall deem necessary for public tranquillity.

ART. XIV. The Government shall guarantee a sufficient salary (*un traitement convenable*) to the bishops and clergy whose dioceses and incumbencies are included in the new boundaries.

ART. XV. The Government will also take measures to enable those French Catholics who desire to do so, to establish ecclesiastical endowments.

The other articles regulate important questions, but such as are comparatively of secondary importance: the alienation of ecclesiastical property, the resignation of the still surviving bishops, the fresh division of dioceses and parishes, the oath to be taken by the bishops and clergy, and the like.

Great moderation was exercised by the Holy See, in order that the Concordat might be arranged; and those who read history in the official documents of the time will easily see, that the part played by Pius the Seventh and his ministers was noble and generous. If there was any spirit of littleness and deceit, it was in the subordinate agents employed by Napoleon. The Holy See sacrificed much; but the

[1] 1800–1814. D'Haussonville, *L'Eglise Romaine et le Premier Empire*. Paris, 1868. Theiner, *Histoire des deux Concordats*. Paris, 1869.

advantages derived from the Concordat were worth the sacrifice, especially its spiritual benefits, which are ever the supreme object of the Church. There was no league with Napoleon, as it has been falsely asserted, for the destruction of the Gallican Church and of its liberties. Such considerations had nothing to do with the Concordat. So far from it, the Government attempted, in the articles termed organic, to re-establish the worst opinions and the most objectionable practices of Gallicanism.

We have seen that the 1st Article of the Concordat speaks of certain "police regulations" to be drawn up for the control of the public worship of the re-established Catholic religion.

It is evident that the Government, in these police regulations, could not meddle with that which was the essential element of the mutual contract just signed. In so doing, they would have taken back with one hand what they gave with the other; and in the case of any sovereign but the Pope, such conduct would have been regarded as a rupture. The maxims of reason and public justice which have been generally accepted may be taken for granted. The Charter of 1830, for instance, was careful to specify in its 13th Article that only those regulations and decrees should be considered constitutional which were necessary for the execution of the laws, and they could not suspend the laws themselves, nor dispense men from their obedience to them.

What was the action of the French Government? Instead of following the dictates of honesty and good sense, and the precepts of public justice, regulations were drawn up in seventy-seven articles, known under the name of Organic Articles, which not only opposed the essential spirit of the Concordat, but that of the Catholic religion. An impartial witness has only to compare the Organic Articles with the Concordat, in order to see that one or the other must be abandoned, for they are inconsistent with each other. It is also evident that these two documents are not of equal value. The Concordat is a treaty between two powers, a treaty which was anxiously discussed, and only concluded after a lengthy negotiation. The organic articles are only a weapon of offence, forged in obscurity and without the knowledge of the opposite party, with which there was outward amity; and it was directed against interests so highly and justly prized by the Church.

This want of good faith on the part of the French Government appears so strange that it has often been asked what motive could have inspired such conduct; and an explanation has been recently suggested which may possibly not be far from the truth.[1] M. Emile Ollivier asserts that since the First Consul was opposed by a strong national party, the party compromised by the Revolution, he devised the Organic Articles in order to pass the Concordat with less difficulty, but that he really intended them to remain undisturbed in the official pigeon-holes. The suggestion is plausible ; and, in fact, no appeal was made to the Organic Articles except in the darkest days of our history, since the beginning of this century. If they were now put in practice, it would become the inauguration of one of the most violent persecutions to which the Catholic Church has ever been subjected. This will appear from the three or four articles which follow :—

ART. I. No bull, brief, rescript, mandate, provision, signature, serving for a provision, nor any other document despatched from the court of Rome, even when it refers only to individuals, can be received, published, printed, nor executed in any other way, unless it be authorized by the Government.

ART. III. The decrees of foreign synods, even those of General Councils, cannot be published in France before they have been submitted to the Government.

ART. XI. The archbishops and bishops may, under the sanction of the Government, establish cathedral chapters and seminaries in their dioceses. All other ecclesiastical establishments are still illegal.

The 2d Article forbade the Papal Nuncio to concern himself in the affairs of the Church of France without permission from the Government. The 4th Article prohibits councils. The 6th regards appeals "*comme d'abus.*" The 17th subjects Bishops elect to an examination conducted by delegates from the Government. The 24th Article prescribes instruction in conformity with the Declaration of 1682. In short, there is scarcely an article which does not contain clauses at war with the freedom of Catholicism, and consequently with the Concordat of 1801. Some of them are even more absurd than objectionable. For example, the 12th Article, by which the Bishop is entitled to be called *citoyen* or *monsieur*, while any other qualification is forbidden. Or, again, the 39th Article, which prescribes one liturgy and

[1] *L'Eglise et l'Etat au Concile du Vatican*, Paris, 1879, vol. ii. I should have more than one exception to make to this remarkable work, especially with reference to the question on which I am now engaged. I am, however, pleased to acknowledge the perfect fairness of M. Emile Ollivier. It is always an advantage to have to do with an opponent of so much justice and courtesy.

one catechism for the whole of France; or the 43d Article, which allows Bishops to carry the pastoral crosier, and to wear violet-coloured stockings—a proof that our legislators did not shrink from trifling details, and that they might take degrees in the art of millinery. Nor is this surprising, since, only the other day, a man whose only title to fame was a treatise on crinoline, has been transformed into a councillor of State.

It need scarcely be said, that the Organic Articles have never been recognized by the Holy See, and that such recognition was impossible. But the Holy See appeared also to believe, as might be inferred from various circumstances, that they were only intended to satisfy revolutionary opinion. Yet, Pope Pius the Seventh did not fail to protest, first in full Consistory, the 24th of May 1802, and on the following day in a letter to Napoleon. Again, on the 18th of August 1803, a protest was made through his ministers. And on the 10th of January 1809, notice of the Organic Articles was taken in the famous Bull of Excommunication. These protests have been frequently renewed by the successors of Pius the Seventh; and, as far as the French clergy are concerned, they have never paid any attention to the injunctions contained in the Organic Articles, so far as they are opposed to the laws of the Church and to the Concordat. Of this we have had a recent instance, and, while these lines are being written, another is on the point of taking place.

Notwithstanding all these facts, of which we have only made a rapid summary, and which are given in detail by several historians—because Pope Pius VII., while he was able to rescue the Church of France from absolute ruin, did not obtain all which he desired, and because he was able to combine great firmness with great moderation—the Concordat and the Organic Articles have sometimes been confounded together; the laborious negotiations of 1801 have been treated as a joint intrigue, and have been described in such terms as the following: "The existing state of affairs is due to the plot of Pius the Seventh with Napoleon the First, against the liberties of the Gallican Church, and therefore has the highest possible Roman Catholic sanction."[1] This

---

[1] "Why Ritualists do not become Roman Catholics: A Reply to the Abbé Martin," by Dr. Littledale. The writer was prevented by a long and painful illness from carrying on the controversy, and can now only observe that if he were to notice in detail all the many errors contained in Dr. Littledale's small pamphlet, he should fill a thick volume. Some of these errors exhibit great ignorance

was asserted in England, and the publication which contains this historical and equitable judgment is widely circulated in that country, and possibly obtains credence elsewhere.

When the Concordat had been concluded in the way we have briefly described, it was necessary to pass from theory to action; from the plan to its fulfilment. The Church of France, which only existed on paper, had still to be made a living reality. But, many difficulties were to be overcome, and obstacles to be set aside, in order to collect the staff of clergy, to restore her institutions, to supply her material wants; for if it is true, as the Gospel says, that man does not live by bread alone, neither can he in this world live only by the Word of God. Let us add, however, that those who do in reality live by the Word of God, do not in general complain that bread is wanting to them. Such was the experience of the Church of France in 1801, and such is still her daily experience. In the critical circumstances in which she then was placed, she trusted in God, nor has God been wanting to her. Let us consider what her material resources really were, and what she did with, or rather without them.

II. We may say that the Church of France possessed absolutely nothing, except some religious buildings, cathedrals, and large churches, a few episcopal palaces, and some large convents which it had not been easy to apply to profane uses, and which had escaped the fury of the destroyers.

By the 18th Article of the Concordat, Pope Pius the Seventh had ratified the alienation of ecclesiastical property; and declared, that neither he nor his successors would disturb those who by more or less unrighteous means had acquired it. In this way he had destroyed, or at any rate diminished, one of the greatest obstacles to the re-establishment of worship; since, as it will be readily believed, those who had most completely despoiled the Church were the most infuriated against her. If the restitution of those ill-gotten goods had been enforced, the enmities between the two classes of citizens would have been perpetuated, and there would have been a serious difficulty in effecting a religious peace. On the contrary, such enmities disappeared in one generation; and either by sale, or inheritance the properties have changed

of Catholic rites and Catholic history, and they prove also that Dr. Littledale does not write with calmness. For instance, what has La Condamine, a traveller of the past century, to do with the devotion to the Sacred Heart? Dr. Littledale has probably mistaken La Condamine for La Colombiére.

hands so often, that all memory of the unjust spoliation of 1789 has now passed away. Religious peace was made, and in this particular will never again be disturbed. The Holy See has, however, been accused of improvidence, and of having encouraged future spoliation. But it does not appear that the circumstances will ever be the same; nor can any one assert that the Pope's action towards Italy, for example, would be the same as it was towards France in 1801.

It is at any rate certain that the concessions of the Holy See in 1801 were attended by the happiest results. The constitutional Church disappeared in the course of a few years, the feeling of bitterness was softened, and union between the despoilers and the despoiled was re-established. It must also be remembered that when the Holy See confirmed the alienation of ecclesiastical property, it obtained three concessions in return: (1) the recognition of its rights of property; (2) an indemnity, or annual restitution, under the form of the Budget for Public Worship; and (3) the right of acquiring fresh property.

We have only one observation to make on the recognition of the rights of property—namely, that it implicitly affirmed the injustice of the spoliation which had been effected to the injury of the Church; and that it was intended to prevent the assumption, that the income allotted to ecclesiastics did not differ in its nature from the salary paid to the State officials. This income cannot be alienated nor confiscated. In fact, even in the darkest days, if we except those of the Commune, no attempt has been made to tamper with the income either of the dignitaries, nor of the inferior clergy.

The value of the ecclesiastical property taken from the Church of France has been estimated at about four milliards of francs, which would be equal to ten milliards at the present time. In return for this sacrifice, the State engaged, by the Concordat of 1801, to make a fitting provision (*un traitement convenable*) for the Bishops and parochial clergy, and to allow the Church to acquire property.

Let us now see how far these two promises have been kept by the State, and what has been done in less than eighty years. Hence we shall be able to judge whether the restoration of the Church of France is not truly miraculous.

The great Revolution deprived the Church of an income of from two hundred to four hundred million francs. By the Concordat, the State guaranteed a budget which, in 1879, after all the additions which have been made to it, does not exceed 51,545,468 francs, or, in round numbers, £2,061,000. It is apportioned in the following manner:—

	francs.
Superior clergy	1,650,000
Parochial clergy	39,963,945
Chapter of St. Denis	219,000
Seminaries	1,032,000
Pensions or donations	992,000
Churches and rectories	7,688,323
	51,545,468

It would be assuredly unjust to accuse the Government of having systematically failed in liberality, and in their duty to the Church. France has passed through critical times; and her budget of expenses is a heavy one. Yet, there is some reason for asking whether the Government has fulfilled all its engagements.

There was a promise that a *sufficient* provision should be made for the Bishops and the parochial clergy. Now the allowance to the Archbishops has never exceeded 20,000 francs, and the allowance to the Bishops is 15,000 francs. This year, the liberality of the Chamber assumed the form of taking from 2000 to 5000 francs from the Bishops' and Archbishops' income, and of the saving effected by this reduction (—viz., 435,000 francs—) 200,000 francs have been distributed among aged and infirm priests. This can scarcely be regarded as the *sufficient* provision by which the Government promised to make compensation for the property confiscated during the Revolution. Even if this provision was sufficient at the beginning of the century, it has ceased to be adequate at the present time, now that prices have risen, and that money is depreciated. The condition of the clergy is very different from that which existed before the Revolution, and from that in other countries at the present day; of the Anglican clergy in England, for example, and of the Catholic priesthood in Austria.

Let us now see what the Government has done for cathedral bodies and for the parochial clergy. The clergy may be divided into five classes, with incomes ranging from 1600, 1500, 1200, 1000, and 900 francs—that is, from £64 to £36 per annum. It must also be observed that, while the Government guarantees an income of £12 to the *vicaires* or curates, of rural parishes, there is absolutely no allowance for those who are employed in large towns. In Paris, for example, some parishes are served by five, six, eight, ten, or even twelve priests, who have never received, and never will receive, a farthing from Government. The income of these priests varies between £120 and £240. The average is about £160, out of which they have to feed, clothe, and lodge themselves.

It will be asked then: how the French clergy are able to live, and what are their resources?——The revenue of the clergy is derived from three sources: first, the Government salary; second, their casual receipts from fees; and third, the offerings of the faithful.

As may be gathered from the foregoing remarks, the income provided by the Budget of Public Worship forms the principal resource of the large majority of the parochial clergy, and in some cases it is perhaps their only means of support. Only a small proportion derive their income from what we have called casual receipts and the offerings of the faithful; and this is the case with the curates of large town parishes, with priests habitually attached to certain parishes, with the aged and the infirm, wherever they are without a superannuation allowance from the diocese. Among all those paid by the State, the clergy alone have not been deemed worthy of a retiring pension to provide for their last days. This omission shows the illiberal spirit of much of our French legislation. The diocesan fund, however, aided by the annual offerings of the faithful, tends to supply this omission.

Let us now see what is the average income of a French priest. It is difficult to ascertain this point, since the data vary much in different dioceses, and even in different parishes. Zeal, effectual ministry, devotion, and the esteem or affection by which these qualities are rewarded, in the first instance, are necessarily the cause of much variation in the latter sources of income. But after instituting many inquiries in many different places, we are inclined to believe that the average revenue of the parochial clergy in country districts may be estimated from £60 to £70 a year. In addition to this sum, there is always a house, almost always a garden, and sometimes a meadow, field, or vineyard. The country priest must be content with this small income, which has to serve for his maintenance and for all other incidental expenses, unless he has private means. We see the differencce between this income and that of parish priests before the Revolution, when it ranged from 10,000 to 30,000 francs (from £400 to

£1200), and compare it also with the condition of priests in some other Catholic countries, and specially with the established clergy in the Anglican Church.

It is true that the French clergy do not desire so large an income. It would sometimes be oppressive and embarrassing, not from any doubt how to employ it in good works; but, because a liberal income would lead people to believe that the priestly office was not accepted for its own sake. A large income would involve the responsibility of spending it on proper objects, and the priest would be naturally exposed to much criticism. Since he has now only just sufficient for his maintenance, he is safe from idle gossip; and on the occasions when he receives liberal gifts, the mode in which they are to be employed is generally indicated, which relieves him from personal responsibility. When he appeals for help to carry on a good work, those who disapprove of it have only to refuse. Those who give know what they are about, and have afterwards no right to complain.

Accustomed from the time when their training begins in the seminary, to regard a plain and simple mode of living as the ideal life of a shepherd of souls, the priest desires to live in poverty, and to be detached from all worldly things. He did not become a priest in order to make his fortune. He is perfectly aware that he has chosen the wrong road for so doing; and that if he were to nourish expectations of wealth or greatness, he would sooner or later be exposed to bitter disappointment. Neither does he propose to advance the interests of his family. He has no children; and he feels that he ought not to give anything to his relations, except in cases of absolute necessity. If he has a modest patrimony, he generally leaves it to his family; but everything else is the portion of the poor, who are his heirs; and for the most part the poor and good works have already absorbed all that he possesses in his lifetime. Having practised St. Paul's maxim, *Habentes alimenta et quibus tegamur, his contenti simus*, he dies poor; and the highest praise which can be given to a priest in the Church of France is to say, that he died leaving no debts behind him, and also no money to pay for his burial. *Pas de dettes et pas de pécule*, is the maxim held in honour by the French clergy. Many priests leave nothing behind them on their death but a few books, and a little furniture—just sufficient to pay for the expenses of their funeral. We have never heard of a French priest who died leaving a fortune acquired during his ministry. Such a scandal is, thank God, almost unknown. We have seen, moreover, that the Budget of Public Worship has taken good care that it shall never occur.

It is true, that the Concordat states in its 15th Article: "The Government will also take measures to permit French Catholics, when they desire it, to make endowments in favour of the Church;" but, it must be added, that these measures are so effectual that endowments are practically almost impossible. So many formalities are necessary, and the individuals capable of receiving bequests are so few, that Catholics cannot be said to possess the privilege of foundations accorded by the Concordat. The documents relating to legacies or donations have to pass through so many offices before they are finally sanctioned, that any official who desires to do so can postpone them indefinitely. The sentiments of the officials who work under M. Jules Ferry may be easily imagined towards those Catholics who desire to make endowments in favour of Catholic Universities and analogous institutions—as, for example, in favour of the excellent Jesuit college in the Rue des Postes, which was last year able to send up to the Government schools 107 pupils out of 167.

The lack of authorization, of which some Religious Orders are accused, is due to this illiberal spirit, and to the tyranny of bureaucracy. The Jesuits and the Dominicans have had, ever since 1870, friends enough in high places to obtain authorization, if they had desired and demanded it. At any rate, if authorization would have been of any real advantage to them, it must be confessed that, in refraining from asking it, they give no proof of the sagacity commonly ascribed to them. The Jesuits must have some reasons for not demanding the authorization which they might have obtained; and their reasons are, evidently, a dislike of the yoke it would impose upon them. It would be impossible for societies devoted to secondary education to introduce any improvements into their establishments, so long as any clerk in office might object to the expenditure of 300 francs, or submit the item to the most vexatious delays. Progress would manifestly be impossible, and the reason is plain why the Jesuits have voluntarily deprived themselves of authorization. Had they been authorized, they would have been no better protected from the attacks directed against them. The fact that they are unauthorized is simply a pretext; and the things which are said and done in France at this moment, with

On the Present State of the French Church. 267

reference to the authorized communities, are an ample proof that such is the case.

The unwillingness of the State to facilitate the endowment of Catholic institutions must also be an obstacle to the separation of Church and State, which has been so much discussed, but for which few people are really anxious. If this separation must be effected, it must not be made in the way desired by Radicals, who only aim at the pure and simple suppression of the Budget of Public Worship, but as it would be understood by honest and just men. Now, the separation, undertaken in a fair spirit, would involve two things: first, the restitution in capital or interest of the sum represented by the Budget of Public Worship; and, secondly, the concession of the rights of acquisition, that is; of endowments in favour of the Church. The first of these two conditions is difficult, and the second is almost impossible, and for this reason men of experience do not believe in the permanent separation of Church and State. The Budget of Public Worship may be suppressed by violence in a crisis like the Commune, but it will be re-established by any regular and legitimate government.

We have seen that the Church in France has not received trom the Government the support promised to her by the Concordat of 1801. Let us now see what she has done for herself under these most unfavourable circumstances.

III. As soon as the re-establishment of religion had been decreed by the Concordat, it became necessary, either immediately or by degrees, to provide churches, a staff of clergy, an administration, and, in fact, all the institutions which, without forming the essence of Catholicism, closely concern its existence, and largely contribute to its well-being and progress. In all these things, it was necessary to act in an orderly way, since it would not be reasonable to undertake everything at once. No time was to be lost in beginning what must be gradually carried out, as time, money, and men should permit.

From this, the only fair point of view, it is clear that the first thing to be done was to provide an ecclesiastical staff. A fresh supply of clergy was wanted before all things, and this was at once undertaken. It would be difficult to ascertain the precise number of clergy who had survived the revolutionary epoch; but, without doing so, we can hardly estimate the resources at the disposal of the Church in 1801, the date of the Concordat. We will therefore give an approximate estimate, taking the episcopate as the standard of comparison.

At the outbreak of the Revolution, there were in the Church of France 150 Archbishops, Bishops, coadjutors, or suffragans. In the year 1801, 82 still survived, of whom only 18 formed part of the new hierarchy. Nearly half of the episcopate, therefore, viz., 68 out of 150, had perished during the Revolution.

It must be remembered, that the parish priests were specially liable to become victims of the Revolution, since their numbers and their duties made it difficult for them to escape the researches of the revolutionary tribunals. It must also be observed, that no ordinations took place for a period of ten years, and that many monks who might have joined the ranks of the parochial clergy were not priests, but merely lay-brothers. We think under these circumstances that 20,000 or 25,000 priests, including those who had subscribed to the constitution, is the maximum estimate. The regular and the secular clergy had amounted together to 97,000 persons, of whom not more than 80,000 were priests. Consequently, we do not think we exaggerate in reducing the number still available in 1801 to a fourth, that is, as we have just said, to 20,000 or 25,000 priests.

To establish this point, we may refer to a well-meant, but somewhat ill-arranged, and consequently badly executed pamphlet. An unfortunate use has recently been made of this publication, especially in England in recent anti-Catholic controversy. M. l'Abbé Bougaud writes as follows:—

"From 1800 to 1815, the number of priests was so small that they only served the towns and important places, and country districts were deserted. Upon his ordination, as l'Abbé Rohrbacher states, he was. though quite a young man, enjoined to serve seven churches. . . . Between 1815 and 1830 much zeal was exerted, but there was no sensible improvement. Witness Mgr. de Frayssinous, who asked in 1820 if it was possible to see without consternation such a terrible number of churches without a pastor. He adds that in the heart of this most Christian kingdom there were 15,000 cures vacant for want of men to fill them."[1]

If in the year 1820 there were still 15,000 vacant cures

---

[1] L'Abbé Bougaud, *Le grand péril de l'Eglise de France*, 4th edition, p. 68. I regret that I cannot examine this work in detail. In spite of some grave exceptions which must be taken to his execution, I should like to do justice to the author's good intentions and to quote some really admirable passages. The first part ought to be re-written. (See also two letters by the present writer, in the "Guardian," 1880, pp. 85, 151.)

among those which formerly possessed or now required an incumbent, no one will dispute that in 1802, the year following the Concordat, there must have been about from 20,000 to 25,000 cures vacant; and this nearly corresponds with our estimate of 20,000 priests who were available in 1801.

Let us now see how the work of restoration was begun. The cure of souls was undertaken; but beside the church school, the clerical seminary was established, which was to ensure a regular supply of clergy. The parish priest became the schoolmaster, at first the teacher of Latin, then of Greek, by and by of history, geography, and mathematics. Each generation added a stone to the building, increasing the quantity, and improving the quality of the instruction given by the parish priest in his character of catechist, visitor of the poor, preacher of more or less distinction, popular teacher, and the maintainer of Catholic tradition.

In each of the ninety dioceses of France there are now two, and sometimes three, minor colleges (*petits séminaires*), generally combined with several ecclesiastical colleges, containing from 150 to 200 pupils, and where as many subjects are studied as in the Government *lycées*. It must be remembered that these have all sprung up within the last seventy or eighty years, in spite of many obstacles to be overcome; and, instead of despairing, as we may be tempted to do after reading the opening pages of M. Bougaud's *Grand Péril*, we should rather praise the goodness and beneficence of God towards the Church of France, in which there were, indeed, some apostates towards the end of the last century, but also thousands of martyrs.

The beginning was necessarily painful and difficult. Everything required reconstruction; and for this, men and money were alike wanting. Happily, all hope in God and for France was not lost. The work was begun, and God alone knows at what cost to our fathers of devotion, of self-denial, and of personal sacrifice, it was carried on. Every school, every college of any standing, possesses a store of pious and affecting reminiscences. Nearly all the *petits séminaires* owe their existence to some zealous priest, who was at once parish priest and schoolmaster. The Concordat in its 11th Article authorised Bishops to establish a seminary, but did not guarantee any support for its maintenance. Sometimes the Government showed liberality, but it was more frequently opposed to the seminaries, which have been subjected to all sorts of annoyances, especially during the first years of the

Government of July. The storm, however, passed by. The *petits séminaires* survived it. And the grain of mustard-seed has become a great tree which offends the eyes of our modern Radicals.

There were several causes for the feebleness of the first start. In the first place, it was opposed by a hostile generation, which had been brought up in the principles of the Revolution. Moreover, everything had to be done at once, and yet, during the first twenty years, there were not recruits enough to fill up the gaps caused by death. The priests who had lived through the Revolution were no longer young. At its downfall the youngest were, probably, not under thirty-five years of age, so that many must have died between 1800 and 1820.

Starting from 1820, the progress was steady, if we make allowance for those disturbed times in which vocations are necessarily fewer; and year by year the gaps in the benefices were filled up, and the ranks of the clergy increased in number. M. Bougaud laments over 3000 vacant cures, and we certainly ought not to lose sight of the reverse side of the medal. Yet, in our opinion, and in that of others we have consulted, the conclusion which he draws from this fact is entirely erroneous. It is enough to observe, in the first place, the difference between this number and the 15,000 vacant cures mentioned by Mgr. de Frayssinous in 1820; secondly, many of these cures have been created from year to year, so that there is an annual increase; thirdly, since the beginning of the century, and especially since 1835, all the ancient Religious Orders have been revived, and several instituted which are absolutely new; and lastly, some cures have been declared vacant which are purely nominal, so that their existence and their vacancy are equally unimportant.

This last remark requires explanation. In several dioceses, the two cases which follow often occur: firstly, a curate is assigned as a temporary arrangement to an aged priest with a laborious charge, but the office of curate, which was created for this special circumstance, is not suppressed on the appointment of a younger incumbent, who does not require help. The office is then set down as vacant, although the vacancy, official or statistical, is not real. Secondly, there are also a number of small rural parishes, closely adjacent to each other, which may easily be served by one priest, but which have each been formed into a separate incumbency.

On the Present State of the French Church. 271

Such cases occur in every diocese, and there are others, merely titular appointments, which have never been filled up since the Revolution. One instance, well known to us, may be given. M. l'Abbé Bougaud declares 26 incumbencies to be vacant in the diocese of Cahors, in which there are about 300,000 souls. In June 1879, however, 28 priests were ordained; and the Bishop himself told the writer of these lines, that he should find it difficult to provide employment for them all. Out of the 459 parishes included in this diocese, the population in 99 parishes is under 300 souls; and 30 parishes out of that number do not contain 150 souls. There are sometimes two, three, and even four churches included within the limited civil division which is termed the commune.

To show that we do not speak at random, we may cite facts obtained in the summer of 1879, during the writer's enforced leisure from illness.

Commune.	Parishes.	Population.	Priests.
Luzech	Fages	140	1
	Camy	330	1
	Luzech	1148	2
	Caïx	300	1
		1918	5

It takes an hour and a quarter to go from Fages to Caïx, passing through Camy and Luzech. Here we have five priests for 1918 souls, and a commune consisting of four parishes; nor is this the only example which might be mentioned in the same diocese.

The conclusions of M. l'Abbé Bougaud, which have been turned to such ill-account, and misrepresented in England—amongst others, by Dr. Littledale in his "Reply to the Abbé Martin"—are therefore not borne out by facts. The conclusions would only be legitimate if the diminution in the supply of priests was regular and steady, but it must be emphatically stated that such is not the case. Cambrai is one of the dioceses painted yellow on M. Bougaud's coloured map of the French dioceses, that is, among those in which there is a deficiency of priests. The Cardinal Archbishop of Cambrai, however, quite recently spoke in public as follows:—

"Vocations to the priestly office are more numerous than ever in our diocese. There is an excellent spirit in all our seminaries: piety prevails in them, and study is vigorous and well directed. As for our numerous institutions for secondary education, their prosperity is always increasing, in spite of the powerful pressure brought to bear against them. The successes achieved in the Government examinations show that they have nothing to fear from a comparison with rival and highly favoured institutions."

Indeed, the figures speak for themselves. The following returns are taken from the censuses of 1866, 1872, 1876.

Year.	Priests.	Increase.
1866	51,100	(?)
1872	52,148	2 per cent
1876	55,269	6.9 ,,

Perhaps the best way of ascertaining if vocations to the clerical life are increasing or falling away, is to study the vocations to the religious life. And the reasons for saying so are these: (1.) Between vocations to religious and to clerical life there is a close connection. (2.) It is certain that many Religious Orders, specially Religious Orders of men, did not exist in France before 1835. (3.) In the last twenty years, the census of these Religious Orders or communities has been taken twice by Government officials (once by command of the Legislature) in order to ascertain the precise number of religious and nuns—that is, in 1861 and 1876. Now, here is the table showing the results of these two censuses [2]:—

	1861.	1876.	Increase.
Men	18,745	30,287	61 per cent.
Women	82,640	127,753	54 ,,

In the space of fifteen years, therefore, the Religious Orders of men have increased by 61 per cent.; and the Religious Orders of women have increased by 54 per cent. Amongst the 30,287 religious, 8006 are designed as *preaching*—that is, as having full priest's orders. These figures do not call for much comment; they are a proof that the vocations to the highest Christian life are not falling off, and we may draw from this fact the like inference as to the clerical life.

The same fact may be also established by another consideration. When we look at the number of incumbencies in the Church of France, we see that there has been a regular and steady increase, although the population has not been

---

[1] *L'Univers*, September 15, 1879.
[2] *Etat des Congrégations, Communautés, et Associations religieuses, autorisées ou non-autorisées, dressé en exécution de l'article* 12 *de la loi du* 28 *décembre* 1876. Paris, Imprimerie nationale, 1878.

largely augmented, nor even much changed in towns and country villages. This is shown by next table :—

	Population of France.
1801	27,349,003
1821	30,461,875
1851	35,783,170
1876	36,905,788

The population of France since 1801 has been augmented by a fourth, since 1821, by a sixth. But, the incumbencies have augmented by a fourth since 1817, and the clergy has been more than doubled. The subjoined table will give a rough idea of the progress made in the parish system in these short periods of time :[1]—

No.	Year.	Cures.	Succursales.	Vicariats.	Total.	Increase.	Decrease.
						Per cent.	Per cent.
1	1817	2859	22,393	4770	30,022	...	...
2	1826	2999	23,190	4520	30,709	2.28	...
3	1835	3263	25,267	5447	33,977	10.64	...
4	1847	3350	27,666	5912	36,928	8.68	...
5	1856	3413	28,984	6958	39,355	6.57	...
6	1866	3533	30,690	8229	42,452	7.81[2]	...
7	1873	3425	29,902	8232	41,559	...	2.10[3]
8	1878	3465	31,500	8929	43,894	5.61 on 1873 / 3.39 on 1866	...

Instead of the somewhat wild declamation which appears in the first part of his work, M. Bougaud would have done better to prove, if it were possible, that in 1830 or in 1850 there were 100,000 secular or regular priests in France, and that there are at the present time only 50,000.

We have thus shown that there has been a steady increase in the number of the clergy since the Church of France was reconstituted in 1801. But, the question may be asked, whether the quality has improved with the quantity? We have no hesitation in answering this question in the affirmative. The education of the French clergy is undoubtedly better and more complete than it was formerly.

[1] This table has been compiled from the following sources :—1. Ch. Jourdain, *Le Budget des Cultes en France, depuis le Concordat de* 1801. 2. *L'Univers* of January 17, 1879. 3. *La France ecclésiastique pour* 1879.
[2] This increase may be explained by the annexation of Savoy and of the county of Nice.
[3] This decrease may be explained by the loss of Alsace-Lorraine in 1871.

IV. Speaking generally, it may be said that the clergy come almost entirely from ecclesiastical colleges, and especially from the *petits séminaires*. It is quite an exception when candidates come from the State colleges. And this is natural; since a vocation for the Church is unlikely to be developed in such an atmosphere, and indeed can with difficulty be kept alive in it. Education in the *lycées* leaves much to be desired from moral and religious points of view, as every one is aware, although it is less easy to point out a remedy than to establish the fact.

After having decided on his vocation while pursuing the course of classical study usual in France, and having, if he so pleases, passed his baccalaureat, the future priest begins his course of philosophy, which generally occupies two years. He studies logic, metaphysics, the Scriptures, history, morals, finally, an elementary treatise of philosophy, either in a *petit séminaire* or in a separate institution, and at the end of two years he is transferred to the *grand séminaire*. It need hardly be said, that he goes through several examinations while pursuing his studies, so as to test his acquirements.

The direct preparation for orders begins at the *grand séminaire*, and the candidate devotes himself to the study of ecclesiastical subjects, to dogmatic theology, to questions of morals and casuistry, to patristic learning, to history, to Holy Scripture and its languages, and to rites. The course in the *grand séminaire* generally occupies four years.

More than this may be, indeed, required in order to become a man of learning, and a teacher of others, but the instruction puts the student in the way to become both, and in any case it trains up good pastors for the Church, men who are qualified to undertake the administration of parishes. The Church needs learned men, but she is still more in need of good pastors. Those who accuse the clergy of France of having produced no illustrious scholars, do not give sufficient consideration to the circumstances of the Church at the beginning of this century, to the struggles through which she has passed, and to the persecutions she has undergone. They do not remember that she has been restricted in light and liberty;[1] that all sorts of privileges

---

[1] The Radicals of France, who call themselves *Liberals*, but whom the late Bishop Dupanloup more properly called *libératres*, are very strongly opposed to the liberty of teaching. One of them said in the French Assembly, December 4th, 1874, during the debates on the superior instruction:—"We do not want

have been refused to her; that it is only within the last few years that the permission to found her own universities was accorded to her. And how was it possible without a university to impress upon a numerous body, like the clergy of France, the ardour and the zeal which lead up to scientific research? It has also been forgotten that time, money, and books, have all been wanting in the case of the mass of the clergy, and without these three requisites it is impossible to go deeply into any subject. Sufficient allowance has never been made for these difficulties; and, while accusing the French clergy of want of learning, more than one jewel in her crown has been unjustly forgotten. What orators, for example, have been more illustrious than Lacordaire, De Ravignan, and Dupanloup, if we seek for instances only among the dead?

It is impossible to do everything at once; and the Church of France, although it was her first thought to train pastors, is very willing that her sons should devote some years to science, now that the gaps which had been made in her ranks are nearly filled. But, we doubt whether she will be permitted to do so. A study of passing events shows that all the attacks made upon liberty of teaching are especially directed against the Church. She is the real object of the blows struck at the Catholic universities, and at the congregationist schools. If our rulers only profess to direct their opposition against the Jesuits and the other unauthorized congregations, their followers attack everything which has to do with the Church. The facts speak for themselves, and belie the assertions which have recently been made on the subject.

There is one reassuring fact amid our present distresses, and that is, the continual progress which has been going on in the reorganization of the Church of France since the beginning of this century. First, we have the institution of seminaries; then, the liberty successively obtained of primary, secondary and higher education; and each success was achieved at the fitting moment. During some years past there has been a revival in theological study, a general desire

---

the liberty of superior education, *ana the Catholics shall be the only ones who shall avail themselves of it.*" This eminent Liberal was quite right in thus speaking, for State education in France is quite irreligious, and Catholics were the only ones wanting liberty; but his speech does not credit himself with a great love of freedom. The freethinker who so spoke was none other than M. Challemel Lacour, the present ambassador of the French Republic in London.

for instruction, something in the air which seem to show that the time is ripe for a complete ecclesiastical organization. Nothing now remains but to expand, enlarge, and invigorate our lives; and time, and men, and money for the work will not be found wanting.

V. The clergy against whom such violent and unseemly attacks are directed display the characteristics of their surroundings. They are sometimes reproached for their origin, and are said to consist only of peasants. It is asked, somewhat ungenerously, why nobles and men of position are not oftener found among them.

It would occupy too much time and space to reply to these accusations in detail, and we must content ourselves with a general answer.[1] Even the question whether it is desirable that the clergy should include many of the nobility in its ranks would demand long consideration. If we regard the Church only in its human aspect, we should undoubtedly desire to see her possessed of great names and great fortunes. But, from a spiritual point of view, we see the wisdom of the precept given by the Council of Trent: the rich and the poor should be the exceptions, the sons of the middle-class should be the rule. It is precisely from this middle-class that the French clergy are drawn—peasant farmers, small landowners, shopkeepers, and merchants — each of these classes furnishes its contingent. This contingent represents, as we have said, the actual state of France. We may think that this is not the case, when we consider France as she once was; or we may deceive ourselves, when we go from one watering-place to another, or spend a few days at the Grand Hôtel or at Versailles. But, those who live in France know at what a headlong pace she is descending the incline of democracy.

Society changes in the course of every ten years. Customs, language, ideas, good manners, all partake of this transformation, which we must deplore from one point of view, but which is irresistible, nor can it now be checked by any efforts of ours. The Church is, however, intended for democracies as well as for aristocracies, perhaps more for the former than the latter; and it is not surprising that the clergy should somewhat resemble the social surroundings in which they

---

[1] I may venture to recommend to the perusal of Englishmen the strictures of Lord Lytton in his "View of the State of Religion," in his work—"England and the English."

live. And if we regard the French clergy as a whole, they are an honour to the class which they represent, and French democracy should be proud of them.

This assertion is so true that the French clergy, as indeed the bulk of the nation, are indifferent to all forms of government, as a matter of duty, and perhaps even of conviction. We say as a matter of duty, for this simple reason; the clergy must do good to all, they can refuse their ministry to none, and they take good care to display no party flag. This impartiality is so general, that we are certain that priests in general regret the warmth with which the cause of monarchy has been espoused by some religious newspapers. The rule dictated by duty prescribes that religion should not be compromised by politics and party spirit.

We have also said that the clergy of France is perhaps by conviction indifferent to forms of government. The clergy, like the mass of the people, only ask for order, and liberty to carry on their good works. It matters little whether they are ruled by a monarchy or by a republic, by the Bourbons or by the Bonapartes; or, it is at all events a matter of secondary importance. Any government which can offer guarantees for order may count upon the hearty support of the clergy, who will never encourage useless opposition.

It follows, as a matter of course, that there is room for many exceptions. The clergy observe passing events with the same eyes as other people, and may end by thinking that a republic is still unsuited to the French temperament, if it lapses into folly and barbarism as it appears to be doing at this moment. The clergy willingly acquiesced in this third experiment, and has done nothing to hinder its success. If unable to sympathise with the present Government, the clergy do not find fault with its form, but with the men who represent it. They have watched with an anxiety, not exempt from fear, the formation of a Ministry consisting of four or five aggressive Protestants, and as many free-thinkers or free-masons. Yet the clergy would have been willing to support the Ministry, if the Ministry had not itself taken the offensive. Its acts have corresponded to its origin. The clergy have defended themselves, and will continue to do so; but they will act with the calmness and moderation befitting their cause. Much has been written during the past months on the present situation; yet, it would be difficult to find, in any episcopal letter, a single word against the Republic, so far as its form of government is concerned.[1]

VI. The clergy of France have therefore reorganized their ranks, both as to numbers and to quality. At no period of their history were the clergy better prepared to fulfil the regular duties of their profession. If we take the parochial clergy alone, we may assert that there are few or none who are not effective ministers. Each has his proper work to do. But now, it may be interesting to see how the machine works; how this army of picked men, trained for a definite moral purpose, moves. This curiosity may be satisfied by recalling the words of the Cardinal of Rouen, uttered in the Senate a few years ago: "My clergy form a regiment; when I say 'March,' they march."

These words have been generally misconstrued, and especially in England. Some people appear to consider it an ideal state of things, when a priest can insult his bishop publicly, in the church or in the newspapers, without any justification for his conduct. But, at no period would such a state of things have been tolerated in the Catholic Church, nor would it have been tolerated in any army. It is only the French Radicals, and the revolutionary spirits in all countries, who wish for an army which reasons before it obeys.

The comparison drawn by the Cardinal of Rouen between the Church and the army is perfectly just; and when that dignitary said, that his regiment would march when he issued the order to do so, he only figuratively expressed the spirit of discipline which prevails among the French clergy. They are in close union with their leaders; there may be differences of opinion, but there are no divisions; and in this union their strength during the present crisis consists. The clergy are united, and will not be scattered by those hostile measures which are manifest, even to the eyes of foreigners.

The Catholic priest at his ordination vows to be ever obedient to his bishop; but obedience, wherever it is due and morally possible, was never more generally practised by French ecclesiastics than it is at this day. English people are apt to ascribe their obedience to other causes.[2] Some

---

[1] I have treated this aspect of the above question in the July number of the "Nineteenth Century," 1880.

[2] I read, for instance, in the "Saturday Review," Nov. 8, 1879, p. 554, vol. ii.: "In the power of moving a priest from a parish where there is nothing to be

writers and journalists speak of the French and Belgian episcopate together, as they have a right to do, since their situation is historically the same, and the present state of the Church in Belgium is due, as in France, to events which occurred at the end of the last century, and at the beginning of the present one. These writers assert that the episcopate both in France and Belgium impose an intolerable yoke upon their clergy. It has even been said that on this account "at least a hundred French priests, and a still larger number of Italian ones, abandon their clerical life yearly, and retire into a lay position." [1]

Speaking generally, the rule of the Church in France is extremely paternal. The bishop in ordinary cases does nothing without his council, that is, his vicars-general and several members of his chapter, who, on account of their age or services, enjoy the consideration and esteem of the public. All the affairs of the diocese are regulated by this council, which meets once or twice a week. Young priests are in the first instance appointed as curates to such charges as happen to be vacant. They are gradually promoted from one charge to another, until they become incumbents, archdeacons, or something higher. In all cases promotion is the reward of past services, rather than an expectation of future efficiency; or at least, the latter motive is an exception which proves the rule. Everything is done paternally, unobtrusively, not perhaps so as to give universal satisfaction, but at any rate, so as to please the majority. A bishop whose rule was arbitrary would soon be checked by the passive resistance of those who work with him, by the complaints which would be made, since the person who is injured, or who claims to be injured, may appeal from the bishop to the

had but the State allowance, to one where the fees form an appreciable increase to the curé's income, the bishop has a lever of very great force. To quarrel with the bishop is to abandon all hope of promotion, and the surest way to avoid a quarrel is honestly to look at everything from the bishop's point of view; this is an accomplishment which the French clergy possess in great perfection. What the bishop thinks, that they think."—To some men it seems well nigh impossible to have opinions different from others without quarrelling. To quarrel with his bishop is a part of the life of every good Anglican, but is this an essential of the Catholic Church? I do not believe it, for if there is anything recommended by our Lord and our first forefathers, it is meekness, love, charity, and respect for those in authority. Quarrels with the bishops are not spoken of in the New Testament. They may occur sometimes, but it ought to be only extraordinary cases.

[1] Dr. Littledale, "Why Ritualists do not become Roman Catholics," p. 61. (This and the next page, although printed for the "Nineteenth Century" of December 1879, were suppressed for want of space.)

metropolitan, and from the metropolitan to the court of Rome. Instances of such appeal have occurred.

Since the Concordat of 1801 France has had no benefices, strictly so-called.[1] The Concordat, or rather the Organic Articles, only recognize the provincial deans as irremovable. Other priests may be removed at the pleasure of the bishop, or rather, of his diocesan council. But practically, changes are only made at the desire of the incumbents themselves. There are cases, however, where the good of the flock makes it imperative that there should be a change of priests; and such a change is therefore made, but with as much consideration and gentleness as possible. What we say of France applies also to Belgium, for the cases are similar, if not identical.

From this it is evident how far we are from the arbitrary acts described by Dr. Littledale, who asserts "that the same policy is being carried out more and more in the Anglo-Roman body, where the State does not meddle at all; that the bishops in Belgium *habitually* extort bonds of resignation from the beneficed clergy" ("Why Ritualists," &c., p. 34).

To this we must make the general reply that there were originally no benefices, and yet that this did not hinder the progress of the Church. There are, moreover, many points of resemblance between the situation of the Church in the early ages of Christianity and her present situation in certain phases of modern society. It is still necessary that the Church should act in whatever way she can, when she is unable to act as she might desire. Does Dr. Littledale suppose that the priests of the primitive Church treated their bishops as the Anglican bishops are treated now by too many of his colleagues, whether Evangelical or Ritualist? Does he really think the English Catholics to blame, because, in the course of the fifty years in which a small liberty has been accorded to them, they have not yet been able to reconstitute a complete Church, with all its institutions and organization? In common justice, when the Church has been despoiled, and suppressed, and when she is fettered by a crowd of restrictive laws, she should not be accused of having failed to do all which seems desirable. After being robbed, she is reproached with poverty. She is forbidden to open schools of higher instruction, and the clergy are accused of want of learning. She is not allowed

---

[1] There is now in progress a movement to alter this state of things.

to educate our young men, especially those of the higher classes; and then she is taunted with the insult that her clergy are a clergy of peasants. We must repeat that these accusations are neither reasonable, nor honest.

After reading the remarks of Dr. Littledale which refer to the Belgian bishops and clergy, we wrote at once to a friend in Belgium, the incumbent of a large rural parish. Two successive letters did not enable this friend to understand what was meant by the rash assertion that the bishops "*habitually* extort bonds of resignation." If Dr. Littledale means—and his language will bear this interpretation—that the Belgian bishops, before installing a priest, exact from him a blank form of resignation, we meet such an assertion by a categorical and authoritative denial. If Dr. Littledale means that the bishops oblige irremovable priests to resign at their own arbitrary desire, without deliberation or serious reasons—and his words must at least bear this sense—to this assertion also, after obtaining information from the episcopal records in Belgium, we oppose a categorical and authoritative denial.

We stated the case as follows:—

"Is it a fact that Belgian bishops habitually extort resignations from their clergy, first, by causing them to sign blank forms of resignation, which may be filled up at the pleasure of the episcopal chancellor; or, secondly, after their institution, by forcing them to resign against their desire, by means of threats, violence, and oppression? It will be understood that we do not enter into cases in which a priest has been accused, tried, and condemned in conformity with the ecclesiastical laws."

We received the following reply to these inquiries:—

"M. le Professeur, the assertions of which you speak, in your letter of October 4, are so absurd and unworthy that they do not seem to require official disproof. The bishops in Belgium conform in such matters, as in all others, to the canonical laws, and to the decisions of the Holy See."

This letter has received the signature of the first ecclesiastical dignitary in Belgium. We have received also a letter from another episcopal officer, in which it is declared to be "really extraordinary that any serious writer should permit himself to utter such strange misstatements."

While we are on the subject of Dr. Littledale's pamphlet, which it would require a volume to refute, we may say in passing that we deny the truth of his assertions respecting the origin of the Papal power (pp. 10, 11, 23), Infallibility

(p. 11, n., p. 38), Catholic theology (p. 41), and the *Démonstrations Evangéliques* (p. 48). We should have much to say on the whole work, both as regards its matter and its form; we must, however, return to the clergy of Belgium and France.

In both countries, the Bishops treat their clergy with justice; and if they were in the habit of compelling the incumbents to resign, for trivial causes or without judicial inquiry, the Holy See would certainly recall them to a sense of their duty. There is more than one instance in which priests have appealed to Rome; but we thank God that, although they have occurred, such instances are rare. The administration of dioceses, both in France and Belgium, is too just and paternal to allow such an appeal to occur often.

VII. We have summed up all that has been done by the Church of France to increase the staff of priests in number, in learning, and in efficiency. Regiments have been formed, troops have been disciplined, the ranks have been filled up, and an army, numbering from 60,000 to 70,000 regular or secular priests, has been formed, of which the union and strength may be estimated by the virulence of the attacks to which they are now exposed.

Meanwhile, the education of youth in ecclesiastical colleges and seminaries has been established. Moreover, the Church being active in other ways, the French missionary is found in every part of the globe. All kinds of charitable and beneficent works have been carried on with success. Under whatever form misery presents itself, Catholic charity is aroused and hastens to relieve it. To estimate the amount of good work accomplished, it would be necessary to give the history of more than four hundred religious congregations of men or women in France, who have devoted themselves to the necessities of mankind in every form, who have taken infants from the cradle, have accompanied them in youth, who have supported, consoled, and relieved them in riper years, who have encouraged them in old age, and have closed their eyes in death. Orphanages, schools, refuges for boys and girls, workshops, farms, houses of correction, asylums for old age—these and other works have been first started in France, and have spread thence into all parts of the Catholic world.

According to the *Etat des Congrégations, &c.*, compiled by order of the Legislature in 1876, we have in France 2363

Religious Orders of every description; they number 5981 houses, schools, convents or colleges; 158,040 members, 13,279 public and 6295 private schools. All these figures are official; but they do not, we think, strictly conform to facts. For instance, we doubt whether the Religious Orders amount to the number of 2363, even taking as an Order every *independent* house or convent. In primary, secondary, or higher schools, the regular and secular clergy educated in 1876–1877, 2,168,643 boys, girls, or young men; whilst all the day-schools contained only 5,092,656. Of these 2363 Orders, the 136 unauthorized exercise on secondary education great influence, as is shown by the subjoined table:—

	Orders.	Schools.	Teachers.	Pupils.
Women	120	555	4857	40,784
Men	16	81	1556	20,235
	136	636	6413	61,019

The Church possesses in public or private schools of all sorts, at least 50,445 teachers, and perhaps 200 or 300 more in the new-founded Catholic universities. The clerical or religious intermediate colleges number 309.

The Tractarian movement in Oxford, and the religious revival effected in Anglicanism, has been sometimes termed an "unparalleled" wonder; and this is true up to a certain point. Protestantism has not prepared us for such a sight, and indeed the Anglican revival was not accomplished by Protestantism, but in opposition to it. We have already rendered homage to whatever is noble in this great event of our day. Yet, after all, what has been the result of the movement? It has led to the restoration of cathedrals which the Anglicans of the sixteenth century had mutilated or destroyed, and which their successors had allowed to fall into neglect and disrepair. It has led men to study the Fathers, biblical history, and theology. It has led to the restoration of the parochial system, which has never ceased to exist in the Catholic Church. It has led to the imitation, under new names and slightly altered forms, of certain Catholic Religious Orders. But, after the struggles, the efforts, the sacrifices, the quarrels of forty years, what is the result? A state of chaos. We admit that all this has been done by the Tractarians and Ritualists, in spite of their episcopate; but this is not precisely to the credit of their work, nor at any rate to the credit of their Church. It cannot be termed an ideal Church of Christ Jesus, in which such relations exist between the Anglican bishops and a small fraction of one party of their clergy. It is true, that the episcopate has opposed the Ritualist movement with the utmost vigour—only with the result of showing their absolute want of power. The machinery is old and worn out, and is only maintained by the State in order to give a certain social relief to the Anglican Church.

Let us now turn to the Church of France to see what she has done, and how much assistance she has received from without. In 1801 there was everything to do. Nothing remained but some deserted churches, ruined either by the Huguenots of the sixteenth century, who were allies of the English Protestants, or by the adherents of the Revolution in the eighteenth century. Besides restoring the old buildings, the Church of France has built hundreds of new ones, and the process of construction or repairs is still going on, and is even more general, for wherever we go, we see that new churches are being built, or that old ones are being restored. After 1801 came the Empire, with its despotism and its persecutions. The Restoration followed, and was scarcely more favourable to the Church. We need not speak of the Government of July, as its conduct is too well known. As for the Second Empire, if we wish to know its sentiments and intentions, we have only to read the memorial presented to Napoleon the Third by one of his Ministers of Public Worship.[1] The official pigeon-holes are full of such documents. In fact, the memorial gives a faithful summary of the policy exercised towards the Church. The Radicals are now carrying out, with their characteristic urbanity, the advice given to Napoleon the Third.

Notwithstanding the silent yet persistent opposition of Government, notwithstanding the ill-will, the vexatious interference, the persecutions of the central or local authorities, the revival of the Church of France is so complete that she would not, taking everything into consideration, exchange her present situation for that which she occupied before the Revolution—not because she has nothing to regret in the past, but because she is more in harmony with the necessities of the day than would be the case with her old organization. She required secular and regular clergy, and could promise

---

[1] Paris, Imprimerie Pillet, Rue des Grands Augustins.

them nothing but poverty, suffering, sometimes even persecution and death, and yet clergy flocked to her standard. In 1801 they scarcely numbered 20,000 or 25,000; and now they amount to more than 60,000. In 1801 the Church encountered suspicion, and often hatred, on all sides, especially among the higher classes. Now, there is not a trace of the constitutional schism, and we find the governing classes are steadily drawn into closer union with her, if we except such men as Waddington, Ferry, Lepère, and De Freycinet, &c., who cannot be said to govern.

The Church, which was destitute of means in 1801, has found money to carry out all her plans. Government has undertaken to keep historical monuments in repair; but the Church is responsible for other ecclesiastical buildings, as well as for the colleges, seminaries, refuges, orphanages, missions, and schools, which she has founded, or is founding every day. French Catholics must not be accused of not knowing how to give, because they do not provide large incomes for the parish priests. Such a state of things would be so contrary to French habits that it would never endure; but they do not allow the priests to lack what is necessary, and for all charitable works money is forthcoming; not, indeed, the millions of the rich—for, as every one knows, large fortunes are rare in France—but the mite of the poor, and that mite is well administered. Charity is ingenious, and such miracles are wrought with small sums, that they excite emotion and surprise.[1]

At the moment when we write these lines a great injustice is in course of perpetration, well calculated to show how much truth there is in the pretended distinction which has been drawn, and which some men have attempted to justify, between the authorized and unauthorized congregations. With a want of loyalty we might expect from those who are now in power, Catholic schools have been suppressed just as they were about to open. Such conduct is simply monstrous; but Catholics do not lose heart, and their courage is equal to the situation. Catholic schools are founded throughout France, and no sacrifice is thought too great for this purpose. The secular schools are empty, or almost empty, and although the majority of the *Conseils Généraux* have blamed the action

---

[1] M. About has disputed my assertion that two or three nuns were able to subsist on the Government allowance of £20: but such is the fact. I have been told of a community in which the average expense of each member amounts to £6 per annum. Their names and addresses are at the disposal of M. About.

of the Government, it has been of no avail. Government will not recognize these two forms of universal suffrage.

Neither the Church nor the clergy of France are opposed to the Republic; and the war which has been declared against them was not begun on their side. But, they passively endure it, and with God's help they hope, in the end, to triumph. The Church already bears signs of more than one wound, but she will not be the last to suffer, nor the most severely damaged. The Republic itself may perish from the senseless war which too many of its adherents have declared against Catholics. M. Thiers is accredited with a picturesque expression which has been verified more than once: "The man who devours a priest ever dies of the meal." And the saying applies equally to monarchies and republics; for it is a fact, that both forms of government have more than once perished in consequence of having partaken of such a repast. The Third Republic may fall from the same causes which destroyed its two predecessors. Therefore, the Church of France feels no alarm, although she deplores, for more than one reason, the conflict into which she has been drawn.

"These times are hard and gloomy for religion, but in the course of the present century we have witnessed still more gloomy days.

"Under the First Empire, any insult to our worship or our persons would have been severely repressed; but, in spite of this apparent protection, no real liberty was accorded to us. Parochial missions were prohibited, priests were not allowed to assemble for a religious retreat, Church schools were constrained to submit to the teaching of the *lycées*, the Sulpicians were expelled from the large seminaries, and the Pope was a prisoner at Fontainebleau. The man who then ruled almost the whole of Europe convoked a national council with a schismatic intention, and imprisoned those bishops who offered a vigorous resistance.

"In 1830 there was a prevailing indifference in matters of religion. In what are called the governing classes, among philosophers and men of literature and learning, religious questions were the object of general and profound disdain; the influence of the Catholic priesthood was supposed to be extinct, and the *funeral rites of a mighty cult*, that is, the end of the Catholic Church, were declared to be imminent.

"This is no longer the case. Religious questions now take precedence of all others; our enemies are amazed and irritated by our energetic vitality; our progress alarms them; and, from their point of view, the influence we have gained is a peril to society.

"The war which has now begun is better than the chill, disdainful indifference of bygone days."

VIII. The words above quoted are taken from a speech lately uttered by one of the princes of the Church of France.

They are a summary of what we have endeavoured to say, and express what we think and hope.

We do not pretend to affirm that everything in the Church of France is perfect, for nothing is or will be perfect in this world. There is room for progress and improvement in more than one direction; but the rulers of the Church are not always able to do what is absolutely the best. They have to be prudent; they must often be silent when they wish to speak, and content themselves with only soliciting a portion of their rights. The Church of France is no longer wealthy. She no longer possesses rich abbeys, and bishoprics of still greater value. Princes of the royal family, counts, and barons no longer become bishops. But, in our age these dignities are not esteemed; and such men as Gambetta, Spuller, Le Royer, and Waddington, are the products of the time. In order to rise to power in France, one might be Genoese, German, Swiss, English, anything in short but French in blood and sentiment. This fact scarcely glorifies the Republic, but the truth remains in spite of it.

While we contemplate the situation of the Church, which she did not create for herself, we do not hesitate to repeat that she is ready to withstand the attack which she deplores and deprecates. If forced to resist, she will do so with charity; but her resistance is certain, and she knows how to follow the example given by her fathers in the faith.

We write these lines almost on the very spot where those massacres occurred which must overwhelm any government with shame. From the window at which we are now sitting, we can mentally follow the phases of this atrocious butchery. In the church hard by were confined the victims doomed to perish by the sword of assassins hired at a salary of six francs a day. The executions took place for the most part in the garden below, and a pillar marks the spot beside the reservoir where the first victim fell. The chapel stained with the blood of these martyrs has only recently disappeared; but the narrow staircase where so many were cut down, and the angle of the wall where from 120 to 170 corpses were piled in ghastly array, may still be seen. On this ill-omened day, the 2d September 1792, nobles and plebeians, bishops and priests, perished together, involved in one common slaughter. Should the present Republic be minded to imitate the doings of its ancestor, the clergy of our time will prove themselves worthy of their predecessors in those days. They will fulfil their mission to the end, and will not shrink from shedding their blood for the cause of God. The heroic spectacle then witnessed will be again enacted, and the clergy of the present century will not be found inferior to the clergy of 1789. May God, however, avert such deeds of blood from France and from the world! *Dî talem avertite casum.*

ADDENDUM.

Additional Note to page 246.

The following Table has been compiled from the XXII. *Tableau* for the years 1872 and 1873, and from the XXIII. *Tableau* for the years 1874 to 1877 of the official publication entitled *Compte Général de l'Administration de la Justice Criminelle en France*, &c. The respective numbers of the clergy and other educated classes are those which are given for the year 1875, in the *Annuaire Statistique de la France* for 1878. To the number of the clergy, there ought to be added, at the least, 8000 regular priests; but, it must be observed, of the gross number of about 70,000 who are computed as ecclesiastical persons, that in round numbers 10,000 are Seminarists, 700 are Protestant Ministers, and 60 are Jewish Rabbis. That the proportion is largely in favour of the clergy is obvious. The distinguishing names have been left in their French form, as the English words are not always rigorously equivalent.

Sentences for crime in the years 1872-1877.

Total Number.	1872.	1873.	1874.	1875.	1876.	1877.	Average.	Proportion.
66,868 *Clergé*	6	6	1	5	13	0	5	1 in 13,000
12,761 *Avocats*	3	6	10	5	4	4	5¼	5 ,,
9,244 *Notaires*	23	11	22	18	16	14	17⅔	23.7 ,,
5,246 *Huissiers*	14	17	18	10	11	10	13½	24.7 ,,

The reader may refer, for further information on this topic, to the recently published volume by Mr. Charles Walker, "The Superiority of the Catholic Church" (Dublin: Duffy), in the note to page 90.

THE END.

1880-81.

A Catalogue

OF

MESSRS. BURNS & OATES' PUBLICATIONS,

ARRANGED ALPHABETICALLY
UNDER THE NAMES OF AUTHORS.

Complete **Church Furniture Catalogue** in preparation.
    Do. **Stationery Catalogue**   Do.
    Do. **Music Catalogue**   Do.
    Do. **Foreign Catalogue** now ready.

London:
17 & 18 PORTMAN STREET, W., AND 63 PATERNOSTER ROW.

Now Publishing, to be completed in 38 Parts (30 of which are now ready), at 1s. per Part,

THE LIFE OF
OUR LORD AND SAVIOUR JESUS CHRIST
AND OF
HIS BLESSED MOTHER.
FROM THE ORIGINAL OF REV. L. C. BUSINGER.

This is the first fully illustrated **LIFE** of **CHRIST** ever published in English. It contains nearly **600 choice Engravings** embodied in the Text, together with a beautiful **Illuminated Title-page**, a **Presentation Plate**, and a **Family Record** printed in colours, **6 exquisite Chromo-lithographs**, and **31** fine full-page **Plates**. In addition,

A SUPERB STEEL ENGRAVING
OF THE
RESURRECTION OF OUR LORD
(Size 20¼ by 27½ inches), is
PRESENTED FREE TO EACH SUBSCRIBER.

Agents wanted in all parts of the country, to whom liberal terms will be given.

THE CATHOLIC BIRTH-DAY BOOK.
COMPILED BY A LADY.

2ND EDITION.

'*Through the Birth-day of Jesus we have been able to celebrate our birth-days.*'—
A BENEDICTINE FATHER.

PRICES.

Cloth plain . . .	2s. 6d.	Calf, with calf cover . . 7s. 6d.
Cloth gilt . . .	3s. 0d.	Russia, in russian cover . 9s. 6d.

LONDON: BURNS AND OATES.

CATALOGUE OF BOOKS

PUBLISHED BY

BURNS AND OATES.

Adolph, W. Simplicity of the Creation . . . £0 5 0
A'Kempis. The following of Christ, in four books; a new translation, beautifully printed in royal 16mo, with borders round each page, and illustrative engravings after designs by the best German Artists. Cloth 0 3 6
    Calf 0 7 0
    Morocco 0 8 6
    Gilt 0 11 0
    Ditto, antique morocco, with clasp, and beautifully illustrated with numerous engravings 1 5 0
    The same, pocket edition. Cloth 0 1 0
    Bound roan 0 1 6
    French morocco 0 2 6
    Calf 0 4 6
    Morocco 0 5 0
    Gilt 0 6 0
    Bound with the NEW TESTAMENT. Calf 0 6 0
    Morocco 0 7 0
    Bound with SPIRITUAL COMBAT. Cloth 0 2 6
    Roan, red edges 0 3 6
    Calf 0 6 0
    Morocco 0 7 0
    Gilt 0 8 0
Alice Leighton : a Tale of the Seventeenth Century 0 6 0
Alice Sherwin : a Tale of the Days of Henry VIII. . 0 4 0
Allies, T. W. See of St. Peter 0 4 6
    Formation of Christendom. Vols. I., II., III., each . . . 0 12 0
Allnatt, C. F. B. Cathedra Petri : the Titles and Prerogatives of St. Peter, and of his See and Successors, as described by the Early Fathers, &c. Second edition, greatly enlarged, demy 8vo . . 0 4 0
    Which is the True Church ? Demy 8vo 0 1 0
    The Church of Rome not the great Apostasy 0 0 6
Anderdon, Rev. Fr. (S.J.) :
    Afternoons with the Saints. Eighth edition 0 4 0
    Antoine de Bonneval : a Story of the Fronde 0 3 0
    Catholic Crusoe. Seven Illustrations. Seventh edition . . 0 6 0
    Christian Æsop. Fifty-one illustrations 0 3 6
    Ditto 0 4 0
    Confession to a Priest 0 0 1

Anderdon, Rev. Fr. (S.J.)—*Continued.*

Controversial Papers. Containing: I. Is Ritualism honest? II. Is there Unity in the Church of Rome? III. Answer to the Protestant Bishop of Manchester. 1 vol., cloth £0 2 0
(These tracts are to be had separately, at the respective prices of 1s., 3d., and 4d).
In the Snow: Tales of Mount St. Bernard. Sixth edition, cloth . . 0 1 6
 Gilt 0 2 6
Is Ritualism honest? New edition, fcap. 16mo 0 1 0
What is the Bible? Is yours the Right Book? 0 0 1

Anderdon, Rev. Fr. (S.J.), edited by:
How Children can write Sermons 0 0 2
Purgatory surveyed; or a Particular Account of the Happy and yet Thrice-Unhappy State of the Souls there. From the edition of 1663 . 0 3 0
What do Catholics really believe? 0 0 1

Andersen, Hans. Select Tales. Cloth gilt . . . 0 2 0
Cheap edition 0 1 4

Andrada, Alphonso de (S.J.):
Daily Meditations on the Mysteries of our Holy Faith, and on the Lives of our Lord Jesus Christ and of the Saints, for all Seasons of the Year. 4 vols. 0 14 0

Anselm, St. Meditations. With Preface by the Cardinal Archbishop of Westminster 0 5 0

Arctic Voyages. Cloth gilt 0 2 0
Cheap edition 0 1 6

Arias, Father Francis (S.J.):
A Guide to the Members of the Spiritual Union, established by the Ven. Domenico Gesù e Maria; The Last Testament of the Soul (by St. Charles Borromeo); Spiritual Contact of the Soul with the Lord our God 0 1 6
The Virtues of Blessed Mary, Mother of Jesus Christ. Second edition . 0 2 6
The Charity of Jesus Christ. 1 vol., 8vo wrapper. 222 pp., . . 0 3 0

Arnold, Rev. Fr. (S.J.) Imitation of the Sacred Heart. 12mo.
Sixth edition 0 4 6
Cloth, red edges 0 5 0
Calf 0 8 6
Morocco 0 9 6
Ditto, with edges turned over 0 13 0
Ditto, antique elegant, with six beautiful engravings, and clasp . 1 5 0

Authority and Anarchy, or the Bible on the Church.
Second edition 0 2 0

Balmez. Catechism of Religion 0 0 6

Baptismal Service, Latin and English, with explanations . 0 0 2

Bedford, Henry. Life of St. Vincent de Paul. A new and complete Biography. Cloth 0 3 0

Bellarmine, Cardinal. Seven Words on the Cross. Translated from the Latin 0 5 0

Benni, Most Rev. C. B., Syriac Archbishop of Mossoul. Tradition of the Syriac Church of Antioch £0 7 6

Catalogue of Publications. 5

Beste, Rev. Kenelm Digby :
A May Chaplet (verses). Blue cloth gilt £0 4 0
Spiritual Reading. See 'Spiritual Reading'.

Bible. 8vo 0 6 0
  ,, French morocco 0 8 0
  12m 0 3 0
  4to . . . . from 1 10 0
Pocket editions . . . . from 0 2 6

Blessed Sacrament, the Centre of Immutable Truth.
A new and revised edition. Cloth 0 1 0

Blois, Henri de. Life of Blosius, a Benedictine
Writer of the Sixteenth Century. Translated by Lady Lovat. 1 vol.,
crown 8vo, cloth 0 6 6

B. N. The Jesuits : their Foundation and History.
2 vols., crown 8vo, cloth, red edges 0 15 0
'The book is just what it professes to be—*a popular history*, drawn from well-known sources,' &c.—*Month*, July 1879.

Bona Mors, Devotion of the. Cloth 0 0 4
Music for do. contained in ' Popular Choir Manual ' 0 10 6

Bonaventure, St., Points for Mental Prayer. Square
32mo. Cloth lettered 0 0 6

Boone on Frequent Communion 0 0 4
 Cloth 0 0 6

Bottalla, Father (S.J.) :
Papacy and Schism 0 2 6
Reply to Renouf on Pope Honorius 0 8 6

Bowden, Rev. H. S., edited by :
Miniature Lives of the Saints. New edition, 2 vols . . . 0 4 0
 Also in separate monthly packets . . . . . each 0 0 4
 Or the complete annual set 0 3 6
Miniature Life of Mary. Cloth 0 0 6
 Cloth extra, with photo. 0 1 0

Bowden, J. E. Spirit of the Curé of Ars . . 0 2 0
Red edges, portrait 0 2 6
Calf 0 5 0
Morocco 0 5 6

Bowles, Emily :
French Eggs in an English Basket. From the French of Souvestre.
Cloth Extra 0 3 6
Life of St. Jane Frances Frémyot de Chantal. (One of the Quarterly
Series vols.) Second edition 0 5 6

Boylesve, Père (S.J.) A Thought for each Day of
the Year. Translated from the French. Second edition, cloth . 0 2 6
 Cloth, red edges 0 3 0
 Calf 0 5 6
 Morocco 0 6 0

Brame, C. M. :
Angels' Visits 0 3 6
Tales from the Diary of a Sister of Mercy. New edition, crown 16mo,
cloth gilt 0 4 0

Breen, J. D. (O.S.B.). Anglican Orders: are they valid? £0 0 8
Anglican Jurisdiction: is it valid? 0 1 0

Bridges, M.:
Popular Ancient History 0 3 6
Popular Modern History 0 4 0

Bridgett, Rev. T. E. (C.SS.R.):
Discipline of Drink 0 3 6
Our Lady's Dowry: how England won and lost that Title. Second ed. . 0 9 0
Ritual of the New Testament: an Essay on the Principles and Origin of Catholic Ritual 0 5 0

Bridgett, Rev. T. E. (C.SS.R.), edited by:
Suppliant of the Holy Ghost: a Paraphrase of the 'Veni Sancte Spiritus'. Now first printed from a MS. of the seventeenth century composed by Rev. R. Johnson, with other unpublished treatises by the same author. Red cloth 0 1 6
Watson's Sermons on the Sacraments 0 7 6

Buckingham, Leicester Ambrose. The Bible in the Middle Ages, with Remarks on the Libraries, Schools, and Social and Religious Aspects of Mediæval Europe. 8vo 0 6 0

Burial Service and Mass. Latin and English . . 0 0 3

Caddell, Miss:
Little Snowdrop 0 0 6
Cloth 0 1 0
Missions in Japan and Paraguay. Cloth 0 3 0
Nellie Netterville: a Tale of the Times of Cromwell . . . 0 3 6
Sœur Marie 0 3 6
Tales for the Young. First Series. Contents: Ellen's Dream, Lucy's Pilgrimage, The Shepherd Boy, Requiescat in Pace, Little Adam, The Cherries, The Rosary, No Virtue without Struggle, Little Martin, Tales of the Ardennes, The Two Mothers, The Two Italians. Paper cover 0 1 6
Cloth 0 2 0
Tales for the Young. Second Series. Contents: Month of Mary, Feast of Corpus Christi, Sacred Heart of Jesus, The Assumption, The Nativity, The Purification, Ash Wednesday, The Annunciation, Holy Week, Easter, Rogation Day, Pentecost. Paper cover . . 0 1 6
Cloth 0 2 0
Tales of the Festivals 0 1 6
Cloth 0 2 0
Three Days' Preparation for Holy Communion. From the French of St. Jure 0 0 8

Callista, as dramatised by Husenbeth 0 2 0

Cambria Sacra. See 'Nédélec'.

Cashel, Hoey, Mrs.:
Life of Madame de la Rochefoucald, Duchesse de Dondeauville, Foundress of the Society of Nazareth. Translated from the French. Cloth extra, with portrait 0 7 6
Nazareth: an Account of the Society of Nazareth 0 2 0

Caswall, Father:
Catholic Latin Instructor in the Principal Church Offices and Devotions, for the use of Choirs, Convents, and Mission Schools, and for Self-Teaching. 1 vol., complete 0 3 6

Caswell, Father—*Continued.*

Or Part I., containing Benediction, Mass, Serving at do., various Latin Prayers in ordinary use £0 1 6
Hymns and Poems. Second edition 0 5 0
May Pageant 0 2 0
Words of Jesus (Verba Verbi). Cloth 0 2 0

Catechism Christian Doctrine, No. 1, per 100, . . . 0 3 0
                                                       No. 2, per 100, . . . 0 5 0

Catechism, Meanings of Words of 0 0 2

Catechism of Confirmation. See 'Richards'.

Catechism of Virtues and Vices. See 'Richards'.

Catholic Belief: Exposition of Christian Doctrine.
Third edition, containing much new matter 0 0 6

Catholic Birthday Book, The 0 2 6

Catholic Christian Instructed. New edition, cloth . . 0 0 9

Catholicity, an Aid thereto. By a Catholic Priest . per doz. 0 0 9

Caussade, Père, (S.J.). The Workings of the Divine Will. From the French. Revised by a Father of the same Society. 18mo, wrapper, 62 pp. 0 0 9

Celebrated Men, Lives of. Cloth gilt 0 3 6

Celebrated Women. Cloth gilt 0 2 0
    Cheap edition 0 1 6

Challoner. Catholic Christian instructed . . . 0 0 9
Meditations for every Day in the Year. New Edition. Revised and edited by the Rt. Rev. Mgr. Virtue, D.D. 8vo . . . 0 6 0

Chancellors, The Three: Wykeham, Waynflete, and More 0 4 0

Children of Mary, The : containing Narratives of Lives of Young Ladies. New edition, cloth elegant, Cheap edition . . . 0 2 6

Children of Mary. Rules, Prayers and Services of the Sodality. 48 pp. 0 0 2

Choppart, Jean Paul, Amusing History of. Gilt . . 0 2 6

Christian Doctrine. Simple Instruction in 0 2 0

Christie, Rev. A. J. (S.J.):
First Christmas : a Mystery Play. Cloth gilt 0 2 6
    Limp cloth 0 0 6
Martyrdom of St. Cecilia : a Drama. Fifth edition, cloth . . 0 5 0
    Cheap edition, limp cloth 0 0 6
St. Cecily : a Drama. Fifth edition, cloth 0 5 0
    Cheap edition, limp cloth 0 0 6

Church History, Manual of, for Families and Schools.
Compiled from the best sources. 12mo, cloth 0 3 0

Clarke, Theodora Lane. Roman Violets, and where they Blossom : a Story for Young and Old. Beautifully bound in cloth, bevelled edges 0 4 0

Clifton Tales:

1. Joe Baker	£0 0 6	
2. Lucy Ward	0 0 6	
3. Rich and Poor	0 0 6	
4. Winefride Jones	0 0 6	
5. Poor Man's Child	0 0 6	
6. Robert May	0 0 6	
7. John Chapman	0 0 6	
The whole may be had in two vols., cloth gilt . . . each	0 3 0	
Or in four parts, limp cloth . . . . . . each	0 1 0	

Clifton Tracts. 4 vols. 0 10 0

Vol. I. The Reformation	0 2 6
II. Historical Fallacies	0 2 0
III. Christian Doctrine	0 3 0
IV. Miscellaneous	0 2 6
Selections in 10 Volumes . . . . . . 6d. to	0 1 0

(The Tracts may also be had separately. List on application).

Code Poetical Reader, with Marginal Notes and Biographical Notices of Authors. By a Teacher. Adapted to the School Boards requirements. Limp cloth. 0 1 0

Coleridge, Rev. H. J.:

Life and Letters of St. Francis Xavier. (Quarterly Series.) Third edition, 2 vols. 0 18 0

Life of Our Life: the Harmony of the Gospels. Arranged with Introductory and Explanatory Chapters, Notes and Indices. (Quarterly Series.) 2 vols. 0 15 0

Prisoners of the King: a Book of Thoughts on the Catholic Doctrine of Purgatory. Cloth 0 6 6

Public Life of our Lord Jesus Christ. (Quarterly Series.) 4 vols. already published . . . . each 0 6 6

*** Other volumes in preparation.

Sermon on the Mount: being three vols. of the Public Life of our Lord, published separately, for convenience of purchasers. (Quarterly Series.) 0 15 0

Vitæ Vitæ Nostræ. Latin Version of Life of our Life. Cloth . . 0 7 6
Calf 0 10 6

Coleridge, Rev. H. J. (S.J.), edited by:

Chronicle of St. Anthony of Padua, the 'Eldest Son of St. Francis.' (Quarterly Series) 0 5 6

Dialogues of St. Gregory the Great. An old English version. (Quarterly Series) 0 6 0

History of the Sacred Passion. By Palma. Third ed. (Quarterly Series) 0 7 6
Cheaper edition, on thin paper 0 5 0

Rogacci. The Christian reformed in Mind and Manners. (Quarterly Series) 0 7 6

In order to meet the convenience of persons who desire to use the Meditations and Considerations in this volume for Retreats, a limited number of copies has been printed, in which each Meditation is on a separate sheet. These copies may be had in a loose cover on application 0 7 6

Communion, Holy, &c., Books on:

Considerations for a Three Days' Preparation for Communion. From the French. By Cecilia Mary Caddell 0 0 8
White vellum, gilt 0 2 0

De Ségur. Practical Counsels for Holy Communion. From the French 0 0 4
Cloth, gilt 0 0 8
White vellum, gilt 0 2 0

Devotions for Confession and Communion (Oratory). Covers . . 0 0 6

Communion, Holy, &c., Books on—*Continued.*

Eucharistic Month	£0	0	6
Cloth	0	1	0
Holy Communion . . . . per doz.	0	1	6
Letters on First Communion	0	1	0
Once every Week . . . . per doz.	0	1	6
Père Bonne on frequent Communion. Cloth	0	0	6
Reflections and Prayers for Holy Communion. From the French. Cloth. Two series . . . . each	0	4	6
Ditto, red edges	0	5	0
Calf	0	9	0
Morocco	0	10	0
St. Alphonso Liguori on the Holy Eucharist	0	3	6
Cheap edition	0	2	0
St. Alphonso Liguori. Visits to the Most Blessed Sacrament	0	1	0
Visits to Jesus on the Altar. By the Author of 'Reflections and Prayers for Holy Communion'. Translated from the French. Approved by the Bishop of Nancy. 32mo, cloth, red edges	0	1	6

Compline Book, The Complete. Third edition . . . 0 1 0

Confession, Manual of 0 0 2

Confession, Instructions and Devotions for. For the use of Convent Schools, &c. Compiled from approved sources by a Priest. 32mo, cloth 0 0 6
 Calf, red edges 0 3 0
 Oratory Book 0 0 2

Confirmation, Manual of 0 0 2

Connolly, Rev. J.:
 Hymns. 32mo, wrapper, 53 pp. 0 0 6
 Melodies and Organ Accompaniments for ditto. 8vo . 0 5 0

Conscience, Hendrik:
Blind Rosa	0	1	0
Conscript	0	1	0
Count Hugo	0	1	4
Curse of the Village. Gilt	0	3	0
Demon of Gold. Gilt	0	3	0
Lion of Flanders. Gilt	0	3	0
Miser	0	1	4
Gilt	0	3	0
Poor Gentleman	0	1	0
Ricketicketack	0	1	0
Tales of Flanders. Gilt	0	3	0
Veva. Gilt	0	3	0

Conversions, Narratives of Remarkable. Cloth . . 0 2 6

Cooke, Rev. Robert (O.M.I.):
 Sketches of the Life of Mgr. de Mazenod, Founder of the Order of the Oblates of Mary, &c. Vol. I. 8vo, cloth 0 10 6
  (Other volumes in preparation.)
 Youthful Holiness. Second edition 0 3 0

Cottage Conversations. Second edition. Cloth . . 0 3 0

Courbon, Père. Mental Prayer. With Preface by the Rev. Fr. Gordon of the Oratory 0 2 6

Crusades, Tales of the. Gilt 0 2 6
 Cheap edition 0 1 8

Cumplido, Father Felix (S.J.). The Perfect Lay
Brother. Translated by Father John G. Macleod, S.J. . . . £0 4 6
Curé's Niece : a Story. From the French. Cloth . . . 0 3 6
Cusack, Miss (Nun of Kenmare) :
Book of the Blessed Ones. Third edition 0 4 6
Cloister Songs :
No. 1. St. Agnes' Eve. Words by Tennyson. Suitable for a mezzo-
soprano voice . . . . 4s for 0 2 0
No. 2. The Bells of Kenmare. Suitable for any compass of voice 4s for 0 2 0
No. 3. The Morning Sacrifice. Words by the Rev. J. Ryan 4s for 0 2 0
Conferences for Ecclesiastical Students. By M. l'Abbé Tronson.
Translated from the French. 0 4 6
Devotions for the Ecclesiastical Year 0 4 6
Illustrated History of Ireland. Eleventh thousand, demy 8vo, 700 pp.,
cloth, gilt edges 0 11 0
Plain 0 10 0
In Memoriam. Mary O'Hagan, Abbess and Foundress of the Convent
of Poor Clares, Kenmare. Cloth gilt 0 6 0
Jesus and Jerusalem ; or the Way Home. Sixth thousand . . . 0 4 6
Liberator, The : his Life and Times, political, social, and religious.
New Library Edition. Seventh thousand, 2 vols . . . each 0 12 0
Life of Father Mathew 0 2 6
Life of St. Patrick, Apostle of Ireland. Demy 8vo, cloth . . . 0 6 0
With illustrations, cloth gilt 0 10 0
Little Book of the Lovers of the Heart of Jesus Crucified . . . 0 0 4
Lives of St. Columba and St. Brigit. Demy 8vo, cloth gilt . . . 0 6 0
New School History of Ireland. Illustrated 0 2 0
Nun's Advice to her Girls, A. Fourth Thousand 0 2 6
Pilgrim's Way to Heaven. Second edition, third thousand. Cloth . 0 4 6
Public Speeches and Letters of the Liberator. A continuation of his
'Life and Times'. 6 vols., demy 8vo . . . . per vol. 0 15 0
Spirit of St. Gertrude. Third edition 0 2 6
Spouse of Christ ; her Duties and her Privileges. Vol. I. . . . 0 7 6
Vol. II. 0 7 6
(This work will be completed in three volumes).
St. Patrick's Manual : a Guide to Catholic Devotion 0 3 6
Visits to the Altar of Mary 0 0 9
Woman's Work in Modern Society. New cheap edition . . . 0 7 6

Day Hours of the Church. Cloth 0 1 0
Also, separately, Prime and Compline 0 0 8
Tierce, Sext, and None 0 0 3
Day Sanctified : The : Select Meditations and Spiritual Readings
from Approved Writers 0 3 6
Red edges 0 4 0
Deharbe, (S.J.) Church History in preparation.
Dering, E. H., Esq., Author of 'Sherborne,' etc.
Freville Chase. 2 vols. 0 12 0
Devine, Rev. Pius, Passionist :
Eutropia, or How to find a Way out of Darkness into Light. 1 vol., cr.
8vo, cloth, boards. 433 pp. 0 7 0
Devotions for Country Missions, with Hymns . . 0 0 6
Devout Life, Introduction to. 'See Richards'.

Dodsworth. Popular Delusions on Catholicism.
Cloth £0 1 0

Dominic, St. :
Life of, with Sketch of the Order. Cloth 0 3 6
Manual of the Third Order 0 2 6
Novena of, in Preparation for his Feast.' With portrait . . 0 0 4

Dominican Hymn Book, in the Press

Douglas, Sir Charles. Long Resistance and Ultimate Conversion. New edition 0 2 6

Drane, Augusta Theodosia :
History of St. Catherine of Siena and her Companions. 1 vol., royal
8vo. 680 pp., cloth gilt 0 12 6

Duke, Rev. H. C. :
King Rodolpho's Will, a Drama in one act, with Prologue. Wrapper . 0 1 4

Eckel, Mrs. St. John. Maria Monk's Daughter. An
Autobiography. Crown 8vo. 411 pp. 0 4 0

Emmerich (Sister) on the Passion 0 3 6

Encyclical Letter of Our Holy Father Leo XIII. on
St. Thomas Aquinas. Translated by Fr. Rawes, D.D., with a Preface
by His Eminence Cardinal Manning 0 1 0

England, History of :
Catechism of 0 0 6
For Schools, Colleges, &c. Post 8vo 0 6 0
For the Young. Illustrations. Cloth 0 3 0
Introductory, for Schools 0 1 8

Epistles and Gospels of the Roman Missal for every
Day in the Year. In English. Arranged, with Index. Cloth . . 0 1 6
For the Sundays and Feasts. Small edition 0 0 6

Estcourt, Very Rev. Canon. The Question of Anglican Ordinations discussed 0 14 0

Faber, Very Rev. Father:
All for Jesus 0 5 0
Bethlehem 0 7 0
Blessed Sacrament 0 7 6
Creator and Creature 0 6 0
Ethel's Book 0 2 6
Foot of the Cross 0 6 0
Growth in Holiness 0 6 0
Hymns 0 6 0
Notes on Doctrinal and Spiritual Subjects. 2 vols. . . . each £0 5 0
Poems 0 7 6
Precious Blood 0 5 0
Sir Lancelot 0 5 0
Spirit of St. Philip 0 2 0
Spiritual Conferences 0 6 0

Faber, Life of Father 0 10 6

Faber's Works, 'Civiltà Cattolicà' on Father . 0 1 0

Fander. Catechism of the Christian Religion.
Cloth £0 2 0

Ferré, Monsignor. St. Thomas of Aquin and
Ideology, Translated by a Father of Charity. Cloth extra . . . 0 2 0

Féval, Paul. The Jesuits 0 3 0

Fifth of November, and other Tales by the Author
of Marion Howard. 1 vol. Cloth gilt 0 5 0

Figuera, Fr. Gaspar de la (S.J.). A Spiritual Compendium. From the Spanish 0 4 6

Finlay, Rev. Thos. A., (S.J.) Freedom of Education under the French Republic. The principles of Liberty and Equality 0 1 0

Fireside Stories; or Tales for the Young. Cloth
gilt 0 2 6

First Communion, Letters on. Cloth 0 1 0
Roan 0 1 6

Fleming, Rev. W. True Church of the Bible. 24mo.
Wrapper 0 1 0

Francis of Assisi. New Life of, by Léopold de Chérancé. 8vo. 0 7 6

Foley, Henry (S.J.). Records of the English Province of the Society of Jesus. Vol. I., Series I. Demy 8vo, 720 pp. nett 1 6 0
Vol. II., Series II. III. IV.. Demy 8vo, ... ,, 1 6 0
Vol. III., Series V. VI. VII. VIII. Demy 8vo, over 850 pages . ,, 1 10 0
Vol. IV., Series IX. X. XI. Demy 8vo, 750 pp., ... 1 6 6
Vol. V., Series XII. Demy 8vo, nearly 1100 pp., with nine Photographs
of Martyrs . . . . nett 1 10 0
Vol. VI. Diary and Pilgrim-Book of the English College, Rome. The
Diary from 1579 to 1773 with Biographical and Historical notes .
The Pilgrim Book of the ancient English Hospice attached to the College
from 1580 to 1656, with historical notes. Demy, 8vo, pp. 796 . . 1 6 0

Formby, Rev. H.
Book of the Holy Rosary : a Popular Doctrinal Exposition of its Fifteen
Mysteries. Embellished with 36 full-page illustrations, designed by C.
Clasen, D. Mosler, and J. H. Powell. In highly ornamental binding. 0 10 6
Catechism of the Christian Doctrine contained in the Fifteen Mysteries
of the Rosary. Super-royal, 32mo. In wrapper 0 0 2
Cloth 0 0 6
Compendium of the Philosophy of Ancient History : a Companion for the
Study of Greek and Roman History, and a book to put into the hands
of Sceptics and Unbelievers 0 4 6
Complete Historical Catechism, from the Beginning of the World, continued down to the Recent Vatican Council, following also the course
of History of the Bible and Church-History Stories, so as to be able to
serve the auxilliary purpose of ' Examination Questions,' either for the
Complete Bible and Church-History Stories or its Abridgment.
Super-royal 32mo, 128 pp., in wrapper 0 0 2
Cloth neat 0 0 6
De Annis Christi Tractatus : sive Chronologiæ Sacræ et Profanæ inter se
et cum Vaticiniis S. Scripturæ Concordia plena. Pars I. Quæstio
Chronologica de Documentis Historiæ. Pars II. Quæstio Theologica
præcipue de Vaticiniis et Interpretatione S. Scripturæ . . . 0 2 0

Formby, Rev. H.—*Continued.*

Five Lectures on the City of Ancient Rome and her Empire over the Nations, the Divinely-sent Pioneer of the Way for the Catholic Church	£0	2	6
Inquiry of a Retired Citizen into the Truth of the Catholic Religion. In the form of a dialogue	0	2	0
Little Book of the Martyrs of the City of Rome. With sixty-one entirely new wood engravings. Crown 8vo, cloth extra, best paper gilt edges	0	3	0
People's edition, cloth plain	0	1	6
Monotheism, the Primitive Religion of the City of Rome: an Historical Investigation. 8vo,	0	12	0
Pictorial Bible and Church-History Stories; abridged and complete in one volume, 320 pp., crown 8vo; with panoramic frontispiece and bird's-eye view of Jerusalem, numerous cuts throughout. Poor-school Edition	0	1	4
Best paper, cloth extra, highly gilt	0	3	6
Pictorial Bible and Church-History Stories, in canvas.			
Part I. Old-Testament History	0	1	3
II. " " "	0	1	3
III. " " "	0	1	3
IV. The Life of Jesus Christ	0	1	3
V. Acts of the Apostles to the Conversion of Constantine.	0	1	3
VI. Constantine to the Martyrdom of St. Thomas of Canterbury	0	1	3
VII. To present Time	0	1	3
Ditto, per doz. to schools	0	12	0
Ditto, Edition for Schools, canvas, 3 vols.	0	8	3
Ditto, Edition for Families, 3 vols., cloth lettered	0	12	0
Superior paper, cloth extra	1	1	0

Formby, Rev. H.:

Pictorial Life of Jesus Christ. Crown 8vo, 64 pp., 30 vignettes in the text. Paper	£0	0	4
Cloth	0	0	6
Allowance to Schools if required in quantities.			
Sacrum Septenarium: or the Seven Gifts of the Holy Ghost, as exemplified in the Life and Person of the Blessed Virgin, the Mother of the Christian Family, for the Instruction of her Children. In cloth, neat red edges	0	3	6

Other Illustrated Works:

1. Parables of our Lord Jesus Christ. Numerous illustrations. Wrapper	0	0	6
Cloth	0	1	0
Gilt, for presents	0	1	6
2. Seven Sacraments of the Church, with 16 illustrations of their types in the Old Testament. Wrapper	0	0	6
Cloth	0	1	0
Gilt, for presents	0	1	6
3. School Keepsake. 4 engravings	0	0	3
Cloth, gilt	0	1	0
4. Twelve Mysteries of the Holy Infancy. 14 engravings, wrapper	0	0	6
Cloth neat	0	1	0
5. Fifteen Mysteries of the Rosary. 18 engravings, wrapper	0	0	6
Cloth neat	0	1	0
6. Stations of the Cross. 14 engravings, wrapper	0	0	4
Cloth neat	0	1	0
7. Seven Dolours of the Blessed Virgin. 7 engravings, wrapper	0	0	4
Cloth neat	0	1	0

School Songs and Music:

Catholic School Song-Book. 210 Songs. 32mo, cover	0	0	4
Cloth	0	0	6

14   Burns and Oates'

Formby, Rev. H.—*Continued.*
Or may be had in two parts:
 Junior School Song-Book £0 0 2
 Senior School Song-Boook 0 0 3
Illustrated Hymn Book 0 0 2
Singing-Class Primer 0 0 2
Music for the above:
 No. I. Melodies of the Junior School Song-Book. Small 4to. For voices and pianoforte 0 2 6
 No. II. Melodies of the Junior School Song-Book. Post 4to. For voices and pianoforte 0 3 6
Catholic Hymns for the Feasts and Saints' Days of the Year. Post 4to . 0 2 6
Rounds and Catches 0 1 0
Roman Ritual, and its Canto Fermo. Cloth flush . . . 0 1 6
Ancient Rome, and its connection with the Christian Religion. An outline of the History of the City from its first foundation by Romulus (B.C. 753), down to the Erection of the Chair of St. Peter in the Ostrian Cemetery (A.D. 42-47), containing numerous illustrations in wood engraving of the Ancient Monuments, Sculpture, Coinage and Localities connected with the History of the City, with the addition of a series of engravings illustrating the formation and the antiquities of the Christian Catacombs. Pp. 448 . . . . 2 10

Formby. An Investigation into the Growing Unbelief of the Educated Classes . . . .

Form for Laying the Foundation Stone of a Church 0 0 2

France, New Popular History of. Many Illustrations . 0 3 6

Franciscan Fathers (of Stratford), Works by:
Manual of the Archconfraternity of the Cord of St. Francis. Cloth . 0 1 6
Month of October, dedicated to the Seraphic Patriarch St. Francis by his Children and Devout Clients. Translated from the Italian of Fr. Candedo Mariotti, with a commendatory letter from Cardinal Manning. Cloth 0 3 0
Presence of God 0 0 6

Franciscan Missions among the Colliers and Ironworkers of Monmouthshire. Dedicated with permission to Cardinal Manning. Cloth 0 2 6

Francis de Sales, St. Devout Life 0 1 6
Manual of Practical Piety 0 3 6

Francis of Assisi. Manual of the Third Order. 2 vols. 0 6 0
Cheap Edition 0 3 6

Frassinetti, Very Rev. Joseph. Consolation of the Devout Soul. Translated by Lady Georgiana Chatterton . . . 0 3 6
Cheap Edition 0 1 6

Freemasonry, Secret Warfare of. Translated from the German, with an Introduction. Crown 8vo. Cloth 0 5 0

Fullerton, Lady Georgiana:
Child of the Sacred Heart, A. Cloth 0 2 0
Countess of Bonneval. New edition 0 2 6
Fire of London. Drama 0 0 6
Germaine Cousin. Drama 0 0 6
Grantley Manor: a Tale 0 3 6
Laurentia, a Tale of Japan 0 3 6
Life of Madame Barat, 1 vol. Cloth 0 7 6

Fullerton, Lady Georgiana—*Continued.*

Life of Madame Duchesne, 1 vol. Cloth	£0	7	6
Life of Mère Marie de la Providence, Foundress of the Helpers of the Holy Souls. Paper	0	2	0
Life of St. Frances of Rome	0	2	6
Cheap Edition	0	1	8
Memoir of Hon. E. Dormer. Cloth	0	2	0
Mrs. Gerald's Niece. New edition	0	4	6
Seven Stories—viz. (1) Rosemary; (2) Reparation; (3) Blacksmith of Antwerp; (4) The Beggar of the Steps of St. Roch; (5) Trouville; (6) Earth without Heaven; (7) Ad majorem Dei gloriam. 1 vol. Cloth	0	3	6
Stormy Life, A. New edition	0	4	6

Gallifet (S.J.) True Devotion to the Blessed Virgin:
in the press.

Gallwey, Rev. Peter (S.J.):

Angelus Bell	0	1	6
An Hour before my Crucifix	0	0	4
Practical Hints on Moral Training. With Preface by the Rev. Father Gallwey	0	2	6
Precious Pearl of Hope in the Mercy of God, The. Translated from the Italian. With Preface by the Rev. Father Gallwey. Cloth	0	4	6
Ritualism: Lecture 1. Introductory	0	0	4
2. Is the Blessing of Heaven on Ritualism?	0	0	4
3. The Sanctity of the Ritualistic Clergy	0	0	4
4. Are Ritualists Protestants or Catholics? (extra size)	0	0	6
5. Ritualism and St. Peter's Mission as revealed in Holy Writ (double size)	0	0	8
6. Do Ritualists owe Obedience to their Directors? Do the Anglican Clergy hold the Place of Christ?	0	0	4
7. Ritualism and the Early Church. The Faith of St. Leo the Great	0	0	6
8. The Faith of the English Church Union, A.D. 1878; of Clewer, A.D. 1878; of the Council of Ephesus, A.D. 431	0	0	6
9. Anglican Orders. Part I.	0	0	4
10. Anglican Orders. Part II.	0	1	0
11. Anglican Orders. Part III.	0	0	8
The Anglican Clergy in the Confessional	0	0	6
Sermons	0	6	0
To the Memory of H.I.H. Prince Louis Napoleon, Funeral Words, July 3, 1879	0	0	6

Galton (Theodore). Gervase Sacheveril: a Tale . . 0 5 0

Garside, The late Rev. C. B.:

Blessed Margaret Mary Alacoque	0	1	0
Helpers of the Holy Souls	0	1	0
Sacrifice of the Eucharist, &c.	0	5	6

Gathered Leaves: Prose and Verse. From the *Lamp.*
By K. O. Illustrated 0 3 0

Gay, Mgr. (Coadjutor to the Bishop of Poitiers).
The Christian Life and Virtues considered in the Religious State. Translated from the French by the Right Rev. Abbot Burder, Order of the Reformed Cistercians. Complete in 3 vols. 0 18 0

Gérard, the Lion-Killer. Cloth . . . 0 2 6
Complete edition, cloth gilt 0 3 0

Gertrude, St., Spirit of 0 2 6
Prayers and Exercises of. See p. 34.

Gilbert (Canon, D.D.):
Love of Jesus, or Visits to the Blessed Sacrament £0 1 6
Reflections on Stations of the Cross 0 1 6
Also in various bindings.
Githa of the Forest; a Tale by the Author of 'The Priory of
Avenham,' &c. 0 3 6
God our Father. By a Father S.J., author of the 'Happiness of
Heaven'. 32mo 0 2 0
Gojos, The Life of Sister Jeanne Benigne, Lay Sister of
the Visitation of Holy Mary. Front., cloth 0 7 6
Golden Words; or Maxims of the Cross, from St. Thomas
à Kempis 0 2 6
Cheap edition 0 1 0
Gospel Stories 0 1 0

Happiness of Heaven. By a Father of the Society of Jesus . 0 2 6
Harper, Rev. Thomas (S.J.):
Manchester Dialogues: a Series of Controversial Tracts, in 2 parts each 0 1 0
Peace through the Truth: or Essays on Subjects connected with Dr.
Pusey's 'Eirenicon.'
1st Series, 8vo 0 15 0
2d Series, 8vo 1 1 0
Hauff. Tales of Wonder. 0 2 6
Cheap edition 0 1 8
Hedley, Bp. Who is Jesus Christ?. 0 1 4
Religion for Children. An Address delivered at the Opening of the
School of Aberkenfig, May 6, 1879 . . . . 0 0 2
Sermons. In the Press.
Spirit of Faith 0 1 6
Herbert, Lady:
Life of Bishop Bruté. Paper Cover 0 2 0
Cloth 0 3 0
Life of Henri Dorié. Second edition. Paper cover . . . 0 1 6
Cloth 0 2 0
Life of Mgr. Berneux, Bishop and Martyr. Paper cover . . 0 2 0
Cloth 0 3 0
Life of Théophane Vénard, Martyr. Paper cover 0 2 0
Cloth 0 3 0
Saint in Algeria, A. Cloth 0 2 0
St. Gaetan 0 1 6
Wilfulness. Paper cover 0 1 0
Cloth 0 2 0
Herbart, Lady, translated by.:
Life of Mother Mary Teresa, by the Abbé Hulst. Portrait . . . 0 4 6
Hergenröther, Dr. Catholic Church and Christian
State. Historical Essays on the Relation of the Church to the Civil
Power. Translated from the German. 2 vols., paper cover . . 1 1 0
Heroines of Charity. Cloth 0 2 6
Cheap Edition 0 1 8
Hill, G. J. (M.A.). Story of the War in La Vendée 0 4 6

Catalogue of Publications.

Hints for Spending profitably the Time of Advent,
Christmas, Lent, Easter, Pentecost . . . . . each £0 0 1
Complete in wrapper 0 0 6
Holy Family, Manual of, with all the Hymns 0 0 6
Strong cloth 0 0 8
Manual separately 0 0 2
Hymns separately 0 0 3
Music 0 1 0
Holy Ghost the Sanctifier. Little Book. Vol. IV.,
Library of the Holy Ghost. Cloth - - - - 1s. 6d. and 0 2 0
Holy Queens, Lives of. Cloth gilt 0 3 0
Holy-Week Book. New and complete edition, with the Psalms pointed for Chanting. *The only edition requiring no turning back or reference.* Cloth 0 1 0
Roan 0 1 6
Gilt 0 2 0
Calf 0 4 0
Morocco 0 4 6
Ditto, according to the Dominican Rite 0 1 6
Hope, Mrs. :
Early Martyrs. Cloth gilt 0 3 0
Ditto, plain 0 2 6
Franciscan Martyrs in England. Cloth 0 2 6
Cloth boards 0 3 0
Life of St. Philip Neri 0 2 0
Cheap edition 0 1 4
Life of St. Thomas of Canterbury 0 4 6
Horæ Sacræ : Latin Prayers for the Clergy . . . 0 6 0
Humphrey, Rev. F. :
Divine Teacher. Third edition 0 2 6
Mary magnifying God. Third edition 0 2 6
Other Gospels; or Lectures on St. Paul's Epistle to the Galatians.
Crown 8vo, cloth 0 4 0
Written Word 0 5 0
Husenbeth, Very Rev. Provost (D.D., V.G.) :
Apparition of the Blessed Virgin at Pontmain . . . 0 1 6
Husenbeth, Very Rev. Provost, edited by :
Bible. Large 4to, calf neat, gilt edges 3 16 0
Morocco 4 10 0
Hymn-Book (St. George's). 20th thousand . . . 0 0 1
Hymn-Book (St. Patrick's). 169 Hymns 0 0 3
Cloth 0 0 6
With Music, cloth 0 1 0
Hymnal, The Catholic. Cloth 0 0 9
Music 0 1 0
Hymns for the Year, complete edition (293 in number) . . 0 0 3
Stout cloth 0 0 5
Hymns for the Year, Music for 0 1 0
Accompaniments 0 10 6
Hymns, Select, for Schools 0 0 1

Ignatius, St., Spirit of. Calendar for the Year 1880.
Richly chromo-lithographed, and printed on red and black on tinted
paper . . . . post-free £0 3 0
Ignatius, St., Spiritual Exercises of ('Manresa').
New edition 0 3 6
Jesuit Sermons. 2 vols . . . . . . each 0 6 0
Jesuits, their History, &c. See 'B. N.'
Joseph, St., Devotions to, for every day in March . 0 0 6
Joseph, St., Devotions to. From the Italian 0 2 0
Joseph, St., His Life and Character 0 3 6
Joseph, St., Protector of the Church, and Model of
Christians. From the French of Madame De Gentelles. Paper . . 0 1 6
Cloth 0 2 0
Kate Kavanagh : a Tale. Gilt 0 2 0
Cheap edition 0 1 6
Knights of St. John. Cloth 0 3 6
Limp 0 2 6
Knox, Fr., Translated by. Life of Blessed Henry Suso 0 4 0
Lady of Neville Court : a Tale of the Times. By the Author of
'Maggie's Rosary,' &c. 0 4 6
Lamp, bound vols., very handsome, in crimson and gold . . . 0 5 0
Landroit, Mgr. Sins of the Tongue. Translated from the
French. Cloth 0 4 6
Law. Letter to his late Parishoners, by Hon. W.
Towry, late Vicar of Horborne, near Birmingham, and late Chancellor
Bath and Wells. 3rd edition. Stitched 0 1 0
Lefebvre, Dr. Louise Lateau, Account of. Edited by
the Rev. Dr. Northcote 0 3 6
Lent, Cookery for 0 1 0
Leuthner, Father Cœl (O.S.B.). Cœlum Christianum :
a Book of Meditations (for Priests) 0 2 0
Library of Religious Biography. See 'Thompson'.
Library of the Holy Ghost :
Vol. I. The Bread of Life, or St. Thomas Aquinas on the Adorable Sacrament of the Altar. Arranged as Meditations by Dr. Raives . . 0 5 0
Vol. II. *In the Press.* St. Thomas Aquinas on the Holy Ghost, with a way of hearing Mass in honour of the Holy Ghost ; Prayers of Saints and other Prayers, Hymns, etc.
Liechtenstein, Princess. Nora : a Tale from the German.
8vo, gilt . . . . 10s. 6d. for 0 5 3
Life and Doctrine of Jesus Christ. With short Reflections
for the help of such as desire to use mental prayer. The second part
wherein every seventh Meditation is an application of the former to the
Most B. Sacrament. 8vo, 1 vol., *edited by Rev. C. Bowden of the
Oratory*, 456 pp., by H. M. of the S.J. 0 7 6

Catalogue of Publications. 19

Liguori, St. Alphonso :

	£	s	d
Devotions to St. Joseph	0	0	3
Cloth	0	0	4
Hymns and Verses on Spiritual Subjects. Cloth elegant	0	1	0
Cheap edition	0	0	6
Music	0	1	0
'Jesus hath loved us,' separately, *new and correct edition* Cloth	0	0	9
Month of Mary	0	1	0
Cloth	0	1	6
Reflections on Spiritual Subjects, and on the Passion of Our Lord. With Memoir and Frontispiece. Cloth	0	2	6
Visits to the B. Sacrament and to the B. V. Mary. An entirely new translation by the Redemptorist Fathers	0	1	0
Way of the Cross	0	0	1

Liguori, St. Alphonso. New and improved Translation of the Complete Works of St. Alphonso, edited by Father Coffin :

	£	s	d
Vol. I. The Christian Virtues, and the means for obtaining them. Cloth elegant	0	4	0
Or separately :			
1. The Love of Our Lord Jesus Christ	0	1	4
2. Treatise on Prayer. *(In the ordinary editions a great part of this work is omitted)*	0	1	4
3. A Christian's Rule of Life	0	1	0
Vol. II. The Mysteries of the Faith—the Incarnation ; containing Meditations and Devotions on the Birth and Infancy of Jesus Christ, &c., suited for Advent and Christmas	0	3	6
Cheap edition	0	2	0
Vol. III. The Mysteries of the Faith—the Blessed Sacrament	0	3	6
Cheap edition	0	2	0
Vol. IV. Eternal Truths—Preparation for Death	0	3	6
Cheap edition	0	2	0
Vol. V. Treatises on the Passion, containing 'Jesus hath loved us,' &c.	0	3	0
Cheap edition	0	2	0
Vol. VI. Glories of Mary New edition	0	2	6
Cloth	0	3	6
With Frontispiece, cloth elegant	0	4	6
Also in better bindings.			

Lindsay, Colin, The Hon. Tracts for the Times :

	£	s	d
1. Church of the New Testament. 24 pp.	0	0	4
2. God or no God, and the Immortality of the Soul. 16 pp.	0	0	4

Little Books of the Holy Ghost, edited by Dr. Rawes :

	£	s	d
Book 1. St. Thomas Aquinas on the Commandments. 32mo, 233 pp. Cloth gilt	0	2	0
Book 2. Little Handbook of the Archconfraternity of the Holy Ghost. Fourth edition, 111 pp.	0	1	0
Gilt	0	1	6
Book 3. St. Thomas Aquinas on the Lord's Prayer. 139 pp. Cloth	0	1	6
Gilt	0	2	0
Book 4. The Holy Ghost the Sanctifier. By Card. Manning, 213 pp.			
Book 5. *In the Press.* St. Basil on the Holy Ghost.			

Lisle, Edwin de. Comparison between the History of the Church and the Prophecies of the Apocalypse. From the German. Crown 16mo 0 2 0

Liturgical Books : (under which heading are included Breviaries, Missals, Horæ Diurnæ, and others) :

Liturgical Books—*Continued.*

Breviarium Romanum :

	£	s.	d.
Mechlin, 4 vols., 4to, red and black	2	8	0
Calf	6	6	0
Morocco	7	8	0
Ratisbon, No. I., 4 vols, 4to, red and black	2	10	0
Calf net	5	10	8
Morocco net	7	2	4
No. II., 4 vols, 4to	3	10	0
No. IV., 4 vols	10	0	0
Mechlin, 4 vols, 8vo, red and black, fine paper	1	18	0
Calf	4	4	0
Morocco	5	6	0
Mechlin, 4 vols, 12mo, red and black, fine paper	1	1	0
Calf	2	11	0
Morocco	3	0	0
India paper	1	6	0
Calf	2	16	0
Morocco	3	4	0
With Franciscan Supplement, fine paper	1	8	0
Calf	2	18	0
Morocco	3	6	0
Mechlin, 4 vols, 18mo, red and black, fine paper	0	19	0
Calf	2	6	0
Morocco	2	12	0
India paper	1	1	0
Calf	2	9	0
Morocco	2	15	0
Tournai, Breviarium S. Ord. Præd. 1 vol, 8vo. Beautifully printed on toned paper, in old faced type, red and black, with red border. Bound in morocco, gilt edges net	0	18	0
Tournai, 4 vols, 18mo, beautifully printed on toned paper, in old-faced type, red and black, with red border. Bound in morocco, gilt edges net	2	12	6
Ratisbon, 4 vols, 18mo, red and black £1 for	0	15	0
Calf	2	4	0
Morocco	2	8	0
Mechlin, 4 vols, 24mo, red and black, fine paper	0	18	0
Calf	2	2	0
Morocco	2	8	0
India paper	1	0	0
Calf	2	4	0
Morocco	2	10	0
Mechlin, 4 vols, 32mo, red and black, fine paper	0	17	0
Calf	1	17	0
Morocco	2	5	6
India paper	0	19	0
Calf	1	19	0
Morocco	2	7	0

Breviarium Romanum totum :

	£	s.	d.
Mechlin, 18mo	0	11	0
Calf	0	18	6
Morocco	1	0	0
Ratisbon, 18mo, very good for travelling, unbound	0	16	0

Breviarium S. Ord. Præd. :

	£	s.	d.
2 vols. 12mo	0	17	0
Calf	1	12	0
Morocco	1	16	0

Liturgical Books—*Continued.*

Breviarum Monasticum:
	£	s.	d.
India paper, 4 vols. 18mo	1	12	0
Calf	3	0	0
Morocco	3	6	0

Cæremoniale Episcoporum:
	£	s.	d.
1 vol. 8vo, unbound	0	3	6
Half Calf	0	8	0

Canon Missæ:
	£	s.	d.
Ratisbon, printed separately from large folio Missal	0	3	0

Cantus Passionis D.N.J.C.:
	£	s.	d.
Ratisbon, folio	0	3	0

Cœleste Palmetum
		£	s.	d.
		0	2	6
Calf	net	0	6	6
Morocco	net	0	8	0
With Plates		0	3	6
Calf	net	0	7	6
Morocco	net	0	9	0

Epistolæ et Evangelia:
	£	s.	d.
Ratisbon, in folio, No. I.	1	0	0
No. II.	3	0	0
No. III.	9	0	0
No. IV.	18	0	0
Mechlin, folio	1	2	0
Calf	2	15	0
Morocco	3	3	0

Graduale Romanum:
Ratisbon, 1871, folio, red and black, 2 vols,
	£	s.	d.
No. I.	5	0	0
No. II.	7	10	0
No. III.	10	0	0
Mechlin, folio	1	10	0
Half calf	2	10	0
Ratisbon, 8vo, (1871)	0	7	6
Half calf	0	11	6
Mechlin, 8vo	0	6	0
Half calf	0	10	0

Horæ Diurnæ:
		£	s.	d.
Ratisbon, 18mo		0	3	0
Mechlin, 18mo. India paper		0	4	6
Calf ,, ,,		0	10	6
Morocco ,, ,,		0	12	0
Tours 32mo, French morocco, gilt edges,	net	0	6	0
Tournai, beautifully printed on toned paper, old-faced type, in red and black, with red border, morocco, gilt edges	net	0	13	0
Ratisbon, 32mo		0	2	6
Mechlin, 32mo		0	3	0
Calf		0	7	6
Morocco		0	8	6
Mechlin, 48mo		0	2	6
Calf		0	6	6
Morocco		0	7	6

Liturgical Books—*Continued.*

Horæ Diurnæ Franciscanorum:

		£	s.	d.
8vo		0	8	6
Calf		1	2	6
Morocco		1	5	6
32mo		0	3	6
Calf		0	8	0
Morocco		0	9	0

Horæ Diurnæ Sac. Ord. Præd.:

		£	s.	d.
Rome, 24mo	net	0	5	0
Calf	net	0	11	0
Morocco	net	0	12	6

Missale Romanum:

		£	s.	d.
Mechlin, large folio (16 in. long, 11½ in. broad), unbound		2	0	0
Calf		3	15	0
Morocco, gilt monogram	net	4	10	0
Red morocco, elegant	from	6	0	0
Tours, folio, unbound		2	13	6
Red morocco, elegant	from	7	0	0
Salviucci, folio, unbound		1	10	0
Red morocco, elegant		6	10	0
Mechlin, folio (14¾ in. long, 10½ in. broad), unbound		1	4	0
Calf		3	0	0
Calf, gilt monogram		3	5	0
Morocco		3	10	0
Morocco, gilt monogram		4	0	0
Red morocco, elegant		5	10	0
Mechlin, large 4to (13¾ in. long, 10½ in. broad), unbound		1	2	0
Calf, plain		2	16	6
Calf, gilt monogram		2	18	0
Morocco, plain		3	1	0
Morocco, gilt monogram		3	17	0
Mechlin, large 4to,				
Morocco, elegant		5	10	0
Mechlin, 4to (13 in. long 9½ in. broad), unbound		0	18	0
Calf, plain		1	17	0
Calf, gilt monogram		2	0	0
Morocco, plain		2	4	6
Morocco, gilt monogram		2	10	6
Red morocco, elegant	from	3	3	0
Ratisbon, 4to, unbound	from 1*l.* to	9	9	0
Bound	from 2*l.* 10*s.* to	15	15	0
Mechlin, small 4to (11 in. long, 8 in. broad), unbound		0	16	0
French morocco, gilt monogram		1	5	0
Ratisbon, 8vo, unbound	from 10*s.* to	1	10	0
Bound	from 1*l.* 4*s.* to	3	4	0
Mechlin, 8vo, white paper		0	9	0
India		0	10	6
Bound in morocco	from	1	10	0
Calf		1	2	0
This new Missal is very serviceable for small Chapels and Oratories.				
12mo, fine paper, unbound		0	6	0
Calf		0	13	6
Morocco		0	15	6
Morocco, gilt		0	19	0
India paper, unbound		0	7	6
Calf		0	15	0
Morocco		0	17	0
Morocco, gilt		1	1	0

Liturgical Books—*Continued.*
  Missale Monasticum :
    Roman edition, folio, morocco £3 15 0
    Gilt monogram 4 4 0
    Ratisbon, small folio 1 6 0
    Calf - 3 0 0
    Red morocco . . . . from 5 10 0
    Mechlin, small 4to, unbound 1 3 0
    Calf, plain 2 2 0
    Gilt monogram 2 10 0
    Morocco, plain 2 12 0
    Gilt monogram 2 15 0
  Missale Sacri Ordinis Prædicatorum :
    Large 8vo, unbound 0 16 0
    Calf 1 10 0
    Morocco 1 13 0
  Missale Rom. Carm. Discalc :
    Small folio 1 6 0
    Calf . . . . from 3 0 0
  Missæ pro Defunctis :
    Mechlin, folio 0 3 6
    Calf 1 5 0
    Morocco 1 10 0
    Ratisbon, in folio . . . . . . from 2s. 6d. to 1 5 0
    Calf 1 1 0
    Morocco 1 5 0
  Officium Hebdomadæ Sanctæ :
    Ratisbon, 8vo 0 6 6
    Mechlin, 18mo, with music 0 4 0
    Calf 0 8 0
    Morocco 0 9 0
    32mo 0 2 6
    Cloth 0 4 0
    Calf 0 6 0
    Morocco 0 7 0
  Rituale Romanum :
    Tournai, good print on toned paper, bound in morocco, gilt edges, net 0 11 0
  Vesperale Romanum :
    Ratisbon, folio, *in the press.*
    8vo 0 10 0
    Half calf 0 14 0
    Mechlin, folio 1 10 0
    Half calf 2 10 0
    Mechlin, 8vo 0 7 6
    Half calf 0 11 6
Livesey, T. J. ;
  Primer of English History. Part I. 0 0 2
  Ditto, Part II. 0 0 3
Lockhart, Father :
  Communion of Saints. Bound 0 1 6
  In paper covers 0 1 0
  Non Possumus 0 1 6
  Old Religion, The 0 3 6
  Secession of Schism 0 0 6
  Who is the Antichrist of Prophecy ? 0 1 0

Maggie's Rosary, and other Tales. Gilt - - - - £0 3 0

Maignen, Maurice. Sketch of the Life of Henri
Planchat, one of the Hostages massacred by the Commune at Belleville,
May 26, 1871. Translated from the French. With Introductory
Preface by Rev. W. H. Anderdon, S.J. 0 5 0

Maltus, Rev. J. H. (O.S.D.). True Love of God,
and other Devotions of Divine Love. Refuge of Mary, &c. - - - 0 1 0
   Calf 0 4 6
   Morocco 0 5 0
   Morocco, extra - 0 5 6

Manning, His Eminence Cardinal:
   Confidence in God. New edition - . - - - . - 0 1 0
   England and Christendom - - - - - - - - 0 10 6
   Fourfold Sovereignty of God. Second edition - - - - 0 2 6
   Cloth - - - - - - - - - - - 0 3 6
   Four Great Evils of the Day. Third edition - - - - - 0 2 6
   Cloth - - - - - - - - - - - 0 3 6
   Glories of the Sacred Heart. Third edition - - - - - 0 6 0
   Grounds of Faith - - - - - - - - - 0 1 0
   Cloth - - - - - - - - - - - 0 1 6
   Holy Gospel of our Lord Jesus Christ according to St. John. With a
     Preface by His Eminence - - - - - - - 0 1 0
   Independence of the Holy See - - - - - - - 0 5 0
   In Memory of the Prince Imperial: Sermon at St. Mary's, Chiselhurst,
     1879 - - - - - - - - - - 0 0 6
   Internal Mission of the Holy Ghost. Second edition - - - 0 8 6
   Love of Jesus to Penitents. Third edition - - - - - 0 1 6
   Miscellanies. 2 vols. - - - - - - - - 0 15 0
   Petri Privilegium - - - - - - - - - 0 10 6
   Praise, A Sermon on; with an Indulgenced Devotion - - - 0 1 0
   Sermons on Ecclesiastical Subjects. Vols. II. and III. - - each 0 6 0
   Sin and its Consequences. Third edition - - - - - 0 6 0
   Temporal Mission of the Holy Ghost. Third edition - - - 0 8 6
   Temporal Power of the Pope. New edition - - - - - 0 5 0
   True Story of the Vatican Council - - - - - - 0 5 0

Manning, His Eminence Cardinal, edited by:
   Life of the Curé of Ars. New edition, enlarged - - - - 0 4 0

Manresa; or the Spiritual Exercises of St. Ignatius 0 3 0

Manual of Instructions in Christian Doctrine - - 0 3 0

Manual of the Cord of St. Francis. Cloth - - - 0 1 6
   Paper - - - - - - - - - - 0 1 0

Manzoni. Promessi Sposi; or the Betrothed. Cloth 0 3 6

Maria Monk's Daughter. An Autobiography by
Mrs. St. John Eckel. Crown 8vo., 411 pp. Cloth - - - - 0 4 0

Marie and Paul. Cloth gilt - - - - - - 0 4 0
   Plain - - - - - - - - - - 0 3 6

Marion Howard. A Tale by the Author of 'Fifth
of November,' etc. - - - - - - - - - 0 6 0

Marriage Service - - - - - - - - - 0 1 0

Marshall, T. W. Christian Missions. 2 vols. 8vo. - 1 4 0

Martin, Abbé, The Church of England, etc. In the press.
Mary, Star of the Sea : a Story of Catholic Devotion.
By the Author of 'Mount St. Lawrence'. New edition - - - £0 5 0
Mass Book for Children's Singing, &c., with Hymns - 0 0 1½
Mass for Serving-Boys - - - - - - - - 0 0 6
Mass, Ordinary of. Latin and English - - - - 0 0 1
May, Books for the Month of, &c. :
Children of Mary - - - - - - - - - - 0 1 8
Gilt - - - - - - - - - - - - 0 2 6
Child's Month of May - - - - - - - - - 0 0 6
Little Book for Marye Month. Compiled and adapted for the use of our Blessed Lady's Sodalists and other Liegemen of Her Dower, as England is called. Blue cloth - - - - - - - - 0 1 0
Lourdes Month of May - - - - - - - - - 0 2 6
Cloth - - - - - - - - - - - 0 3 0
Mary in Sorrow and Desolation - - - - - - - 0 1 0
Calf - - - - - - - - - - - - 0 4 0
Mary magnifying God. (Humphrey.) Second edition - - - - 0 2 6
Month of Mary, for Children and Schools - - - - - 0 0 1
Per 100 - - - - - - - - - - - - 0 7 0
Month of May, consecrated to the Glory of the Mother of God, the Queen of Heaven - - - - - - - - - - - 0 2 0
Month of May for Interior Souls - - - - - - - 0 2 0
Cloth - - - - - - - - - - - - 0 2 6
Music and Hymns for the Month of Mary, in 'Hymns for the Year' and Music - - - - - - - - - - - 0 2 0
Muzzarelli's Month of Mary. Cloth - - - - - - 0 1 0
New Month of Mary. By Bishop of Namur. Cloth - - - 0 3 0
Oratory Month of May - - - - - - - - - 0 0 1
Our Lady's Manual of the Sacred Heart - - - - - 0 2 0
Cloth, elegant - - - - - - - - - - 0 2 6
Calf - - - - - - - - - - - - 0 5 6
Pilgrim's May Wreath. By Rev. F. Thaddeus, Stratford. Blue cloth - 0 2 6
Rosary Hymns and Music for Children - - - - - 0 0 2
St. Alphonsus' Month of Mary - - - - - - - 0 1 0
Cloth - - - - - - - - - - - - 0 1 6
Tickets for May, per packet - - - - - - - - 0 0 4
Virtues of Mary. Second edition - - - - - - - 0 2 6
Visits to the Altar of Mary - - - - - - - - 0 0 9
McCabe. Florine : a Tale of the Crusades. New edition 0 5 0
M'Carthy, Rev. D. Epistles and Gospels, complete in 1 vol. - - - - - - - - - - - - 0 12 0
Meditations for each Day of the Year on the Life of our Saviour. By a Father of the S.J. New and improved edition. 2 vols., cloth, - - - - - - - - - - 0 9 0
Calf - - - - - - - - - - - - 0 16 0
Morocco - - - - - - - - - - - 0 17 0
Meditations on the Passion. Translated by a Sister of Mercy, Coventry - - - - - - - - - - - 0 2 0
Meditations on the Passion ; with Account of the Scapular, Form of conferring the Habit, Litanies, &c. - - - - - 0 0 2
Molitor, William. Burning Questions - - - - 0 3 0

Montgomery, Hon. Mrs. The Eternal Years. Introduction by Rev. George Porter, S.J. Cloth · · · · · £0 3 6
Divine Sequence · · · · · · · · · · · 0 3 6

Morris, Rev. John (S.J.):
Condition of Catholics under James I. Second edition · · · · 0 14 0
Devotions of the Lady Lucy Herbert of Powis · · · · · 0 3 6
Letter Books of Sir Amias Poulet, Keeper of Mary Queen of Scots.
Demy 8vo · · · · · · · · · · · · · 0 10 6
Troubles of our Catholic Forefathers, related by themselves. Second
Series. 8vo, cloth · · · · · · · · · · 0 14 0
Third Series · · · · · · · · · · · · 0 14 0

Morris, Rev. J., edited by:
Formularium Sacerdotale; containing the Form of erecting the Via
Crucis; Blessing of Scapulars, Rosaries, &c. Cloth · · · · 0 2 6

Morris, Rev. W. B. (of the Oratory). Life of St.
Patrick, Apostle of Ireland. Second edition, revised, cloth · · · 0 4 0

Mumford, Rev. James (S.J.) A Remembrance for
the Living to pray for the Dead. Third edition · · · · · 0 2 0

Nédélec, Rev. Louis. Cambria Sacra; or the History of
the Early Cambrian-British Christians. 1 vol., 8vo, xxx. 580 pp. · 0 10 6

Newman, Cardinal:
Annotated Translation of Athanasius · · · · each vol. 0 18 0
Apologia pro Vitâ suâ · · · · · · · · · · 0 6 0
Arians of the Fourth Century, The · · · · · · · 0 7 0
Callista: an Historical Tale. New edition · · · · · 0 5 6
Difficulties of Anglicans. Two volumes:
Vol. I. Twelve Lectures · · · · · · · · · 0 7 6
Vol. II. Letters to Dr. Pusey and to the Duke of Norfolk · · 0 5 6
Discussions and Arguments. 1. How to accomplish it. 2. The Antichrist of the Fathers. 3. Scripture and the Creed. 4. Tamworth
Reading-Room. 5. Who's to blame? 6. An Argument for Christianity. 0 6 0
Doctrine of Justification · · · · · · · · · 0 5 0
Essay on Assent · · · · · · · · · · · 0 7 6
Essay on the Development of Christian Doctrine · · · · 0 6 0
Essays Critical and Historical. Two volumes with Notes. 1. Poetry.
2. Rationalism. 3. De la Mennais. 4. Palmer on Faith and Unity.
5. St. Ignatius. 6. Prospects of the Anglican Church. 7. The
Anglo-American Church. 8. Countess of Huntingdon. 9. Catholicity of the Anglican Church. 10. The Antichrist of Protestants.
11. Milman's Christianity. 12. Reformation of the Eleventh Century.
13. Private Judgment. 14. Davison. 15. Kemble · · · 0 12 0
Essays on Miracles, Two. 1. Of Scripture. 2. Of Ecclesiastical History. 0 6 0
Historical Sketches. Three volumes. 1. The Turks. 2. Cicero.
3. Apollonius. 4. Primitive Christianity. 5. Church of the Fathers.
6. St. Chrysostom. 7. Theodoret. 8. St. Benedict. 9. Benedictine
Schools. 10. Universities. 11. Northmen and Normans. 12. Mediæval
Oxford. 13. Convocation of Canterbury · · · · · 0 18 0
Idea of a University. 1. Nine Discourses. 2. Occasional Lectures and
Essays · · · · · · · · · · · · · 0 7 0
Loss and Gain · · · · · · · · · · · 0 5 6
Occasional Sermons · · · · · · · · · · 0 6 0
Parochial and Plain Sermons. 9 vols. · · · · · each 0 5 0
Present Position of Catholics in England. New edition · · · 0 7 0
Sermons on Subjects of the Day · · · · · · · 0 5 0
Sermons to Mixed Congregations · · · · · · · 0 6 0

Catalogue of Publications.

Newman, Cardinal—*Continued.*
Theological Tracts. 1. Dissertatiunculæ. 2. Doctrinal Causes of Arianism. 3. Apollinarianism. 4. St. Cyril's Formula. 5. Ordo de Tempore. 6. Douay Version of Scripture - - - - - - £0 8 0
University Sermons - - - - - - - - - - 0 5 0
Verses on Various Occasions. New edition - - - - - 0 5 6
Via Media. Two volumes with Notes - - - - - - 0 12 0
Complete set of his Works in, half bound, in 34 vols. - - - nett 13 0 0

Neumayr, F. (S.J.) Science of the Spiritual Life - 0 2 0

New Testament. Royal 8vo, large type, with notes - - - 0 2 0
Per dozen - - - - - - - - - - - 0 12 0
Also in better bindings.
New Pocket Edition, in beautiful type. Neat cloth - - - 0 1 0
Embossed roan - - - - - - - - - - 0 1 6
French morocco - - - - - - - - - - 0 3 0
French morocco, gilt - - - - - - - - - 0 3 6
Calf - - - - - - - - - - - - - 0 4 6
Best morocco - - - - - - - - - - 0 5 0
Best morocco, gilt - - - - - - - - - 0 6 0

Noble, Frances. Gertrude Mannering. Second edition 0 4 0

Northcote, Very Rev. J. S. (D.D.) :
Roma Sotterranea ; or an Account of the Roman Catacombs, especially of the Cemetery of St. Callixtus. Compiled from the Works of Commendatore De Rossi, with the consent of the Author, by the Very Rev. Canon Northcote and the Very Rev. Canon Brownlow. New edition, re-written and greatly enlarged. This work is in three volumes, which may at present be had separately :
Vol. I. History - - - - - - - - - - 1 4 0
II. Christian Art - - - - - - - - - 1 4 0
III. Epitaphs of the Catacombs - - - - - - 0 10 0
The Second and Third Volumes may also be had bound together in cloth - - - - - - - - - - - - 1 12 0
Sanctuaries of the Madonna - - - - - - - - 0 6 6
Visit to Louise Lateau. Written in conjunction with Dr. Lefebvre of Louvain - - - - - - - - - - - - 0 3 6
Visit to the Roman Catacombs, being a popular abridgment of the larger work - - - - - - - - - - - - 0 4 0

Novena to St. Francis Xavier, from the 4th to the 12th March. Wrapper - - - - - - - - - - 0 0 3

Novum Testamentum - - - - - - - - 0 1 0
Bound neat - - - - - - - - - 3s. and 0 3 6
Also a Miniature Edition, with 'Imitatio' - - - - - 0 8 0
Or with 'Imitatio Christi' and 'Psalterium,' calf - - - - 0 8 0
Morocco - - - - - - - - - - - 0 9 0

Oakeley, Rev. Canon :
Catholic Worship : a Manual of Popular Instruction on the Ceremonies and Devotions of the Church. Second edition - - - - 0 1 0
Fabiola, dramatised - - - - - - - - - 0 1 4
Lyra Liturgica : Verses for the Church Seasons. 18mo - - 0 3 6
Calf - - - - - - - - - - - - - 0 7 6
Morocco - - - - - - - - - - - 0 10 0
Office and Ceremonial of the Mass explained. New edition - - 0 1 0
Voice of Creation as a Witness to the Mind of its Divine Author - 0 1 6

October, The Month of, dedicated to the Seraphic Patriarch, St. Francis, by his Children and devoted Clients. Translated from the Italian of Fr. Candido Mariotti by a Religious of the Convent, Woodchester, for the Franciscan Fathers of Stratford. With a Notice by his Eminence Cardinal Manning, Archbishop of Westminster. Cloth - £0 3 0

Office and Burial of the Dead, with Mass. Latin and
English. Cloth 0 1 0
Burial of the Dead and Mass alone 0 0 3

Office, Little, of the Immaculate Conception . . 0 0 2

Office of the B.V.M., Latin and English 0 0 6
Cloth 0 1 0
And in various bindings.

Office of the B.V.M., for the Carmelite Order - . 0 0 6
Cloth 0 1 0

Officium Parvum, B.V.M. Latin only. Miniature edition;
neatly bound, gilt edges 0 1 0

O'Hanlon, Alice :
Erleston Glen : a Lancashire Story of the Sixteenth Century. Crown 8vo,
cloth 0 5 0
Which is Right ? 0 5 0

O'Meara, Kathleen (Grace Ramsay) :
Bells of the Sanctuary. New edition, containing May Benedicta, Agnes,
Aline, One of God's Heroines, Mgr. Darboy. Red cloth, gilt - 0 4 6
Iza : a Story of Life in Russian Poland. Second edition. Cloth - 0 8 6
Life of Bishop Grant. A few copies at half-price, *i.e.* - - 0 8 0

Oratory Books :
Book of the Sacred Heart 0 0 2
Confraternity of the Precious Blood 0 0 1
Devotions to Infant Jesus 0 0 2
Devotions to the Holy Ghost 0 0 2
How to be a Saint 0 0 2
Hymn-Book of the Oratory 0 0 6
Limp cloth 0 0 9
Boards 0 1 0
Jesus Risen 0 0 1
Manual for Confession and Communion 0 0 3
Covers 0 0 6
Month of Mary 0 0 1
Octave for the Souls in Purgatory, and Novena of the Immaculate Conception 0 0 2
Passion of Jesus 0 0 2
Prayer-Book 0 0 4
Covers 0 0 6
Way of the Cross 0 0 2
The whole may also be had, done up in 1 vol. cloth . . 0 3 6
French morocco 0 4 6
Calf 0 6 0
Morocco . . . . 7s. and 0 8 0

Ordinary of the Mass. Latin and English 0 0 2

O'Reilly, Rev. Fr. Martyrs of the Coliseum - . 0 6 0
Victims of the Mamertine 0 8 0

Catalogue of Publications. 29

Ornsby, R. Life of St. Francis de Sales. To which is
added Selections from the 'Spirit of St. Francis' - - - £0 3 0

Pagani, Rev. Dr. :
Altar Companion, or Manna of the New Covenant
   New edition - - - - - - - - - - 0 2 0
   Red edges - - - - - - - - - - 0 2 6
Manna of the New Covenant: Meditations for Communion. Cloth, neat 0 2 6
Way of the Cross - - - - - - - - - - 0 0 1

Pallotti, Rev. Fr. (of Rome), Life of - - - - 0 4 0

Palma, Luis de la (S.J.) :
History of the Sacred Passion. Quarterly Series - - - - 0 7 6
   Cheaper Edition - - - - - - - - 0 5 0
Treatise on the Particular Examen of Conscience - - - - 0 2 6

Parochial Hymn Book. New edition in the Press.

Parochial Vespers-Book ; containing the Complete Vespers for
all Sundays and Holidays of the Year, with Compline and Benediction.
   Cloth - - - - - - - - - - - 0 1 0
      Neatly bound - - - - - - - - - 0 1 6
      Gilt - - - - - - - - - - 0 2 0
      French morocco - - - - - - - - - 0 3 0
      Gilt - - - - - - - - - - 0 3 6
      Calf, red edges - - - - - - - - - 0 4 6
      Morocco - - - - - - - - - 0 5 0
      Gilt - - - - - - - - - - 0 6 0

Parsons, Mrs. :
Afternoons with Mrs. Maitland. Cloth, gilt - - - - 0 2 0
   Cheap edition - - - - - - - - 0 1 6
Heath-House Stories. Cloth - - - - - - - 0 1 6
Life of St. Colette, the Reformer of the Three Orders of St. Francis,
especially of the Poor Clares, among whom she revived the first
fervour of their illustrious Founder. Crown 8vo, x. 290 pp. - 0 6 0
St. Ignatius, Life of *- - - - - - - - - 0 2 6
   Ditto - - - - - - - - - - 0 1 8
Tales for Young Men and Women - - - - - - 0 2 6
Twelve Tales for the Young :
   1st Series, cloth plain - - - - - - - - 0 3 0
      Gilt - - - - - - - - - - 0 3 6
   2nd Series, cloth plain - - - - - - - - 0 3 6
Twelve Tales for Children - - - - - - - - 0 2 0
Wrecked and Saved. Cloth - - - - - - - - 0 5 0

Passion Flower : a Catholic Story - - - - - - 0 5 0

Passion, Works on the :
Meditations on the Passion - - - - - - - - 0 0 1
   Ditto, with Account of the Scapular - - - - - 0 0 2
Meditations on the Sufferings of Christ. By Sister Emmerich. Cloth - 0 3 6
Passion of Jesus and Woes of Mary - - - - - - 0 0 2
Stations of the Cross (from Golden Manual) - - - - 0 0 1
St. Liguori, Treatises and Meditations on the Passion. Containing 'Love
of Jesus to Souls' (otherwise entitled, 'Jesus hath loved us,' or
'Clock of the Passion') - - - - - - - - 0 3 0
   Cheap edition - - - - - - - - 0 2 0
Way of the Cross. By St. Liguori - - - - - - 0 0 1
Via Crucis. By Dr. Pagani - - - - - - - - 0 0 2
   Fine edition, borders - - - - - - - - 0 0 4

Passing Away : being some Account of the Last Illness of my adopted Child. Cloth - - - - - - - - - £0 3 0
Peter's Journey ; and other Tales. Cloth - - - - - 0 3 0
Pictures of Christian Heroism. Cloth - - - - 0 3 0
Pictures of Missionary Life. Cloth - - - - - 0 3 0
Pictures, Tales, and Parables. Many cuts - - - - 0 3 0
Pilgrim, The ; or Truth and Beauty in Catholic Lands - - - 0 5 6
Pinamonti, John Peter (S.J.). The Art of Knowing Ourselves. The Looking-Glass which does not Deceive. With Twelve Considerations on Death, by Luigi La Nuya, S.J., and Four on Eternity, by John Baptist Manni, S.J. - - - - - - 0 3 0
Pious Youth, Lives of. Cloth elegant - - - - - 0 1 6
   Gilt - - - - - - - - - - - - 0 2 0
Place Vendome, and La Roquette - - - - - 0 3 6
Planchat, Life of. See 'Maignen'.
Poetry for the Young ; a First Book. With 30 Illustrations - 0 1 0
Poetry, Popular ;. a Second Book - - - - - - 0 2 0
Poetry ; a Third Book. Selections from the Writings of our chief Poets ; adapted for family use and the higher classes of schools. Edited by Aubrey de Vere, Esq. Cloth - - - - - - - - 0 3 6
Poor Man's Catechism, or 'People's Catechism.' A new and revised edition, suited for young or old - - - - 0 1 0
Points for Mental Prayer from St. Bonaventure. Sq. 32mo. Cloth lettered - - - - - - - - - 0 0 6
Popular Ballads - - - - - ♦ - - 0 1 0
Popular Books :

At 1s.

Amusements of Travel	Emma's Cross, and other Tales
Anecdotes, 300, Book of	Enterprise and Peril, Tales of
Cardinal d'Amboise, or the Story of a Bell	Footsteps of Spirits
Catholic Legends	Floreat Etona : a Catholic College in Old Times
Catholic Worship and Devotions	France, Tales of
Child of the Sacred Heart	Francis, St., and Clare, St., Lives of
Christian Heroism, Tales of	Francis of Sales, St., Spirit of
Clare Maitland	George Morton, and Boy and Man
Conscience's Conscript	Gérard the Lion-Killer (abridged)
Ricketicketack	Gospel Stories
Poor Gentleman	Harry O'Brien, and other Tales
Blind Rosa	Historical Tales and Legends
Conversions, Narratives of	Hymns and Verses, by St. Alphonsus
Cookery for Lent	Joe Baker, and James Chapman
Crusade of the Children, &c.	Joy and Sorrow, Tales of
Crusade of Hungary	Kings and Queens, Tales of
Dodsworth on Popular Delusions	Land and Sea, Tales of
Dormer, Hon. E., Life of	Lazaretto Keeper, The
Elizabeth of Hungary, St.	Little Snowdrop. Cloth

Catalogue of Publications.

Popular Books (at 1s.)—*Continued.*

Madeleine the Rosière
Manor of Mont Cruel
Mary and Elizabeth
Monks of Lerins
Narratives and Dialogues
Naval and Military Life, Tales of
Oakeley (Canon) on the Mass Catholic Worship
Paraguay, Missions in
Popular Ballads
Points of History
Ratisbonne, Conversion of
Rich and Poor, and Lucy Ward
Robert May, and Poor Man's Child
Sainted Queens, Lives of
Sœur Rosalie, &c., Lives of
Suffering for the Faith
Tales and Traditions
Tales for the Many
Wilfulness, by Lady Herbert
William of Waynflete, Life of
William of Wykeham, Life of
Winefride Jones
Wiseman's Hymn of St. Casimir

At 1s. 4d.

Ancient History : Greece, &c.
Columbus and La Pérouse
Conscience's Miser
Count Hugo
Fabiola, a Drama by Canon Oakeley
Formby's Compendious Sacred History
Historical Tales of Old Time
Life of St. Philip Neri
Missions in the East and West
Roman History
Saints Once of the Working Classes
Scenes and Incidents at Sea
Tales of Bandits, &c.
Tales of Catholic Artists
Tales of Daring and Peril
Tales of Faith and Loyalty
Tales of the French Revolution
Tales of Shipwrecks

At 1s. 6d.

Andersen's Popular Tales
Bickerton, or the Emigrants
Celebrated Men, Tales of
Heath-House Stories, by Mrs. Parsons
Holiday Tales, by Miss Taylor
In the Snow
Kate Kavanagh, or the Pretty Plate
Life of St. Francis of Sales
Life of Sir Thomas More
Life of Henri Dorié, Martyr
Lives of Pious Youth
Parables and Stories of Père Bonaventure
Tales for the Many. Gilt
Tales of Celebrated Women
Tales of Remarkable Men

At 1s. 8d.

Anecdotes and Incidents
Breton Legends. Limp cloth
Hauff's Tales of Wonder. Do.
Heroines of Charity. Do.
Introduction to English History
Life of St. Frances of Rome
Lives of the Children of Mary
Pictures and Parables. Gilt, elegant
Pictures and Tales. Do.
Tales of the Crusade. Limp cloth

At 2s.

Afternoons with Mrs. Maitland. Gilt
Andersen's Tales. Gilt
Arctic Voyages. Gilt
Bonaventure's Parables. Gilt
Celebrated Women. Gilt
Dyrbington. By Mrs. Parsons
Fables and Parables
Gérard the Lion-Killer. Fancy boards
Gospel Story-Book. Plates, gilt
Graces of Mary. Cloth
Holiday Tales. Gilt
Kate Kavanagh. Gilt
Life of St. Philip Neri
Life of St. Ignatius
Life of St. Paula
Life of Henri Dorié. Cloth
Life of Du Guesclin. Gilt
Lives of Pious Youth. Gilt
Maggie's Rosary
Missions in Japan
Popular Church History. Cheap edition
Popular Poetry
Robinson Crusoe. Limp cloth
Spirit of St. Philip Neri
Tales for the Young. Cloth
Tales for Home Circle. Gilt
Tales of the Festivals. Cloth
The Corean Martyrs. Cloth
Twelve Tales for Children
Wilfulness. By Lady Herbert

Popular Books—*Continued.*

At 2s. 6d.

A Noble Lady. By Mrs. Craven
Anecdotes and Incidents. Gilt
Children of Mary. Gilt
Early Martyrs. By Mrs. Hope
Fireside Stories. Gilt
Gérard the Lion-Killer. Gilt
Hauff's Tales of Wonder. Gilt
Heroines of Charity. Gilt
Knights of St. John
Legends of our Lady
Life of St. Frances of Rome. Gilt
Life of St. Ignatius. Gilt
Lives of Children of Mary
Remarkable Conversions
Robinson Crusoe
Tales of Duty and Affection. Gilt
Tales of the Crusades. Gilt
Tales for the Home Circle. Gilt
Tales for Young Men and Women
Twelve Tales for Children. Gilt
Vessels of the Sanctuary, &c.

At 3s.

Bonneval. By the Rev. Father Anderdon
Breton Legends. Gilt
Catholic Legends. Cloth
Clifton Tales. 1st Series.—Do., 2d do.
Conscience's Veva. Gilt
   Curse of the Village. Gilt
   Demon of Gold. Gilt
   Lion of Flanders. Gilt
   Miser. Gilt
   Tales of Flanders. Gilt
Cottage Conversations
Early Martyrs. By Mrs. Hope
Gérard the Lion-Killer. Gilt
History of England for the Young
Life of St. Vincent de Paul
Life of St. Francis de Sales
Lives of Holy Queens. Gilt.
Maggie's Rosary
Missions in the East and West
Missions in Japan and Paraguay
Pictures of Christian Heroism
Pictures, Tales, and Parables
Popular Church History
Robinson Crusoe. Gilt
Romantic Tales of Great Men
Tales of Land and Sea. Gilt
Tales of Enterprise and Peril
Tales of Brigands and Daring and Peril
Tales of the French Revolution. Gilt
Tales and Legends from History
Tales of Celebrated Men
Théophane Vénard, Martyr. Gilt
Twelve Tales for the Young
Youthful Holiness

At 3s. 6d.

Abyssinia. By Lady Herbert
Angels' Visits. By C. M. Brame
Bridges' Ancient History
Catholic Legends. Full gilt, gilt edges
Christian Æsop
De Vere's Selections from the Poets
Fabiola
French Eggs in an English Basket
Grantley Manor. Large edition, gilt
Life of St. Charles Borromeo
Manzoni's Betrothed. Gilt
Marie and Paul
Not Yet. By Miss Oxenham
Popular History of France
Tales of Humour
The Knights of St. John
The Old Religion. By Father Lockhart
Twelve Tales for the Young. Gilt
Tyborne. By Miss Taylor
Workwoman of Liège. By C. M. Brame

At 4s.

Alice Sherwin
Bridges' Modern History
Christian Æsop. Gilt
Diary of a Sister of Mercy
Fabiola. Gilt
Gertrude Mannering
Life of Blessed Henry Suso
Life of Olier
Life of the Curé d'Ars
Patriots of the Tyrol
Roman Violets
The Three Chancellors

At 4s. 6d.

Allies' See of St. Peter
Bells of the Sanctuary
Countess of Bonneval
Kathleen O'Meara
Mrs. Gerald's Niece
Life of St. Thomas of Canterbury. By Mrs. Hope
Lydia: an Historical Tale
Sins of the Tongue
Waterworth's England and Rome
Waterworth's Protestantism

Popular Books—*Continued*.

At 5s.

Afternoons with the Saints
Life of Marie Eustelle
Life of Marie Lataste
Life of St. Aloysius Gonzaga

Life of St. Stanislas Kostka
Martyrs of the Coliseum
Passion Flower
Wild Times

At 6s.

A Sister's Story. By Mrs. Craven
History of England. Enlarged
Life of Ven. Anna Maria Taigi

Mrs. Gerald's Niece
St. Francis of Sales. By Lady Herbert

Popular Choir Manual. 1 vol., cloth - - - - - £0 10 6
Or Two Parts, viz. { Morning Offices - - - - - - - 0 3 6
{ Evening Offices - - - - - - - 0 5 6

Popular Hymn and Tune Book. 1 vol., cloth - - - 0 10 6
Or Three Parts - - - - - - - - - - each 0 3 0

Power, Rev. Patrick. Catechism of Christian Doctrine, approved for the Use of the Faithful in all the Dioceses of England and Wales. Familiarly explained. With the Imprimatur of the Cardinal Archbishop of Westminster. 2 vols. fcap. 8vo, cloth - - 0 7 6
Catechism: Doctrinal, Moral, Historical, and Liturgical. Fourth edition. 3 vols., cloth - - - - - - - - - - - 0 10 6

Prayer-Books:

Catholic Child's Guide to Devotion: a First Prayer-Book for the Young. In large type, with Engravings. Cloth - 0 0 6
Bound, with 16 extra Plates and Hymns - - - - - 0 1 6
Morocco - - - - - - - - - - - 0 2 6
Gilt - - - - - - - - - - - - 0 3 0

Catholic Piety. Roan - - - - - - - - 0 1 0
French morocco, gilt - - - - - - - - - 0 2 6
Calf - - - - - - - - - - - - 0 4 0
Morocco - - - - - - - - - - - 0 4 6
Gilt - - - - - - - - - - - - 0 5 6

Catholic's Daily Companion. Roan - - - - 0 1 0
French morocco - - - - - - - - - - 0 2 6
Gilt - - - - - - - - - - - - 0 3 0
Calf - - - - - - - - - - - - 0 3 6
Morocco - - - - - - - - - - - 0 4 0
Gilt - - - - - - - - - - - - 0 4 6
Ivory - - - - - - - - - - - - 0 12 0
Elegantly ornamented - - - - - - - - 1 1 0

Catholic's Vade Mecum: or Select Prayers for Daily Use. New and beautiful edition, with red borders, ornaments, &c. Calf - - - - - - - - - - - 0 5 6
Morocco - - - - - - - - - - - 0 6 0
Ditto, gilt - - - - - - - - - - - 0 7 0
Ditto, with clasp - - - - - - - - - 0 9 0
Antique morocco, with clasp - - - - - - - 0 15 0
Ditto, extra gilt - - - - - - - - - - 1 1 0
Ditto, tooled edges, &c. - - - - - - - - 1 5 0
Ivory, with rimmed clasp - - - 1*l*. 1*s*., 1*l*. 5*s*., & 1 11 6
Ditto, very elegant - - - - 2*l*. 2*s*., 3*l*. 3*s*., & 3 10 0
A few copies from the original plates still on sale, cloth - 0 2 0

Prayer Books—*Continued.*

	£	s.	d.
Child's Mass Book	0	1	0
Coloured	0	1	6
Church Manual, with Epistles and Gospels.			
Roan	0	2	0
Neatly bound, gilt edges	0	3	6
Calf	0	5	0
Morocco	0	5	6
Gilt	0	6	6
Also in various elegant bindings: ivory, elegantly ornamented 15s. &	1	1	0
Daily Exercise. New Edition, with beautiful engravings.			
Cloth	0	0	6
Bound and gilt	0	1	0
Devotions to the Sacred Heart. With Frontispiece	0	0	6
Exercises of St. Gertrude · from	0	1	6
The Prayers and Exercises may be had, bound in one very neat pocket volume, calf	0	6	6
Morocco	0	7	6
Ditto, gilt	0	8	6
Calf, flexible boards	0	9	0
Morocco, flap and band, illustrated with sacred photographs, adapted for a present	0	14	0
The Prayers of St. Gertrude, bound with the Catholic's Vade Mecum, same prices.			
Flowers of Devotion. Diamond type. Roan	0	1	0
Tuck	0	1	6
French morocco	0	2	6
Calf	0	3	0
Morocco	0	3	6
Ditto, gilt	0	4	0
Morocco or russia, in case	0	9	6
Morocco, antique, and clasp	0	10	6
Ivory	0	8	6
Garden of the Soul. New edition with all the additional Devotions in general use. Two hundredth thousand. Cloth	0	0	6
Large paper, superior	0	0	8
Embossed, gilt edges, with Ordinary	0	1	0
French morocco, gilt	0	2	0
Ditto, rims and clasps	0	3	0
Calf	0	3	6
Best morocco	0	4	0
Gilt	0	5	0
With Epistles and Gospels:			
Cloth, red edges	0	1	0
Ditto, clasp	0	1	6
Roan, embossed, gilt edges	0	1	6
French morocco	0	2	0
Gilt	0	2	6
Calf	0	4	0
French morocco, gilt, rims and bar	0	4	0
Best morocco	0	4	6
Gilt	0	5	6
Velvet 6s. to	1	1	0
Ivory	0	15	0
Ditto, elegantly ornamented	1	1	0

Catalogue of Publications. 35

Prayer Books—*Continued*.

	£	s.	d.
18mo edition, good type. Cloth	0	1	0
With Epistles and Gospels, roan	0	1	4
Ditto, French morocco	0	3	0
Ditto, calf	0	4	6
Ditto, morocco	0	5	6

Golden Manual: or Complete Guide to Catholic Devotion, Public and Private. Thick or thin paper. Roan, gilt

		£	s.	d.
edges		0	6	0
French morocco		0	7	0
Calf		0	8	6
Morocco		0	9	6
Gilt		0	11	0
Velvet, rims and clasp, very elegant		1	4	0
Ivory		1	5	0
Ditto, beautifully ornamented		2	2	0
Morocco, antique	1*l*. 1*s*. to	2	5	0
Limp morocco, edges turned over		0	12	0

With Missal complete, 6*s*. 6*d*. extra.
With Epistles and Gospels, 1*s*. extra.

Key of Heaven. Cloth

		£	s.	d.
Cloth		0	0	6
Roan		0	1	0
French morocco, gilt		0	2	6
Calf		0	4	0
Morocco		0	4	6
Gilt		0	1	6

With Epistles and Gospels:

		£	s.	d.
Roan, gilt edges		0	1	6
French morocco, gilt		0	3	0
Ditto, rims and bar		0	4	6
Gilt		0	5	6
Velvet	6*s*. to	1	1	0
Ivory		0	12	0
Ornamented Ivory		1	1	0

Manual of the Holy Family, with the Hymns

	£	s.	d.
	0	0	6
Strong cloth	0	0	8

Manual of the Sacred Heart. New and beautiful edition.

	£	s.	d.
Cloth	0	2	0
Red or gilt edges	0	2	6
Calf	0	5	6
Morocco	0	6	6

Manual of the Sacred Heart of our Lady.

	£	s.	d.
Cloth	0	2	0
Red or gilt edges	0	2	6
Calf	0	5	6
Morocco	0	6	6

Missal for the Laity. Abridged edition, 32mo.

		£	s.	d.
Cloth		0	1	0
Roan		0	1	6
French Morocco		0	3	6
Gilt		0	4	0
Calf		0	4	6
Morocco		0	5	0
Gilt		0	6	0
Ivory, ornamented	12*s*. &	1	1	0

Prayer Books—*Continued.*

Missal. New and Complete Pocket Missal, in Latin and English, with all the New Offices and the Proper of Ireland, Scotland, and the Jesuits. Roan, embossed gilt edges · · · · · £0 5 0
    Calf flexible, red edges · · · · · · · 0 8 6
    Morocco, gilt edges · · · · · · · · 0 9 6
    Ditto, gilt · · · · · · · · · · 0 11 0
    With plates · · · · · · · · · · 0 13 0
    Also, beautifully printed in red and black, morocco elegant, with engravings · · · · · · · · from 1 10 0
    Also in morocco, russia, vellum, &c., with metal edgings, clasp, &c. · · · · · · · · from £1 1s. to 3 0 0
    Ivory, beautifully ornamented · · · · · · 2 2 0
    Ditto, elegantly carved · · · · · · · 5 5 0
    Velvet, rims and clasp, very elegant · · · · · 1 4 0

Paradise of the Christian Soul. By Horstius.
New edition. Cloth · · · · · · · · · 0 6 0
Roan · · · · · · · · · · · · 0 8 0
Calf · · · · · · · · · · · · 0 10 0
Morocco · · · · · · · · · · · 0 12 0
Ditto, extra · · · · · · · · · · 0 14 0

Path to Heaven. The cheapest and most complete Book of Devotions for public or private use ever issued. Cloth lettered · 0 2 0
Neatly bound, red edges · · · · · · · 0 2 6
Ditto, clasp and rim · · · · · · · · 0 4 0
Roan, lettered · · · · · · · · · 0 3 0
Ditto, full gilt, clasp · · · · · · · · 0 4 6
French morocco, gilt edges · · · · · · · 0 4 0
Calf, red edges · · · · · · · · · 0 5 0
Best calf, tooled · · · · · · · · · 0 7 6
Morocco · · · · · · · · · · · 0 6 0
Ditto, gilt · · · · · · · · · · 0 7 0
Ditto, gilt extra · · · · · · · · · 0 8 0
Ditto, gilt, rim and clasp · · · · · · · 0 14 0
Velvet, rim and clasp · · · · · · · · 0 10 6
Best Turkey morocco · · · · · · · · 0 8 6
Ditto, gilt · · · · · · · · · · 0 10 0
Ivory · · · · · · · · · · · 0 12 0
Ditto, best ornamented · · · · · · · 2 2 0
Best Velvet, rim and clasp · · · · · · · 1 10 0

Prayer-Book of the Oratory of St. Philip Neri.
With Special Devotions for various Seasons, &c. Cloth · · 0 3 6
French morocco · · · · · · · · · 0 4 6
Calf · · · · · · · · · · · · 0 6 0
Morocco · · · · · · · · · · · 0 7 0
Ditto, gilt · · · · · · · · · · 0 8 0

Prayers of St. Gertrude & St. Mechtilde. Neat
cloth, lettered · · · · · · · · · 0 1 6
    Cheap edition, limp cloth · · · · · · 0 1 0
    French morocco, red edges · · · · · · 0 2 0
    Best calf, red edges · · · · · · · 0 4 6
    Best morocco, plain · · · · · · · 0 5 0
    Ditto, gilt · · · · · · · · · · 0 6 0
    On thin vellum paper · · · · · from 0 1 6
    Also in various extra bindings.

Prayer Books—*Continued.*

Quarant' Ore, Devotions for. Edited by Cardinal
Wiseman. Stiff cover · · · · · · · · · · £0 1 6
   Cloth, gilt · · · · · · · · · · · 0 2 0

Raccolta, or Collection of Indulgenced Prayers.
Translated by Father St. John (with authority). Cloth · · 0 3 0
   Calf · · · · · · · · · · · · 0 6 0

Septem; or Seven Ways of Hearing Mass.
By Father Rawes. New edition. Cloth · · · · · 0 1 0
   Boards · · · · · · · · · · · 0 2 0
   Red edges · · · · · · · · · · 0 2 6
   Calf · · · · · · · · · · · 0 4 0
   Morocco · · · · · · · · · · · 0 4 6
   Ditto, extra · · · · · · · · · · 0 5 0

Vita Devota. Cloth · · · · · · · · 0 0 9
   Roan · · · · · · · · · · · · 0 2 0

Preces Xaverianæ. Devotions, Novena, &c., in honour of St.
Francis Xavier · · · · · · · · · · 0 1 6

Presence of God, translated from the French of Fr. Simon de
Bussières, O.S.F. Wrapper · · · · · · · · 0 0 6

Psalterium Davidis. 32mo, cloth, very neat edition · · 0 1 6

Psalter, The; or Psalms of David in English · · · · 0 1 6

Purbrick, Rev. J. (S.J.). May Papers. 2nd edition · 0 2 0

Quarant' Ore, Popular Devotions for · · · · 0 0 1

Quarterly Series (edited by the Managers of the 'Month'):
Christian Reformed in Mind and Manners, The. By Benedict Rogacci, of the Society of Jesus. The Translation edited by the Rev. H. J. Coleridge, S.J. · · · · · · · · · · · 0 7 6
   [In order to meet the convenience of persons who desire to use the Meditations and Considerations in this volume for Retreats, a limited number of copies has been printed, in which each Meditation is on a separate sheet. These copies may be had in a loose cover on application.]
Chronicle of St. Anthony of Padua, the 'Eldest Son of St. Francis'. Edited by the Rev. H. J. Coleridge, S.J. · · · · · 0 5 6
Dialogues of St. Gregory the Great: an old English Version. Edited by the Rev. H. J. Coleridge, S.J. · · · · · · 0 6 0
English Carmelite, An. The Life of Catharine Burton, Mother Mary Xaveria of the Angels, of the English Teresian Convent at Antwerp. Collected from her own Writings, and other sources, by Father Thomas Hunter, S.J. · · · · · · · · · · 0 6 0
Gracious Life, A (1566-1618); being the Life of Madame Acarie (Blessed Mary of the Incarnation) of the Reformed Order of our Blessed Lady of Mount Carmel. By Emily Bowles · · · · · · 0 6 0
History of the Sacred Passion. By Father Luis de la Palma, of the Society of Jesus. Translated from the Spanish. With Preface by the Rev. H. J. Coleridge, S.J. Third edition · · · · · 0 7 6
Also a cheaper edition of the same, on thin paper, and in black cloth · 0 5 0
Ierne of Armorica: a Tale of the Time of Chlovis. By J. C. Bateman · 0 6 6
Life and Letters of St. Francis Xavier. By the Rev. H. J. Coleridge, S.J. Vol. I., third edition · · · · · · · · 0 7 6
   Ditto, Vol. II., third edition · · · · · · · 0 10 6
Life of Anne Catharine Emmerich. By Helen Ram. With Preface by the Rev. H. J. Coleridge, S.J. · · · · · · · 0 5 0
Life of Christopher Columbus. By the Rev. A. G. Knight, S.J. 0 6 0

Quarterly Series—*Continued.*

Life of Henrietta D'Osseville (in Religion, Mother Ste. Marie), Foundress of the Institute of the Faithful Virgin. Arranged and edited by the Rev. John George M'Leod, S.J.	£0	5	6
Life of Margaret Mostyn (Mother Margaret of Jesus), Religious of the Reformed Order of our Blessed Lady of Mount Carmel (1625-1679). By the Very Rev. Edmund Bedingfield, Canon of the Collegiate Church of St. Gomar, and Confessor to the English Teresians at Lierre. Edited, from the Manuscripts preserved at Darlington, by the Rev. H. J. Coleridge, S.J.	0	6	0
Life of Our Life : The Harmony of the Gospel, arranged with Introductory and Explanatory Chapters, Notes, and Indices. By the Rev. H. J. Coleridge, S.J. 2 vols.	0	15	0
Life of Pope Pius the Seventh. By Mary H. Allies	0	6	6
Life of St. Jane Frances Fremyot de Chantal. By Emily Bowles. With Preface by the Rev. H. J. Coleridge, S.J. Second edition	0	5	6
Life of the Blessed John Berchmans. Second edition. By the Rev. F. Goldie, S.J.	0	6	0
Life of the Blessed Peter Favre, First Companion of St. Ignatius Loyola. From the Italian of Father Boero. With Preface by the Rev. H. J. Coleridge, S.J.	0	6	6
Prisoners of the Temple ; or Discrowned and Crowned. By M. O'C. Morris. With Preface by the Rev. H. J. Coleridge, S.J.	0	4	6
Public Life of our Lord Jesus Christ. By the Rev. H. J. Coleridge, S.J. 4 vols. each	0	6	6
Story of St. Stanislaus Kostka. With Preface by the Rev. H. J. Coleridge, S.J.	0	3	6
Sufferings of the Church in Brittany during the Great Revolution. By Edward Healy Thompson	0	6	6
Suppression of the Society of Jesus in the Portuguese Dominions. From Documents hitherto unpublished. By the Rev. Alfred Weld, S.J. [This volume forms the First Part of the General History of the Suppression of the Society.]	0	7	6
Three Catholic Reformers of the Fifteenth Century. By Mary H. Allies	0	6	0
Thomas of Hereford, Life of St. By Fr. Lestrange	0	6	6
Life of King Alfred the Great. By A. G. Knight. Book I. Early Promise ; 2. Adversity ; 3. Prosperity ; 4. Close of Life. 1 vol., 8vo. Pp. 325	0	6	0

Raccolta; by Ambrose St. John (of the Oratory). New edition, cloth	0	4	0

Raphael, Sister Frances :

History of England for Schools and Families	0	6	0
Introduction to English History	0	1	8
Knights of St. John. Cloth	0	3	6
St. Catherine of Siena and her Companions	0	12	6
Songs in the Night, and other Poems	0	5	0

Rawes, Rev. Fr. (D.D., S.H.G.) :

Beloved Disciple, or St. John the Evangelist, The. 1 vol., neat cloth. Second edition, with a Sermon on St. John by St. Charles	0	3	6
Devotions for the Souls in Purgatory. Fourth edition. To which are added, A Way of Hearing Mass for the Dead, and The Doctrine of Suarez on Purgatory. 233 pp., paper	0	1	6
Cloth	0	2	0
Devotions for the Way of the Cross. With Drawings by N. H. J. Westlake. Boards	0	2	6
Cloth, neat	0	4	6
Eucharistic Month. Translated from the Latin of Father Lercari, S.J. Third edition	0	0	6
Cloth	0	1	0

Catalogue of Publications.

Rawes, Rev. Fr. (D.D., S.H.G.)—Continued.

God in His Works: a Course of Five Sermons preached in the Pro-Cathedral, Kensington. Cloth - £0 2 6
Great Truths in Little Words. Third edition, neat cloth - 0 3 6
Homeward. Second edition - 0 3 6
Little Handbook of the Archconfraternity of the Servants of the Holy Ghost. To which has been added, A Way of Hearing Mass in Honour of the Holy Ghost. Fourth edition - 0 1 0
Nine Visits to the Blessed Sacrament. From the Canticle of Canticles. Third edition - 0 0 6
Septem : Seven Ways of Hearing Mass. New edition, flush - 0 1 0
  Bound - 0 2 0
  Red edges - 0 2 6
  Calf - 0 4 0
*Twelve Visits to our Lady and the Heavenly City of God. Third edit. 0 0 8
  * Or in one volume, Visits and Devotions, neat cloth, 3s.

Rawes, Rev. Fr., edited by ;

The Library of the Holy Ghost :
Vol. I. St. Thomas Aquinas on the Adorable Sacrament of the Altar. With Prayers and Thanksgivings for Holy Communion. Red Cloth 0 5 0
Vol. II. St. Thomas Aquinas on the Holy Ghost. With a Way of Hearing Mass in Honour of the Holy Ghost ; Prayers of Saints and other Prayers ; Hymns ; and the Little Handbook of the Archconfraternity. (Ready for the press.)
This will be the Large Handbook of the Archconfraternity. The Little Handbook will always be printed as now.

Little Books of the Holy Ghost :
Book 1. St. Thomas Aquinas on the Commandments. 32mo, 233 pp. Cloth gilt - 0 2 0
Book 2. Little Handbook of the Archconfraternity of the Holy Ghost. Fourth edition, 111 pp. - 0 1 0
  Gilt - 0 1 6
Book 3. St. Thomas Aquinas on the Lord's Prayer. 139 pp. Cloth - 0 1 6
  Gilt - 0 2 0
Book 4. The Holy Ghost the Sanctifier. By Card. Manning, 213 pp.
Book 5. *In the Press.* St. Basil on the Holy Ghost.

Reeve and Challoner. Bible History. New and improved edition - 0 2 0
Set of Illustrations for ditto, coloured - 0 12 0
Larger size - 0 16 0

Reflections and Prayers for Holy Communion.

Translated from the French. With Preface by the Cardinal Archbishop of Westminster. Fifth edition. Foolscap 8vo, cloth - 0 4 6
Red edges - 0 5 0
Calf - 0 9 0
Morocco - 0 10 0
Ditto. Second Series. Same prices as above.

Ricards, Right Rev. Bishop (Bishop of Retimo and
Vicar-Apostolic of the Eastern Vicariate of the Cape Colony). The Catholic Church and the Kaffir. A brief Sketch of the Progress of Catholicity in South Africa, and the Prospects of extensive Catholic Missions on the point of being founded for the Natives of British Kaffraria - 0 1 6

Richards, Rev. Walter J. B. :

Catechism of Confirmation - 0 0 1
Worship of Sacrifice : Catechetical Instruction on the Holy Mass - 0 0 1
Manual of Scripture History in the press.

Richards, Rev. Walter J. B., edited by :
  Book of Psalms. Translated from the Latin Vulgate, being a Revised
    Edition of the Douay Version. With Preface by and Imprimatur of
    Cardinal Manning. 32mo, cloth, red edges - - - - - £0 1 6
  Catechism of Virtues and Vices, compiled chiefly from Bellarmine - 0 0 2
  Francis of Sales, St., Introduction to the Devout Life. New translation.
    Third edition, cloth, red edges - - - - - - - 0 1 6

Ritualism, Lectures on. See 'Gallwey'.

Robinson Crusoe. Revised. Gilt - - - - - 0 2 6

Rodriguez on Christian Perfection. For the Laity. 2
  vols., neat cloth, lettered - - - - - - - 0 6 0
  Also in calf and morocco

Rogacci, F. (S.J.). Holy Confidence. Cloth. Second
  edition - - - - - - - - - - 0 2 6
  The Christian Reformed. See 'Quarterly Series'.

Romantic Tales of Great Men. Cloth - - - - 0 3 0

Rosary Book ; containing Meditations on each Mystery, with 15
  Engravings - - - - - - - - - - 0 0 2
  Rosary with Music for Children - - - - - - 0 0 2

Rosary Tickets, on a Sheet (for Circles of the Living Rosary).
  Beautiful engravings - - - - - - - - 0 0 1½
  Per 100 - - - - - - - - - - 0 10 0

Rosmini. Catechism. - - - - - - - 0 2 6
  Cheaper edition - - - - - - - - 0 1 6
  Life of - - - - - - - - - - 0 2 0

Sacrament, Blessed, Novena and Devotions for - - 0 0 1

Sacred Heart, Guard of Honour of the (Tickets) - - per 100 0 1 0
  Account of the Origin and Object of the Devotion - - - 0 0 1
  Association of our Lady of the Sacred Heart - - - - 0 0 6
  Print of ditto, with Devotions - - - - - - 0 0 3
    Ditto - - - - - - - - - - 0 0 1
  Guard of Honour (Dial) - - - - - - - 0 0 2
  Novena - - - - - - - - per 100 0 1 0
  33 Tickets for each Friday in the Month - - - - 0 0 4

Sacred Heart of Jesus, Devotions for. With photograph,
  borders, &c. - - - - - - - - - 0 0 3
  Manual of the Sacred Heart of Jesus - - - - - 0 2 0
    Red or gilt edges - - - - - - - - 0 2 6
    Calf - - - - - - - - - - 0 5 6
    Morocco - - - - - - - - - 0 6 6

Sacred Heart, Our Lady of, Devotions for. Same
  prices as the above.

Saldanha, Duc De. Truth - - - - - - 0 2 0

Sander, Nicolas, D.D., sometime Fellow of New College, Oxford.
  Rise and Growth of the Anglican Schism. Published A.D. 1585, with
  a Continuation of the History by the Rev. Edward Rishton, B.A., of
  Brasenose College, Oxford. Translated with Introduction and Notes,
  by David Lewis, M.A. Full price, 14s. ; now offered for - - 0 7 0

Sarasa (S.J.). Art of always Rejoicing - - - - 0 2 6

Scapular of Mount Carmel explained. With Engraving - £0 0 1
 The Scapular itself 0 0 4
 Per Dozen 0 3 6
Scapulars of the Holy Passion and of the Sacred
 Hearts of Jesus and Mary (Account of.) With red wrapper . . 0 0 1
 Per 100 - 0 7 0
 The same, with Meditations on the Passion 0 0 2
 Per 100 - 0 14 0
 Scapular of the Passion ; made up in red cloth 0 0 4
 Per dozen 0 3 6
 Scapular of the Immaculate Conception 0 0 4
 Per dozen 0 3 6
Scapulars (The Four), Explanation of 0 0 2
School Literature.
 History (Church and Bible):
  1. Darras' History of the Church, from the French. 4 vols. 4to . 2 8 0
  2. Alzog's History of the Church, from the German. 3 vols. 4to . 3 0 0
  3. Noethen's History of the Church (American) 0 8 0
  4. Formby
   a. Pictorial Bible and Church History Stories. 3 vols . . 0 12 0
    Better edition 1 1 0
    Also to be had in parts separately. See under 'Formby' in
     general catalogue
   β. An Abridgement of the above, suitable for schools . . 0 1 4
  5. Manual of Church History, approved by Cardinal Wiseman . 0 2 0
  6. Reeve and Challoner's Bible History 0 2 0
  7. Wenham. Readings from Old Testament. New Testament
    Narrative. See under 'Wenham' in general catalogue.
  8. Bible History. By a Priest of Cincinnata. Illustrated . . 0 2 0
  9. Historical Catechism, or Chronology for Schools. Cloth . . 0 0 6
    Paper 0 0 4
    Historical Chart for Schools. Plain 0 1 6
     Coloured 0 2 6
     Rollers 0 5 6
  10. Old-Testament Stories 0 1 6
    Ditto, gilt 0 2 6
    Gospel Stories 0 1 0
    The two volumes together 0 3 0
  11. Children's Bible History. 180th thousand. Per dozen - . 0 1 6
    Children's Explanatory Catechism. 88 pp. 100th thousand.
     Per dozen 0 1 6
    Children's Companion to Bible and Explanatory Catechism.
     72 pp. Per dozen 0 1 6
 History (English):
  1. History of England for Colleges and Families. By Author of
    'Christian Schools and Scholars.' Illustrated - . . . 0 6 0
  2. History of England for Children. By Miss Emily Bowles . 0 3 0
  3. Introduction to English History 0 1 8
  4. Catechism of the History of England. By the Author of 'History of England for Colleges and Families' 0 0 6
  5. Primer of English History, Part I. For title, see 'Livesey' in
    general catalogue.
    Primer of English History, Part II. For title, see 'Livesey' in
    general catalogue.
 History (French):
  A Popular History of France. Illustrated 0 3 6

School Literature—*Continued*.

Poetry :

	£ s. d.
De Vere's Selections from the Poets. Cloth	£0 3 6
Code Poetical Reader. Adopted by the School Board	0 1 0

Reading Books :

		£ s. d.
Primer, with woodcuts	Per doz.	0 1 0
Book I. (woodcuts)	,,	0 1 6
Primer and Book I. together	,,	0 3 0
Book II. (woodcuts)	,,	0 3 9
Book III., more advanced Lessons	,,	0 6 0
Book IV., Lessons for the Higher Classes	,,	0 9 0
Supplement to Book I. (woodcuts)	,,	0 3 0
Supplement to Book II. (woodcuts)	,,	0 4 6
Tablet Lessons, including Alphabet and Figures, in very large type	Per set	0 1 2
Alphabet and Figure Sheet by itself		0 0 2
New Standard Lesson-Books for Catholic Schools. Adapted to the Revised Code of 1871. Children's Primer. Cloth.	Per doz.	0 3 0
Part I. Cloth		0 1 11
Part II. Cloth		0 2 8
Book I. for Standard 1. Cloth	Per doz.	0 4 6
Book II. ,, 2. Cloth	,,	0 5 3
Book III. ,, 3. Cloth	,,	0 7 6
Book IV. ,, 4. Cloth	,,	0 9 0
Book V. for Standards 5 & 6. Cloth	,,	0 12 0
Primer, Part I., stitched wrapper	,,	0 1 2
Lesson Sheets, large type, per set	,,	0 13 6

Religious Instruction :

		£ s. d.
The new Penny Catechism, issued by command of the Cardinal Archbishop and Bishops of England	Per doz.	0 0 9
Catechism No. I., an abridgment of No. II.	,,	0 0 5
Fander. Catechism of the Catholic Religion	,,	0 2 0
Wenham : Manual of Religious Instruction. 8th thousand		0 3 0
Religious Reading Books ;		
No. I.		0 0 10
No. II.		0 1 0
No. III.		0 1 6
Schouppe. Abridged Course of Religious Instruction, 3rd edition		0 3 0
Balmes. Demonstration and Catechism of Religion		0 0 6

Various :

		£ s. d.
The Young Scholar's Table Book for school and Home use ; with notes on the decimal coinage and the metric system of weights and measures. 5th thousand. 20 pp.	Per doz.	0 0 6
A new Compendious English Grammar. Wrapper	,,	0 2 0
Cloth	,,	0 3 0
Pocket Grammar of the French Language	,,	0 6 0
Cloth	,,	0 12 0
Vade Mecum of French Conversation. Cloth	,,	0 12 0
A Sunday School Register, drawn up for the use of Catholic Schools. In this register provision is made for showing the *weekly, quarterly,* and *annual* results *in attendance* on Sundays and in progress in religious knowledge	each	0 0 6

Schouppe (S.J.). Abridged Course of Religious Instruction, Apologetic, Dogmatic, and Moral, for the use of Catholic Colleges and Schools. 1 vol. crown 16mo, xii. 405 pp. New edition, cloth. Approved by Cardinal Manning — 0 3 0

Segneri. Manna of the Soul : Meditations for every Day of
the Year. Vol. I. - - - - - - - - - - £0 6 6
Vols. II. III. and IV. - - - - - - - - each 0 7 6
Ségur (Mgr. de) :
Familiar Instructions and Evening Lectures on all the Truths of Religion.
16mo, Vol. I. 261 pp. - - - - - - - - 0 3 0
Do., Vol. II. - - - - - - - - - - 0 3 0
Holy Communion (the tract distributed by Pope Pius IX. to the Priests
of Rome), - - - - - - - per doz. post free 0 1 8
Once every Week : a Treatise on Weekly Communion per doz, post free 0 1 8
Select Hymns for Schools - - - - - - - 0 0 1
With cover - - - - - - - - - - - 0 0 2
Music for ditto - - - - - - - - - - 0 1 0
Shaw, the MacPhersons, or England's glory, the
Roll Call of Honour, cloth - - - - - - - - 0 2 6
Shapcote, Emily Mary, Compiled by :
Legends of the Blessed Sacrament ; gathered from the History of the
Church and the Lives of the Saints. With Illustrations. 4to, cloth gilt 0 10 6
Rhythmical Prayer to the Sacred Members of Jesus hanging on the Cross,
ascribed to St. Bernard ; rendered into English rhythm. 32mo, wrapper 0 0 6
Shipley, Orby :
Truthfulness and Ritualism, 1st series - - - - - - 0 1 0
2nd series - - - - - - - - - - 0 2 0
1 vol, cloth - - - - - - - - - 0 4 0
Shortland, Canon :
Corean Martyrs. New edition - - - - - - - 0 2 0
Persecutions of Annam - - - - - - - - - 0 6 0
Sœur Eugénie. Life and Letters of a Sister of
Charity. Second edition - - - - - - - - 0 3 0
Ditto - - - - - - - - - - - - 0 4 6
Southwell, Fr. Robert (S.J.). A Hundred Medita-
tions on the Love of God - - - - - - - - 0 6 6
Calf, red edges - - - - - - - - - - 0 12 0
Spiritual Combat ; a new and careful translation. 18mo, cloth - 0 3 0
The same, pocket size, cloth - - - - - - - - 0 1 0
Spiritual Exercises of St. Ignatius, The Text of the.
Translated from the Spanish, with Preface. Imitation morocco - - 0 2 6
Spiritual Man. From the French of St. Jure. Cloth - - - 0 6 0
Spiritual Reading for every Day : an Introduction to the Interior
and Perfect Life, for the use alike of persons in the word and in religion.
By Rev. Dom Innocent Le Masson (forty-ninth General of the Order of
Carthusians, 1677). Arranged in Fifty-three Lessons, made up from
Holy Scripture (over 500 verses), the Devout Life (nearly all), and the
whole of the Imitation of Christ. Translated and slighty abridged by
Kenelm Digby Beste, Priest of the Oratory of St. Philip Neri. *Suitable
for all readers, young and old* - - - - - - - 0 2 0
Stewart, Agnes :
Life of Bishop Fisher. Cloth (with 2 portraits) - - - - 0 7 6
Gilt (3 portraits) - - - - - - - - - 0 10 6
Life of Sir Thomas More - - - - - - - - 0 6 0
Life of Cardinal Wolsey - - - - - - - - 0 6 0
Life of Margaret Roper - - - - - - - - - 0 6 0
The Yorkshire Plot - - - - - - - - - 0 6 0
Tried in the Furnace - - - - - - - - - 0 4 6

St. John, Fr. Ambrose. Raccolta of Indulgences.
New edition, incorporating all the later Indulgences - - - - £0 4 0
St. John, Fr. Sarra. Doctrine of Holy Indulgences 0 1 0
Stone, Mrs. Our Flag, a Lay of the Pontifical Zouaves; and other Poems. Cloth - - - - - - - - - - 0 3 0
Stoneleighs of Stoneleighs, and other Tales by the Author of Tyborne. 1 vol, cloth - - - - - - - - - 0 5 0
Strike, The; and the Drunkard's Death. Reprinted from "The Sick Calls," - - - - - - - -
Sweeney, Right Rev. Dr. (O.S.B., Abbot of St. Alban's):
Church a Light unto the Nations, The: a Sermon preached at the Opening of St. Benedict's Monastery and College at Fort Augustus, Inverness - 0 1 0
Few Words of Comfort, A : a Sermon preached at the Funeral of Monsignor Bonomi, V.G., at St. John's Bath - - - - - 0 0 6
Grounds of Faith - - - - - - - - - - 0 3 6
Joys of a Consecrated Church ; a Sermon preached at the Consecration of the Church at Stanbrook Convent - - - - - 0 1 0
Jubilee of Catholic Emancipation : a Paper read in the Assembly Rooms, Bath, before the Catholic Association - - - - - 0 0 6
Pope and the Emperor, The - - - - - - - - 0 2 0
Lectures on Catholic Faith and Practice. 3 vols - - - - 0 9 0
Lectures on the Œcumenical Council - - - - - - 0 5 0
Lectures on the Nature, the Grounds, and the Home of Faith - 0 3 6
Life of Father Augustine Baker - - - - - - - 0 2 6
Pius IX., Teacher, Ruler, and Martyr : a Sermon preached on the Occasion of the Death of Pope Pius IX - - - - - 0 0 6
Priest and Patriarch : a Sermon preached at the Funeral of Monsignor Brindle, at St. Mary's, Bath - - - - - - - 0 0 6
Sancta Sophia ; or Directions for the Prayer of Contemplation. By Father A. Baker : edited by Dr. Sweeney - - - - - 0 10 6
Sermons for the Sundays and Festivals of the Year. Second ed., in 1 vol. 0 10 6
Switzerland in 1876 : a Lecture read in the Assembly Rooms, Bath - 0 1 0
Vir Fidelis : a Sermon preached at the Funeral of the Very Rev. Canon Shattock, at St. Mary's, Bath - - - - - - - 0 0 6

Tales : See Popular Books, page 30.
Taylor (Miss) :
Dame Dolores - - - - - - - - - - 0 4 0
Holiday Tales - - - - - - - - - - 0 1 6
Gilt - - - - - - - - - - - - 0 2 0
Stoneleighs of Stoneleigh, and other Stories - - - - 0 4 6
Tyborne, and who went thither - - - - - - - 0 3 6
Teresa (St.), Spirit of - - - - - - - - 0 2 0
With portrait, cloth - - - - - - - - - 0 2 6
Testament, New. Stories for Children - - - - 0 1 0
Gilt - - - - - - - - - - - - 0 2 0
Testament, Old. Stories for Children - - - - 0 1 6
Gilt - - - - - - - - - - - - 0 2 6
Text of the Spiritual Exercises of St. Ignatius, The.
Translated from the Spanish, with Preface. Imitation morocco - 0 2 6
Thaddeus, Rev. F. (O.S.F.). Pilgrim's May Wreath 0 2 6
Think well on't. New edition, clear type - - - - 0 0 6

Catalogue of Publications.

Thompson, Edward Healy:
Devotions to the Nine Choirs of Holy Angels, and especially to the Angel Guardians. Translated from the French of Henri-Marie Boudon, Archdeacon of Evreux - - - - - - - £0 3 0
Hidden Life of Jesus, a Lesson and Model to Christians. Ditto. Second ed. 0 3 0
Holy Ways of the Cross; or a short Treatise on the various Trials and Afflictions, interior and exterior, to which the Spiritual Life is subject, and the means of making a good use thereof. Ditto - - - - 0 3 6
Life of M. Olier, Founder of the Seminary of St. Sulpice - - - 0 4 0
Missionary Life in the East and West - - - - - - 0 3 0
Sufferings of the Church in Britanny during the Great Revolution (Quarterly Series) - - - - - - - - - - - 0 6 6
Unity of the Episcopate - - - - - - - - - 0 4 6

Thompson, Edward Healy, edited by:
Library of Religious Biography:
Vol. I. Life of St. Aloysius Gonzaga, S.J. Third edition - - 0 5 0
Vol. II. Life of Marie-Eustelle Harpain, the Angel of the Eucharist. Third edition - - - - - - - - - 0 5 0
Vol. III. Life of St. Stanislas Kostka, S.J. Second edition - - 0 5 0
Vol. IV. Life of Baron de Renty. Second edition - - - 0 6 0
Vol. V. Life of Ven. Anna Maria Taigi, the Roman Matron (1769-1837). With Portrait. Third edition - - - - 0 6 0
Vol. VI. Life of Marie Lataste - - - - - - - 0 5 0
Du Guesclin: or the Hero of Chivalry. Cloth - - - - 0 2 0
Cheap edition - - - - - - - - - - 0 1 6
Life of St. Charles Borromeo - - - - - - - 0 3 6
Patriots of the Tyrol - - - - - - - - - 0 4 0
Life of Henri-Marie Boudon, Archdeacon of Evreux.
In preparation.
Letters and Writings of Marie Lataste, with Critical and Expository Notes by two Fathers of the Society of Jesus. Translated from the French. Uniform with the Life. Two vols.
Life of Armelle Nicolas, the Servant Girl of Campenéac.
Life of Jean-Jacques Olier, Founder of the Seminary of St. Sulpice. New and enlarged edition. Two vols.

Tickets for each Month - - - - - - per packet 0 0 4

Tracts for the Times. No. 1. The Church of the
New Testament. By C. L. - - - - - - - each 0 0 4
Ditto - - - - - - - - - - per 1000 0 14 0

Treasury of Prayer, The: a Manual of Popular Devotion. Dedicated to the frequenters of the Oratory of St. Philip Neri. 1 vol., cloth, 16mo - - - - - - - - - - - 0 2 0

True to Trust; or the Story of a Portrait - - 0 4 0

Ullathorne, Bishop:
Convent Life - - - - - - - - - - 0 1 0
Paper - - - - - - - - - - - 0 0 6
Ecclesiastical Discourses - - - - - - - - 0 6 0
Restoration of the Hierarchy - - - - - - - 0 2 6
Sermon at the Synod - - - - - - - - - 0 1 0
Church Music; a Discourse given in St. Chad's Cathedral, Birmingham.
Endowments of Man, &c., in the Press.

Unravelled Convictions; or 'My Road to Faith.'
By a Convert. Cloth - - - - - - - - 0 3 0

Vere, de. Selections from the Poets. Cloth neat - - 0 3 6

Vespers Book:

For Chanting; contains all the Psalms of Vespers and Compline, with the Notes of the Tones, and the Antiphons, Versicles and Responses, &c.	£0	1	0
Introductory, for Chanting. Containing the Psalms for *Sunday* Vespers, with the Musical Notes	0	0	1
For the Laity. Containing the Office of Vespers (including Compline and Benediction) complete for the first time for *every day in the year*, with the New Offices and Supplements. Roan, gilt edges	0	3	6
Calf	0	6	0
Morocco	0	7	0
Gilt	0	8	0
On thin vellum paper, half an inch thick, same prices.			
Compendius. Including Compline, &c. Cloth	0	0	8
With 'Hymns for the Year'	0	1	0
Little, with Compline	0	0	2
Parochial. Cloth	0	1	0
Roan, neat, red edges	0	1	6
Roan, gilt edges	0	2	0

Visits to Jesus on the Altar, by the Author of "Reflections and Prayers for Holy Communion," translated from the French.

32mo, cloth, red edges	0	1	6

Vita Devota: a Manual of Devotion. Edited by the Redemptorist Fathers.

New edition, cloth	0	0	9
Roan	0	2	0

Ward, W. G. (D.Ph.):

Commendation of Pope Honorius. An Essay republished and newly arranged from the 'Dublin Review,' with a few notes in reply to Rev. F. Willis, of Cuddesdon Theological College. One vol., 8vo, paper cover, 64 pp.	0	1	6
Doctrinal Definitions	0	5	6
Essays on Devotional and Scriptural Subjects. Reprinted from the 'Dublin Review'. Contents: 1. Catholic Devotion to our Blessed Lady; 2. Catholic Doctrine concerning our Blessed Lady; 3. Mary in the Gospels; 4. The Sacred Heart; 5. St. Paul's relations with St. Peter; 6. St. Mary Magdalen in the Gospels; 7. Father Coleridge on the Gospels; 8. Gospel Narrative of the Resurrection; 9. Father Coleridge's Life of our Life. One vol., crown 8vo, cloth, xxxii, 467 pp.	0	9	0
Nature and Grace. 8vo	0	12	0
Essays on the Church's Doctrinal Authority, mostly reprinted from the 'Dublin Review'. 1 vol., crown 8vo, 565 pp., cloth	0	10	0

Ward, Mrs. Biographical Sketch of St. Thomas of Canterbury.

Small 8vo, pp. 180, cloth	0	4	0

Wardour, Lord Arundell of:

Nature-Myth Theory untenable from the Scriptural Point of View. Demy 8vo	0	6	0
Scientific Value of Tradition: a Correspondence between Lord Arundel and Mr. E. Ryley, with a letter from Rev. H. Formby on the Christian Science of Tradition. Demy 8vo	0	5	0
Tradition: Principally with Reference to Mythology and the Law of Nations. Demy 8vo	0	8	0

Warmoll (Canon). Little Book of the Most Holy Child Jesus: a Prayer-Book for His Children.

Second edition	0	1	0

Waterworth, Rev. W.:

England and Rome	0	4	6
Origin and Developments of Anglicanism	0	4	6

Catalogue of Publications. 47

Way of the Cross. Illustrated by Westlake - - - - £0 2 6
   Fine paper - - - - - - - - - - - - 0 4 6
   Large edition - - - - - - - - - - - 1 11 6
Weld. Mission of the Zambesi. With a Map of the Mission 0 1 0
   Suppression of the Society of Jesus (see 'Quarterly Series ').
Wenham (Canon) :
   Manual of Instruction in Christian Doctrine. For Pupil-teachers or
     Advanced Classes - - - - - - - - - - 0 3 0
   New-Testament Narrative in the Words of Sacred Writers. Suitable for
     private reading - - - - - - - - - - 0 2 6
   Old Testament Readings. The 'Readings' are divided into four historical
   periods :
     Part I. The Patriarchs ; II. The Israelites - - - - - 0 2 0
     Part III. The Kings ; IV. The Prophets - - - - - 0 3 0
   Religious Reading Books :
     No. I. Suitable to Standards I. and II. - - - - - - 0 0 10
       II. ,, ,, III. and IV. - - - - - - 0 1 0
       III. ,, ,, V. and VI. - - - - - - 0 1 6
   School Manager : his Office and Duties in regard to Elementary Deno-
     minational Schools - - - - - - - - - 0 4 6
Wilberforce, F. Bertrand (O.S.D.). Sketches of the
   Lives of Dominican Missionaries in Japan, including those of the
   Martyrs beatified by Pius IX. Preface by Cardinal Manning. Cloth - 0 1 6
Wilfrid of Galway, Translated by. Life of Blessed Joseph
   Hermann. Cloth - - - - - - - - - - 0 4 6
Willibrord, St., Life of. To which is added the Life of St.
   Lioba. Cloth - - - - - - - - - - - 0 3 0
Winefride (St.) ; or Holywell and its Pilgrims. By
   the Author of 'Tyborne'. Third edition, revised - - - - 0 1 0
Wiseman, Cardinal :
   Fabiola : a Tale of the Catacombs. New edition, cloth - - - - 0 3 6
     Gilt - - - - - - - - - - - - 0 4 0
     Morocco - - - - - - - - - - - 0 9 0
   Few Flowers from the Campagna - - - - - - - - 0 2 0
   Hidden Gem - - - - - - - - - - - 0 2 0
   Holy Week - - - - - - - - - - - - 0 4 0
   Last Four Popes - - - - - - - - - - - 0 5 0
   Lectures on Science and Revealed Religion - - - - - 0 5 0
   Lectures on the Church - - - - - - - - 0 3 6
   Real Presence - - - - - - - - - - 0 1 8
   Sermons on our Lord and His Blessed Mother - - - - 0 7 6
   Sermons on Moral Subjects - - - - - - - - 0 7 6
Witch of Melton Hill, The : a Tale. By the Author of
   'Mount St. Lawrence'. Cloth - - - - - - - - 0 3 0
Wyndham Family, The : a Story of Modern Life. By the
   same. 2 vols., 10s. 6d. - - - - - - - - for 0 5 6
Xavier, St. Francis, Life of. Cloth - - - - - 0 2 0
   Cheap edition - - - - - - - - - - - 0 1 6
Yeatman, John Pym (Barrister-at-Law). The She-
   mitic Origin of the Nations of Western Europe, and especially of the
   English, French, and Irish Branches of the Gaelic Peoples. Post 8vo 0 5 0
   Ditto, cloth - - - - - - - - - - - 0 6 0

THE
NEW STANDARD COPY BOOKS.

Price 2d. each,

ADOPTED BY THE LONDON SCHOOL BOARD.

STANDARD I.

1. ELEMENTS; SIMPLER OF SMALL LETTERS; EASY WORDS. *(Medium Text).*
2. MORE DIFFICULT OF SMALL LETTERS; EASY WORDS. *(Medium Text).*

STANDARD II.

3. LONGER WORDS; CAPITALS; FIGURES. *(Medium and half text).*
4. GRAMMAR; GEOGRAPHY; CAPITALS; FIGURES. *(Medium and half text).*

STANDARD III.

5. GRAMMAR; CAPITALS; FIGURES. *(Small round hand).*
6. GEOGRAPHY (ENGLAND); CAPITALS; FIGURES. *(Small round and small hands).*

STANDARD IV.

7. GEOGRAPHY (SCOTLAND, IRELAND); FIGURES. *(Small hand).*
8. GRAMMAR; GEOGRAPHY (COLONIES); HISTORY. *(Small hand).*

STANDARD V.

9. GRAMMAR; GEOGRAPHY (EUROPE—PHYSICAL); HISTORY. *(Small hand).*
10. GRAMMAR; GEOGRAPHY (EUROPE—POLITICAL); HISTORY. *(Small hand).*

STANDARD VI.

11. GRAMMAR; GEOGRAPHY (ASIA—AFRICA); HISTORY. *(Small hand).*
12. GEOGRAPHY (N. AND S. AMERICA, OCEANIA); HISTORY. *(Small hand).*

'A splendid set of copy books. Every aid is furnished to the beginner in the form of ruled, measured, and marked spaces, and the graduation is skilfully maintained throughout. The headlines, or, as we should say, the lines to be copied, for they are not confined to the head of each page, are beautifully written in a moderately-sized round hand; and, as each line teaches something in History, Grammar, and Geography, the writing-lesson may include one or more of these subjects.—*The Educational News.*

'These books contain a good selection of models, in figuring as well as word and letter writing. They are well suited for instruction.'—*The Schoolmaster.*

'These books are well "got-up". The writing is good, that of the higher numbers being simply faultless; and judicious aids are given to prevent the learner copying his own writing. We give them a hearty welcome.'—*The Teacher.*

'The headlines are designed to impress upon the minds of children grammatical, historical, and geographical facts, that will be useful in preparing for the Standard Examinations. The writing is round and bold, and the paper in the books is good.'—*The School Guardian.*

'This is a very useful set of copy books. The style is good, legible, and plain, and fairly within the reach of boys and girls. This is more than can be said of many of the models now in use.'—*The Student's Magazine*, April 2, 1880.

'This is undoubtedly an excellent series of copy books. The headlines are written in a bold, clear style, the paper is of the very best quality—the graduation and arrangement are most commendable—and the price (twopence) extremely moderate. The numbers are deserving the attention of teachers.'—*Educational Chronicle*, April 17, 1880.

'We have carefully examined these copy books and have great pleasure in bearing testimony to their excellence in every respect. . . . The style of writing throughout the series is of the most approved and finished kind, the printing is clear, bold, and admirably executed; and the paper and general appearance of the book excellent.'—*The Irish Teaching Journal*, Feb. 21, 1880.

Other 100 letters have been received from School Inspectors highly approving of the style of writing and general execution of these copy books.

BURNS AND OATES, LONDON.

www.ingramcontent.com/pod-product-compliance
Lightning Source LLC
Chambersburg PA
CBHW030323240426
43673CB00040B/1252